Canada and the Korean War

Studies in Canadian Military History
Series editor: Tim Cook, Canadian War Museum

The Canadian War Museum, Canada's national museum of military history, has a threefold mandate: to remember, to preserve, and to educate. Studies in Canadian Military History, published by UBC Press in association with the Museum, extends this mandate by presenting the best of contemporary scholarship to provide new insights into all aspects of Canadian military history, from earliest times to recent events. The work of a new generation of scholars is especially encouraged, and the books employ a variety of approaches – cultural, social, intellectual, economic, political, and comparative – to investigate gaps in the existing historiography. The books in the series feed immediately into future exhibitions, programs, and outreach efforts by the Canadian War Museum. A list of the titles in the series appears at the end of the book.

CANADIAN WAR MUSEUM
MUSÉE CANADIEN DE LA GUERRE

Canada and the Korean War
Histories and Legacies of a Cold War Conflict

Edited by Andrew Burtch and Tim Cook

UBCPress · Vancouver

UBC Press is a Benetech Global Certified Accessible™ publisher. The epub version of this book meets stringent accessibility standards, ensuring it is available to people with diverse needs.

Printed in Canada on FSC-certified ancient-forest-free paper (100% post-consumer recycled) that is processed chlorine- and acid-free.

Library and Archives Canada Cataloguing in Publication

Title: Canada and the Korean War : histories and legacies of a Cold War conflict / edited by Andrew Burtch and Tim Cook.
Names: Burtch, Andrew Paul, editor. | Cook, Tim, editor.
Series: Studies in Canadian military history.
Description: Series statement: Studies in Canadian military history | Includes bibliographical references and index.
Identifiers: Canadiana (print) 20230595464 | Canadiana (ebook) 20230595499 | ISBN 9780774868631 (hardcover) | ISBN 9780774870535 (EPUB) | ISBN 9780774870528 (PDF)
Subjects: LCSH: Korean War, 1950–1953—Participation, Canadian. | LCSH: Canada. Canadian Army—History—Korean War, 1950–1953. | LCSH: Cold War.
Classification: LCC DS919.2 .C32 2024 | DDC 951.904/2371—dc23

Canada Council for the Arts Conseil des arts du Canada

Canada

British Columbia Arts Council

British Columbia

UBC Press gratefully acknowledges the financial support for our publishing program of the Government of Canada, the Canada Council for the Arts, and the British Columbia Arts Council.

This book has been published with the help of a grant from the Canadian Federation for the Humanities and Social Sciences, through the Scholarly Book Awards, using funds provided by the Social Sciences and Humanities Research Council of Canada.

Publication of this book has been financially supported by the Canadian War Museum.

UBC Press is situated on the traditional, ancestral, and unceded territory of the xʷməθkʷəy̓əm (Musqueam) people. This land has always been a place of learning for the xʷməθkʷəy̓əm, who have passed on their culture, history, and traditions for millennia, from one generation to the next.

UBC Press
The University of British Columbia
www.ubcpress.ca

Contents

Acknowledgments / vii

List of Abbreviations / viii

Note on the Romanization of Korean Names and Terms / ix

Introduction / 3
Andrew Burtch and Tim Cook

Part 1: Canada, Korea, and Politics

1 Alignment without Illusions: Canada's World, 1945–50 / 17
Hector Mackenzie and Norman Hillmer

2 Canadian Political Leadership and the Korean War / 31
Ryan M. Touhey

Part 2: Canada, Korea, and the War

3 The US Army and the Battle for Korea, 1950: Lessons Learned / 53
Brian McAllister Linn

4 The Canadian Naval Experience Off Korea / 71
Michael Whitby

5 Cut and Thrust: The Canadian Army in Korea, June 1950–October 1951 / 90
William Johnston

6 Canada's Defensive Battle, 1951–53 / 110
William Johnston

7 The Commonwealth Division / 128
S.P. MacKenzie

8 The Royal Canadian Air Force in the Korean War / 142
Richard Mayne

9 China's Battles for Korea / 160
Xiaobing Li

10 Flesh and Blood: The Commonwealth Division and Medical Care in the Korean War / 176
Meghan Fitzpatrick

11 Canada's Korean War Dead / 192
Andrew Burtch

Part 3: Korean War Memories and Legacies

12 The Korean War's Prisoners / 213
Jonathan Vance

13 Returning Home: The Canadian Veterans' Experience / 234
Ted Barris

14 The Korean War's Impact on the Republic of Korea Army and the Korean People's Army / 247
Youngjun Kim

15 Canadian-Korean Relations since the Korean War / 258
Tina J. Park

16 Canada's Korean War in Commemoration, Memorials, and Memory / 272
Tim Cook and Andrew Burtch

Selected Bibliography / 292

Contributors / 298

Index / 301

Acknowledgments

THE EDITORS ARE grateful to the contributors to this volume for their collaborative spirit, their receptiveness to feedback, and the desire shared with us to make this volume a success. We appreciate all we learned from assembling this volume, which we believe to be an important contribution to the national and international scholarship about the Korean War. The book would not have been possible without the generous assistance of many of our colleagues at the Canadian War Museum who offered resources, expertise, and support. Staff of the Military History Research Centre provided important access to interviews, photographs, and archival resources that helped shape several of the chapters in this volume. Robyn Jeffrey financially supported the inclusion of colour images. Other colleagues at the museum, and those beyond it, such as at the Library and Archives Canada and the Directorate of History and Heritage, made this a better book.

Our manuscript readers offered incisive and constructive commentary that helped refine the work and its organization. The editorial and production staff at UBC Press are some of our favourite people with whom we work, providing helpful guidance at the outset of this project and during the peer review process, and stickhandling the manuscript through the various phases of copyediting and proofing to produce the volume in hand. We are grateful for the financial assistance of the Canadian War Museum in supporting the Studies in Canadian Military History Series, of which we have been past and present series editors.

We thank our families – Virginia, Graham, and Jas; and Sarah, Chloe, Emma, and Paige – for their support and good humour during the writing, review, and editing processes. Finally, we are grateful to the veterans whose stories, photographs, artwork, artifacts, and experiences we have drawn upon in this volume, and whose determined advocacy has done so much to ensure that the Korean War will not be forgotten.

Abbreviations

3 RAR	3rd Battalion, the Royal Australian Regiment
25 FDS	25th Canadian Field Dressing Station
CANDU	Canada deuterium uranium
CPVF	Chinese People's Volunteer Force
DPRK	Democratic People's Republic of Korea (North Korea)
EHF	epidemic hemmorhagic fever
EUSAK	Eighth US Army Korea
KPA	Korean People's Army (see also NKPA)
MASH	mobile army surgical hospital
NKPA	North Korean People's Army
PPCLI	Princess Patricia's Canadian Light Infantry
R22eR	Royal 22e Régiment
RAR	Royal Australian Regiment
RCAF	Royal Canadian Air Force
RCN	Royal Canadian Navy
RCR	Royal Canadian Regiment
ROKA	Republic of Korea Army
UNF	United Nations forces
UNSC	United Nations Security Council
USAF	United States Air Force

Note on the Romanization of Korean Names and Terms

THE ROMANIZATION OF Korean scripts and language has changed over time. This volume, following Library of Congress standards, uses, wherever possible, the revised McCune-Reischauser (M-R) Romanization system, which originated in the 1930s and was revised in 2009. This system differs in significant ways from official revised Korean romanization, which came into effect after 2002. The M-R system employs apostrophes to indicate aspirated consonants among other visual signifiers. Where the pronunciation of the word differs from the M-R system, the editors give preference to the romanization of the pronounced version – that is, *Busan* rather than *Pusan.* An exception to this rule is cases where the traditional romanization has taken hold and recognized in battle honours, such as *Kap'yong* instead of the official revised romanization of *Gapyeong.* Where applicable, the editors and authors indicate the newer romanization in brackets.

Canada and the Korean War

Introduction

Andrew Burtch and Tim Cook

Major (Ret'd) Donavan "Reg" Redknap, a veteran of the Korean War, was a volunteer at the Canadian War Museum in 2005. The new museum, in Ottawa, had just opened to the public. Wearing a blazer bedecked with medals, the aged veteran freely shared his wartime experiences with visitors. In conversations with staff, he lamented that few of the people coming through the galleries knew about the Korean War, what Canadians did during the conflict, or even much about the region.

Over the following years, the museum's displays would help introduce the war and its history to millions of visitors. Reg was indefatigable in his desire for younger people to understand the war, particularly the complexity and importance of gunnery that his unit, the Royal Canadian Artillery's 81st Field Regiment, provided in support of soldiers such as his friend Ed Hollyer. On the night of 2–3 May 1953, as a superior Chinese force raided the platoon position defended by Canadian and South Korean soldiers, Lieutenant Hollyer's 3rd Battalion, Royal Canadian Regiment, ordered a request for Reg's guns to rain fire onto his own lines to drive off the attack. After confirming the order, Reg complied, and by the morning of 3 May, the seventy-two guns of the Commonwealth Division had poured eight thousand shells onto the attacking force.

Ed survived the raid and the barrage and was later awarded the Military Cross. When the museum's Korean War displays opened, a photograph of Reg and Ed was displayed to help explain the importance of firepower in defending UN lines. In the fall of 2022, after sharing his knowledge with so many visitors to the museum, Reg passed away, joining most veterans from the Korean War, including his old friend Ed, who had died in July 2013, shortly before the sixtieth anniversary of the Korean War armistice. Both men's stories live on through the museum's displays.

Reg's comments on the public's lack of knowledge about the Korean War might well be extended to most wars and conflicts in Canadian military history,

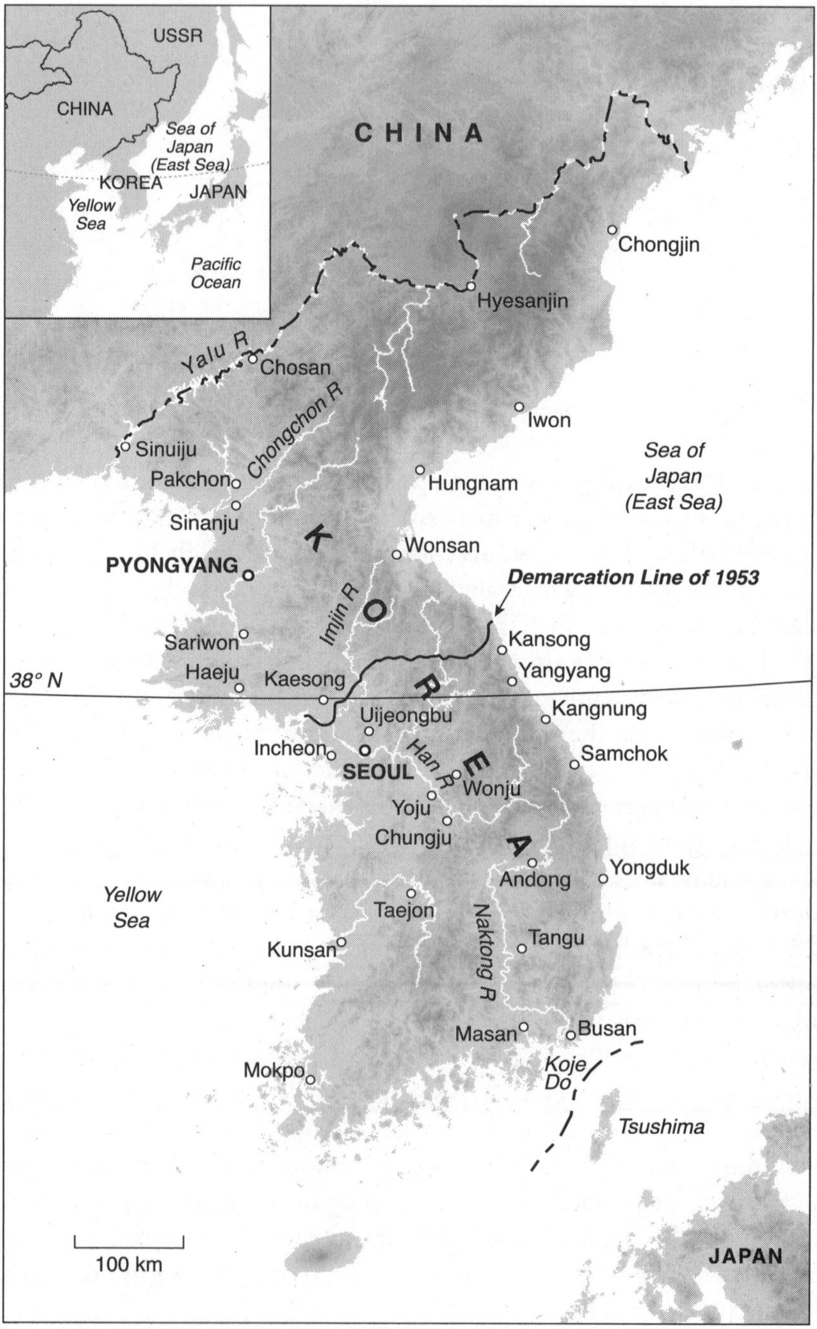

Map 1 The Korean Peninsula, 1950–53

Cartography by Eric Leinberger. Reprinted from Meghan Fitzpatrick, *Invisible Scars: Mental Trauma and the Korean War* (Vancouver: UBC Press, 2017).

save, perhaps, for the world wars, which dominate the historiographical and commemorative landscape. The Korean War has had few historical, cultural, or public affairs champions, and it holds little place in the collective imagination of Canadians. This is notwithstanding detailed scholarly works that document Canada's involvement in the war such as David Bercuson's *Blood on the Hills*, Brent Byron Watson's critical examination in *Far Eastern Tour*, and William Johnston's signature volume, *A War of Patrols*, to name a few.[1]

However, most of these works tend to focus either on the performance of a particular arm of the Canadian military or on the war's implications for areas of greater national interest, such as managing the Canada–United States relationship in the early Cold War, or Canada's involvement with the budding North Atlantic Alliance.[2] In the United States, which has a far greater body of historical study on the Korean War, the war has sometimes been painted as a disappointment when set against the record of unconditional victory in 1945. General Omar Bradley's caution against escalating the war and risking a global conflict has often been mistakenly summarized as standing for the entire war: "The wrong war, at the wrong place, in the wrong time, against the wrong enemy."[3] Bradley's (and, by extension, the Joint Chiefs of Staff's) warning was not to lose sight of the real priority – preparing for and deterring conflict in Europe.

Yet Bradley's evocative phrase has also provided fodder for historians to interpret Korea – and some of the American missteps before, during, and after the war there – as a prelude to Vietnam and its controversies.[4] In much of Canadian and international historiography, the Korean War tends to be a weigh station employed to shape or sharpen other early Cold War events, whether as a foreign-policy orientation, lessons for urgent budgetary allocations, military reforms, or deployments elsewhere in the world. Korea, in terms of Canadian military and foreign-policy historiography, is generally used to help illustrate other Cold War trends.[5]

As Masuda Hajimu points out in *Cold War Crucible*, however, the spectre of unsettled outcomes of the Second World War led many in the West to view the Korean War as a possible global war. "World War II was not simply an event in the past," wrote Masuda Hajimu, "it was an image of the future."[6] Much of the world was living with the legacy of the Second World War. Refugee crises and independence movements, countries divided by the war, and the rise of new superpowers were but a few of the war's key legacies. With its 60 million dead, the Second World War was very much a spectre that continued to haunt the survivors of the remade world.

In East Asia, the years leading up to the Korean War were not setting the table for the forthcoming Cold War. The cultural and, in some cases, violent purges of "counterrevolutionaries" in Eastern Europe, China, and North Korea; the concurrent Red Scares in western Europe, Canada, and the United States; the rebuilding of nations, such as a destroyed Japan, or in fending off Communist aggressions in West Berlin or South Korea – these were *all,* to some extent, a settling of accounts from the recent world war, undertaken to produce a promised stability, with long-term and often unforeseen consequences.

In turn, Stalin's Soviet Union, Mao's unified China, and Kim Il Sung's North Korea were all seeking to make or remake the divided world that had emerged from the great trauma of 1945. In victory over fascism, a new ideological war was born, pitting, in broad terms, the Western democracies and their allies against the emerging Communist Bloc. Korea was where these tensions came to an abrupt and costly head.

The Korean War gave rise to many of the defining themes of the Cold War, including domestic anti-Communist campaigns, increased defence spending, and a general sense of urgency that spread to almost every aspect of foreign policy and domestic politics. The Korean War was the catalyst that fired the Cold War, in East Asia and elsewhere. While many of these streams of thought can be seen in earlier crises, such as in responses to the Berlin Blockade or the Czechoslovakia coup, it was during the Korean War that ideological, diplomatic, and actual battle lines hardened in ways that had far-reaching consequences.[7]

Scholarship during the Cold War routinely depicted the North Korean invasion of the South as a local satellite acting under orders from the Soviet Union, if not Stalin himself. And while more recent scholarship drawn from previously shuttered archives clearly reveals that Stalin gave Kim his tacit approval, it also confirms that the Korean War was firstly a local affair fought between nationalists who leveraged their sponsoring states for support.[8] Historian Bruce Cumings' studies, some of the first to make use of Korean sources, did much to illustrate the domestic political circumstances that contributed to the outbreak of the Korean War.[9] Kim Il Sung wanted to reunite the divided Korean peninsula; he saw discontent over the continued American presence in South Korea as an opportunity. Kim's counterpart, Syngman Rhee's government, seemed at times at war with its own people, waging a vicious internal conflict against left-leaning militants and northern infiltrators, with security forces often unable to discriminate between militants and innocents caught in the middle.[10] Until recently, American scholarship has tended to cast the United States as a relative bystander in Rhee's internal war, though critical studies have revealed the extent to which American foreign policy empowered or facilitated Rhee's excesses.[11] The end product was the same: the South appeared as though it would be an easy target. For Kim, the invasion of 25 June 1950 was the right war, in the right place, at the right time, and against the right enemy. Were it not for the stiff resistance offered by South Korea's defenders, he might well have been correct.

With a green light from the Soviet Union and a restless neighbour, Kim envisaged a rapid war where his soldiers would be greeted as liberators and uniters of the divided country. The continuous internecine fighting in South Korea accounted, to some extent, for South Koreans' lax response to the North's invasion on 25 June 1950. When the war was announced, it did not immediately precipitate widespread panic. News of the invasion did not even disrupt a baseball game being played in Seoul, but the capital city soon fell to a rapidly moving column of North Koreans. These invaders, who spoke the same language, if in a rougher Northern dialect, were welcomed by some who saw them as brothers rather than as an alien force that characterized the Japanese imperial presence.

These delusions were put to rest, first by North Korean brutality towards captured military personnel and political elites and then by the vicious fighting that destroyed the capital city before it could be recaptured – and captured again by Chinese forces, and then recaptured by the UN forces – in the fall of 1950. But the poorly organized South Korean defenders recovered from the initial blow. Backed by American garrison units, which arrived first from Japan, and then by more combat-effective formations from the United States, they made a successful but costly stand in the southeast of the country. The history of the subsequent long, grinding land campaign is recounted in this book, as is the context for the war and its many stages of combat on land, at sea, and in the air from 1950 to 1953. When the armistice was finally struck on 27 July 1953, the war's impact did not end there. Its legacy continued to shape the Korean peninsula and reverberate around the world.

With the seventieth anniversary of the Korean Armistice Agreement behind us, an anniversary that passed with little recognition outside of the Koreas, we sought to present some of the newest research and writing about the Korean War.[12] Part of this effort was to synthesize in a single volume a reference point for future scholars aiming to learn more about Canadian attitudes towards the Korean War, and the operational history of the Royal Canadian Navy, Canadian Army, and Royal Canadian Air Force. Recognizing that Canada was but one of sixteen countries to contribute to the UN's war effort in Korea, and that Canadian warships, aircraft, and soldiers all operated with or within Commonwealth and American formations, we felt it was important to draw together scholarship that illustrated the scope and nature of Allied commitment. These international operations fundamentally shaped the nature of Canada's wartime experience in Korea and were often, in turn, affected by Canadian martial efforts. The books and articles written about the Cold War, though dwarfed by studies of the world wars, is nonetheless vast. Yet this literature is divided between national studies of individual contributions, on the one hand, and experiences of the multinational war, on the other, notwithstanding trends to create more "global studies" of the war by scholars such as William Stueck, Hajimu, and others. The contributors to this volume synthesize the applicable historiographies and situate their work among national and international streams of Korean War scholarship.

To build on the foundation of Canadian and allied military historical study, we also include studies from the "other side of the hill." Canadian war diaries, contemporary press accounts, and oral histories failed to grasp the scope and complexity of operations of Canada's principal opponent on the battlefield, the Chinese People's Volunteer Force, whose vast efforts and ambitions in Korea irrevocably shaped the war. The essays collected here address the contribution of the Korean armies, often ignored in the literature, as well as the war's enduring military and cultural legacy in North and South Korea. Cumulatively, these histories help us grasp the scope, nature, and impact of the war effort of the United Nations Command and provide a fuller picture of the war's legacy. They will help future readers grasp the roots of the present situation surrounding the Korean peninsula, as the armistice agreement did much to freeze the Cold War into place. In the decades since, the test of maintaining military preparedness, the politics and diplomacy of the war, the challenge of working with and through international and local allies, and the larger competition between North and South Korea and the Chinese and American superpowers all remain intractable problems.

This volume unfolds in three thematic and largely chronological parts. Part 1, "Canada, Korea, and Politics," establishes the nature of international and domestic political affairs that successive Canadian governments faced in the early Cold War. A close focus on Ottawa's political response to the Korean crisis tells us much about Canada's evolving attitude towards entanglements with its allies, as well as its caution in engaging with East Asia, which its traditional foreign policy generally ignored in favour of North America and European affairs. Canada's initial indifference to Korea was not indicative, as Hector Mackenzie and Norman Hillmer note in their chapter, of any trepidation about what role the country should play in the Cold War. Key government officials were united in solidarity with American and western European allies against the Soviet and Chinese threat. Canada never approached the Cold War as a neutral participant.

However, even when the die was cast in favour of intervention, as Ryan Touhey describes in his chapter, Canadian political leaders had to carry out a balancing act between satisfying the demands of the United Nations and, more importantly, the United States. They did this while keeping a worried eye on public opinion that was, as ever, divided between those who believed Canada needed to respond with vigour to the crisis and those who urged caution because they recalled previous wars had led to lasting social disruptions. Surging economic good fortune in North America eased some of these concerns. Canada's limited war effort yielded electoral dividends for the government's management of the crisis far from the country's borders.

Part 2, "Canada, Korea, and the War," examines the conflict itself from the perspectives of the different parties to the conflict, including allies and enemies. More than thirty thousand Canadians served in the Korean War theatre from the war's start until 1957, when the last units returned home years after the armistice.[13] Within the UN's war effort, Canada's contribution was the fourth largest, but it was still a fraction of the colossal commitment of soldiers and personnel arrayed against the North Korean and Chinese war efforts. As William Stueck notes in his work *Rethinking the Korean War*, "The Korean War was a multifaceted event, the mastery of which challenges the capacity of the most diligent of historians."[14] One cannot understand the war solely through Canadian eyes – a wider study of the international war is required. Ottawa's decision to support the UN took place against a backdrop of a war already raging. The main combatants, to that point, were the Republic of Korea and American garrison and reinforcements fighting a vital battle for control of the peninsula.

Brian McAllister Linn's chapter addresses the US Army's transformation during and after the war, with an emphasis on the hard-fought battles of 1950 and 1951, which prevented South Korea's fall. As the Canadian government weighed the benefits and drawbacks of deeper involvement in the UN war effort, the United States fought what some thought was an existential struggle against communism. Its regional and international reputation was on the line. But the US Army's ill-preparedness and poor initial performance created both near and long-term consequences not only for the American effort in Korea but also for reforms that would extend to NATO operations and concepts about the atomic battlefield.

The initial American (and British) experiences during the 1950–51 campaign in turn shaped Canada's war on the ground. William Johnston's two chapters concerning the Canadian Army in Korea also analyze the war on the ground by comparing the successful campaign conducted by the Canadian volunteers who formed the first rotation of soldiers to fight in 1950 and 1951 and their Regular force successors, who largely ignored the lessons learned in combat in favour of a more rigid and unimaginative approach to operations.

In examining the "Commonwealth spirit" that united the Canadians, Australians, British, and other members of the Commonwealth Division, S.P. MacKenzie shows that the fondness with which the division's work in Korea was recalled was often achieved despite significant differences between its members. The division's success owed much to the clear-eyed management of the formation by its leadership. Meghan Fitzpatrick's study of the Commonwealth units' medical management, both near the battlefield and farther afield, notes the advancement of both the physical and psychological treatments offered to soldiers and the battlefield medical advances that were brought back to Canada at war's end. Both chapters indicate that the way forward from Korea pointed to greater integration and coordination between national contingents.

A successful war in the air and at sea was built on the foundations of close cooperation between the Canadian, British, and American forces, and these United Nations forces triumphed because of technological superiority and their extensive combat experience. In their analyses of the Royal Canadian Navy and the Royal Canadian Air Force, Michael Whitby and Richard Mayne argue that while the service arms had to manage competing priorities – wartime needs, domestic defence duties, and contributions to NATO – they nonetheless contributed to victory.

Whether at sea, in the air, or on the ground, service in Korea came at a cost, and Andrew Burtch unearths how the Canadian military tallied its war dead, the circumstances leading to losses, and how families at home responded during and long after the war. In his study of the Chinese Volunteer Peoples' Force in Korea, Xiaobing Li highlights China's stunning initial successes and subsequent struggles against the United Nations Command. The stakes for China's intervention were high, and its strategic goals hinged on transforming the Cold War in East Asia, cementing its regional influence, and persuading the UN that China was a power in its own right. The Korean War is not forgotten in China but etched into its founding mythos as the War to Resist the United States and Aid Korea. The United States was forced to withdraw from North Korea, which survived, and so the Chinese war aims were achieved. The war, and Chinese victories against US forces, was the subject of the 2021 film *The Battle at Lake Changjin*, the second highest-grossing film of the year. It earned $200 million, more than the most recent James Bond sequel.[15]

Part 3, "Korean War Memories and Legacies," focuses on the many legacies of the so-called forgotten war. Jonathan Vance considers the dilemma that prisoners of war faced as they waited for negotiations leading to the armistice. Even when freed, the prisoners had to deal with allegations of "brainwashing" and concerns about the conduct of Western service personnel after capture. Canada, for its part, seemed eager to leave behind Korea after the war, though, as Tina J. Park notes in her study of Canada-Korea relations over the past seventy years, this aversion was short-lived as Korea emerged as an important market and regional partner with shared points of interest.

Because the war ended with an armistice rather than a peace treaty, a renewal of the conflict was still possible. Youngjun Kim dissects the war's legacy for the armed forces of the Koreas. Each country learned foundational if opposing lessons that shaped their militaries, societies, and alliances. Canadian veterans returning home from the war, as Ted Barris shows, did not enjoy a warm reception either from their communities or from veterans of past wars, and they were forced to build their own associations over time. Unlike in China or in North and South Korea, Canadians had the luxury of distance and geography to protect them from these still fraught battlegrounds, and they easily moved on from a war that had involved relatively few men and women and left no great divisive legacy in the country.

We conclude by examining how the war came to be remembered and commemorated during decades when the Canadian government failed to put much effort into marking the war or honouring those who served in it. Veterans stepped into this gap with privately coordinated remembrance. They were supported by the South Korean government, which had benefited from their service and the sacrifice of their comrades who never came home.

What shapes a country's military history? Do all wars carry equal weight in framing our understanding of the world in which we live? Clearly not. The world wars have an outsized presence and place in public memory for many reasons, not least their titanic impact on shaping global affairs, their staggering loss of life, and their cultural resonance. For Canada, narratives surrounding peacekeeping in the Cold War were woven into public perceptions of the country's military disposition, partly out of a nationalist desire to distance Canada from the United States. More recently, the costly Canadian contribution to the Afghanistan War from 2001 to 2014 led to much public debate about the role of Canada's armed forces abroad, as well as a resurgence in public efforts to commemorate the service of those who served in Afghanistan and past wars.

Amid these historical and social developments, it is unsurprising that the Korean War often faded from the public's view. Korea was referred to as a "forgotten war" while it was still ongoing. The term was coined in Canada by Anglican Primate the Reverend Walter Foster Barfoot after he returned from ministering to Canadians in Korea in November 1951.[16] Although veterans of the war and their families never forgot, Barfoot was correct in lamenting that Canadians were fighting and dying far from home and would return to a largely indifferent country.

While few wars are forgotten during the fighting – and this was not the case with Canada and Korea, despite Barfoot's claim – most wars fade over time, treading lightly on Canada's public memory. They are rarely taught in classrooms and ignored in general histories, and save for lesser-known memorials and monuments, there are few cultural products to stir the imagination. Rarely do Canadians think of the many battles of the Seven Years War, the clash between Canadians and Americans in the War of 1812, the internal struggle and strife of the 1837–38 rebellions, the South African War of 1899 to 1902, or even more recent conflicts, missions, or wars. Added to that amnesia is a mythos of Canada as a peaceable kingdom, at least when compared with the United States. National narratives about Canadians as natural peacekeepers are a by-product of this reading of military history.

A greater understanding of our complex past has emerged since the late twentieth century in response to bursts of commemorative activities, books, exhibitions, and other cultural output. Yet during this resurgence, the Korean War was often overshadowed, as Canadian scholars and commemorative efforts focused heavily on the impact and importance of Canada's participation in the world wars.[17] The absence of major commemorative events about Korea didn't surprise some veterans. "Well, we weren't met with any fanfare," recounted Reg Redknap about his homecoming from Korea in an oral history conducted at the Canadian War Museum. "I don't think any of us really cared. By this stage, all we wanted to do was get on that train in Seattle and go home."[18] Much of the scholarly literature from the Korean War points to the lessons countries drew from the conflict and moved on to new Cold War crises.

However, the scholarship showcased here shows how rewarding it is to engage with the war in its own right and to more carefully understand its origins, its contradictions, and how the public memory of the war has been framed and reframed over nearly three-quarters of a century. Now, as most of the war's veterans have passed away, and as more archival evidence from participating countries has been opened, historians can further public understanding of this watershed war. This obligation extends to keeping alive the memories of all those affected by the war (civilian and military), those who never had a chance to come home, those veterans still living, and the many other Canadians who have come to share a connection to the war in Korea and its enduring legacy.

Notes

1 David Bercuson, *Blood on the Hills: The Canadian Army in the Korean War* (Toronto: University of Toronto Press, 1999); Brent Byron Watson, *Far Eastern Tour: The Canadian Infantry in Korea, 1950–1953* (Montreal/Kingston: McGill-Queen's University Press, 2002); William Johnston, *A War of Patrols: Canadian Army Operations in Korea* (Vancouver: UBC Press, 2003); and Meghan Fitzpatrick, *Invisible Scars: Mental Trauma and the Korean War* (Vancouver: UBC Press, 2017). These studies build on the dated yet still relevant official histories such as Lieutenant-Colonel Herbert Fairlie Wood's *Strange Battleground: The Operations in Korea and Their Effects on the Defence Policy of Canada* (Ottawa: Queen's

Printer, 1966) and Thor Thorgrimsson and E.C. Russell's *Canadian Naval Operations in Korean Waters, 1950–1955* (Ottawa: Naval Historical Section, Canadian Forces Headquarters, 1965). The editors discuss official histories and historiography in the concluding chapter of this volume.

2 Some important studies include Denis Stairs, *The Diplomacy of Constraint: Canada, the Korean War, and the United States* (Toronto: University of Toronto Press, 1974); and John Price, *Orienting Canada: Race, Empire, and the Transpacific* (Toronto: UBC Press, 2011).

3 Michael O'Hanlon, *Military History for the Modern Strategist: America's Major Wars since 1861* (Washington, DC: Brookings Institution Press, 2023), 211.

4 For an example of the former study, see Bevin Alexander, *Korea: The War We Lost* (New York: Hippocrene Books, 1986); for an example of critical scholarship that draws parallels between the Korean War, the Vietnam War, and the Iraq and Afghanistan Wars, see Mark Philip Bradley and Mary L. Dudziak, eds., *Making the Forever War: Marilyn B. Young on the Culture and Politics of American Militarism* (Amherst: University of Massachusetts Press, 2021). The relevant twentieth-century historiography is detailed in Allen R. Millett, "The Korean War: A 50-Year Critical Historiography," *Journal of Strategic Studies* 24, 1 (2001): 188–224.

5 Although it touches on the military course of the war, Denis Stairs's seminal volume, *The Diplomacy of Constraint,* focuses on understanding how the war shaped Canadian foreign policy and how multilateralism was a method of constraining the American superpower through Canada's admittedly limited means. A more recent work, John Price's *Orienting Canada,* examines the Korean War more in passing, as part of an overall effort to correct the perspective that Canada was solely an "Atlantic" country. Using race as a filter, Price re-establishes the importance of the Pacific and East Asian populations and politics to the formulation of Canadian foreign and domestic policy. Like American historian Bruce Cumings, Price is critical of the Korean War as an exercise in American imperialism and marshals evidence to reveal the role that racist attitudes towards Koreans and East Asians played in the prosecution of the war. Both Stairs and Price account for an important chapter in Canadian military and diplomatic history – not the Korean War per se, but how Canada reacted to the replacement of the British Empire with the American empire at the end of the Second World War and the dawn of the Cold War. See Francine Mackenzie, "The Conundrum of Canadian-American Relations," *International Journal* 69, 1 (2014): 110–17. See also Andrew Burtch, *Give Me Shelter: The Failure of Canada's Cold War Civil Defence* (Vancouver: UBC Press, 2012); and Andrew Godefroy, *In Peace Prepared: Innovation and Adaptation in Canada's Cold War Army* (Vancouver: UBC Press, 2014).

6 Masuda Hajimu, *Cold War Crucible: The Korean Conflict and the Postwar World* (Cambridge, MA: Harvard University Press), 285.

7 Hajimu, *Cold War Crucible,* 6–9. A Canadian exploration of this trend can be found in Robert Bothwell, "The Cold War and the Curate's Egg: When Did Canada's Cold War Really Begin? Later Than You Think," *International Journal* 53, 3 (1998): 407–18.

8 John Lewis Gaddis, *We Now Know: Rethinking Cold War History* (Oxford: Oxford University Press, 1997), 70–77. For a full inventory of the seminal work carried out through the *Cold War International History Project,* see Yeseul Lee and Jihan Kim, "The Korean War: A Bibliography of Wilson Center Publications," *Wilson Center: Sources and Methods,* 23 June 2020, https://www.wilsoncenter.org/blog-post/korean-war-bibliography-wilson-center-publications.

9 Bruce Cumings, *The Origins of the Korean War,* vol. 1, *Liberation and the Emergence of Separate Regimes, 1945–1947,* and vol. 2, *The Roaring of the Cataract, 1947–1950* (Princeton, NJ: Princeton University Press, 1981, 1990). Often classified as "revisionist" scholarship,

owing to its sharply critical interpretation of the United States' role in the origins of the Korean War, its ongoing military presence in South Korea, and the extensive nature of the bombing campaigns against North Korea, Cumings' work offers indispensable insight into the origins and ongoing impacts of the Korean War and the legacies of atrocities committed by all sides in the conflict.

10 Su-kyoung Hwang, *Korea's Grievous War* (Philadelphia: University of Philadelphia Press, 2016); and Brendan Wright, "Politicidal Violence and the Problematics of Localized Memory at Civilian Massacre Sites: The Cheju 4:3 Peace Park and the Kŏch'ang Incident Memorial Park," *Cross-Currents: East Asian History and Culture Review* 4, 1 (2015): 151–80, https://doi.org/10.1353/ach.2015.0023.

11 For a summary of this scholarship, see Bruce Cumings, "A Murderous History of Korea," *London Review of Books*, 18 May 2017, https://www.lrb.co.uk/the-paper/v39/n10/bruce-cumings/a-murderous-history-of-korea.

12 As in other arenas, North and South Korea differ on the commemorative dates attached to the war. The North Koreans mark the armistice of 27 July 1953 as Victory Day in the Fatherland Liberation War. South Korea, meanwhile, marks 25 June, the anniversary of the North's invasion, as the key commemorative date, though the government often marks the armistice date.

13 The phrase most often employed is "more than 26,000 Canadians." This includes 21,940 Canadian soldiers (not including the 484 soldiers who served more than one tour), approximately 3,600 sailors, and an indeterminate number of air personnel. These figures do not include the approximately 7,000 military personnel who served in the theatre (Korea and Japan) between 1953 and 1957. In all, the number exceeds 30,000. We have chosen to include the more expansive number in this volume. For a discussion of troop deployments, see Wood, *Strange Battleground*, 257.

14 William Stueck, *Rethinking the Korean War: A New Diplomatic and Strategic History* (Princeton, NJ: Princeton University Press, 2004), 8. The move towards an international approach was itself a major change in the American historiography, which Stueck contributes to greatly with his work *The Korean War: An International History* (Princeton, NJ: Princeton University Press, 1997).

15 Its 2022 sequel, *The Battle at Lake Changjin II*, was the ninth highest-grossing film worldwide that year.

16 "Primate Sorry Korea Forgotten War," *Globe and Mail*, 15 November 1951.

17 See Tim Cook, *The Fight for History: 75 Years of Forgetting, Remembering, and Remaking Canada's Second World War* (Toronto: Allen Lane, 2020); and Tim Cook, *Vimy: The Battle and the Legend* (Toronto: Allen Lane, 2017).

18 Canadian War Museum, Oral History with Donovan Redknap, 14 January 2004, 31D 4 Redknap.

Part 1
Canada, Korea, and Politics

1

Alignment without Illusions: Canada's World, 1945–50

Hector Mackenzie and Norman Hillmer

At the end of the Second World War, Canada's global position was one of exceptional, unprecedented, and unaccustomed international standing, a result of its wartime military and economic contribution to victory and the devastating impact of that conflict on other nations. Its armed forces – by various measures, the fourth military, naval, and aerial power of the Allied wartime alliance – were prominent in the final offensives of 1944–45. Canada was also the fourth industrial power, with a disproportionate share of its output contributed to its allies, usually without asking for anything in return. That financial approach reflected its economic strength as the second greatest creditor nation in the world, after only the United States. Though loans and grants underwrote its exports to a considerable extent, Canada was unquestionably a major trading nation and a key source of goods vital not only for the war effort but also for postwar reconstruction in Europe. These goods included manufactured products, food, and mineral resources, notably uranium, essential for the peaceful and military development of atomic power.[1]

Canada was a steadfast postwar partner and ally of the United States and the United Kingdom. Close association in defence and foreign policy was reinforced by Canada's financial and trade interests. The country's wealth was determined by its commerce within the North Atlantic Triangle, which linked Canada, the United States, and the United Kingdom.[2] Canada was a major player in the global economy as its allies and enemies recovered from six years of conflict and even more years of economic and political disruption. In the new global institutions that it helped to shape – the International Monetary Fund, the World Bank, and the General Agreement on Tariffs and Trade – Canada's greatest preoccupation and its largest benefits centred on the reconciliation of American and British policies and interests. The rewards of reducing international barriers to trade and exchange were expressed and gained in traditional markets for Canada's exports. The economic world outside the North Atlantic Triangle was not nearly as important to Canada.[3]

Policy-makers at the heart of government were under no illusion that the increase in the country's stature and influence was permanent. But the circumstances that gave Canada clout when the war ended were expected to last for some time. There was a firm resolve to wield the country's temporary authority to help its principal allies, the United Kingdom and the United States, in establishing an international regime that favoured its long-term interests and values. Whatever the forum or issue, Canada's stance was remarkably consistent and unambiguous. There were occasional differences over priorities or specific actions, but Canada's North Atlantic alignment was unshakable. Most of the time, Canada could rely on its allies to pursue objectives and outcomes that were consonant with its own aims. Taking the initiative was seldom seen as necessary, although there were times when the Canadian government took a leadership role, as it did in the establishment of the General Agreement on Tariffs and Trade and as it would in the talks that led to the North Atlantic Treaty in 1949.

The country's armed forces had a small presence in the Pacific, most notably at the doomed defence of Hong Kong and in airlift operations over Burma, as well as a short-lived naval contribution. Canada's significant participation in the global conflict and its major contributions to victory in the Second World War were predominantly in the North Atlantic, alongside its long-time partners in world affairs. An Anglo-American perspective framed all aspects of Canada's international outlook and determined how and when it would act. There was no notion of an independent path for Canada. It was hoped that, when the war was over, the victorious coalition would implement and uphold the noble aims that they had elaborated in wartime – in effect, that the victors would collaborate to win the peace much as they had done to defeat their enemies.

Central to the Allied alliance's grand design for the postwar world was the United Nations, established at the 1945 San Francisco peace conference and intended as the continuation of the victorious wartime alliance, with the UN's membership, structure, and distribution of powers reflecting that origin and purpose. San Francisco was the occasion for much idealism about the new organization's potential to act as the fulcrum for multiple levers of global co-operation, but the making of the UN was, at bottom, an exercise in unsentimental politics and diplomacy. Here as elsewhere in the war-winning partnership, the contradictory interests that weakened the UN from the beginning were in evidence.[4]

Canada's international engagement after 1945 stood in marked contrast to its deliberately limited involvement before the war. In the poet W.H. Auden's "low dishonest decade" of the 1930s, Canadians stood aloof from the conflicts of Europe and Asia. Within the evolving British Commonwealth, however weighty the bonds of sentiment and self-interest, Canada's relationship with the United Kingdom was, at best, an informal alliance. There were strong military ties but no definite obligations.[5] Canada and the United States, despite mostly cordial relations and high-minded rhetoric, were not certain partners or allies. At the League of Nations, Canada evaded responsibility, claiming that the troubles of Europe were a world away from a young country with problems of its own. In early 1937, aware of what was at stake if aggression overseas went unchecked, Prime Minister William Lyon Mackenzie King instituted a program of modest rearmament. Against the grain of a reluctant Canada, he eased his country's politics towards participation in the coming war.[6]

During the Second World War, repeating a frequent complaint of the 1930s, King's critics did not think that his foreign policy amounted to much.[7] The Department of External Affairs, small in numbers but bursting with ideas, was "always at me to be asserting more strongly Canada's position," the prime minister complained.[8] Hume Wrong, the brightest of Canada's diplomats, provided the idea that became rooted in wartime policy as the functional principle, which argued for greater representation in allied decision-making bodies where Canada had resources or other assets that justified its participation.[9] Lester Pearson, serving in senior External Affairs posts in London, Washington, and Ottawa during the war, explored the notion of Canada as an in-between or middle state, residing somewhere between a little big power and a big little power. Soon enough, expanding on the theme, External Affairs was using the term *middle power* to claim that Canada was close to being a great power by reason of its size, stability, material resources, and willingness to accept responsibility.[10] In a widely distributed 1944 pamphlet, Pearson promoted Canada's powerful war effort and enhanced international standing in what he called the emerging "world community." Yet he made clear that Canada's relationships with the United States and Britain and its Commonwealth mattered most. Nothing could be allowed to bring "Canada's American and British interests" into conflict.[11] A similar pragmatism characterized thinking at the San Francisco peace conference. Canada's delegation at the peace table was out to "get what it could," in the words of historian Robert Bothwell, "but not at the price of offending the great powers, meaning the Americans and the British."[12]

Canada's moderate stance at San Francisco reflected what came before and what came after. There was no sudden break with the past that ushered in a course of disinterested internationalism that revolutionized Canadian foreign policy.[13] Mackenzie King, fully in control and uncomfortable with taking on too much international responsibility, remained prime minister until the end of 1948. His officials at External Affairs themselves found in postwar geopolitics the advantages of caution and restraint.[14] At the same time, there was a much greater role for Canada in world affairs and a significant shift in the appreciation of how best to advance its interests. Politicians and policy-makers acknowledged that Canada and the world had changed and grasped the opportunities and dangers that lay ahead, as well as what remained constant. This interplay of change and continuity happened within the decisive and familiar context of the North Atlantic. Charles Ritchie, who joined External Affairs before the Second World War, remembered that time well. "We were all Atlantic men," he told an audience in the 1980s.[15]

At the beginning of 1947, shortly after King appointed him foreign minister, Louis St. Laurent gave a landmark address at the University of Toronto describing the "foundations of Canadian policy in world affairs." There were, he announced, five principles that guided the government's thinking – national unity, political liberty, respect for the rule of law, Christian values, and a willingness to take on global responsibilities. To the speaker and his audience, these tenets were not expressions of a new international outlook, as some commentators have insisted.[16] Instead, they had been identified and verified by experience. The Second World War demonstrated that St. Laurent's principles were best upheld in concert with like-minded and more powerful allies. Beliefs about what was right for Canada, furthermore, were enhanced by the extent to which they were shared with Canada's closest partners in world affairs and other nations with which it might collaborate in pursuit of constructive international cooperation. St. Laurent went out of his way to emphasize the limited influence of "any secondary power" such as Canada. He saw "little point in a country of our stature recommending international action, if those who must carry the major burden of whatever action is taken are not in sympathy."[17] The fluently bilingual St. Laurent was presented to the Toronto audience by his hosts as the embodiment of the "Canadian unity" imperative of the nation's life and politics.[18] Already the obvious choice to become the country's next leader, St. Laurent became prime minister the following year and brought Lester Pearson into his government as foreign minister. They were a formidable team for the next decade. They were also, as Ritchie put it, "the inheritors of Mackenzie King."[19]

When the Allied wartime coalition fractured and divided into the hostile camps that ultimately defined the Cold War, there was never any question about which side Canada would take in the transcendent clash of interests and ideas.[20] As the North Atlantic partners split from their former ally, the Union of Soviet Socialist Republics (USSR), and confronted their adversary over contested terrain in Europe, the Middle East, and Asia and the Pacific, Canadians and their government employed their newfound wealth and power steadfastly in support of the policies and actions of its Cold War allies. In late-1940s meetings of Commonwealth prime ministers, which included representatives from the new

South Asian dominions of India, Pakistan, and Ceylon, Canada was instrumental in redefining the criteria of membership so that republican members could remain in an increasingly multiracial organization. The government hoped to employ that goodwill to strengthen the Commonwealth as a Cold War bulwark, establish key links to South Asia, and sway the new dominions in favour of positions consistent with Canada's global purposes.[21] Similarly, in the novel setting of the UN, no matter the question on the agenda, the paramount purpose was to bolster the Western side in a bipolar world.

Canada played a leading part, not of its own volition, in the revelation of Soviet espionage that did so much to initiate and sustain the bipolar division of the world. The first evidence of USSR spying in North America came from the testimony of a cipher clerk in the Soviet embassy in Ottawa, Igor Gouzenko, who defected in September 1945, carrying with him incriminating documents.[22] Mackenzie King hesitated for a moment – the Soviets, after all, were "close friends" – but he took firm hold of Ottawa's response to the crisis while he and his officials kept in close contact with their Anglo-American counterparts and took their advice seriously. The world had taken on an "appalling outlook," King wrote in his diary, fearing another war that would bring "total destruction" and "come against America by way of Canada from Russia." Canada, the United Kingdom, and the United States, he counselled, had to form a united front to meet an existential threat.[23]

Days after Gouzenko's revelations were made public in February 1946, Winston Churchill spoke in Fulton, Missouri, about the breakdown of the wartime alliance and the descent of an "iron curtain" dividing eastern from western Europe. Churchill's visit to the United States fit the purposes of President Harry Truman, who introduced the former British prime minister to his audience and sat approvingly nearby as the speech hit its mark. According to the Cold War historian Melvyn Leffler, Churchill's "warning of a totalitarian menace intent on geopolitical domination resonated deeply" in the minds of Americans, accelerating "a widespread hostility to the Soviet Union. Changing perceptions of the Kremlin permitted Truman and his advisers to go on the offensive."[24] In Ottawa, Mackenzie King saw in Churchill's Fulton plea for Anglo-American collaboration another chance to line Canada up with its two closest economic and defence partners in the anti-Soviet fight. Lester Pearson had a folksy image at hand that captured King's thinking. Canadians liked to play the triangle in the international symphony. They were happiest when the British and American instruments were in harmony.[25]

Alongside the United States and Britain, Canada worked during the Second World War on the development of atomic energy and its application to nuclear weapons. That program, which had been one of the principal targets of Soviet espionage, carried on after 1945, with American leadership even more pronounced than before. Canada was represented on the Combined Policy Committee, established in 1943 and designed to continue the Anglo-American-Canadian wartime cooperation into the peace. The committee was chaired and directed by the United States, but increasingly the Americans acted unilaterally, with minimal consultation with their allies. That tendency for the United States to go it alone and to withhold highly secret information from even its closest partners was reinforced when the USSR successfully tested its own atomic weapon in the late summer of 1949. The Soviet bomb's accelerated development was attributed to spies linked to the Anglo-American scientific contribution to the trilateral program. Canada participated actively in the UN Atomic Energy Commission, with General A.G.L. McNaughton serving as its first chair, though that institution was effectively sidelined by the independent and adversarial actions of the two superpowers.[26]

Canadian engagement with the UN was shaped by its role as a forum in which the government articulated its alignment with the Western alliance in a divided world. This was demonstrated by Canada's conduct during its 1948–49 term as a temporary member of the UN Security Council (UNSC), where the consistent aim was to bridge differences within its own grouping of member countries, not with the West's principal adversaries in the Cold War. Canada sought to avoid or limit the damage from contradictory interpretations by the United States and the United Kingdom of regional conflicts, whether in Asia or the Middle East. That intent, rather than any dedication to the UN as an institution whose membership was far from universal, explains Canada's stance on a succession of major issues that came before the UNSC. Canada donned the armour of a Cold Warrior rather than the garments of a peacemaker. Its attempts at mediation or conciliation, the professed avocation of responsible middle powers such as Canada in the postwar international system, were directed at easing interallied tensions rather than seeking the best outcome for the antagonists. The overwhelming, almost exclusive, focus of Canada's interest and activity was Europe and the North Atlantic, even when the locus of the dispute before the UNSC was elsewhere.[27]

The most inflammatory dispute dealt with by the UNSC during Canada's term, and the one that most seriously divided the United Kingdom and the United States, concerned the fate of the mandate in Palestine, which the British had abandoned in 1948. Canada had withstood considerable pressure to serve on the UN Special Commission on Palestine. At the UNSC, its foremost aim, as stated by Foreign Minister St. Laurent, was to avoid "a bitter public controversy between the United Kingdom and the United States on this matter," since that could only benefit the USSR.[28] Prime Minister King agreed that reconciliation of British and American views was Canada's priority. Part of the strategy, reminiscent of Canada's stance at the League of Nations in the 1930s, was to be as quiet as possible. Its discretion brought a success – an Anglo-American agreement to appoint a regional mediator – but that accord did not last. Even as the disagreements became wider and more public, compounded by sympathies for the Jewish cause in Washington and sentiment falling on the Arab side in London, Canada treated the restoration of Anglo-American harmony as far more important than the fate of Palestine or the United Nations.

The clash between India and Pakistan over Kashmir was already on the UNSC's agenda when Canada took its seat. Canada was again determined not to take sides, only assuming a mediatory role when obliged to do so by its presidency of the UNSC in the final month of its term in 1949. Canada's representative, General McNaughton, side-stepped continuing involvement by stressing that Canada's time on the UNSC was coming to an end. The suspicion was that the British and Americans wanted Canada to assume a responsibility that neither country was prepared to accept. However, at least Canada's principal allies were not divided on the question. Instead, it was the Commonwealth relationship that was threatened. As did its key partners, Canada interpreted the dispute over Kashmir from the perspective of its implications for the Western alliance rather than on the basis of an assessment of what might be best for the UN, South Asia, or Kashmir.

The third major conflict to come before the UNSC while Canada was a member was Indonesia's struggle for independence from the Netherlands. Once again, the local questions and even the broader issue of colonial rule versus national self-determination were subordinated in Canadian assessments and actions to the implications of the problem for the West. The Netherlands was expected to join the North Atlantic Treaty Organization, and negotiations to that end were underway by the autumn of 1948. What most worried the Canadians, along with the British and Americans, was that the Dutch government's harsh suppression of the Indonesian independence movement was alienating the rest of the world, with potentially "grievous consequences in the relations between the Western world and Asiatic community generally."[29] Canada's cautious approach upset India and Australia especially, both firm supporters of Indonesian independence, so the Commonwealth, which Canada hoped could play a pro-Western role in world affairs, was divided on this question as well. Canada's efforts to persuade the Dutch to moderate their stance succeeded only after worldwide condemnation forced the Netherlands to seek a way out through a ceasefire and negotiated agreement to establish an Indonesian republic, a path illuminated by McNaughton's persistent diplomacy.

The most emphatic expression of Canada's Atlanticist alignment was its zeal to transform the nebulous sense of shared Western perspectives and fears of the USSR into the firm commitments that underpinned the North Atlantic Treaty. That outlook and resolve prompted Louis St. Laurent to warn the UN General Assembly in September 1947 that the West, "if forced," might "seek greater safety in an association of democratic and peace-loving states willing to accept more specific international obligations in return for a greater measure of international security."[30] St. Laurent's speech highlighted perceptions and concerns not only in Canada but elsewhere in what was increasingly seen as a North Atlantic world, encompassing western Europe, with Britain included, and North America. At the invitation of the American and British governments, Canadian delegates participated in the highly secret and ultimately decisive talks in the Pentagon with their British and American counterparts during March and April 1948.

The Canadians made vital contributions to drafting a document that provided the rationale and framework of a prospective treaty, particularly in persuading the Americans that a unilateral guarantee of support, subject to reversal by another president (or even the current president), would not meet the needs of a threatened and vulnerable western Europe. Those "security conversations" not only outlined the provisions that must be included in a treaty, but also set out the requisite obligations of the signatories for collective self-defence in unmistakable and unambiguous language. Throughout the early "ABC talks" and the wider negotiations that followed, it was an irrevocable American commitment to the defence of western Europe that was indispensable. Canadian negotiators, like the British and later their European colleagues, were determined to obtain a binding American pledge. The North Atlantic Treaty, signed on 1 April 1949, gave them just that.[31]

Later Canadian commentaries would stress how the representatives of Canada strove to broaden the purposes of the North Atlantic alliance with the Treaty's Article 2, the clause affirming the need for political, social, and economic collaboration.[32] The pursuit of that goal, though, was always a lesser consideration than Article 5, which especially assured the European members of immediate and substantial American help in the event of an attack by the unnamed but obvious enemy, the USSR. Canada understood and supported the European position. Article 2 was desirable. Article 5 was vital, and, for all signatories, it was the essence of the alliance. The illusion that the UN might herald an era of global cooperation and peaceful collaboration had been dispelled. The concept and means for collective security were redefined by the treaty and limited to a regional pact, whose geographical scope included those nations most important for Canada's prosperity and security, as well as its most likely partners in international affairs. As before, Canada's international perspective was dominated by the North Atlantic, but it was now to be protected by a military alliance in peacetime, a significant departure for Canada as well as the United States, and an advance on past British commitments to Europe. Hume Wrong, Canada's chief treaty negotiator, welcomed the prospect of the pieces of the North Atlantic Triangle being brought into a regularized defence partnership. His hope was that the presence of Britain might ease some of the pressures that were accumulating in the ever-tighter Canada–US military relationship.[33] As the influence of the United States in North American affairs grew, the notion that multilateral alignments could counter the power of the United States took hold in Canada's foreign policy.[34]

Even as it was pledging its support for the territorial integrity of those states lying in the potential path of the Red Army, the Canadian government stayed aloof from an early test of Western resolve in Europe, the dramatic 1948–49 allied airlift in response to the land blockade of West Berlin by the USSR and its authorities in the eastern zone of occupied Germany. This failure to match Canada's actions to its internationalist rhetoric cannot be entirely attributed to the chronic anxiety of the departing leader, Mackenzie King. The policy was emphatically supported by his defence minister, Brooke Claxton, who was not keen to risk Canadian personnel and equipment in a dangerous mission that might spark a third world war. Nor was the decision to turn a deaf ear to British entreaties for help reversed by King's successors after he left office.[35] Canada's abstention from the Berlin airlift has been ignored in later commemorations of the event, to which the Canadian ambassador is invariably invited to mark the successful defiance of the USSR by the Western allies.

The other place where American and Soviet forces confronted one another after the war was in the Korean Peninsula, with occupation zones divided by the armistice at the thirty-eighth parallel. Canada's involvement there initially came through a back door that was opened by the delegation of the United States to the UN, not because of any direct Canadian interest or commitment. That engagement provoked a serious controversy within the Canadian government, prompting one of the more unexpected and bizarre Cabinet crises in the country's political history, especially since it was a group of notably harmonious ministers.

The United States was keen to extricate itself from its costly role as an occupying power in the southern part of the peninsula, preferably by shifting the burden to the UN, where it might advance its aims by proxy. It hoped to provide a pretext for the withdrawal of Soviet as well as American forces from the peninsula and unify Korea as perhaps a democratic and preferably a pro-Western country. The first step on this path would be the establishment of what the United States proposed as a United Nations Temporary Commission on Korea (UNTCOK). Without warning or consultation, the United States nominated Canada as a member in a resolution passed by the UN General Assembly in mid-November 1947. This happened while King was in London for the wedding of Princess Elizabeth, so St. Laurent was acting prime minister. St. Laurent and Pearson approved the recommendation of the Canadian delegation to accept this role, not out of any concern for the fate of Korea, but as a favour to the United States.[36]

When King learned of this decision taken in his absence, he was apoplectic, not only because he opposed an active role in Korea but also because he had not been consulted. At the first Cabinet meeting after his return, he opposed the Order-in-Council required to appoint a Canadian representative to UNTCOK. An acrimonious dispute followed between King and his anointed successor, St. Laurent, who threatened to resign over the matter. His deputy minister, Pearson, also intended to resign in support of his minister if King did not relent. The Cabinet in the end agreed to name the Canadian diplomat and Asian expert George Patterson to UNTCOK, with the explicit understanding that he would quit the body if it attempted to extend its authority beyond the south of Korea, where it had permission to function. Should the commission attempt to intervene where it was not welcome – above the thirty-eighth parallel – Canada would play no part in that endeavour. That King did not follow up on this condition to remove Canada from UNTCOK's membership when the commission ventured, at American behest, to sponsor elections ostensibly governing the whole peninsula in May 1948 does not alter the fact that the Canadian government's decision surrounding the appointment was a compromise.[37] These were not, as King's defence minister claimed, "the last bellows of the leader of the herd before he cashed in the cheques."[38]

Moreover, when an opportunity presented itself, shortly after King's retirement, for the government to extricate itself from this unwelcome responsibility, it did so promptly and effectively. The UN General Assembly decided in December 1948 to reconstitute UNTCOK as the United Nations Commission on Korea. In the circumstances, the Canadian government volunteered to resign, with the disingenuous argument that the commission would function better with fewer members. Canada's formal involvement in the affairs of the North Pacific came to an end barely a month after St. Laurent succeeded King as prime minister.

In the aftermath of that withdrawal and with its preoccupation with the North Atlantic Treaty and the fate of Europe, the Canadian government paid little attention to what was happening on the Korean peninsula and in that part of the world. Even the establishment of the People's Republic of China on 1 October 1949, after the Communist triumph in the Chinese Civil War, was treated as a secondary concern since there was no "strong sense that vital Canadian interests were engaged."[39] Pearson, then secretary of state for external affairs, made his first visit to Asia early the next year. In Tokyo, he was told by General Douglas MacArthur, supreme commander for the Allied powers in Japan and the senior American officer in Asia, that the United States would not defend South Korea, now the Republic of Korea. Pearson never forgot what MacArthur told him: "It would be embarrassing, it would be disappointing, it would be worrying if an enemy took Korea, but it is not vital to our security."[40] MacArthur's assurance was bound to be good news to Pearson. He, like most of his colleagues and subordinates, wanted the Western allies to keep their focus on Europe, the source of the most significant threat to world order.[41]

The American intervention in the summer of 1950, under the auspices of the UN, to defend the Republic of Korea against invasion from the north came as a shock to policy-makers in Ottawa. "At almost the exact time on 26 June when President Truman was deciding that the United States would be giving air and sea support to the South Koreans," Pearson wrote in his memoirs, "I was talking to some press people in Ottawa and telling them, off the record, that I did not expect a US military response to the invasion."[42] In the weeks and months that followed, the Canadian government scrambled to define and defend its initial tentative and somewhat limited commitment and then to enlarge that contribution, less from a determination to support South Korea than in response to persistent pressure from the government of the United States.[43] As the crisis unfolded and the conflict and its costs escalated, the Canadian government still cast a sharp eye on developments in Europe, as it worried that the conflict on the Korean peninsula might be a Soviet-inspired diversion to take attention and resources away from the principal battleground of the Cold War. A third world war might result.

The story of Canada's involvement in the Korean War and its surrounding diplomacy is one for other contributors to this volume. What is critical for an understanding of Canada's world before the Korean War is an appreciation of the extent to which Canada's international outlook and policies were shaped by a North Atlantic perspective. In the aftermath of the Second World War, the part Canada played in international affairs was that of an ally, not a bystander or disinterested activist. Canada's alignment was unequivocal, and there were no illusions about a peaceful new world order.

Notes

1 Roger Sarty, "Canada's Military Effort in the World Wars," in *Canada: Confederation to Present* (Edmonton, AB: Chinook Multimedia, 2001); Hector Mackenzie, "Sinews of War and Peace: The Politics of Economic Aid to Britain, 1939–1945," *International Journal* 54, 4 (1999): 648–70. The standard histories of Canada's Second World War politics and policies are C.P. Stacey, *Arms, Men and Governments: The War Policies of Canada, 1939–1945* (Ottawa: Queen's Printer, 1970); and J.L. Granatstein, *Canada's War: The Politics of the Mackenzie King Government, 1939–1945* (Toronto: Oxford University Press, 1975).

2 John Bartlet Brebner, *North Atlantic Triangle: The Interplay of Canada, the United States and Great Britain* (New Haven, CT: Yale University Press, 1945). Brebner's geometric image had its greatest application in the economic realm in the 1940s and early 1950s, and the triangle was always more visible and important for Canada than it was for Washington or London. See Hector Mackenzie, "Delineating the North Atlantic Triangle: The Second World War and Its Aftermath," *Round Table* 95, 383 (2006): 101–12.

3 Hector Mackenzie, "North Atlantic World: Canada and the Wartime Plans for the Postwar Global Economy, 1941–1947," *London Journal of Canadian Studies* 36, 1 (2022): 109–32.

4 Paul Kennedy, *The Parliament of Man: The Past, Present, and Future of the United Nations* (Toronto: HarperCollins, 2006), 24–47.

5 Norman Hillmer, "Defence and Ideology: The Anglo-Canadian Military 'Alliance' in the Nineteen Thirties," *International Journal* 33, 3 (1978): 588–612.

6 Hillmer, "Defence and Ideology," 609–11; and Norman Hillmer, *O.D. Skelton: A Portrait of Canadian Ambition* (Toronto: University of Toronto Press, 2015), chaps. 11–14.

7 See, for example, a survey of Canadian newspaper opinion by the British United Press, "Canada's Foreign Policy," *Canada Digest* 2, 3 (1945): 34–38; and Norman Hillmer, "The Foreign Policy That Never Was, 1900–1950," in *Canada, 1900–1950: A Country Comes of Age*, ed. Serge Bernier and John MacFarlane (Ottawa: Organization for the History of Canada, 2003), 149–50.

8 Quoted in F.H. Soward, "Some Aspects of Canadian Foreign Policy in the Last Quarter Century," *Transactions of the Royal Society of Canada* 4, 4 (1966): 141.

9 J.L. Granatstein, *The Ottawa Men: The Civil Service Mandarins, 1935–1957* (Toronto: Oxford University Press, 1992), 124–33.

10 James Eayrs, *In Defence of Canada*, vol. 3, *Peacemaking and Deterrence* (Toronto: University of Toronto Press, 1972), 164, and his "Defining a New Place for Canada in the Hierarchy of International Powers," *International Perspectives* (May-June 1975): 20. For a critique of the ways that middlepowerhood took hold in Canadian foreign policy, see Adam Chapnick, "The Canadian Middle Power Myth," *International Journal* 55, 2 (2000): 188–206.

11 L.B. Pearson, "Canada and the Post-War World," *Canadian Affairs* 1, 6 (1944): 14.

12 Robert Bothwell, *Alliance and Illusion: Canada and the World, 1945–1984* (Vancouver: UBC Press, 2007), 21.

13 Hector Mackenzie, "Golden Decade(s): Reappraising Canada's International Relations in the 1940s and 1950s," *British Journal of Canadian Studies* 23, 2 (2010): 179–206.

14 John English, "'A Fine Romance': Canada and the United Nations, 1943–1957," in *Canada and the Early Cold War, 1943–1957*, ed. Greg Donaghy (Ottawa: Department of Foreign Affairs and International Trade, 1998), 80–81.

15 Charles Ritchie, "After Dinner Thoughts" (presented at "Canada, the United States, and the Atlantic Alliance," Ryerson Polytechnical Institute, Toronto, Ontario, April 1987).

16 Hillmer, "Foreign Policy That Never Was," 51–52; and Hector Mackenzie, "Shades of Gray: 'The Foundations of Canadian Policy in World Affairs' in Context," *American Review of Canadian Studies* 37, 4 (2007): 459–73.

17 Louis St. Laurent, "The Foundations of Canadian Policy in World Affairs," Duncan and John Gray Memorial Lecture, University of Toronto, 13 January 1947, in Department of External Affairs, *Statements and Speeches*, 1947, 33.
18 St. Laurent, "Foundations," 9. The lecture was published with French and English side by side.
19 Quoted in English, "Fine Romance," 88.
20 On the Cold War importance of ideas, "and ideas in the broadest sense," see Louis Menand, *The Free World: Art and Thought in the Cold War* (New York: Farrar, Straus and Giroux, 2021), 5.
21 Hector Mackenzie, "An Old Dominion and the New Commonwealth: Canada and Republican India, 1947–49," *Journal of Imperial and Commonwealth History* 37, 3 (1999): 215–50.
22 Amy Knight, *How the Cold War Began: The Gouzenko Affair and the Hunt for Soviet Spies* (Toronto: McClelland and Stewart, 2005).
23 Hector Mackenzie, "Canada's International Relations in the Early Cold War: The Impact and Implications of the Gouzenko Afffair," in *The Gouzenko Affair: Canada and the Beginnings of Cold War Counter-Espionage*, ed. J.L. Black and Martin Rudner (Ottawa: Penumbra Press, 2006), 15–19, 20–27 (quotations on 16, 17, 22).
24 Melvyn P. Leffler, *A Preponderance of Power: National Security, the Truman Administration, and the Cold War* (Stanford, CA: Stanford University Press, 1992), 109.
25 Norman Hillmer, "The Canadian Diplomatic Tradition," in *Canadian Culture: International Dimensions*, ed. Andrew Fenton Cooper (Waterloo, ON: Centre on Foreign Policy and Federalism, University of Waterloo/Wilfrid Laurier University, 1985), 56–57; and Bothwell, *Alliance and Illusion*, 46–47.
26 Eayrs, *In Defence of Canada*, 3, 258–318; and John W. Holmes, *The Shaping of Peace: Canada and the Search for World Order, 1943–1957*, vol. 2 (Toronto: University of Toronto Press, 1982), 45–56.
27 The analysis here and in the three paragraphs that follow is from Hector Mackenzie, "Knight Errant, Cold Warrior or Cautious Ally? Canada on the United Nations Security Council, 1948–1949," *Journal of Transatlantic Studies* 7, 4 (2009): 453–75. See also Adam Chapnick, *Canada on the United Nations Security Council: A Small Power on a Large Stage* (Vancouver: UBC Press, 2019), chap. 2.
28 Quoted in Mackenzie, "Knight Errant," 458.
29 Quoted in Mackenzie, "Knight Errant," 464.
30 Quoted in Escott Reid, *Radical Mandarin: The Memoirs of Escott Reid* (Toronto: University of Toronto Press, 1989), 226.
31 Hector Mackenzie, "Canada, the Cold War and the Negotiation of the North Atlantic Treaty," in *Diplomatic Documents and Their Users*, ed. John Hilliker and Mary Halloran (Ottawa: Department of Foreign Affairs and International Trade, 1995), 145–73.
32 The essential source on Article 2 of the North Atlantic Treaty is John C. Milloy, *The North Atlantic Treaty Organization, 1948–1957: Community or Alliance?* (Montreal/Kingston: McGill-Queen's University Press, 2006).
33 Mackenzie, "North Atlantic Treaty," 81. For the ups and often downs of Canada's history in NATO, see Norman Hillmer, "Canada, the North Atlantic Treaty Organization and the Boundaries of Alignment," in *Activism and (Non)alignment: The Relationship between Foreign Policy and Security Doctrine*, ed. Ann-Sofie Dahl and Norman Hillmer (Stockholm: Swedish Institute of International Affairs, 2002), 55–70.
34 Hillmer, "Canadian Diplomatic Tradition," 57.
35 Leigh E. Sarty, "The Limits of Internationalism: Canada and the Soviet Blockade of Berlin, 1948–1949," in *Nearly Neighbours: Canada and the Soviet Union from Cold War to Détente and Beyond*, ed. J.L. Black and Norman Hillmer (Kingston, ON: Frye, 1989), 56–74.

36 John Price, in "The 'Cat's Paw': Canada and the United Nations Temporary Commission on Korea," *Canadian Historical Review* 85, 2 (2004): 297–324, argues that Pearson (but not King) acted as an agent of US imperialism.
37 Denis Stairs, *The Diplomacy of Constraint: Canada, the Korean War, and the United States* (Toronto: University of Toronto Press, 1974), 6–17.
38 Quoted in Bothwell, *Alliance and Illusion,* 81. See also Eayrs, *In Defence of Canada,* 3, 13–14.
39 Robert Bothwell, "Eyes West: Canada and the Cold War in Asia," in Donaghy, *Canada and the Early Cold War,* 67. See also Stephen Beecroft, "Canadian Policy toward China, 1949–1957: The Recognition Problem," in *Reluctant Adversaries: Canada and the People's Republic of China, 1949–1970,* ed. Paul M. Evans and B. Michael Frolic (Toronto: University of Toronto Press, 1991), 44–45.
40 John A. Munro and Alex. I. Inglis, eds., *Mike: The Memoirs of the Right Honourable Lester B. Pearson,* vol. 2, *1948–1957* (Toronto: University of Toronto Press, 1973), 147.
41 John English, "Lester Pearson and China," in Evans and Frolic, *Reluctant Adversaries,* 135.
42 Pearson, *Mike,* 2, 145.
43 Greg Donaghy, "The Road to Constraint: Canada and the Korean War, June-December 1950," in Hilliker and Halloran, *Diplomatic Documents,* 189–212.

2

Canadian Political Leadership and the Korean War

Ryan M. Touhey

In his first federal campaign as leader of the Liberal Party, Louis St. Laurent won a crushing majority on 27 June 1949 with 190 seats. Foreign policy issues, particularly Ottawa's relations and interests in Asia, did not feature in the campaign. But less than a year later, events in East Asia strained Canada's defence ties with the United States and challenged Ottawa's commitment to multilateralism. St. Laurent and his Cabinet were confronted with their first major foreign policy test as a government when North Korea invaded South Korea on 25 June 1950.

Between the election and the invasion of South Korea, tensions in Asia had forced the government to pay increasing attention to its policy towards the region, to debate whether to recognize the People's Republic of China following the Communists' mainland victory on 1 October 1949. Three weeks later, in this changing foreign-policy landscape, Jawaharlal Nehru, India's charismatic prime minister, made his first state visit to Ottawa. He impressed St. Laurent's secretary of state for external affairs, Lester Pearson, and senior members of the government as he urged Ottawa to become more engaged in Asia.

In January 1950, Pearson travelled to Colombo, Ceylon, for a Commonwealth conference before moving on to India and Pakistan. He returned to Ottawa and promoted what would become the Colombo Plan, the Commonwealth's foreign aid plan directed at stabilizing South Asia while blunting potential Communist inroads. At no point, however, was conflict in Korea expected to be an issue for the St. Laurent government, a problem that would lead to massive rearmament and the dispatch of Canadian forces to fight in Korea under the UN's flag.

St. Laurent's election as prime minister and the appointment of Pearson as secretary of state for external affairs are sometimes seen by historians as a refreshing new chapter that closed the door on the hesitant statecraft of the Mackenzie King era. A study of Ottawa's initial response to the Korean War suggests that this is not entirely the case. King's legacy lingered. In the early stages of the conflict, the Cabinet – echoing King's hesitation to commit Canada to international causes – reacted with caution, even disbelief, as it struggled to understand the invasion's significance and the expectations of its main ally, the United States. As a result, Canada's response was halting and uncertain, even as public rhetoric about supporting democracies against Communist aggression sharpened. However, by late summer 1950, Ottawa's actions showed a government catching up to events and conservatively managing an expanded involvement in the conflict as it kept its eye on public opinion. Reflecting politics over principle, the Canadian government sought to forget Korea and promoted economic stability and prosperity at home rather than trumpeting Canada's role abroad.[1]

The first major casualty of the Korean War for Canada came within days of its outbreak. Long-debated plans to formally establish diplomatic relations with the People's Republic of China came asunder. For months, the St. Laurent Cabinet had considered giving its chief diplomat on the ground, Chester Ronning, the green light to enter negotiations with the Chinese. The North Korean invasion put paid to that idea. With China as an ally of Pyongyang, and given a likely ferocious reply from the Americans if Ottawa were to proceed, the government looked to avoid any further diplomatic crises.

As summer unfolded, the St. Laurent government cautiously considered the scope of its response to the Korean War while looking to galvanize the public to stand behind it. On 27 June, two days after the invasion, St. Laurent met with Conservative leader George Drew, Co-operative Commonwealth Federation leader Stanley Knowles, and the Social Credit leader Solon Low. All three Opposition parties favoured the government's early decision to support a UN Security Council resolution to "furnish such assistance to the Republic of Korea as may be necessary to repel armed attack."[2] In the House of Commons, Pearson added a caveat: "We would do our full duty, but only as a member of the United Nations in concert with other members."[3] The Conservatives, the Co-operative Commonwealth Federation, and Social Credit even supported Pearson's explanation to the House of Commons – that "it was impossible to say what contribution, if any, Canada could make to the United Nations collective action" given the fluidity of the evolving situation.[4]

Cabinet met on 28 June and listened as Pearson outlined a sombre situation. North Korean forces had captured Seoul, South Korea's capital, and the security situation continued to deteriorate rapidly as the North Koreans advanced southwards. Noting that the United States would soon respond with greater force, Pearson informed his colleagues that the British government was considering whether to contribute naval units and possibly ground forces from Hong Kong. Rather than suggesting the Cabinet consider a similar military commitment, Pearson mentioned a request from the UN's secretary-general to provide two military officers for the UN Observer Corps in Korea. Pearson explained the secretary-general believed such a role "would be an indication" of Canada's goodwill.[5]

Recalling the extent to which the Canadian military had demobilized following the Second World War, Brooke Claxton, minister of national defence, added that "the only practical contribution that could be made at the present time appeared to be a provision of a number of Canadian destroyers," possibly supplemented with "a small squadron of transport aircraft." Claxton thought such a specific contribution "might be a desirable gesture."[6] Although prominent English-language newspapers such as the *Montreal Star* and *Winnipeg Free Press* were urging "unconditional support of the military effort Washington was hastily mounting under the UN flag," no decision was made.[7] In the House of Commons, Claxton and Pearson offered the government's argument for a cautious approach. However, Claxton deflated the Opposition's demands for immediate or precipitous defence spending: "We would be doing exactly what the communists want us to do. Consequently it is necessary for us to strike a balance between what might be needed ... and what we think it is proper and useful to do."[8] And on 30 June, Parliament rose for the summer. Cabinet ministers departed Ottawa uncertain as to whether South Korea and the American garrison could survive. Evidently, they were still sufficiently at ease to go on vacation.[9]

St. Laurent, however, instructed both Pearson and Claxton to determine what sort of participation the UN expected from Canada in Korea; until then, no decision on military assistance would be forthcoming.[10] Publicly, Ottawa emphasized its support for the multilateral, UN-led response in Korea. Officials were nevertheless wary that the United States was now taking the lead in organizing a UN-sanctioned military response. With safety in numbers, Pearson recalled in his memoirs that Ottawa "felt that we should participate as a member of the United Nations ... we wanted to be absolutely certain that this would be a United Nations and not a United States operation."[11] Behind the scenes, Ottawa grappled to understand what Washington wanted. The next six weeks would see a commitment gradually pieced together by St. Laurent, Pearson, Claxton, Finance Minister Douglas Abbott, and Minister of Trade and Commerce C.D. Howe, the key ministers directing the diplomatic, military, and economic response to the war.

Just over two weeks after the initial invasion, with Parliament still on summer recess, Cabinet decided on a small and contained naval offering that echoed

Mackenzie King's hope in the early days of the Second World War for a limited military contribution. Caution remained a key pillar of Canadian foreign relations. The St. Laurent Cabinet learned that the US commander for Korea, General Douglas MacArthur, would welcome three destroyers to the Korean theatre, and so on 5 July, HMCS *Cayuga*, HMCS *Sioux*, and HMCS *Athabaskan* set sail for Korean waters. Although the Cabinet understood "the present military situation was bad," there was no sign that Ottawa was prepared to send soldiers to fight in Korea. Pearson was adamant that "the contribution was in support of the United Nations only and that U.N. operations against Korea should not be confused with U.S. operations in other parts of the Far East," referring to tensions between the People's Republic of China and the United States over Taiwan.[12] Ottawa accordingly refused UN Secretary-General Trygve Lie's 14 July plea to UN members to send soldiers to help the Americans and South Koreans.[13] As historian David Bercuson has noted, in the days following Lie's appeal, St. Laurent was fishing, Claxton was in Newfoundland meeting American military officials, and the Chiefs of Staff Committee did not reconvene until 18 July, despite the calamitous security environment the Americans and South Koreans were engaged in against superior North Korean forces.[14]

Any hope that Ottawa could limit its involvement in Korea faded in mid-July. On 19 July, Cabinet met to discuss Lie's public request – now sent as a formal communication to the government – for "effective assistance," including ground forces. St. Laurent expressed annoyance with what he believed was a pressure tactic. Cabinet, caught off guard by the undiplomatic message, listened as Claxton detailed the chiefs of staff's view that "Canada was not in a position to contribute ground forces," largely because of five years of defence cuts. Concerned that the Soviets were using the conflict to deplete Western military capabilities, both Claxton and the chief of the general staff, Charles Foulkes, did not want Canada to become significantly embroiled in Korea.[15]

Air transport in East Asia, however, was in short supply, and a Canadian contribution of North Star aircraft could quickly be made available to help the Americans.[16] Claxton also argued that events in Korea had made it necessary to reflect on "steps which might be taken to strengthen Canadian defences generally." But here, too, Claxton expected such actions to be modest in cost and scope, "with additional expenditures" across the armed services to "be between $40 and $50 million and the over-all increase in personnel would be between 5 and 6 thousand men."[17] Considerable political pressure to contribute troops was coming from the Americans, Pearson added.

Washington was annoyed with what it regarded as Canada's slow response to contribute to the mission. For example, on the evening of Lie's appeal, Pearson gave a public speech in which he declared that deploying three Canadian destroyers was "no mere token." He suggested that if one of the destroyers was sunk, it would lead to a tremendous loss of life, surpassing American casualties in the first month of the conflict. Pearson's remark went over poorly in Washington. One State Department official replied acidly, "Okay, let's call it three tokens."[18] Reconsidering the scope of Canada's contribution at a Cabinet meeting, Pearson supported Claxton's position that Ottawa could recruit Canadian volunteers to form a brigade under the UN flag to relieve the converging diplomatic and military pressures. Cabinet agreed to proceed with the deployment of a squadron of North Star aircraft to supply and reinforce UN forces in Korea and approved Claxton's request for a limited increase in defence expenditures.[19]

Following the Cabinet meeting, St. Laurent briefed the press, updating them on Canada's expanded contribution. Pearson, who believed the Americans were putting undue pressure on their allies to send ground troops, quietly fumed. He put pen to paper and wrote a blunt letter to his friend Hume Wrong, the Canadian ambassador in Washington. "I think that we can and should do considerably more than we have done," he admitted, but the decision to send aircraft and to boost defence expenditures represented "the first step in that direction; no doubt it will have to be followed by others." However, taking additional steps would not be helped if "the impression is given that the U.S. is bringing pressure on us, or suggestions are made that we are not pulling our weight." Public opinion had to be considered, and Ottawa would need to weigh its actions in light of what Canadians would support. This was especially true given that conscription during the world wars had provoked deep distrust in Quebec and elsewhere in Canada towards overseas commitments. St. Laurent and other Cabinet members remembered the political crisis that conscription had created. Pearson continued, "So far, we have carried the Canadian people along," and Quebec "has been relatively calm and is becoming friendlier to stronger Canadian action." Given the emerging, but delicate consensus, Pearson believed it imperative for Ottawa and Washington to avoid taking any action that would "destroy that general support."[20] Pearson had reason to closely observe domestic opinion. A Gallup poll released two weeks after his reply to Wrong revealed that only 21 percent of Quebecers approved of Canada sending soldiers to fight in Korea. Across English Canada, that number was only marginally higher at 41 percent.[21] Despite the Communist invasion of the South, in the summer of 1950, this was not a popular war.

Pearson also informed Wrong that the most recent Canadian contribution was "as far as we intend to go here in participation in U.N. action in Korea at this time."[22] Pearson, however, had not let Wrong know that a decision to commit ground forces had fostered "considerable division" within Cabinet just as American and UN political pressure intensified.

Ironically, Mackenzie King's death afforded the Cabinet the opportunity to travel together by train to Toronto for his funeral on 27 July. A frank discussion about Korea unfolded during that journey. King's legacy of exercising caution in foreign relations was evident. Pearson reflected in his memoirs, "For almost the entire trip we argued about what we should do." He was now convinced, the Gallup poll notwithstanding, that the Cabinet had not properly gauged the mood of the country. He argued in favour of sending an expeditionary force. Others, such as the labour minister, Humphrey Mitchell, reflected on what King would have done and concluded that "he wouldn't be getting involved."[23] Also wary of sending Canadian soldiers to Korea were the minister of national health and welfare, Paul Martin, and the agriculture minister, Jimmy Gardiner, a long-standing member of Cabinet with clout because of his seniority. Historian Robert Prince has noted that Pearson came close to resigning until St. Laurent backed his judgment, expressing support for a small contribution of infantry.[24]

In the final week of July, the Cabinet continued to debate Ottawa's next steps. This process was aided when the US ambassador, Stanley Woodward, delivered a specific request from Washington seeking Canadian ground forces. Speaking to the American request, Pearson noted that other UN countries, particularly Australia, Britain, and New Zealand, had now made similar commitments. He reiterated his support "for a brigade group [to] be specially recruited as volunteers" as part of a UN force. His rationale was forthright and couched in Pearson's broader foreign-policy goals for Canada in the Cold War: "Canada had every interest in strengthening the U.S. position as [a] leader in the struggle against communism. The lesson of effective United Nations co-operation would not be lost" on Moscow.[25] If Cabinet had been divided earlier about any such decision, the opponents quietly held back as the likes of Brooke Claxton, C.D. Howe, and the Cabinet veteran Robert Mayhew lined up behind Pearson, who was instructed to discuss the deployment of Canadian soldiers with his American counterpart, Dean Acheson.[26] The next day, Pearson and the secretary to the Cabinet, Norman Robertson, discreetly travelled to Washington for direct and far-ranging discussions with Acheson at the Canadian embassy and, afterwards, with Trygve Lie in New York before returning home to meet with Cabinet in the first week of August.

Frustrated with the slow pace of Ottawa's decision making, the conservative-leaning but nationally prominent newspaper the *Globe and Mail* blasted the St. Laurent government in two blunt editorials on 3 and 5 August. Declaring that "Public Opinion Asserts Itself," *The Globe* asserted, "For weeks virtually every daily newspaper in Canada has been expressing disappointment and dissatisfaction with the Federal Government's attitude on Korea ... When decisiveness and boldness were called for, Ottawa was hesitant and timid."[27] Adding to its pointed criticism, *The Globe* printed snippets of critical editorials from eleven newspapers from across the country, some of them Liberal friendly, and all voicing their frustration with Ottawa's handling of the crisis. Two days later, while the Cabinet gathered in Ottawa to discuss the next steps in Korea, *The Globe* continued its barrage with an editorial, "Is This Leadership?," while calling for Claxton to be replaced "with a full time, interested, vigorous and competent Minister."[28]

Finally, on 7 August 1950, the St. Laurent government announced its commitment to support the UN-led effort in Korea with a contribution of ground forces coinciding with a significant rearmament pledge to strengthen the armed services. The government's preliminary hope of accepting limited liability in the Korean War had evaporated in part because of public demand from the English-language press but especially because of direct and repeated requests from the United States and the United Nations. Ottawa now sought to raise a Canadian Army Special Force of between five thousand and ten thousand men separate from the Permanent Force and would spend a further $90 million on the armed forces for 1950–51. The minister of finance, Douglas Abbott, cautioned that Canada likely faced moving towards "a semi-war economy during the next few years," but he expressed confidence that the national economy, in addition to a sizable budget surplus, could absorb defence spending increases. Indeed, it is striking the extent to which the Cabinet now supported Claxton's requests.[29] Later that day, St. Laurent announced the decision nationwide in a radio address. Claxton initially believed that few would volunteer for combat in Korea, although he was pleasantly surprised when crowds of men eagerly volunteered to join the Canadian Army Special Force, initially overwhelming recruitment centres.[30] Claxton monitored the establishment of the force with great interest, insisting he be told "of every proposed development" while working closely with the chief of defence staff, Charles Foulkes.[31]

A special parliamentary session convened on 29 August with the speech from the throne. Hopes of a sleepy summer were long over, and Korea had not been the only crisis. The first national railway strike in Canadian history began on 22 August, threatening the national economy just as Ottawa was planning a war and rearming. Unusually (and a clear sign that Korea was deeply on his mind, as noted by his secretary, Dale Thomson), St. Laurent met with railway management and workers and urged them to find a consensus for the sake of the national interest.[32] Neither party appeared willing to budge, and a frustrated

St. Laurent moved swiftly to intervene. Parliament would now debate legislative action to send the workers back to the railyards and urgently discussed deploying Canadian soldiers to Korea, defence spending, and how to pay for the conflict.

In his memoir, former clerk of the Privy Council and St. Laurent-era Cabinet minister Jack Pickersgill suggested that "St. Laurent and the Cabinet had shown no hesitation about deciding to send Canadian troops to fight in eastern Asia." That is not true as the sequence of events mentioned above illustrates. Unsurprisingly, given that St. Laurent had been mentored by King and was strongly attuned to Quebec politics and public opinion, the prime minister was sensitive to the fact that past participation in both world wars had severely tested national unity. He was determined that Korea would not tear the nation asunder. He also demanded that any deployment of additional forces to Korea would be made transparent to the Canadian public.[33]

During the next few months, St. Laurent "spoke frequently to groups of Canadians on the new situation" that the country found itself in while dismissing suggestions that conscription was imminent.[34] When Parliament resumed in early September, the government could bask in the fact that only one member of Parliament, P.E. Gagnon, representing Chicoutimi as an Independent, opposed Canadian participation in Korea.[35] Still, this one outlier – along with a critical article by journalist Pierre Laporte in the nationalist Montreal newspaper *Le Devoir* that began with the question, "Are we to return to the era of Mr. King's lies?" – was troublesome. Laporte wrote, "Mr. St. Laurent has deceived us about Korea – 5000 men who turn out to be 15,000."[36] St. Laurent brushed the criticism aside and promised governmental transparency in the event Ottawa needed to commit additional forces to Korea. He needn't have worried. French Canadian volunteers had come forward in greater numbers than anticipated. Despite this positive outcome, Ottawa remained cautious in selling the war to Canadians. Blair Fraser, *Maclean's* editor, reflected, "The Government seems to think, and perhaps rightly, that too much enthusiasm, too much talk of war and preparedness might boomerang in Quebec and produce, not a growing support, but a revival of the old-anti-war hysteria."[37] Ottawa's sensitivity to maintaining national unity had the effect of containing what hostility existed on the Opposition benches and in the press.

Confirmation is evident in political scientist J.I. Gow's study of Quebec French-language newspaper editorials from 1950. Gow explored whether newspaper editors promoted or condemned the idea of greater Canadian involvement in Korea. The study revealed that eight newspapers were in support, two reserved judgment, and two were opposed to Canadians fighting in Korea.[38] Good news from Korea in mid-September 1950 provided another boost to the government. Coast to coast, Canadians read or heard on the radio that General MacArthur's daring landing at Inchon had not only succeeded but also threatened to cut North Korean forces off from their lines of communication northward. The Americans were on the march to liberate Seoul.

Some, even some in Cabinet, believed the war might be over before the first draft of Canadian soldiers crossed the Pacific. There was also a growing consensus that Canada should be involved in Korea to oppose communism, which no doubt helped the St. Laurent government carry the public with its gradualist approach. Another mitigating factor was the enthusiastic rush of volunteers to join the Canadian Army Special Force, along with St. Laurent's firm statements opposing the need for conscription. Events had progressed so smoothly for the government that by 15 September, Parliament was adjourned, and key Cabinet ministers like Abbott, Claxton, and Howe got on with the business of managing the defence and economic side of the war.

Reflecting on the preceding two weeks, Claxton confided to his close friend and Canada's high commissioner to South Africa, Terry MacDermot, that the last parliamentary session has "been a miracle. We met torn and divided about labour relations, Korea and all that. We shall leave more united then ever before because of the pattern of conduct set by the Liberal leaders, Laurier and King, to whom he [St. Laurent] has succeeded and whom he almost excels."[39]

Before adjourning, Douglas Abbott presented a supplementary budget in September. Despite the increase in military spending, the budget was balanced. To offset increased federal spending, a modest increase to the corporate tax rate was introduced "from 10 p.c. on the first $10,000 and 33 p.c. on the remainder to 15 p.c. and 38 p.c., respectively." Consumers looking to purchase cars, radios, and jewellery would also pay more. Alcohol taxes, too, increased, and soft drinks and candy were now taxed for the first time.[40] These were prudent choices that largely avoided a day-to-day impact on the lives of Canadians while also raising revenue and reminding them that support of the war had a cost, if a minor one.

China's entry into the Korean War dramatically altered Ottawa's rearmament plans: the government would be forced to spend much more than originally envisaged. At the same time, Canada's new commitments to NATO also demanded more service personnel and weapon systems, higher training costs, and the formation of new units. Despite this new spending, under the direction of Douglas Abbott and C.D. Howe, the Canadian economy absorbed the shocks from the international tumult in East Asia. Under Howe, the St. Laurent government had brought in legislation the previous September ensuring that defence production and defence-related activities had unhindered access to the resources they required under an Essential Materials (Defence) Bill so that "if there were a conflict between military needs and civilian demand," Howe had the means "to resolve it – in favour of the military."[41] But direct government control of resources was rare, with the exception of the use of steel. From autumn 1950 to the end of 1952, "places of amusement, stores, hotels, banks, [and] restaurants" would have to wait if expansion or renovation plans required steel. Canadians and businesses took the legislation in stride.[42] Consumers responded to China's entry into the war with a spasm of panic. Some Canadians, with fresh memories of wartime rationing, began stocking up beyond their needs. The government drafted plans to introduce price controls and rationing, if necessary. The cost-of-living index rose 14 percent between July 1950 and December 1951, but Ottawa monitored the situation closely and did not have to introduce severe measures.[43] In 1952, consumer prices began to decline when it became evident that Canada's economy could balance defence needs "without ... dislocation in the civilian economy."[44]

Along with carefully managing the economy and maintaining forces in Korea, Cabinet had to address its NATO allies, who pressured Ottawa to deploy significant forces to defend western Europe. Soon enough, a permanent Canadian force was on its way across the Atlantic. On 29 December 1950, the government announced a tripling of the defence budget from $403 million in 1950–51 to approximately $1.45 billion for 1951–52.[45] Within approximately eighteen months, defence spending went from 2.75 percent of Canada's GDP in 1950 to 8 percent in 1952.[46] This number would grow as Ottawa announced a rearmament and continental defence package of $5 billion over three years in February 1951, much of which would be managed through a new department created in April 1951, the Department of Defence Production. The experienced C.D. Howe was tapped to lead its mission.

Howe was a steady and safe hand. The renowned "Minister of Everything" had directed Ottawa's Second World War production programs as head of the Department of Munitions and Supply. In 1944, he became minister of reconstruction as the King government prepared for the postwar peace. For the new department, and for Brooke Claxton in Defence, there was no shortage of work. As his biographer observed, "For the next few years, Claxton's portfolio would be one of the most important" as defence needs had significant impacts on government budgets and fiscal policy.[47] The St. Laurent government now led the largest peacetime mobilization in Canadian history; at its peak in the early 1950s, the armed forces consumed more than 50 percent of the total federal budget.[48] During 1951, defence production "was primarily one of preparation, of designing and constructing plants and equipment, of determining types of military goods to be produced, of undertaking development work and of placing some of the more important contracts."[49] Between April and December 1951, Department of Defence Production "placed almost $1.5 billion worth of defence orders," of which just over "$100 million was for foreign customers."[50] The new department ran efficiently. At no point did Howe use his considerable powers as minister to direct manufacturers to produce what he deemed necessary at the government's set price. In Howe's estimation, the "need for speed" in rearmament pushed Ottawa to provide the minister with additional powers. Nor would Howe need to "seize a manufacturer's premises" and take control of any business, although he had these powers for a five-year window.[51]

Throughout the war, Cabinet was sensitive to the rise in consumer prices as well as the need to pay for substantial defence expenditures without significantly raising taxes, if possible. The Conservative Opposition, led by George Drew, had tried to attack the St. Laurent government on the issue in early 1951. Claxton confided to Terry MacDermot that despite the key legislative and financial work Parliament had undertaken since January, "This has been a very quiet session with Drew working under wraps. I suppose he's been told by friends that he was getting nowhere by his other tactics." The cost of living had been the only issue to trouble the government so far, Claxton continued, "and while everyone feels bitterly about this, I don't think anyone for a second credits the conservatives on the sincerity of their attack on us on this account."[52]

Perhaps the most resounding endorsement that the government was managing the Korean conflict capably came from Blair Fraser in his biweekly *Maclean's* editorial, "Backstage at Ottawa." Although an election remained well over two years away, Fraser raised the question as to who the next Liberal leader would be. Answering the question, Fraser asserted that St. Laurent would return for another election. So long as the Korean War continued, "St. Laurent is the man supremely qualified to lead Canada in a time of crisis. No one else in any party could equal him. St. Laurent is a conscientious patriot."[53]

Nonetheless, there were glimmers of political dissatisfaction across the country. To what extent this reflected Ottawa's handling of the Korean War as the Chinese and the United Nations Command entered a prolonged stalemate is difficult to tell. Just as Parliament prepared to recess for the summer of 1951, four by-elections occurred in Brandon, Winnipeg South Centre, Waterloo South, and Queen's in Prince Edward Island. All four of the ridings (three of which were previously held by the Liberals) turned to the Progressive Conservatives.[54] Muddying the waters, national public opinion polls suggested that the Canadian public remained pleased with the St. Laurent government's overall direction: 50 percent of respondents agreed that if an election were held, they would vote Liberal, as opposed to the 29 percent who favoured the Progressive Conservatives.[55]

The Liberals' close relationship with the nation's media undoubtedly helped. Historian Patrick Brennan in his study of government-press relations observes that prominent journalists such as Grant Dexter (*Winnipeg Free Press*), George Ferguson (*Montreal Star*), Bruce Hutchinson (*Victoria Daily Times*), and Blair Fraser fostered close relationships with Liberal politicians and other government sources. In return, these journalists acted as "confidential intermediaries" or even as conduits for prominent civil servants to test ideas and reach the public; "the pressures of the Korean crisis merely served to cement the relationship more firmly than ever."[56] A cogent example of these close relationships at work is apparent in how Hutchinson offered his journalistic and editorial support to Pearson. In the weeks following the Chinese entry into the conflict, Hutchinson wrote reassuringly to Pearson, "be sure that everything you are doing at the U.N. is being closely and sympathetically watched and that if there is any way at all in which we can help you it will not only be a personal pleasure but a national privilege."[57] For his part, Fraser offered Pearson a glowing profile in *Maclean's*. The columnist gushed about the minister's "knack for getting on with other people"; perhaps "one reason we all like him – he trusts us. But a more important reason is his astonishing gift for making friends."[58] Certainly the government's handling of the nation's finances, defence stimulus, and international demand for Canada's resources buoyed the country.

After a shaky start between June and August 1950, the St. Laurent government settled into a confident and organized path to managing Canadian military efforts in Korea while competently steering the domestic economy. Nearly full employment existed as the economy expanded, and the country welcomed an increased flow of 194,400 immigrants in 1951, followed by 164,500 immigrants in 1952.[59] The brief period of consumer hoarding in late 1950 disappeared in early 1951 as Canadians realized shortages would not be as severe as initially believed, while increased government taxes and credit controls placed a break on consumer demand. Credit restrictions were lifted in 1952 as incomes continued to increase and retail prices declined, especially food prices. "By the beginning of 1953 the domestic consumer market had strengthened appreciably," and it continued to do so throughout the year. Indeed, according to *Canada Year Book,* as early as mid-1952, the growing domestic market had begun to replace defence spending "as the principal stimulus to expansion in the Canadian economy."[60] Finally, the birth rate continued to soar throughout the Korean War, as it had from 1946 in the aftermath of the return of veterans from the Second World War.[61]

Canadians weren't just confident in the times they lived in; they were confident in their government as 1952 dawned. A Canadian Institute of Public Opinion poll concluded that the "best argument to get people to vote Liberal in any election held this year in the opinion of people interviewed throughout the country is that Canada is prosperous. The second argument was the "calibre of the Liberal leadership," and a "close third, the record of the Liberal government with respect to social measures, such as old age pensions, and family allowances."[62] Although Korea was not reflected in the poll, the war was not entirely remote to Canadians. In late August 1952, Gallup released another poll that acknowledged that while previous polls demonstrated that high living costs vexed Canadians – more than any single identified issue – 22 percent of Canadians felt "that the greatest problem facing the Federal Government at the present time is military. Inflation rates as a poor second to such matters as civil defence, rearmament, and the Korean War." By contrast, 8 percent of Canadians cited inflation and the high cost of living as the greatest problem facing Ottawa.[63] As thousands of service personnel were sent overseas, and as news of casualties and prisoners of war trickled in, the stalemated front in Korea did not negatively impact the Liberals. In fact, Liberals had been the "government party" since October 1935, and preliminary polls in late winter 1952 showed they had a ten-point lead over the Conservatives (43 to 33 percent) and were well positioned for the 1953 election.[64]

On 19 February 1953, Douglas Abbott announced a budget intended to revert the economy to a peacetime setting. Income tax was reduced by 11 percent, placing it back to 1949 levels; small businesses would benefit from a reduced corporation tax rate; cigarette taxes were reduced; and personal deductions were increased.[65] Defence spending was set to level off. One political commentator noted, "For the first time since Korea, we're coasting."[66] High taxes had been a sensitive political topic for the Liberals during the early part of the war, which required a jump in defence spending, but the Liberals were announcing to Canadians that they were now the party of tax relief.

A key organizer for the 1953 election campaign, Brooke Claxton followed the budget reaction closely and read the polls even more carefully. In a memorandum to St. Laurent, he suggested the prime minister call an election before Queen Elizabeth II's coronation on 2 June 1953. Claxton believed a spring writ would favour the Liberals and outlined fourteen factors to explain his reasoning, including economic prosperity, agricultural plenty, an Opposition not yet prepared to go to the polls, and people feeling positive in the spring. Not one of the fourteen factors related to Korea, reflecting the government's initial discomfort with becoming embroiled in a war that even Claxton regarded as a sideshow.

St. Laurent, however, opted to wait for the coronation to pass before calling the election.[67] The polls were solid, St. Laurent was confident of his government's record, and there were no good reasons to distract Canadians ahead of the coronation. In the meantime, preparation for the election went ahead, and Claxton lobbied for St. Laurent to be at the centre of campaign publicity and strategy. The Liberals were "united behind a leader in whom the people of this country have the greatest possible confidence, Louis St. Laurent." Outlining a list of government accomplishments, Liberal strategist Ross Martin emphasized that the country possessed "the greatest sense of national unity we have ever had," along with the largest expansion of social welfare programs in Canadian history. Further down the list came defence. Martin reasoned the government "had developed the largest defence forces we ever had in peacetime, provided them with equipment ... and enabled them to create an enviable record for themselves by their service in Korea and in Europe."[68] Given the two world wars had led to deep divisions in the country, the Liberal's handling of the Korean War effort appeared successful to the Canadian public.

Within days of returning home from the coronation, Louis St. Laurent met with the governor general on 12 June to dissolve Parliament for a general election on 10 August 1953. The Korean War and its resolution would play a role in the campaign. A Canadian Institute of Public Opinion poll commissioned just before the election call placed the Liberals with a boost at 47 percent and the Conservatives at 30 percent. Liberal popularity remained strong across all regions of Canada, as during the 1949 election, the major difference being in western Canada, where the Social Credit had eaten into Conservative and Liberal support.[69]

A confident prime minister took to the airwaves on 22 June for the first national campaign broadcast. During his chat with Canadians, St. Laurent presented a vigorous outline of his government's achievements since 1949. Remarkably, the government's defence record was at the bottom of the prime minister's list of twenty points. Korea would not be an election issue for the government. Rather, the government championed its record of overall competence, management, and St. Laurent's steady hand overseeing the nation's fortunes.[70] From afar, the *Times of London* weighed in, favouring the Liberal record, which had benefited from its willingness to send approximately thirty thousand soldiers to war in Korea. It asserted, "Canada during these four years has continued to advance in international authority. She is an indispensable buttress of the North Atlantic alliance."[71] As the campaign entered its penultimate week, news came on 27 July that the Chinese, North Korean, and UN forces had signed a long-awaited armistice. Over the three years of the Korean War, 471 Canadians had died, and approximately 1,500 Canadians had been wounded.[72]

Yet as election day came closer, Canadian voters remained preoccupied with their domestic well-being rather than issues of international security. When asked in a late July poll, "What would you say is the main issue to be decided in this election?," a quarter of respondents suggested taxation. Only 5 percent raised the war.[73] In what can only be considered a smashing endorsement while managing a limited war in East Asia, the dispatch of forces to western Europe, and the economic dislocation of massive spending, the St. Laurent Liberals won in every single region of the country, returning with 170 seats to the Conservatives' 51. Between the ceasefire in Korea and a majority electoral return, the government could rightfully celebrate its handling of an arduous parliamentary term.

Jack Pickersgill observed that "the attack from North Korea on the South in June 1950 marked the beginning of a period of stress for St. Laurent and his government." At least initially, this was not the case. The first few weeks of the war appeared to have the opposite effect on the prime minister, who appeared relaxed enough to take a fishing vacation in mid-July at his summer home in St. Patrick, Quebec. When a reporter located him to question him about Trygve Lie's appeal for Canadian troops, St. Laurent replied curtly, "I wish reporters wouldn't bother me when on holiday," and hung up.[74]

There is little doubt that the prime minister and his Cabinet were slow to realize the complexity of the environment they found themselves in during the summer of 1950. That Korea of all places had become a potential global flashpoint undoubtedly shocked Ottawa, as did the sudden hawkish mood of American policy-makers. In many respects, the government's blend of inaction and caution was no surprise. The Cabinet was composed predominantly of King-era ministers who had learned from their former leader's wariness of international crises. Certainly, St. Laurent was deeply attuned to Quebec's wariness of Ottawa's historical responses to international conflict, particularly given the legacies of conscription. To that end, apart from an initial hesitancy, the government's record during the war was one of considerable achievement, although it was leery of championing its military record come election time. The public hardly expected it to do so.

While the war demanded much attention from the Cabinet, it was not the sole issue over three years. The economy expanded, hundreds of thousands of immigrants were welcomed and subsequently employed, Canadians were more prosperous than ever before, and in response the birth rate and consumer demand spiked. Cabinet managed the war, allayed fears of conscription, and kept the country united, all while overseeing a massive increase in military budgets and formations. And, of course, the government achieved this while dispatching another significant military force to defend western Europe as part of its NATO obligation and providing, for the first time, tens of millions of dollars in foreign aid to South Asia under the auspices of the Colombo Plan.[75] St. Laurent and his Cabinet proved considerably adept at providing calm and consistent leadership in the face of the domestic and international challenges that accompanied the first major international crisis of the atomic age. In a fitting assessment of the era, ever the political partisan, Jack Pickersgill described the government's record as "splendid."[76] It is difficult, though, to disagree with him: quite simply, the government's political leadership and accomplishments during the Korean War were, indeed, splendid, at least to the audience that counted: the electorate, who rewarded the St. Laurent Liberals at the ballot box.

Notes

1 There are few histories of Canadian political leadership during the Korean War. A recent and important collection on Prime Minister Louis St. Laurent does not touch on the Korean War: see Patrice Dutil, ed., *The Unexpected Louis St. Laurent: Politics and Policies for a Modern Canada* (Vancouver: UBC Press, 2020). Likewise, although St. Laurent–era Cabinet minister Jack Pickersgill wrote an illuminating memoir of the prime minister, he devotes only 6 pages of his 334-page study to the Korean War: see J.W. Pickersgill, *My Years with Louis St. Laurent* (Toronto: University of Toronto Press, 1975). J.L. Granatstein's important biography of Norman Robertson, prominent diplomat and secretary to the Cabinet during the Korean War, barely mentions the conflict and the government's response: see *A Man of Influence: Norman A. Robertson and Canadian Statecraft, 1929–68* (Toronto: Deneau, 1981). In other cases, memoirs of key civil servants who worked closely with St. Laurent or his key Cabinet colleagues opted not to discuss, or barely mention, the Korean War. See, for example, Gordon Robertson, *Memoirs of a Very Civil Servant: Mackenzie King to Pierre Trudeau* (Toronto: University of Toronto Press, 2000); Mitchell Sharp, *Which Reminds Me ... A Memoir* (Toronto: University of Toronto Press, 1994); and Arnold Heeney, *The Things That Are Caesar's: The Memoirs of a Canadian Public Servant* (Toronto: University of Toronto Press, 1972). Arguably, the most useful, if patchy, study of the government's political leadership of the Korean War is the sole biography of Louis St. Laurent: Dale C. Thomson, *Louis St. Laurent: Canadian* (Toronto: Macmillan, 1967). David J. Bercuson's biography of Defence Minister Brooke Claxton offers the most useful study of a key St. Laurent Cabinet minister's political influence in shaping Ottawa's response to the war: see *True Patriot: The Life of Brooke Claxton, 1898–1960* (Toronto: University of Toronto Press, 1993).

2 See UN Security Council, *Security Council Resolution 83 (1950)* [*Complaint of aggression upon the Republic of Korea*], 27 June 1950, S/RES/83 (1950), https://www.refworld.org/docid/3b00f20a2c.html.

3 "Extract from Memorandum from Secretary of State for External Affairs to Prime Minister," 27 June 1950, in *Documents on Canadian External Relations* (*DCER*), vol. 16 (1950), https://epe.lac-bac.gc.ca/100/206/301/faitc-aecic/history/2013-05-03/www.international.gc.ca/department/history-histoire/dcer/details-en.asp@intRefid=7051.

4 "Extract from Memorandum."

5 Cabinet Conclusions, 28 June 1950, Library and Archives Canada (LAC), RG 2, Privy Council Office, series A-5-A, vol. 2645.

6 Cabinet Conclusions, 28 June 1950.

7 Patrick Brennan, *Reporting the Nation's Business: Press-Government Relations during the Liberal Years, 1939–1957* (Toronto: University of Toronto Press, 1994), 136.
8 *House of Commons Debates,* 21st Parl., 2nd Sess., No. 4 (26 June 1950) (Brooke Claxton), https://www.lipad.ca/full/permalink/1615100/.
9 See Greg Donaghy, *Grit: The Life and Politics of Paul Martin Sr.* (Vancouver: UBC Press, 2015), 107.
10 Cabinet Conclusions, 28 June 1950.
11 John A. Munro and Alex I. Inglis, eds., *Mike: The Memoirs of the Right Honourable Lester B. Pearson,* vol. 2, *1948–1957* (Toronto: University of Toronto Press, 1973), 148.
12 Cabinet Conclusions, 12 July 1950.
13 On Canadian defence spending for the period 1945–49, see Robert Prince, "The Limits of Constraint: Canadian-American Relations and the Korean War, 1950–51," *Journal of Canadian Studies* 27, 4 (1992): 139.
14 David Bercuson, *True Patriot: The Life of Brooke Claxton, 1898–1960* (Toronto: University of Toronto Press, 1993), 209.
15 Bercuson, *True Patriot,* 210.
16 Cabinet Conclusions, 19 July 1950.
17 Cabinet Conclusions, 19 July 1950.
18 Blair Fraser, "Backstage at Ottawa: Uncle Sam Thinks We Let Him Down," *Maclean's Magazine,* 1 September 1950, 4.
19 For more information about how Canada's involvement in air support to the Korean War unfolded, see Richard Mayne, Chapter 8, this volume.
20 Pearson to Wrong, 20 July 1950, *DCER,* vol. 16 (1950), https://epe.lac-bac.gc.ca/100/206/301/faitc-aecic/history/2013-05-03/www.international.gc.ca/department/history-histoire/dcer/details-en.asp@intRefid=7070.
21 See Mildred A. Schwartz, *Public Opinion and Canadian Identity* (Berkeley: University of California Press, 1967), 81.
22 Pearson to Wrong, 20 July 1950.
23 Munro and Inglis, *Mike,* 148–49.
24 For the Cabinet ministers opposed to sending troops to Korea and Pearson's threat, see Prince, "The Limits of Constraint," 136, 149.
25 Cabinet Conclusions, 28 July 1950.
26 Cabinet Conclusions, 28 July 1950.
27 "Public Opinion Asserts Itself," *Globe and Mail,* 3 August 1950.
28 "Is This Leadership?" *Globe and Mail,* 5 August 1950.
29 Cabinet Conclusions, 7 August 1950.
30 Bercuson, *True Patriot,* 216–17.
31 Bercuson, *True Patriot,* 217.
32 Thomson, *Louis St. Laurent,* 297.
33 Pickersgill, *My Years with Louis St. Laurent,* 130.
34 Thomson, *Louis St. Laurent,* 301.
35 Gagnon was not entirely alone. During the early days of the conflict, fellow Quebec Liberal member of Parliament Jean-François Pouliot, representing Témiscouata, suggested Ottawa do nothing. See "Extract from Memorandum from Secretary of State."
36 Pickersgill, *My Years with Louis St. Laurent,* 130.
37 Blair Fraser, "Backstage at Ottawa: The Whisper of Conscription," *Maclean's Magazine,* 1 November 1950, 53.
38 See J.I. Gow, "Les Québécois, la guerre et la paix, 1945–60," *Canadian Journal of Political Science* 3, 1 (1970): 98.

39 Claxton to MacDermot, 9 September 1950, LAC, MG 32 B5, Brooke Claxton Fonds, vol. 52, file 1.
40 *Canada Year Book* (Ottawa: Statistics Canada, 1951), xxxv.
41 Robert Bothwell and William Kilbourn, *C.D. Howe: A Biography* (Toronto: McClelland and Stewart, 1979), 253.
42 *Canada Year Book* (Ottawa: Statistics Canada, 1952–53), xiv.
43 *Canada Year Book,* 1952–53, xiv. On price controls and rationing, see Sharp, *Which Reminds Me,* 54.
44 *Canada Year Book,* 1952–53, xii.
45 J.L. Granatstein, *Canada's Army: Waging War and Keeping the Peace* (Toronto: University of Toronto Press, 2002), 321.
46 *Canada Year Book,* 1952–53, xviii.
47 Bercuson, *True Patriot,* 215.
48 Bercuson, *True Patriot,* 227.
49 *Canada Year Book,* 1952–53, vxiii.
50 Bothwell and Kilbourn, *C.D. Howe,* 257.
51 Bothwell and Kilbourn, *C.D. Howe,* 256.
52 Claxton to MacDermot, 23 April 1951, LAC, MG 32 B5, vol. 52, file 1; see also Thomson, *Louis St. Laurent,* 308.
53 Blair Fraser, "Backstage at Ottawa: Aroused but Not Rattled," *Maclean's Magazine,* 1 April 1951, 5.
54 Thomson suggests that the four defeats were a sign that "Canadians were evidently becoming restless under the higher taxes, rising prices, and shortages resulting from the Korean War and were responding to opposition charges of arrogance and heavy-handedness": Thomson, *Louis St. Laurent,* 315.
55 See *Ottawa Citizen,* 11 August 1951.
56 Brennan, *Reporting the Nation's Business,* 139.
57 Hutchinson to Pearson, 29 November 1950, LAC, MG 26 N1, Lester Pearson Fonds, vol. 6, file 6.
58 See Blair Fraser, "Backstage at Ottawa: Meet Mike Pearson," *Maclean's Magazine,* 15 April 1951.
59 "150 Years of Immigration in Canada," *Canadian Megatrends,* 29 June 2016, https://www150.statcan.gc.ca/n1/pub/11-630-x/11-630-x2016006-eng.htm; and *Canada Year Book* (Ottawa: Statistics Canada, 1953), xi.
60 *Canada Year Book,* 1953, xi–xii.
61 For instance, in 1952, 400,000 babies were born, and that number steadily increased in 1953. See Doug Owram, *Born at the Right Time: A History of the Baby Boom Generation* (Toronto: University of Toronto Press, 2007), 4.
62 *Montreal Star,* 11 February 1952, LAC, MG 32 B5, vol. 166, file: Elections 1953, Clippings and Gallup Polls.
63 *Montreal Star,* 27 August 1952, LAC, MG 32 B5, vol. 166, file: Elections 1953, Clippings and Gallup Polls.
64 *Montreal,* 7 March 1953, LAC, MG 32 B5, vol. 166, file: Elections 1953, Clippings and Gallup Polls.
65 Liberal newsletter, March 1953, LAC, MG 32 B5, vol. 30, file 1: Dominion General Elections 1953. See also "Smile in Every Line of Budget," *Ottawa Citizen,* 20 February 1953.
66 See Blair Fraser, "Backstage at Ottawa: The False Bottom in Abbott's Hat," *Maclean's Magazine,* 1 April 1953.
67 Claxton to St. Laurent, 2 March 1953, LAC, MG 32 B5, vol. 123, file: Prime Minister, the Rt. Honourable St. Laurent.

68 Claxton to Pickersgill and Kidd, 19 March 1953, LAC, MG 32 B5, vol. 30, file 1: Dominion General Elections 1953.

69 *Toronto Daily Star,* 24 June 1953, LAC, MG 32 B5, vol. 166, file: Elections 1953, Clippings and Gallup Polls.

70 "Battlegrounds Chosen," *Montreal Star,* 27 June 1953, LAC, MG 32 B5, vol. 166, file: Elections 1953, Clippings and Gallup Polls.

71 "Battlegrounds Chosen," *Montreal Star,* 27 June 1953, LAC, MG 32 B5, vol. 166, file: Elections 1953, Clippings and Gallup Polls. Quoted in *Ottawa Journal,* 1 July 1953.

72 The figure of 516 dead includes deaths to December 1956. For more information, see Andrew Burtch, Chapter 11, this volume.

73 "Taxation Problems Tower as Main Election Issue," *Montreal Daily Star,* 1 August 1953, LAC, MG 32 B5, vol. 166, file: Elections 1953, Clippings and Gallup Polls.

74 Blair Fraser, "Backstage at Ottawa: Uncle Sam Thinks We Let Him Down," *Maclean's Magazine,* 1 September 1950.

75 See Ryan Touhey, *Conflicting Visions: Canada and India in the Cold War World, 1946–1976* (Vancouver, UBC Press, 2015).

76 Pickersgill, *My Years with Louis St. Laurent,* 156.

Part 2
Canada, Korea, and the War

3

The US Army and the Battle for Korea, 1950: Lessons Learned

Brian McAllister Linn

Regardless of whether it will always be "the forgotten war" within the greater historical discipline, the Korean War's impact on the US Army is inescapable. When the war began in June 1950, the army numbered roughly 591,000 soldiers: three years later, it totalled over 1.5 million personnel. Almost as revolutionary was the service's social composition, transforming from volunteer and segregated to conscripted and racially, economically, and regionally integrated. The war accelerated the transition from temporary occupation forces to large permanent overseas garrisons in West Germany and Japan. It witnessed one of the most controversial civil-military confrontations in American history, between President Harry S. Truman and General Douglas MacArthur. The Korean experience had other lasting effects, not least that both civil and military leaders were determined to never again engage in a land war with China. In the Cold War context, the first months of Korea confirmed to both policymakers and the army leadership that the Asian mainland was of secondary strategic importance to defending western Europe. Even as its soldiers were fighting in Korea, the army accelerated its focus on preparing for a war with the Soviet Union.[1]

In American military historiography, the Korean War narrative is dominated by analyses of the performance of two generals (MacArthur and Lieutenant General Matthew B. Ridgway) and a few dramatic events: the Task Force Smith debacle, the Inchon landing, the Chinese intervention, and MacArthur's relief.[2] It is a narrative that usually excludes the South Koreans and the other UN forces. And it focuses on the military defeats of the war's first months, paying little attention to how the US Army interpreted and assimilated the war's early lessons. This chapter seeks to balance this last omission by focusing on three tasks. First, it will provide a summary of the US Army's experience leading up to and in the first months of the war. Second, it will discuss the service's interpretation of those lessons and how they were assimilated in the immediate aftermath.

Last, it will examine the longer-term lessons the army drew from the conflict and how they were applied to the Cold War army.

Background

Although the Korean People's Army's (KPA) invasion of the Republic of Korea on 25 June 1950 caught American military and political leaders by surprise, their response was rapid and decisive. From their Cold War perspective, the North Koreans were acting as agents of the Soviet Union; to remain neutral would encourage more Communist aggression. Within two days of the North Korean attack, US Air Force fighters were engaged in combat. President Truman authorized the commitment of American ground forces from Japan. The government called up reservists, instituted large-scale conscription, and deployed air, land, and sea components to the Far East. Yet American policy-makers did not impose full national mobilization, as they had in the Second World War, nor did they focus all the nation's military efforts on Korea. They were uncertain whether the KPA invasion was merely a distraction intended to suck American military resources into the Far East to allow a Soviet attack in western Europe.[3] Although war aims shifted from defending the Republic of Korea (ROK) to an invasion of North Korea and then, again, after the Chinese intervention, to defending the ROK, Washington was determined not to trigger a nuclear war. Korea, in the words of the chairman of the Joint Chiefs of Staff, Omar N. Bradley, was "the wrong war, at the wrong place, at the wrong time, and with the wrong enemy."[4] Bradley might have added that in 1950 Korea was a war fought with the wrong army.

The half-decade following the Second World War was a period of unusual turmoil, even by the traumatic standards of most postwar demobilizations. It was not just that in the three years since the surrender of Japan army manpower had dropped from 8 million to 538,000. It was that the army's personnel was widely scattered across the globe with nearly half invested in occupying Japan, another third posted in various countries in Europe, and, after 1950, many more committed to a massive buildup of antiaircraft units to defend the continental United States against Soviet bombers. The post-Second World War plans reflected a conviction that the next war would be much like the last. They were predicated on a sudden Soviet onslaught in Europe, with the service conducting a fighting retreat then, in an expeditionary role, seizing airfields in the Middle East, landing on the continent, and mopping up resistance and occupying conquered territory, all after the nuclear strategic bombardment campaign had shattered Soviet resistance. The army's contribution was based on the perceived lessons of the previous two global conflicts. The service's leaders envisaged the professional (or regular) army serving as a cadre to provide the training, organizing, and leadership for a several-million-man citizen-soldier army, a process that would take several months.[5]

Mobilization plans, in turn, led the army to maintain a far larger force structure than it had personnel to support. Except for one airborne division, all five divisions in the continental United States were skeletonized to the point of ineffectiveness, as were all elements of nondivision strength such as corps artillery, maintenance, and training units. With the civilian economy booming, too many recruits were immature (half were under twenty-one) or lacked the education, intelligence, and social abilities to be soldiers. Overriding all of this was personnel turbulence at both the junior officer and enlisted levels, with many units annually suffering 100 percent turnover. Compounding the problem was that few remained in uniform: one service journal estimated the army would discharge 200,000 of its 530,000 enlisted men by April 1951.[6]

The troops in the US Eighth Army, on occupation duty in Japan, which in mid-1949 numbered some 110,000 soldiers, typified the poor state of the postwar army. In part because of Truman's inability to decide on either a national-security or military-personnel policy, the service stumbled along, every year losing personnel, budgets, and resources. MacArthur, who was both supreme commander for the Allied Powers in Japan and commander-in-chief, Far East, viewed the Eighth Army as primarily an agency for reconstructing that nation. But he was also desperate to remain a viable presidential candidate for the Republican Party, a priority that often conflicted with his roles as general and de facto shogun. In one particularly egregious example of pandering to public war weariness, he undercut the army by claiming he needed only half the troops Washington had planned to allocate and that they needed minimal training.

The results were disastrous. "The combat troops of the Eighth Army practically disintegrated," its commander wrote to MacArthur in January 1948. To maintain force structure, it implemented the "one-third slice," eliminating a battalion from each infantry regiment, a battery from each artillery battalion, the infantry's tank companies, and so on. Even then, the remaining combat and support units were between a third and a fifth of their authorized strength of about 18,000 men in an infantry division.[7] To its credit, Eighth Army carried out MacArthur's nation-building priorities. It disarmed more than 4 million Japanese troops, repatriated 2.5 million refugees, destroyed 100,000 airplanes and 1 million tons of explosives, and built hospitals, schools, railroads, airfields, and many other public works. It also laid the cornerstones for a permanent military presence with bases, training and repair facilities, athletics, post exchanges, commissaries, housing, and on and on. But whether justified or not, Japan became known as a comfortable place for field officers to go into early retirement and for junior officers who had started families.[8]

In early 1949, the soldiers in the Eighth Army began part of a service-wide transition from occupation to preparation for war. This shift was in part an acknowledgment of the success of the occupation, but its primary impetus was the heightening of Cold War tensions following the coup in Czechoslovakia, the Berlin blockade, and the Communist triumph in China. By the end of the year, the infantry divisions in Japan had been built up, but only to 66 percent of their authorized strength. The Eighth Army's personnel problems were exacerbated by its limited facilities, especially in locations where tanks and artillery could manoeuvre and cooperate with the infantry. Much of the equipment had seen hard service in the war and had been rebuilt to varying degrees of effectiveness; spare parts, repair shops, and skilled mechanics were all in short supply. In the months preceding the war, Eighth Army's tactical units began a rigorous training program that, despite numerous obstacles, brought companies and battalions up to qualification. Yet this training regimen was focused on defending Japan against Soviet attack, not on mobile operations across the sea. Throughout this period, Korea was viewed in both Washington and Tokyo as of little to no strategic interest: in May 1950, US military advisers to the Republic of Korea Army (ROKA) numbered 494.[9]

In the days following the North Korean attack, MacArthur ordered Eighth Army's commander, Lieutenant General Walton H. Walker, to take operational command of the American land forces on the peninsula, designated as Eighth US Army Korea (EUSAK). Both MacArthur and Walker grossly underestimated the size and the efficiency of the KPA and the limits of their own forces. From the four infantry divisions on occupation duty in Japan, they culled together battalions and regiments from three to bring just one division to its full peacetime authorization (12,000 men) and dispatched them to the front with little regard for morale, coherence, or tactical ability. In the war's first months, soldiers often fought with unfamiliar comrades under unknown officers, and they were frequently equipped with insufficient war surplus equipment, from artillery rounds to radios.

On 5 July, the 4th Division of the KPA quickly overran the first US contingent, Task Force Smith, at Osan. This humiliating defeat for the understrength battalion (440 personnel) remains a cautionary watchword within the army on the dangers of unpreparedness.[10] In the next few weeks, Task Force Smith's parent organization, the 24th Infantry Division, suffered a similar fate: its commander was captured and 3,600 soldiers were killed, wounded, or missing. As the 24th crumbled, two additional occupation divisions, the 25th Infantry and the 1st Cavalry, were committed but proved unable to stop the North Korean advance; they and the ROKA forces fell back towards the port of Busan. On 3 August, engineers demolished the last bridge over the Natkong River, confining the defence to a perimeter 160 kilometres long and 80 kilometres wide around the crucial logistical centre of Busan. [11]

From 4 August to 16 September, ROKA, American, British, and Australian forces engaged in a brutal battle of attrition against the North Koreans along what quickly became known as the Battle of the Pusan Perimeter. By then, the United States had 90,000 soldiers and Marines in Korea, but none of these units arrived fully trained or with a full complement of authorized personnel or equipment. Walker was never able to concentrate overwhelming forces to decisively counterattack and destroy the KPA in any area. Instead, reinforcements were committed on an emergency basis, often lacking sufficient troops, armour, and artillery support. The Busan campaign became a grinding battle of attrition that sucked KPA combat units in and ground them up, allowing the Allied forces, in conjunction with an amphibious landing at Inchon in mid-September, to drive the North Koreans back to the thirty-eighth parallel. The subsequent expansion of the war aims – to unite all Korea under the US-sponsored southern regime and advance to the Yalu River bordering China – proved a strategic blunder. The Chinese intervention in November 1950 led to what MacArthur insisted was a "retrograde manoeuvre" but the troops termed it "the Great Bugout." In the face of the third major Chinese offensive on 31 January, EUSAK, now under Ridgway, abandoned the defence of Seoul and fell back to a new defensive line. To many, it appeared the war was lost.

Historical Analysis

The 1950 campaign required a sustained effort by the army to establish both an internal and external narrative. The latter, typified by the secretary of the army's end-of-the-year report to Congress, was "the war in Korea unquestionably had already affirmed in the eyes of the world the imperative necessity for the ground soldier in war."[12] The army interpretation – backed by evidence – was aggressive in its explicit criticism of the national strategy of strategic nuclear deterrence and the privileging of the air force and navy. But it was also a desperate effort to counteract what one public affairs officer termed "the destruction of public esteem of the Army by poor, unbalanced reporting of the first six months of the Korean conflict."[13] That media reporting was often biased and unfair was admitted by veteran correspondents with experience covering operations in the Second World War. Between MacArthur's headquarters and EUSAK, by July the theatre had over two hundred accredited reporters with little official guidance beyond self-censorship. In some cases, such as being briefed on the Inchon landing, reporters demonstrated exceptional self-policing. But in too many instances during the fallback to Busan, inexperienced or hostile journalists interviewing a few dazed, exhausted, and frustrated soldiers elevated minor firefights into epic defeats. In the process, some drew an invidious comparison between the mythological GIs who had defeated the Axis and their allegedly inferior successors. After the Chinese intervention and the "Great Bugout," the coverage became more critical: to the martial and moral inadequacies of the soldiers was added increasing questioning of the leadership and the war's purpose. By December, the hammering in the press compelled even the publicity-hungry MacArthur to impose censorship.[14]

Despite its journalistic origins, the initial denigration of the enlisted ranks – what might be termed the "blame-the-troops narrative" – suited the army's own version of military unpreparedness and early defeats.[15] This interpretation is manifest in one of the first overviews, a 1952 EUSAK study that argued that "a relatively untrained and consequently unprepared army was sent into the field, poorly equipped and understrength, against an underrated enemy" with the result that the "the Eighth Army was, in large part, trained by combat and taught by disaster."[16] Army historian Russell A. Guegler's 1954 textbook, *Combat Actions in Korea,* began by quoting the poet Rudyard Kipling's denigration of the troops first sent into combat as "rotten 'fore we started."[17] Guegler's contempt was reserved for the enlisted personnel and junior officers; it did not extend to the career officers responsible for this rot. The first volume in the army's official history of the Korean War, Roy E. Appleman's 1961 *South to the Natkong, North to the Yalu,* also highlighted the failures of the soldiers – "not trained, equipped, or ready for battle" – and exculpated the senior commanders.[18] Ridgway, who emerged as one of the few heroes among the senior officers, contributed to the blame-the-troops narrative, and his own reputation, by highlighting his role in restoring the troops' morale, discipline, and fighting spirit.[19] But by far the most influential propagator of the blame-the-troops narrative was the Korean War veteran T.R. Fehrenbach's 1963 *This Kind of War: A Study of Unpreparedness.* Fehrenbach, who arrived in Korea in 1952, concluded that the defeats in the early months were essential to transforming weak civilian soldiers of the occupation into hardened warriors: "For underneath the misconceptions of their society, the softness and mawkishness, the human material was hard and good."[20]

This blame-the-troops narrative minimized many inconvenient truths. Most notable was the absence of accounting for South Koreans – who comprised most of the combatants – and the United Nations units, the British Commonwealth Forces, the Turkish brigade, or the battalions from the Netherlands, the Philippines, Greece, and six other countries. Almost as notable as these omissions was how the service chose to allocate blame. With much justification, the military criticized the Truman administration, Congress, and the public for insufficient budgets, personnel and training deficiencies, and reducing the service to a skeleton force. The critique of lower-level leadership overshadowed criticism, far more warranted, of the senior US Army leadership's passivity in the debate over postwar strategy and force structure; its overoptimistic assessment of military readiness; its decision to commit the least prepared division (the 24th) to combat first; and the failings of far too many division and regimental commanders, both before and during the first months of the war. From a detached perspective, it is difficult not to concur with historian Kelly C. Jordan's assessment that rather than criticize EUSAK for what it did not do, historians (and army intellectuals) should be impressed that in only a few months of combat it managed to stop the KPA's onslaught and drive it back across the border.[21]

The Lessons of 1950

"The Department of the Army," one historical summary explained, "sensed the importance of recording wartime experience as speedily as possible to enable the Army to meet similar situations in the future."[22] The Second World War had left the service with a multitude of ways and means to document that experience. Eighth US Army's Headquarters established its own analytical branch, which provided its own perspective on its problems and accomplishments. Within a few months, Far East Command's Military History Section was compiling, summarizing, and disseminating reports on personnel, operations, intelligence, logistics, tactics, and so on. Military history detachments toured the theatre, reporting on combat actions and support operations. Units in Korea prepared monthly command chronologies and other studies that were reviewed by the Office of the Chief of Army Field Forces and then disseminated in "lessons learned" publications. The office, charged with doctrine, tactics, equipment, and training, also sent eight separate survey teams to the combat zone.[23] The Office of the Chief of Military History collected information and wrote reports, and much of its primary material would be incorporated in official histories.[24] Throughout the conflict, the professional military education system – branch schools and staff and war colleges – provided a venue for lectures, conferences, and research papers covering everything from national strategy to tactics and equipment.[25]

The combat branches conducted the most immediate analysis of the 1950 experiences and made the most immediate changes. Perhaps not surprisingly, the Infantry Branch was at the forefront, in part because it was so heavily criticized, and because its soldiers did most of the fighting. Critics, including many within the branch, argued that the infantry had become too road-bound, too burdened with equipment, too bloated – one survey found a quarter of the 150 soldiers in an infantry company were detailed to nonfighting occupations – and too dependent on close air support, artillery, and tanks rather than its own weapons and tactics. This criticism was endorsed by the branch's own analysis, which admitted that the troops were poorly trained, with many tactical withdrawals degenerating into "mob movements."[26]

In response, the 1951 Infantry School curriculum expanded to include more emphasis on the defence, on mountain and night fighting, and on massing fires. The army also developed experimental elite light infantry units, the Rangers. Although they performed some meritorious actions, these units were soon disbanded as they removed highly motivated soldiers from line units and were ill-suited for the sustained, attritional trench warfare that characterized the Korean front. But as was the case with the other branches, the Infantry Branch concluded that its doctrine, tactics, and equipment had all been validated: the problem was training, execution, coordination, and poor leadership at the junior level.[27]

The other branches were less attuned to the Korean War's lessons, in part because, quite correctly, they viewed the conflict as of little importance for their own future. The Field Artillery Branch was on the defensive from the beginning. Much of the blame for the defeat of Task Force Smith and subsequent engagements fell on the branch for its lack of adequate supporting fires, insufficient ammunition, and the failure of artillerymen to defend their positions and to instead abandon their guns. As with the Infantry Branch, most of these criticisms were based on the Department of the Army's and Far East Command's decisions to skeletonize units, reduce training, and limit equipment without modifying doctrine to reflect these major changes. Once the artillery had sufficient guns, gunners, transport, and ammunition, it became the most lethal force on the battlefield. Artillery played a vital role in shattering the Chinese offensives in 1951.

The war helped spur the modernization of equipment, particularly atomic-capable missiles and cannon, but the Field Artillery recognized its future lay in the missiles and atomic cannon destined for Europe. The Armor School was more proactive. It had incorporated the initial lessons of Korea into its curriculum by the end of 1950 and published a two-volume history of armour operations in the first year of the war. In common with the infantry, the Armor Branch reaffirmed the validity of its equipment and doctrine and blamed most problems on a lack of coordination, a failure to follow proper procedures, and the lack of combined arms training. But the branch was most interested in applying the perceived lessons of Korea to win the next war. Indeed, according to one officer at the Armor School in 1954, "The Korean War was hardly mentioned in the basic course. This was a shock to all of us. They mainly talked about the emerging Soviet threat in Europe because that was where the majority of the active armor forces were at that time."[28]

The army solicited analysis on its performance in Korea through conglomerations of boards, inspections, and surveys by both its own agencies and contractors. Perhaps the most significant of these for the future was the Weapons System and Evaluation Group team that included Major General James M. Gavin and several scientists. Once stateside, they initiated Project Vista, a 1950 to 1952 study that incorporated tactical atomic weapons into the defence of Europe.[29] The Human Resources Research Organization's Project Fighter was tasked with explaining the uneven performance of US combat troops in the war's first months. It sought to "define the characteristics of fighters and non-fighters" and "to determine the proportion of low-potential men who can be used effectively in a combat unit without seriously impairing the effectiveness of the unit."[30] Perhaps the most prestigious independent analysis came from noted military journalist S.L.A. Marshall, who was employed by the Operations Research Office. While acknowledging problems early in the war, Marshall refuted the blame-the-troops narrative: "The American infantry within the Eighth Army in Korea is a battle-worthy foot force as efficient in the employment of its arms during combat and as disciplined in the face of enemy fire as any we have yet produced."[31]

The first months of the Korean War radically transformed the size and composition of the US Army. The need was for combat forces, particularly in the infantry and field artillery as replacements for casualties. In the first months, stateside units were repeatedly culled for replacements, and after a call for volunteers fizzled, the army involuntarily recalled almost 8,000 company-grade officers, 1,600 medical specialists, and 62,000 enlisted personnel. The individual reserve pool – which soon adopted the nickname "retreads" – however, could not accommodate the demand for both replacements for Korea and the rapid expansion of the force. The National Guard and Organized Army Reserve units were kept intact, which left conscription as the only source for individual replacements.[32] Within weeks of the outbreak of war, Congress passed a new Selective Service Act; the Selective Service Administration, scheduled for oblivion, was instead ordered to draft 50,000 recruits by the end of September. This allowed for a rapid increase in army strength: from 593,526 in May 1950 to 1,414,182 the following March. However, the critical problem was not calling up young men but finding a place to put them. The peacetime training centres were inadequate in both numbers and facilities for such a rapid expansion. The first 100,000 selectees did not start arriving in Korea in significant numbers until early 1951; in March, 67 percent of the army's manpower was still in the continental United States. But by the middle of that year, draftees not only provided the majority of the combat forces in Korea; they flooded into West

Germany to prepare for the feared Soviet invasion. At war's end, conscripts accounted for well over half of the army's incoming soldiers. The war also transformed the officer corps: by 1952, West Point Military Academy graduates, historically the primary source of officers in peacetime, represented only a tiny subgroup among company-grade officers (lieutenants and captains) compared to the products of the Reserve Officers' Training Corps and branch-sponsored Officer Candidate Schools. In fiscal year 1952, for example, the Military Academy graduated and commissioned 552 second lieutenants compared to the 7,000 that graduated from Officer Candidate Schools.[33]

Another result of the manpower crisis in Korea was the end of the army's historical policy of racial segregation. Truman had ordered the armed forces to be desegregated in 1948, but army commanders ignored the directive with impunity, abetted by senior uniformed and civilian leaders who slow-rolled desegregation policy within the army. Losses among infantry and gunners in EUSAK were such that almost every soldier capable of firing a rifle was pressed into frontline service. Under such conditions, racial segregation proved impractical, and within a few months, some units were assigning replacements regardless of race. By the end of the Korean War, the forces in Korea were probably the most racially integrated institution in the United States.[34]

Racial integration of another kind began with the creation of the joint EUSAK-ROKA KATUSA program (Korean Augmentation to the US Army) in August 1950. Some forty thousand Koreans were sent through a perfunctory ten-day basic training course in marksmanship, discipline, and sanitation then assigned to American infantry companies and field artillery batteries. When the 7th Infantry Division landed at Inchon, eight thousand soldiers, almost half its combat strength, were KATUSAs. The program went through numerous ups and downs over the course of the war, but as with Black integration, after a rocky beginning, the KATUSA program was acknowledged as a positive initiative.[35]

One of the great lessons of 1950 was the need to improve the service's relationship with the press. "The first six months of the Korean conflict," concluded the Army Public Information Office, witnessed "the destruction of public esteem of the Army by poor, unbalanced reporting."[36] Much of the unfavourable coverage came from the army's failure to impose either censorship or standards until December 1950. This resulted in sensationalized stories of US defeats at the hands of the Communists by even veteran combat reporters such as Homer Bigart, Carl Mydans, and Keyes Beech. The negative tone of such coverage led S.L.A. Marshall to demand of reporters in Korea: "For God's sake quit writing stories aimed to doom your country and its cause."[37] Press coverage improved in 1951 because Ridgway was a master of public relations and also because, by then, reporters had sufficient time in the country to recognize, in the cynical words of one officer, that "you can't mix Ernie Pyle and straight reporting."[38] One lesson the army drew from the first months of Korea was that managing the press was no job for amateurs. In the next decade, its public affairs office would insert itself into movies, television, radio, sports events, and virtually every other public event to sell the army to its citizens.[39]

The first months of the Korean War had an immediate impact on US Army training methods, particularly infantry combat training. From the beginning, army leaders had to deny media accusations "that the United States troops thrown into the line in Korea were raw recruits who had never heard the sound of artillery fire"[40] Responding to public outrage, Congress mandated that no soldier could be sent overseas without at least sixteen weeks of training. The army's response was to reinstate many of the realistic practices implemented during the final year of the Second World War that had been banned as too dangerous, such as live-fire exercises and hand-to-hand combat. However, the soldiers of Eighth Army sent to Korea in June 1950 were all products of the pre-1949 basic training program, not its updated versions.[41] In response to complaints in the early months of the war that US troops were unfit and unable to fight in heat or mountains, it implemented a new physical training program emphasizing marching, obstacle courses, and complete body conditioning.[42]

On a short-term basis, army efforts at applying the lessons of the Korean War to training were less successful. The tripling of manpower, the deployment of tens of thousands of troops to Korea as replacements, and the lack of sufficient training cadre and facilities proved challenges that took most of the war to overcome. One training division suffered a 130 percent turnover rate in officers and a 108 percent turnover rate in enlisted trainers in less than six months. Two years after the war began, inspectors still reported numerous replacements arriving in Korea insufficiently prepared for combat. To provide this needed instruction, most combat divisions created special training programs for replacements.[43]

The 1950 operations affected not only how the army trained soldiers but also how they were mentally conditioned. To raise morale, the army shifted the focus of its Troop Information and Education from lectures on sanitation and morality to an emphasis on patriotism and martial values. As one general informed his subordinates, it was a chance to make direct contact with soldiers and "tell them why our lads are fighting in Korea. It is a lot better to fight a war to protect our country in Korea, than in California or in Georgia, or in any place in the U.S. That is a thought that does not occur to them. They are fighting to protect their own country over there."[44] The Command Conference program, still in existence, provided a way for senior officers to give direct guidance to subordinate commanders and principal staff officers without having to either moderate their comments or issue them as orders. Ideally, it provided a means to receive feedback, assess leadership, and identify problems in the unit.

A further lesson the army drew from the first months of the war was that the air force was an unreliable source of support. When the war began, these services were already locked in a dispute over doctrine; it escalated to involve the US Navy and Marine Corps once operations began. Air officers complained that too many field officers lacked a sufficient appreciation of the capabilities and limits of air power; air personnel were inexperienced, untrained in working with land forces, and had high turnover. The result, as one authority summarized, was that air operations in 1950 were typified by "confusion, frustration, and inefficiency."[45] The Korean War magnified the army's interest in aerial transport that was neither under air force control nor required the construction of airfields. The army had experimented with the helicopter before the war. By its end, many were convinced that it provided "the mobility so vital to Atomic warfare ... [and would] allow us to disperse our units, offering unprofitable targets to enemy A-weapons and then allow us to mass our forces for a decisive blow at the critical time and space."[46]

Long-Term Lessons?

The editors of *Armor* spoke for many army officers when they concluded in 1953: "Korea's most potent lesson lies in the fact that ... it is not the kind of war to fight."[47] The terrain, the supremacy of the defence, the tactical stalemate and limited political objectives after 1951, and the low-level commitment of resources to a secondary theatre frustrated those who served.[48] Many concluded, correctly, that they could have achieved far more than Washington and the United Nations allowed. Deprived of the opportunity to achieve clear battlefield success, army analysts tended to draw the specific lessons that best suited their service and branch. For example, the fact that President Truman had committed US combat troops rather than launching atomic strikes against Pyongyang, Beijing, or Moscow was cited as proof that the nation needed both strong overseas garrisons and rapidly deployable land forces to support them. When President Dwight D. Eisenhower returned to the pre-Korea strategy of relying on an all-out nuclear attack on the USSR, army spokesmen argued, "Korea stands as a precedent for the acceptance of limitations in the atomic era."[49] To Ridgway, the Korean War demonstrated the fallacy of a US national-security strategy predicated on massive retaliation with the USSR, and nothing else. He believed future wars were likely to be limited in both objectives and force; to fight these limited wars, the United States would require powerful, mobile, and immediately deployable ground forces.[50] But many army officers were determined that the lessons of Korea would not be interpreted to mean that the army should be organized to fight similar conflicts in the Far East. They shared with political leaders a conviction that NATO and Europe were the decisive theatres. They were pessimistic about future land wars in Asia. MacArthur might fulminate that there was no substitute for victory, but one frontline journalist noted that "one of the most striking facts encountered in Tokyo and Seoul is the generals' profound aversion to a war-to-the-finish with China in China."[51]

The early months of the war also had a profound impact on the US Army's tactical and strategic thought, demonstrating US forces would need more firepower, specifically atomic firepower, to compensate for their inferiority in personnel. In the years immediately after Hiroshima, the army largely conceded the use of atomics to the air force, but by the end of the decade, senior leaders recognized that if the national strategy was predicated on atomics, without these weapons their service was doomed to irrelevance. Three weeks before the North Korean invasion, Army Chief of Staff J. Lawton Collins announced on television that the army was researching atomic warheads for artillery and guided missiles. In November 1950, Major General James M. Gavin published an article that criticized the current view of atomics as strategic weapons against cities, populations, and economies. Referencing Korea, he suggested that atomic bombs concentrated on a five-to-eight-kilometre front would provide the equivalent firepower of eight thousand medium artillery shells per square mile. The result would replicate the carpet bombing that had blown open the German defences in Normandy.[52] On 25 May 1953, the US Army shot a fifteen-kiloton atomic shell from a modified 280 mm cannon. Politicians who witnessed the test urged it as a solution to the Korean deadlock, though there is no conclusive evidence this contributed to the Communists' decision to sign the armistice two months later.[53]

Gavin's article was one of several appearing during the war that emphasized the service's need for an arsenal of tactical atomics. By mid-1951, the Office of the Chief of Army Field Forces had concluded: "If by mass destruction of combat personnel the enemy can be forced to revise steamroller tactics and disperse units more thinly over a given area, conventional operations in conjunction with tactical air can defeat enemy land forces on any selected objectives. Under favorable circumstances, the Atomic Bomb is a weapon which can produce mass battle casualties."[54] Korea also provided evidence that a future US-USSR war (or proxy war) would not necessarily escalate to a mutual thermonuclear exchange. In place of a nuclear holocaust, army theorists provided a limited tactical war scenario in which American and Soviet politicians would agree to limit their use of atomic weapons to purely military targets. War could again be decided on the battlefield (no Korean War stalemate) and, thus, it followed, victory would go to the first army to transform its doctrine, organization, and equipment to wage atomic war.[55]

Conclusion

The Korean War has entered American popular military history as a contest dominated by a few generals, a few battles, and long periods in which little happened other than grinding attritional warfare, ultimately ending in a ceasefire and status quo ante bellum. In the broader context of the Cold War, Korea is seen as a necessary test of "Free World" resistance to Soviet and Communist aggression and as a strategic victory. The performance of the US Army, especially in 1950, remains a source of controversy. The early defeats and retreats, symbolized by the fate of Task Force Smith, prompted a great deal of internal and external criticism of the service's performance, particularly of its enlisted personnel. Much of this criticism was accepted by the service because it fit into the army's own traditional unpreparedness narrative.[56] For the US Army, the impact of the early months was two-fold. In the short term, it led to more emphasis on realistic combat training and increased focus on morale. In the long run, the lessons of the early battles in Korea found their way into the army's doctrine of limited atomic war, new weapons, more emphasis on mobility, and reorganizing combat forces for high-tempo, mobile operations that would be employed, perhaps inappropriately, in Vietnam.

Notes

1 On the US Army before the Korean War, see Thomas E. Hanson, *Combat Ready? The Eighth U.S. Army on the Eve of the Korean War* (College Station: Texas A&M University Press, 2010); Brian McAllister Linn, *Elvis's Army: Cold War GI's and the Atomic Battlefield* (Cambridge, MA: Harvard University Press, 2016), 9–47; and William W. Epley, *America's First Cold War Army, 1945–1950* (Arlington, VA: Association of the United States Army, 1999). An earlier version of this chapter, "From the Nat-dong River Battle to the Nuclear Battle," was presented at the International Academic Seminar of the Korean War, Daegu, Republic of Korea, in 2013. This chapter was greatly assisted by the expertise of William M. Donnelly and Thomas Hanson.

2 The best military history is Allan R. Millett, *The War for Korea, 1950–1951: They Came from the North* (Lawrence: University Press of Kansas, 2011). For popular military histories that emphasize the poor performance of the US Army in the first months of the war, see Alexander Bevin, *Korea: The First War We Lost* (New York: Hippocrene Books, 1986); Clay Blair, *The Forgotten War: America in Korea* (New York: Anchor Books, 1987); T.R. Fehrenbach, *This Kind of War: A Study of Unpreparedness* (New York: Macmillan, 1963); David Halberstam, *The Coldest Winter: America and the Korean War* (New York: Hyperion Books, 2007); and Max Hastings, *The Korean War* (New York: Simon and Schuster, 1988). On the historiography of Inchon, see Paul M. Edwards, *The Inchon Landing, 1950: An Annotated Bibliography* (Westport, CT: Greenwood, 1994).

3 Millett, *They Came,* 107–25; and Glenn D. Paige, *The Korean Decision: June 24–30, 1950* (New York: Free Press, 1968).

4 Cited in Millett, *They Came,* 440. On the US Army in Korea, see William M. Donnelly, "The US Army during the Korean War," in *Raise, Train, and Sustain: Delivering Combat Power,* ed. Peter Dennis and Jeffrey Grey (Canberra: Australian Military History Publications, 2010), 127–59.

5 JPS 789/1, Sub: Staff Studies of Certain Military Problems Deriving from "Concept of Operations for PINCHER," 13 April 1946, Strategy and the Army Files, folder 4, box 1, RG 319, National Archives and Records Administration, College Park, Maryland (NARA); and Edward Kaplan, *To Kill Nations: American Strategy in the Air-Atomic Age and the Rise of Mutually Assured Destruction* (Ithaca, NY: Cornell University Press, 2015), 19–76.

6 "Dodging the Draft," *Armed Force* 6 (15 April 1950): 2.

7 Robert L. Eichelberger to Douglas MacArthur, January 1948, box 12, Robert L. Eichelberger Papers, Perkins Library, Duke University, Durham, North Carolina. When separate from MacArthur as commander-in-chief, Far East, the organization was designated Far East Command.

8 Eighth Army Fact Sheet, 2 June 1965, box 272, entry 1A1, RG 550, NARA; Briefing at GHQ, Report of the Department of the Army Training Inspection: Far East Command, 24 September to 29 October 1949, box 7, entry 1, RG 337, NARA. On the occupation, see Susan L. Carruthers, *The Good Occupation: American Soldiers and the Hazards of Peace* (Cambridge, MA: Harvard University Press, 2016); and John Dower, *Embracing Defeat: Japan in the Wake of World War II* (New York: W.W. Norton, 1999).

9 Hanson, *Combat Ready?*; and Donnelly, "US Army during the Korean War," 128–34. On US Army assessments of the Republic of Korea Army (ROKA) prior to the North Korean invasion, see Bryan R. Gibby, "The Best Little Army," *Journal of Military History* 77, 1 (2013): 173–201.

10 On Task Force Smith, see Roy E. Appleman, *South to the Natkong, North to the Yalu (June-November 1950)* (Washington, DC: Office of Chief of Military History, 1961), 65–76; and Roy K. Flint, "Task Force Smith and the 24th Division: Delay and Withdrawal, 5–19 July, 1950," in *America's First Battles, 1776–1965,* ed. Charles E. Heller and William A. Stofft (Lawrence: University Press of Kansas, 1986), 266–75.

11 On the first weeks of the war and the retreat to Pusan, see Appleman, *South to the Natkong,* 59–181; William T. Bowers, William M. Hammond, and George L. MacGarrigle, *Black Soldier, White Army: The 24th Infantry Regiment in Korea* (Washington, DC: CMH, 1996), 67–123; and Millett, *They Came,* 1–231.

12 *Semiannual Report of the Secretary of the Army, January 1 to June 30 1950* (Washington, DC: Government Printing Office, 1950), 67.

13 "Public Information Segment, Command and Management Program, 1 July 1951–31 December 1951," box 1, entry 55A, RG 319, NARA.

14 Marshall Andrews, "What Can You Believe?," *Combat Forces Journal* 1 (October 1950): 20–21; "Responsible Journalism," *Combat Forces Journal* 1 (March 1951): 6; Headquarters (HQ), Eighth US Army Korea (EUSAK), "Special Problems in the Korean Conflict," 1952, Combined Arms Research Library, Fort Leavenworth, KS (CARL); Eric Larrabee, "Korea: The Military Lesson," *Harper's* 201 (November 1950): 51–57; Garrett Underhill and Ronald Schiller, "The Tragedy of the U.S. Army," *Look* 15 (13 February 1951): 27–31. On media, see Robert T. Davis, *The US Army and the Media in the 20th Century* (Fort Leavenworth, KS: Combat Studies Institute Press, 2009), 53–57; and Hanson, *Combat Ready?*, 1–12.

15 The argument that US military policy consists of cycles of unpreparedness, military defeat, mobilization, victory, and unpreparedness dates back to the nineteenth century and is

often attributed to Emory Upton, *The Military Policy of the United States* (Washington, DC: Government Printing Office, 1904).

16 HQ, EUSAK, "Special Problems."

17 Russell A. Gugeler, *Combat Actions in Korea* (Washington, DC: Government Printing Office, 1954). The quotation is from Rudyard Kipling's poem "That Day."

18 Appleman, *South to the Natkong,* 180.

19 Matthew B. Ridgway, *The Korean War* (Garden City, NY: Doubleday, 1967).

20 Fehrenbach, *This Kind of War,* 167.

21 Kelly C. Jordan, "Three Armies in Korea: The Combat Effectiveness of the United States Eighth Army in Korea, July 1950–June 1952" (PhD diss., Ohio State University, 1999), 228. The state of Korean War historiography and US military policy up to the invasion is expertly summarized in Millett, *The War for Korea,* 1–84.

22 Allison R. Hartman, "Foreword," Charles G. Cleaver, "History of the Korean War," vol. 2, "Personnel Problems," [1952?], Military History Section, HQ Far East Command, CARL.

23 HQ, EUSAK, "Special Problems"; and John E. Dahlquist, "OCAFF Role in Support of Overseas Theaters and Area Commands," lecture, Armed Forces Staff College, 17 February 1954, folder 350.001, box 22, entry 55F, RG 337, NARA.

24 Robert K. Sawyer, "United States Military Advisory Group to the Republic of Korea," 1955, CARL. The official histories of operations were Appleman, *South to the Natkong*; Walter G. Hermes, *Truce Tent and Fighting Front* (Washington, DC: Office of the Chief of Military History, 1966); and C. Billy Mossman, *Ebb and Flow: November 1950–July 1951* (Washington, DC: Center of Military History, US Army, 1990).

25 "Conference on United Nations Military Operations in Korea," 1951, Army War College, CARL; remarks of General J. Lawton Collins, Infantry School Conference, 5 April 1951, Service School Speeches file (5), box 43, J. Lawton Collins Papers, Dwight D. Eisenhower Presidential Library, Abilene, Kansas.

26 Infantry School, "Lessons from Korea," 1954, CARL. Robert G. Turner, R.J. Darnel, and Robert R. Summers, "Comments," Infantry Instructors Conference, 16–32 June 1952, Maneuver Center of Excellence Donovan Research Library, Fort Benning, Georgia; Office of Armed Forces Information and Education, Attitude Research Branch, "What Soldiers Think about the Infantry," September 1951, Report 118-338, box 1008, entry 93, RG 330, NARA; Frank T. Mildren, "What Has Korea Taught Us?," *Infantry School Quarterly* 43 (October 1953): 6–13; and Edward L. Rowney, "Going to Korea?," *Infantry School Quarterly* 43 (July 1953): 99–103.

27 Turner, Darnel, and Summers, "Comments."

28 Oral History, Louis C. Wagner Jr., Papers, 15, Army Heritage and Education Center, (AHEC), Carlisle, Pennsylvania; George B. Barth, "The First Days in Korea," *Combat Forces Journal* 2 (March 1952): 21–24; George B. Pickett, "Tanks in Korea," *Armor* 59 (November–December 1950): 6–9; Armor School, "Employment of Armor in Korea: The First Year," vol. 2, 1952, Maneuver Center of Excellence Donovan Research Library; and Boyd L. Dastrup, *King of Battles: A Branch History of the U.S. Army's Field Artillery* (Fort Monroe, VA: US Army Training and Doctrine Command, 1992), 252–61.

29 David C. Elliot, "Project Vista and Nuclear Weapons in Europe," *International Security* 11 (Summer 1986): 163–83.

30 Office, Chief of Army Field Forces, Introductory Narrative, Summary of Major Events and Problems, FY 1955, vol. 1, TRADOC Archives, Fort Eustis, Virginia; and Willard Wyman, "Mobile Forces Concepts," lecture, Army War College, 8 January 1957, AHEC.

31 S.L.A. Marshall, "Commentary on Infantry Operations and Weapons Usage in Korea," October 1951, vii; and S.L.A. Marshall, "Technical Memorandum ORL-T-7 (EUSAK): Notes on Infantry Tactics in Korea," 11 December 1951, both in CARL. On Operations

Research Office, see Charles R. Shrader, *History of Operations Research in the United States Army,* vol. 1, *1942–1962* (Washington, DC: Office of the Deputy Undersecretary of the Army of Operations Research, 2006), 86–98.

32 William M. Donnelly, *Under Orders: The Army National Guard during the Korean War* (College Station: Texas A&M University Press, 2001); and George Q. Flynn, *The Draft, 1940–1973* (Lawrence: University Press of Kansas, 1993), 110–33.

33 Semiannual Report of the Secretary of the Army, 1 January 1952 to 30 June 1952 (Washington: Government Printing Office, 1952), 91–92.

34 Bowers, Hammond, and MacGarrigle, *Black Soldier, White Army,* 125–78; and Richard M. Dalfiume, *Desegregation of the Armed Forces: Fighting on Two Fronts, 1939–1953* (Columbia: University of Missouri Press, 1969), 200–15.

35 Richard T. Cranford, "The Impact of Racial Integration on Combat Effectiveness of Eight (US) Army during the Korean War" (master's thesis, School of Advanced Military Studies, Command and General Staff College, 2012).

36 Public Information Segment, Command and Management Program, 1 July 1951 to 31 December 1951, box 1, entry 55A, RG 319, NARA.

37 S.L.A. Marshall, *Bringing Up the Rear: A Memoir* (San Rafael, CA: Presidio Press, 1979), 183.

38 "Responsible Journalism," *Combat Forces Journal* 1 (March 1951): 6.

39 Linn, *Elvis's Army,* 230–67; G.P. Welch, "Public Information, Troop Information and Education," lecture, Army War College, 23 November 1953, AHEC; and Lon Smith, "The Effects of Civilian Control on Current Military Affairs," student paper, Army War College, 23 February 1951, AHEC.

40 "Army Denies Use of Green Troops," *New York Times,* 10 September 1950; William M. Donnelly, "From Sergeant Snorkels to Drill Sergeants: Basic Training of Male Soldiers in the U.S. Army, 1953–1964," *Journal of Military History* 86, 2 (2022): 399–426.

41 Hanson, *Combat Ready?,* 26–27.

42 On the difference between basic training before and after the Korean War, see Bill Davidson, "The New GI Joe: He Never Had It So Good," *Colliers* 126 (30 September 1950): 24–25, 71–75; Bill Safire, "Shape Up or Ship Out," *Colliers* 131 (11 April 1953): 17–19; and Patrick H. Devine, "Recruit Training for the Future Army," student paper, Army War College, 1957, AHEC.

43 HQ, EUSAK, "Special Problems"; "Note from the Korean Battlefield," in *Training Bulletin* 11, 23 October 1952, box 215, entry UD-5, RG 547, NARA; "Sinews of War ... Training the Men," *Newsweek* 37 (2 April 1951): 22–24; and John L. Romjue and Richard P. Weinert, *A Brief Survey of the U.S. Army Experience in Mobilization and Training* (Fort Monroe, VA: CONARC, 1977).

44 Remarks by Major General Chase during 3rd Army Troop Information and Education Conference, April 1951, box 29, entry NC3-38-81-4, RG 338, NARA. Christopher S. DeRosa, *Political Indoctrination in the U.S. Army from World War II to the Vietnam War* (Lincoln: University of Nebraska Press, 2006).

45 Allan R. Millett, "Korea," in *Case Studies in the Development of Close Air Support,* ed. Benjamin F. Cooling (Washington, DC: Office of Air Force History, 1990), 353, see also 345–405; and Infantry School, "Lessons from Korea."

46 Joseph W. Stilwell Jr., "Remarks," Infantry Instructors Conference.

47 "For Continental Warfare ... an Armored Corps," *Armor* 52 (January-February 1953): 21.

48 Bryan R. Gibby, *Korean Showdown: National Policy and Military Strategy in a Limited War, 1951–1952* (Tuscaloosa: University of Alabama Press, 2021); and William M. Donnelly, "The Best Army That Can Be Put in the Field in the Circumstances: The U.S. Army, July 1951–July 1953," *Journal of Military History* 71, 3 (2007): 809–47.

49 Thomas J.H. Trapnell, "The Army Views on the Use of Force in Limited War," lecture, Air War College, 12 April 1957, K239.716257-37, Air Force Historical Records Research Agency, Maxwell Air Force Base, Alabama.
50 Matthew B. Ridgway, "The Army's Role in Today's World," lecture, Army War College, 24 August 1953, AHEC.
51 John Osborne, "Little Known Facts about the GIs and Generals," *Life* 34 (16 March 1953): 59.
52 James M. Gavin, "The Tactical Use of the Atomic Bomb," *Combat Forces Journal* 1 (November 1950): 9–11.
53 Richard L. Miller, *Under the Cloud: The Decades of Nuclear Testing* (New York: Free Press, 1986), 178–80.
54 Office, Chief of Army Field Forces, "Tactical Employment of the Atomic Bomb," 7 October 1951, 000.9/35, box 4, entry 55B, RG 337, NARA.
55 On the US Army's transition to atomic war planning, see Linn, *Elvis's Army*, 73–98.
56 Hanson, *Combat Ready?*, 7–9.

1 Major (Ret'd) Reg Redknap (*left*) and Lieutenant-Colonel (Ret'd) Ed Hollyer (*right*) together at the Canadian War Museum's Vimy House in 1997. | Canadian War Museum, 19970045-002

2 Lieutenant Robert Peacock captured this view of the opposing hills from a Canadian machine-gun emplacement in UN lines, 1953. | Canadian War Museum, 20070056-003_028

3 Brian Meredith, an information officer with the United Nations Commission for the Unification and Rehabilitation of Korea, took this photo of the ruins of Seoul in the fall of 1950. | Canadian War Museum, 19950074-037_168

4 Prime Minister Louis St. Laurent (*second from left*) visiting 25 Field Dressing Station, 1953. | Canadian War Museum, 19840027-065-001

5 US soldiers fighting in the streets of Seoul, 1950. | US National Archives, 111-SC-351392

6 Soldiers of the 24th Infantry Regiment assist a wounded comrade following a battle near Chor'won, 22 April 1951. | US National Archives, 111-SC-365537

7 HMCS *Nootka* fires a salvo at a target at Songjin, 26 May 1951. | Canadian War Museum, 20020045-1761

8 Soldiers of the Royal 22e Régiment take up a hillside position. | Canadian War Museum, 19900076-566

9 *Left to right*: Gunners R.J. Galarneau, G.W. North, and Sergeant V.K. Cornish, 2 Royal Canadian Horse Artillery, fire at a target in Korea, 28 May 1951. Cornish was killed in action on 20 November 1951. | Canadian War Museum, 20020045-2725

10 Ted Zuber's depiction of the battle of Hill 355, October 1952. | *Contact,* Ted Zuber, 1978, Beaverbrook Collection of War Art, Canadian War Museum, 19890328-001

11 A wiring party in Korea, 1951–52. | Canadian War Museum, 20030176-001_19

12 Lieutenant H.R. Gardner with a Chinese soldier taken prisoner on the night of 2–3 September 1952. | Courtesy of the Mahar family

13 Artist and Korea veteran Ted Zuber's depiction of a night patrol in no man's land halting as a Chinese flare lights up the landscape. | *Freeze!,* Ted Zuber, 1978, Beaverbrook Collection of War Art, Canadian War Museum, 19890328-012

14 Soldiers of the 1st Commonwealth Division pose in front of an observation post in Korea. | C.N. Barclay, *The First Commonwealth Division: The Story of British Commonwealth Land Forces in Korea, 1950–1953*

15 Canadian airmen at Shemya Air Force Base in the Aleutians, likely in 1951. | Canadian War Museum, 20100087-037_001

16 Emergency crews respond to a crash of a 426 Squadron North Star aircraft at Sea Island Airport in Vancouver, in December 1953. The forty-three passengers and eight crew all survived. | Department of National Defence

17 The CVPF's 172nd Regiment attacks the US Marines, 1951. | Courtesy of Xiaobing Li, author's private collection

18 Medical officers, nursing officers, and patients of 25 Canadian Field Dressing Station, Korea, 1953. | Canadian War Museum, 19840072-002_140

19 Private Andrew LaRiviere served with 3 Princess Patricia's Canadian Light Infantry in Korea in 1953, where he was wounded. His family donated this sketch of the dressing station to the Canadian War Museum. | *Just Outside Hospitle,* 1953, artist unknown, Beaverbrook Collection of War Art, 20150290-001

20 Private Elliott Gordon Mackay was one of the first Canadian soldiers killed in action in Korea. He enlisted under his cousin's name. For many years, his gravesite in Busan was wrongly labelled "J.M. Mackay." | Canadian War Museum, 20030290-005

21 A woman lays a wreath at the gravesite of Able Seaman Wallis Burden in Yokohama, Japan. Burden was one of three sailors killed in action aboard HMCS *Iroquois* in October 1952. | Canadian War Museum, 19920085-1188

22 Former prisoner of war Lance Corporal Paul Dugal *(left)* speaks with 25 Canadian Infantry Brigade commander Brigadier J.V. Allard, April 1953. | Canadian War Museum, 19900576-62-001

23 New Year's Eve, 1953, moments before the grenade went off. | *New Year's Eve,* Ted Zuber, 1978, Beaverbrook Collection of War Art, Canadian War Museum, 19890238-007

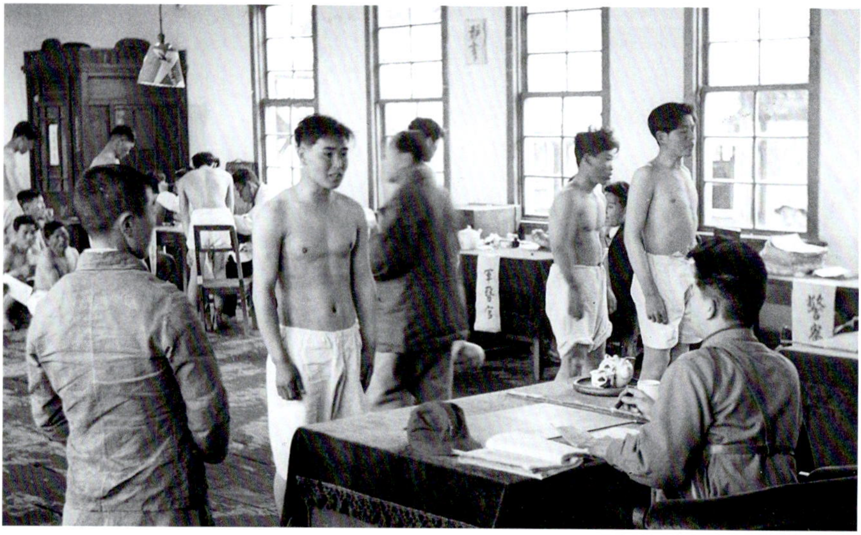

24 Recruits for the Republic of Korea Army line up to be processed, fall 1950. | Canadian War Museum, 19950074-037_128

25 A Canadian gunner hands out rations to orphans gathered at the railyard at Tokchon, 1953. | Canadian War Museum, 20110039-004-030

26 The Kap'yong memorial stone, unveiled in 1975 near the site of the battleground. | Canadian War Museum, 20020045-1557-2

27 The Korea Veterans' National Wall of Remembrance in Meadowvale Cemetery, Brampton, Ontario. | Photo courtesy of the Embassy of the Republic of Korea

28 The Korean government's Korean War Ambassador for Peace Medal. This medal was issued posthumously to Private Elliott Gordon Mackay, the youngest Canadian to die in Korea. | Canadian War Museum, 20030290-003-002

29 A remembrance ceremony at The Ambassador of Peace Monument in Burnaby, British Columbia, July 2023. | Photo courtesy of Andrew Burtch

4

The Canadian Naval Experience Off Korea

Michael Whitby

Late on the sun-drenched afternoon of Wednesday, 5 July 1950, the cruiser HMCS *Ontario* led three destroyers westward through the spectacular beauty of British Columbia's Strait of Juan de Fuca. *Ontario* soon peeled off for home, but *Cayuga, Athabaskan,* and *Sioux* held a steady course across the Pacific for Korea. Forming Canada's first, and initially only, military commitment to the Korean War, which had exploded the previous month, they were spurred on by a message from the chief of the naval staff: "First at bat as usual. Good luck with your mission."[1]

Nobody knew when the ships would come home, but, in the end, five years would pass before the final Royal Canadian Navy (RCN) destroyer returned from duty off Korea – a period not much shorter than the Second World War. For most of that time, the navy maintained a force of three destroyers in theatre and eight of the RCN's eleven destroyers ultimately deployed. By carrying out blockade duty similar to that conducted in the age of sail, the force made a meaningful contribution to the UN's successful application of sea power in aid of campaigns ashore. Just as important, the experience gave the RCN a much-needed boost that helped jolt it from its so-called sickly season, which followed the Second World War. Thus, as perpetually occurs, the war had ramifications beyond the actual fighting.

The Sickly Season

Despite growing pains from its almost unparalleled expansion, during the Second World War, the RCN played an indispensable role in the Battle of the Atlantic and the Normandy invasion and made a contribution to the war at sea beyond any reasonable expectation. But no matter how consequential, the experience was an aberration. Peacetime has rarely been kind to the navy. In the period between the First and Second World Wars, the navy had been starved of resources and, at the leanest times, barely survived. The years following the Second World War were better, but not much so. The navy was cut back to peacetime proportions, and even though the fleet – comprising an aircraft carrier, two carrier air groups, two cruisers, eleven destroyers, and a handful of frigates – was a significant step up from the tiny prewar navy, it suffered from a sea of troubles, including limited budgetary support, severe manpower shortages, and poor morale, that contributed to a series of mutinies.

At the outbreak of the war, the RCN's personnel strength was fixed at 9,600 officers and men. Many were permanent force professionals, but these had been augmented by former wartime volunteer reservists who had chosen the navy as their career after the war; although they knew war, many lacked the overall training and experience of professionals, and it would take time for that to be accrued. The situation began to improve at the end of the 1940s due to rising tension between the Western allies and the Soviet Union. The maritime obligations that accompanied the formation of the North Atlantic Treaty Organization brought a boost in both purpose and resources – naval expenditures spiked dramatically from $44.7 million in 1949 to $260.3 million in 1953.[2] Personnel limits were also increased, and the RCN launched a vigorous recruiting drive to meet the new allowance of 13,440 officers and men.

In an address on the CBC, the chief of the naval staff, Vice-Admiral Harold Grant, explained, "We want the best type of young Canadian we can get – stout hearted lads with brains as well as brawn and who understand the value of teamwork." He added the caveat "that our new entries should appreciate at the outset that life at sea is not always comparable to life ashore."[3] Korea would prove all that to be true, and the RCN's positive experience in Korea would serve as another catalyst in rallying the navy's fortunes.

Early Innings

On 30 June 1950, Naval Services Headquarters (NSHQ) in Ottawa directed Pacific Command to place three destroyers on five days' notice to join the UN naval forces gathering to meet the Korean emergency. Although the ships were preparing for a European cruise, much had to be done to meet the rush to war. *Sioux* was in dry dock for routine maintenance; *Athabaskan* was in the midst of her annual leave period, and the last of her crew was not expected back until 6 July; and *Cayuga* had only just emerged from refit and had not yet begun the task of storing ship.[4] Nonetheless, the three ships sailed on time, but they left the situation behind them in disarray. To bring them up to wartime strength, the barracks and other ships based on Esquimalt were stripped of personnel, and the hurried deployment left storeroom shelves bare.[5]

On 30 July, after a long trek across the Pacific, the destroyers put into Sasebo, Japan, their primary base throughout the conflict. They were not given much opportunity to adjust to their new surroundings; within twenty-four hours,

Athabaskan was dispatched to escort an American troop convoy to embattled Busan. Meanwhile, Captain Jeffry Brock, *Cayuga*'s commanding officer, who had served in the Second World War and was the senior Canadian naval officer in the Korean theatre, ascertained where his ships stood in the UN Command structure: "Each ship individually joined TG 96.5 under Rear Admiral Hartman, USN for service with TE 96.50 (Captain Jay) and TE 96.53 (Rear Admiral Andrews, RN)."[6] Among this confusing nomenclature was the critical designator *individually,* which signified that Canadian ships would be deployed piecemeal and not as a national force. Nobody seemed to object to this, but it brought an inevitable loss of prestige and less effective public relations.[7]

The maritime environment off the Korean peninsula varied greatly between its two coasts, and the difference shaped naval operations. The East Coast, bordering the Sea of Japan, is distinguished by a narrow coastal plain and deep water close inshore. In contrast, the West Coast on the Yellow Sea features a broad littoral, innumerable islands, severe tidal currents, and shifting shoals and sandbanks, all of which tested seamanship. Although Canadian destroyers worked both coasts, they more often operated off the West Coast with other Commonwealth forces while occasionally cruising the Sea of Japan with US Navy carrier task groups.

In conducting these operations, RCN sailors worked alongside other navies that joined the UN cause. Although they had little or no experience with services from France, the Netherlands, or South Korea, they shared common doctrine and training with their Commonwealth brethren from Great Britain, Australia, and New Zealand and were cementing an increasingly close bond with the US Navy through partnership in NATO and continental defence. As will be seen, though they did not always agree with the decisions and practices of their allies, they did know how to work with them. Moreover, the continual rotation of three modern, capable destroyers into the theatre during the conflict, all of which gave effective service, was a valuable contribution and buttressed the navy's reputation, hard-earned in the Second World War.

North Korea had no seagoing forces capable of disrupting UN naval operations or affecting military activities ashore. "It is evident from the nature of the North Korean invasion of the South," the Australian official history of the Korean war opined, "that Kim Il-Sung gave little thought to the strategic importance of the sea."[8] That was an error since command of the sea played a decisive role in shaping the course of the war, enabling UN troops to launch direct assaults on – or be evacuated from – most of the peninsula. When carrying out blockade operations, naval forces were typically most concerned with threats from submarines, aircraft, mines, and coastal artillery, but none of these proved decisive during the conflict. North Korea had no submarines, and although there was concern the Soviets or Chinese might deploy them, that did not occur. The threat of air attack was more ominous but, again, had little impact on the war at sea. With evident relief, Captain Brock reported, "It is fortunate that the enemy did not possess sufficient air strength to enable him to place the blockading and bombarding forces in any real danger [as] the efficiency of the Long and Close range AA armament [in RCN destroyers] was dangerously low when the division was first committed to the Korean campaign."[9] North Korea had no sea-mining capability, but it profited from weapons and expertise provided by the Soviets, masters in that form of warfare. When minefields frustrated an assault on the East Coast port of Wonsan, an American admiral despaired, "We have lost control of the seas to a nation without a Navy, using pre-World War I weapons, laid by vessels that were utilized at the time of the birth of Christ."[10]

So the threat was real, but apart from a few well-defended ports, North Korea laid mines "only in piecemeal fashion as part of a harassment campaign, and not as a part of an integrated coastal defense."[11] Although no RCN destroyers fell victim to mines, the ships dispatched dozens of mines by gunfire or demolition. Fire from shore batteries was the greatest sustained danger for warships operating inshore, and the North Koreans proved adept at siting artillery in range of well-travelled coastal routes. Several UN ships, including HMCS *Iroquois,* took hits, and sailors found the best defence against coastal artillery to be effective intelligence, prompt avoiding action, and accurate counterbattery fire. When all the enemy threats are considered, the lack of any deadly, sustained menace enabled UN maritime forces to clamp down an aggressive inshore blockade off Korea. The situation was reminiscent of an episode in classic naval fiction. When the sloop HMS *Hotspur* blockaded the coast of Napoleonic France in a C.S. Forester novel, Lieutenant William Bush observed to his captain, "We're the terrier at the rat hole, Sir." "Exactly," Commander Horatio Hornblower agreed. That same sense of confident superiority endured among UN naval forces off Korea.[12]

On 15 August 1950, *Cayuga* fired the first Canadian shots in anger in Korea. Yosu, a small port west of Busan, had been taken by the North Koreans, and UN commanders wanted its port facilities demolished before any use could be made of them by the enemy. *Cayuga* anchored six kilometres offshore and, assisted by a spotter aircraft from the carrier HMS *Theseus,* fired some ninety-four four-inch rounds over fifty minutes.[13] Several hits were noted, and the results were assessed as "fair."[14] Effective gunnery requires constant exercising, but Brock complained that "control teams were unpractized [sic] at this particular phase of gunnery, so that it was not until two or three actual bombardments were carried out that a satisfactory state of efficiency was achieved." "This," he emphasized, "would seem to indicate a requirement for a bombardment range on the West Coast, and for bombardment training to be an important part of a ship's gunnery exercises." There were other problems. The Americans and British used different spotting systems, forcing Canadians to become proficient in both. There was also trouble with ammunition. The cordite propellant came from different production lots, each slightly different, which affected uniformity, a key element of accurate fire control.[15] Ultimately, experience remedied these irritants, and the Canadian destroyers built a reputation for prompt and accurate shooting.

There was an interesting aside to *Cayuga*'s initial bombardment. In late August, the British commander of the UN naval forces on the West Coast responded to a query from his commander-in-chief:

> You asked recently whether we were wearing the United Nations Flag and if so, what are the regulations; I replied that we were not wearing it and indeed none of us were very clear as to how it should be worn.
>
> I find now that our Canadian ships have orders or permission to wear the United Nations flag at the foremasthead and HMCS *Cayuga* wore it the other day when bombarding, "Just for the hell of it." Personally I have not sighted it since this war started though this must have been due to not looking out as I am told it flies over General MacArthur's Headquarters in Tokyo.[16]

Captain Brock may have noticed the flag at MacArthur's headquarters during a visit there and adopted its use; whatever the inspiration, *Cayuga* appears to have been the first warship to fly the UN flag off Korea.

Along with blockade missions, screening American, British, and Australian aircraft carriers during flight operations became another enduring activity for the Canadian destroyers. While blockade activity was typically slow and steady, screening was fast and erratic. Destroyers had to manoeuvre constantly at high speed to keep station on carriers as they turned into the wind to launch and recover aircraft and then shifted back to base course. This proved a bane to watchkeepers, signals staff, helmsmen, and engine-room personnel who had to constantly stay on their toes. Canadians derogatorily termed such duty the "Corpens Club," for the Course Pennant flown from the carrier before course alteration signals. Lieutenant Andrew Collier, *Cayuga*'s navigating officer, recalled: "Corpening yourself to death with all the alterations of course and screen orientations and everything else ... we were just going around in circles."[17] Lest their ship suffer the embarrassment of being caught out of position or, worse, causing a collision (and destroyers always came out worse in collisions with much larger carriers), sailors could never relax.

Inchon and Chinnamp'o

Blockade duty and "corpening" dominated the RCN's initial deployment to Korea; "unglamorous and dull," Brock described the duty.[18] Two major operations, the amphibious assault on Inchon and the evacuation of Chinnamp'o, broke the routine and focused sailors' attention. They also highlighted the startling contrasts of the first half-year of the war as armies yo-yoed up and down the Korean peninsula.

The landing at Inchon – Operation Chromite – saw the UN go on the offensive. General Douglas MacArthur envisaged the assault as a way to break free of the Busan perimeter. He had utilized a "leap-frogging" strategy successfully in the South West Pacific during the Second World War, and he thought the UN's dominance of the seas off Korea presented a similar opportunity. The Inchon plan, a historian observed, "Rested on seapower, on its flexibility, adaptability, and, above all, its capacity for *surprise.*" From 15 to 19 September 1950, UN naval forces overcame severe tides, currents, mudflats, and shoals to put some seventy thousand soldiers ashore. It was a stunning success.[19] The Canadian destroyers were limited to a support role, escorting reserve convoys and guarding against a submarine threat that proved nonexistent (one positive was that, for the first time, the destroyers operated together). But there is more to a successful amphibious operation than putting soldiers ashore. The destroyers' contribution to Chromite was "small."[20] But like the dozens of RCN warships that filled support roles off Normandy in 1944, their activity was a necessary component in the application of sea power. As it was, the assault on Inchon enabled UN ground forces to break out of the Busan pocket and begin a relentless advance up the peninsula and into North Korea.

While Inchon was an assault based on an aggressive strategy, Chinnamp'o was an evacuation incited by a whiff of panic. On 25 November, the Chinese army launched a massive counterattack against UN forces approaching its frontier. Within hours, the Allies were in retreat on all fronts. In a hurriedly drawn-together plan, commanders of naval amphibious groups were given control of naval forces at evacuation points, some of which were on the verge of being overrun by the enemy as UN armies retreated. One such point was Chinnamp'o, North Korea's major port situated about fifty kilometres southwest of Pyongyang. Captain S.G. Kelly, US Navy, had taken five transports upstream to the port on 4 December. Captain Brock – with *Cayuga, Athabaskan,* and *Sioux,* the Australian destroyers *Warramunga* and *Bataan,* and the American destroyer *Forrest Royal* – waited offshore, prepared to cover Kelly's transports and provide fire support as the evacuation proceeded. Typical of the West Coast, the problem at Chinnamp'o was exacerbated by its maritime geography. The city lay about thirty-five kilometres from the sea, at the end of a shallow, narrow, serpentine channel known as the Daido-ko, through which UN minesweepers had swept an even narrower channel.

On the evening of 4 December, Brock was informed his ships would be required at Chinnampo by noon the next day. While this was difficult seafaring under the best circumstances, he promptly queried Kelly, "Indicate degree of urgency for destroyer support [in] inner harbour. Will attempt night passage if essential otherwise arrive early morning." Meanwhile, he called a meeting of his commanding officers, who advised against a night passage because of extreme navigational hazards. Soon after, a panicked signal arrived from an American ship alongside at Chinnampo. "We are uncovered," it complained. "Take necessary action immediately." Shortly afterwards, Kelly signalled that the situation at Chinnampo "may reach emergency basis."[21] Brock took this to mean the circumstances were grave, and he ordered his force upriver immediately to provide support. *Athabaskan*'s commander, Robert Welland, an experienced, dynamic destroyer officer, observed that the passage was one "that a prudent navigator would regard with misgivings [even] with a high tide or a sunny day."[22] Brock's destroyers would have neither.

At 2230, the six destroyers headed upstream at five knots in the following order: *Cayuga, Athabaskan, Bataan, Forrest Royal,* and *Sioux. Warramunga* proceeded separately. *Warramunga* ran aground shortly before midnight, and about a half hour later, *Sioux* also touched bottom. Commander Paul Taylor worked his ship free, only to run afoul of a buoy that had broken loose from its mooring. The damage caused heavy vibrations in the starboard shaft. Not wanting to break down completely and block the channel, Taylor reluctantly followed *Warramunga* back to sea. Brock was down to four destroyers.

The burden of getting their ships safely upriver fell on the navigation officers, and the heaviest burden was carried by Lieutenant Andy Collier in *Cayuga*, at the head of the line. In a letter home, he admitted, "I was pretty well twitched and not at all happy with the prospect of leading six destroyers up-river but the task was there and as a trained navigator I was supposedly trained for this sort of operation and just got on with it." The night "was dark as the inside of a cow's belly up top [on the bridge] and the only thing we had to rely on was radar which thank God really did its stuff."[23] *Cayuga*'s hard-pressed radar operators provided some 132 navigational fixes during the four-hour passage – about one every two minutes. "We only got a bit of a scare once," Collier remembered, "when the ship didn't seem to be answering her helm fast enough, that was mainly because of the flood tide. She just caught it a bit." When the four destroyers reached Chinnampo shortly before 0300 on 5 December, the urgency behind their treacherous passage was nowhere in evidence – lights, not guns, blazed ashore. When Brock contacted Kelly to arrange an immediate meeting, he was told it could wait until after breakfast. "That made old Brock pretty furious, I'll tell you!" recalled Collier.[24] As it turned out, although they were pressing south, the enemy was not yet within thirty kilometres of the city.

By late afternoon, Kelly's transports had embarked some 7,700 evacuating soldiers and set off downstream. Thirty-five minutes later, *Cayuga, Bataan,* and *Forrest Royal* opened fire on targets along the harbour front, including railway yards, oil tanks, and supply dumps – nothing was to be left for the enemy. The result was spectacular:

> The fires started by the military [demolition squads] were sufficient, in the dusk, to indicate very clearly the target areas, and more fires were started by the opening broadsides. As darkness fell, the fires became more and more brilliant, making the whole waterfront as bright as day; great balls of fire rose from the explosions to dissolve into the huge pall of black smoke which was drifting slowly to the southeast. Whenever a fresh oil tank was hit, which was often, sprays of molten glowing metal were radiated in all directions, adding spectacularly to the show. Fires were observed and explosions heard until 0615 the following morning.[25]

At 1845, the three destroyers joined *Athabaskan* downstream to anchor for the night. The next morning, they transited safely down the Daido-ko – the daytime passage, Welland remarked, "was relatively easy." The rush into Chinnamp'o won acclaim. The commander of the naval forces on the West Coast declared that it "was a fine feat of seamanship on the part of all concerned, and its bold execution was worthy of the finest traditions of the naval service." *The Crowsnest,* the RCN's in-house journal, observed more informally, "Though it bred a few gray hairs, the Canadian-commanded withdrawal was completely successful."[26] Chinnamp'o was arguably the RCN's finest moment in the Korean War.

On the Ocean Wave

Even though actual warfighting was limited, the heavy operational load took its toll on Canadian sailors. During one stretch in September 1950, *Sioux* was at sea for twenty-two days. During a seven-week period in October and November, *Athabaskan* burned 3,100 tons of fuel, 100 tons more than her entire annual peacetime allowance.[27] Such activity required efficient logistical support, but in Korea, according to Captain Brock, the Canadian destroyers fell under the definition "of beggars and borrowers." With no afloat logistics capability or supply facility of their own, they had to acquire most *matériel* from American and British sources. One supply officer noted, "Virtually all fresh provisions and approximately 90 per cent of dry provisions, [come] from the USN; rum from the RN; consumable naval stores and stationary (other than printed forms) from either as convenient."[28] That said, it was often difficult to obtain purely naval stores from navies who were understandably reluctant to part with *matériel* they might need themselves – replacing RCN pattern clothing was a particular problem as it could only be obtained from Canada at the other end of a three-month supply line. The situation was partially resolved when the RCN established a small supply depot at Sasebo, but logistical support remained a continual challenge.

Sailors could endure delays in acquiring kit or canteen items, but they were not nearly as patient when it came to mail delivery. The personal lifeline to home was critical to morale, and in those days, you could not call home from sea. Sailors needed to know what their families or friends were up to, and, just as importantly, needed to know that the home front knew what *they* were up to, but for the first two months of the deployment to Korea, mail delivery was sporadic and prone to long delays. Brock, who as the RCN administrative authority had to bear the brunt of the criticism, pointed the finger squarely at the Fleet Mail Offices. "It appeared," he complained to headquarters, "that attempts were being made to follow slavishly a set of inadequate peace-time regulations regarding mails to and from ships cruising [in peacetime], and to overlook such aspects as operational commitments, wireless silence, communication difficulties, movements of ships without notice, separation of Canadian units, etc."[29]

In other words, they were at war, and peacetime red tape should not thwart the needs of fighting sailors. Regular Royal Canadian Air Force flights to Korea helped to alleviate the mail problem, and other popular items began to flow. Church groups, service organizations, and others donated popular magazines such as *Saturday Night, Readers Digest,* and *Esquire*; perhaps more important, copious amounts of cigarettes found their way to the ships – at one point, the Legion Branch in Sarnia, Ontario, donated some 10,800 Buckingham brand cigarettes to the destroyers.[30] Movies also brought a taste of home and were readily available from the US Navy and Royal Navy, although those from the former were more to Canadian tastes.

Sailors managed to stay relatively healthy. Overcrowding was a problem: only *Sioux* was fitted with bunks, and sailors in the other destroyers slept in hammocks (which some old salts preferred). Their messing was excellent; Brock thought his men had the best food of any Commonwealth navy. Medical stores had been augmented before they left Esquimalt to treat the range of tropical diseases that might be encountered, and most complaints involved the usual colds, skin infections, and influenza. The major medical problem was venereal disease: brothels were plentiful in Sasebo, and the incidence was high.[31] When considering things medical, one cannot avoid mentioning the infamous Walter

DeMara, an American without any medical training or experience whatsoever, who used stolen documents to pose as an RCN surgeon lieutenant. "The Great Imposter," as a Hollywood film dubbed him, treated *Cayuga*'s hands for months before he was finally exposed.[32]

Weather is a ubiquitous factor in life at sea, and although they were on the far side of the world, Canadian sailors found themselves in a familiar climate with variable seasons. Summer was hot, winter cold, and spring and fall lay somewhere in between. Reporting from *Cayuga* in February 1951, *The Crowsnest* noted, "The patrols of last summer, when the rig of the day was shorts and sandals (and even then, the heat was oppressive), have certainly become a thing of the past. Now the 'Cayugans' wear toques, mittens, sea boots, woolen stockings, and, of course, winter coats."[33] As with mail, magazines, and the like, Canadian sailors had another reminder of home.

Sailors' morale changed like the seasons. Often it was poor. Historian Edward Meyers observed:

> The nights during those [early] patrols were generally sleepless because of the continuous action. The lack of sleep took its toll as each wearying day passed into yet another wearying night. Tempers grew short as the sailors, forced by circumstance to spend the night in the close confinement of their various action stations found the mornings offered no change. The overcrowded mess decks seemed like prisons.[34]

In contrast, the mood changed when sailors met operational success. Such is normal at sea, and the establishment of elected Welfare Committees helped to ease problems by initiating reforms such as allowing Coke instead of water as the mix for the daily rum ration and issuing baseball hats for use at sea.[35] The seemingly small steps were important to sailors. Most importantly, despite the ebbs and flows in morale, the overall experience gave Canadian sailors a sense of pride. Their performance showed they did their job as well, and often better, than their allies. That lifted spirits across the entire navy.

The War from Naval Headquarters

The RCN devoted a higher proportion of its assets to Korea than the other Canadian services. Eight of Canada's eleven destroyers saw duty between the outbreak and the armistice in July 1953. *Athabaskan* completed three tours; *Cayuga, Huron, Iroquois, Nootka,* and *Sioux* two; and *Crusader* and *Haida* one each. The commitment did not end there. After the armistice, RCN destroyers completed six more tours, and the final deployment by *Sioux* only ended in

September 1955.[36] This five-year effort in the wake of the "sickly season" exacted a heavy toll.

Keeping three destroyers on station in the Far East required five ships: three in Korean waters and two "relief" ships prepared to go. Although Pacific Command met the early burden, it soon realized the effort had to be navy-wide. In January 1951, HMCS *Huron* sailed from Halifax. The personnel ramifications of this ongoing commitment were immense: 3,621 sailors ultimately served in Korean waters, and many of them did more than one tour. As previously mentioned, Pacific Command had to "borrow" personnel from other duties to bring the three ships in the first deployment up to wartime establishment, and this policy of robbing Peter to pay Paul continued throughout the conflict, straining the navy to the limit. Twenty months into the commitment, the director of naval plans and operations at NSHQ warned that "the training of personnel has been seriously affected" and that "the planned expansion of RCN forces with which to meet our NATO obligation is also being seriously affected as unless the manpower situation can be improved ... an adequate number of trained men will not be available to man additional new construction and modernized ships as they become available."[37] He recommended a reduction of the effort. Beyond the manpower challenge, the need to continually rotate destroyers to Korea delayed the program to convert the ships into more capable antisubmarine destroyer escorts and at one point forced the navy to ask the British to provide a plane guard destroyer for the aircraft carrier *Magnificent*'s European cruise.[38] In short, Korea was in danger of bankrupting the service.

Despite this, senior officers never flagged in their determination to maintain the commitment. As Rear-Admiral Harry DeWolf, vice-chief of the naval staff for much of the Korean period, later emphasized, "The Navy saw it as more important to have destroyers in Korea than it was that they actually be there."[39] As one historian observed, Korea enabled the navy to "raise its political profile."[40] It demonstrated that the RCN had a role in the changing Cold War environment, one that could bring prestige to Canada. There was little risk involved, and the ongoing presence of three ships in Korean waters demonstrated Canada's backing of the UN to both domestic and international audiences. It also gave Canada additional clout at the proverbial bargaining table. In short, there was little that was not attractive from a political point of view; thus, if Korea caused some internal upset, naval leaders, who yearned for government support, were willing to accept that price.

Even as they sustained the commitment, naval leaders rebuffed efforts to alter its shape. A cadre of RCN officers who decried the navy's identity as a "destroyer navy" pushed to deploy a light cruiser to demonstrate it had "big ship" capability similar to other major fleets. Since *Ontario* and *Québec* served as essential training platforms and it would be difficult to bring the ships to wartime complement, naval leaders swatted that suggestion aside. A recommendation to deploy frigates instead of destroyers was also rejected. External pressure to contribute their aircraft carrier proved more difficult to resist. Suffering from its own constraints, the Royal Navy prodded the RCN to send *Magnificent* to Korea, following the model of Australia, which deployed HMAS *Sydney* in late 1951. This idea gained traction at NSHQ since it would highlight the importance of naval aviation and provide "incomparable experience" to *Magnificent*'s air department.[41] Nonetheless, the notion was finally rejected because *Magnificent* was a key element of the RCN's NATO contribution, her deployment would strain thin naval aviation resources, and her specialized antisubmarine air wing was unsuited to the strike role carriers fulfilled in Korea. However, NSHQ did gain approval to deploy one of its two Hawker Sea Fury fighter-bomber squadrons to Korea to operate from a British carrier; VF-871 was working up in preparation for the deployment when the ceasefire was announced, and the government cancelled the deployment.[42] Destroyers would shoulder the entire load.

Islands and Trains

After the Chinese surged down the Korean peninsula in late 1950, the front eventually stabilized around the thirty-eighth parallel, transforming the land war into a relatively static campaign. For the RCN destroyers that rotated into the theatre after the initial deployment, not all that much changed. Their primary task remained coastal blockade; the screening of carrier forces was a secondary, and still unpopular, duty. On the West Coast, operations focused on defending what became known as the "friendly islands"; on the East Coast, the interdiction of rail transport – "trainbusting" – dominated.

Grouped in six clusters midway up the West Coast, the friendly islands were important strategic assets that became valuable bargaining chips in the ongoing truce negotiations. Operations typically involved supporting South Korean forces trying to maintain a foothold in the face of enemy assaults. The maritime geography made this challenging work. Strong tides, shoals, and mud flats abounded, while the nearby mainland was studded with shore batteries, some radar-controlled. Commodore J.C. Hibbard, RCN, an experienced destroyer officer who had shone at inshore warfare during the Second World War, commented after an inspection tour, "I am amazed at the confined waters in which our [destroyers] are operating. There is the ever-present knowledge that if they run aground they would, with daylight, be under fire from eight enemy batteries – sometimes at point blank range."[43]

Happily, the Canadian destroyers had an advantage. The ships that followed the initial cadre had new Sperry High Definition Warning Surface (HDWS) Mk 1 radar that could detect small objects at close range. It proved invaluable for inshore navigation, and no other UN ships had sets nearly as accurate. For much of the Second World War, the RCN had struggled with ineffective radar; now it had the best first. The RCN's HDWS-equipped destroyers became so treasured that UN naval commanders selected them for hazardous missions close inshore.[44]

A patrol during *Cayuga*'s second tour in July 1951 gives a flavour of the campaign. Receiving a request to support a South Korean guerrilla landing near Ch'o-do, the largest of the islands, the destroyer fired some two hundred four-inch rounds at an artillery bunker, a gun emplacement, and a mining plant thought to be providing material for concrete fortifications. After *Cayuga* moved out beyond Ch'o-do for the night,

> five junks came alongside with some ninety South Korean guerrillas who were proceeding on a raiding party to the mainland in the vicinity of Pungchon. They required information which was given them as well as a small map. Their leader seemed a most energetic and enterprising person.
>
> At 0700 on the following morning some explosions and smoke were heard and seen in the direction of the guerrillas. At 0810 considerable rifle and machine-gun fire came from the beach in that sector. At 0830 a motor fishing boat with more guerrillas from Ch'o-do came alongside. From the officer that came onboard and remained throughout the operation it appeared that with no wind the guerrilla force was trapped on the beach and was unable to withdraw in junks. *Cayuga* closed to within 2,500 yards of the beach and the firing ceased. The junks came out from shore ... one junk was towing a "liberated" cow – still alive. The cow did not appear to appreciate its new political freedom.[45]

Evaluating the situation afterwards, Commander James Plomer, *Cayuga*'s commanding officer during her second tour, thought the level of enemy activity to be ominous. "There is no doubt that a fair build up is underway"; "shelling by naval forces could improve the situation."[46] Not all agreed. Considerable discord existed among senior UN naval officers about how aggressive their forces should be during the ongoing peace talks; in particular, Plomer became aware of a "go-easy" policy among senior British officers.

> The first clear impression we had of this "go easy" policy was after particularly successful results in supporting a Guerrilla raid on the enemy mainland, with no

> losses to the friendly Guerrillas but approximately 170 killed among the enemy forces. I was received on the return to harbour in an atmosphere of strong disapproval. No encouragement was given in any way and no [congratulatory] messages were made. It so happened that the Flag Officer, Second in Command [Rear-Admiral Alan Scott-Moncrieff] was having lunch onboard *Cayuga* the following noon. He said to me in front of my officers after mentioning feuds against mothers-in-law and money-lenders and generally throwing cold water on the event, "We do not want to upset these people," however, there had never been any written orders or instructions stating a definite policy in such operations.

In contrast, Plomer observed that Rear-Admiral George Dyer, US Navy, the principal UN naval commander at that time, was more pessimistic about the peace talks with the result "he has consistently followed an aggressive warlike policy."[47] That was more the Canadians' cup of tea.

The difference of opinion between the RCN's main allies continued to fester. After a May 1952 inspection tour, Commodore Hibbard noted:

> Admiral Scott-Moncrieff is of the opinion that our operations [on the West Coast] are a great waste of effort and a drain on the British economy. He is greatly concerned with the risks we are taking with our ships from the navigating point of view and cannot believe they are justified. Admiral Dyer is of the opinion that we do not yet use seapower to the best advantage. He feels we that must press close inshore with our blockade.[48]

Disagreements are a staple of coalition warfare, but in this case, the sniping became quite poisonous, and Plomer deprecated the open criticism directed by certain British officers at their American allies. The solution, he thought, was to establish an integrated UN naval staff in the theatre.[49] That was never done, but the actions of the commanding officers of Canadian ships demonstrate they shared Dyer's aggressive stance; they were at war and wanted to keep pressure on the enemy. Moreover, whereas a decade previously the RCN probably would have automatically followed British direction, it had now gained the confidence and maturity to choose its course.

The island campaign lingered until the armistice but accrued benefits. The ongoing presence of UN naval forces fuelled enemy fears of a repeat amphibious flanking operation like Inchon. "That this threat has been appreciated," opined a senior British officer in April 1953, "is shown by the large numbers of troops the enemy has had to disperse in a purely defensive role over the past year. On the West Coast alone these forces have been increased from about 40,000 to approximately 80,000 – forces which otherwise could have been employed in the battleline, or in immediate reserve."[50] Again, sea power influenced matters ashore.

Whereas the island campaign generated controversy, "trainbusting" generated friendly competition. The UN's overwhelming advantage in air power forced the enemy to move the bulk of their supplies at night, and rail was the most efficient way to do that. But at certain points along the East Coast, the rail lines lay within easy range of destroyers, who could manoeuvre comfortably inshore. One captain observed, "After the somewhat treacherous coast of western Korea it was a pleasure to be able to operate so close in and yet still be in deep water."[51] In July 1952, after the destroyer USS *Orleck* mauled two trains, an American officer organized the "Trainbusters Club" to lift morale. By the end of the competition with the armistice, twenty-eight trains had been destroyed by eighteen different UN destroyers; with four "kills," HMCS *Crusader* was declared the club's undisputed champion.[52]

After arriving in theatre in June 1952, *Crusader* went to the West Coast, where she spent three months on the coastal blockade and screening carriers. When the destroyer shifted to the East Coast, she arrived on the heels of bad news. On the morning of 2 October, HMCS *Iroquois* and USS *Marsh* were bombarding a rail line when an enemy battery hit the Canadian destroyer abreast "B" gun. In the only battle casualties suffered by the RCN in Korea, Lieutenant-Commander John Quinn and Able Seaman Elburne Baikie were killed instantly while Able Seaman Wallis Burden succumbed to his wounds that night. Ten more sailors were wounded.[53]

By the time *Crusader* turned to her new duty, trainbusting had developed into a settled routine. At night, destroyers waited off one of five designated "Package" areas, navigating with the aid of prepositioned radar reflectors. The missions often became a cunning cat-and-mouse game as the enemy railwaymen, knowing the danger that lurked offshore, masked their movements or hid their trains in tunnels; then again, sometimes they just barrelled down the line at high speed, hoping to beat the odds.[54] That is what confronted *Crusader* one night off Package 2, a two-hundred-metre stretch of track between two tunnels. At 0345 on 24 October, she sighted a southbound train, but only B and X guns were "closed up" – the other gun crews were grabbing sleep in their hammocks – and the train managed to escape before *Crusader*'s guns engaged. From then on, *Crusader*'s commanding officer, Lieutenant-Commander John Bovey, closed up all guns at night, accepting any fatigue and resultant loss of work during daytime.[55]

Two nights later, again off Package 2, Bovey trained his guns on the northern tunnel since a southbound train "would be more valuable than one going north, as it would probably have food, stores, equipment and even troops for the front line, whereas a north-bound train might contain nothing." At 2020, *Crusader* sighted white smoke billowing from the tunnel:

> Using ranges from Sperry radar, which has proved better then [Type] 275 for this particular type of operation, fire was opened. The train was hit and stopped with the first salvo along the whole length of the embankment.
>
> The locomotive was observed disappearing into the south tunnel. Fire was held until it emerged again to the south of Package Two and immediately re-opened as it left the tunnel. However, it was thought it had escaped. There was no mistaking the remainder of the train. With starshell illumination the train was worked over completely with 4.5[-inch], causing fires and explosions. The ship was brought into a range of 1800 yards [1,650 metres] at 2035 and fire opened with 40-mm to give the close-range guns' crews a chance to join in the kill and to work over the battery area. [USS] *DeHaven* ... was called in to give support and he joined in the destruction at 2130, proceeding inshore of *Crusader* and using his 40-mm and 5-inch guns.
>
> With daylight, the wreck of the train could be clearly seen extending over the whole length of the cutting. The rails were hanging down the embankment to the south and the boxcars, 13 in number, appeared reduced to broken flat cars.[56]

The next morning, aircraft sighted the locomotive on its side down the far side of the embankment – *Crusader* and *DeHaven* had destroyed the entire train. After a rest, *Crusader* returned to the duty in April 1952 and increased her score to four trains to become the "Ace of Train Busters."[57]

When *Crusader* shaped course for Canada in May 1953, two months before the armistice, her captain noted the destroyer had "covered the enemy coast from the Yalu River to the Soviet border and, at various times had been attached to all the different inshore patrol units, as well as the West coast carrier element – The Corpen Club – and Task Force 77."[58] Chasing this theme, *The Crowsnest* reported that *Crusader* had steamed 114,231 kilometres on 14 operational patrols, replenished at sea 68 times, screened 10 different UN carriers, and worked in close partnership with 109 different UN ships from seven countries.[59] The seven other Canadian destroyers deployed to Korea racked up experiences and statistics as impressive as *Crusader*'s. Marred only by *Iroquois*' casualties from shellfire and *Huron*'s running aground on Korea's East Coast two weeks before the armistice, Canadian sailors demonstrated they could fulfill a wide range of capabilities and do so as ably as their allies.[60] They played a significant role in enabling the UN to accrue the advantages of commanding the seas off Korea.

In a wider sense, Korea helped the RCN recuperate from the "sickly season" of the post-Second World War years, when its resources and personnel levels had been cut to the bone and it suffered serious morale problems. The international tension that boiled over on the Korean peninsula triggered an Accelerated Defence Program, which increased the RCN's budget, raised personnel ceilings, and enabled new warship construction – one of the navy's first moves under the program was to acquire the invaluable HDWS radars.[61] Challenges remained, particularly with lingering personnel deficits, but the navy was on a steady course out of the doldrums. Perhaps most importantly, the Korean experience brought a much-needed lift to morale across the entire service, creating pride, satisfaction, and an increased sense of purpose. Considering that aspect as well as their performance at sea, the Korean experience was significant in preparing the navy for its role as an integral element of NATO's naval capability during the Cold War.

Notes

1 CNS to TF 214.4, 5 July 1950, Department of National Defence, Directorate of History and Heritage (DHH), 81/520 1650-239/187.

2 Dan Middlemiss, "Economic Considerations in the Development of the Canadian Navy since 1945," in *RCN in Transition, 1910–1985*, ed. W.A.B. Douglas (Vancouver: UBC Press, 1988), 257.

3 Quoted in *The Crowsnest* (October 1950): 22.

4 *Cayuga, Athabaskan,* and *Sioux*, Reports of Proceedings (ROP), June-July 1950, DHH, 81/520.

5 W.G.D. Lund, "The Rise and Fall of the RCN, 1945–1964: A Critical Study of the Senior Leadership, Policy and Manpower Management" (PhD diss., University of Victoria, 1999), 237.

6 *Cayuga*, ROP, July 1950, 1.

7 When Canada faced a similar situation during the 1991 Persian Gulf War, Cabinet insisted that the three-ship force remain together even though it meant operating in a support role.

8 Robert O'Neill, *Australia in the Korean War, 1950–1953*, vol. 2, *Combat Operations* (Canberra: Australian War Memorial, 1985), 413.

9 Captain J.V. Brock, "Korean War Report," 4 April 1951, App. 1, 2, DHH, 81/520 1650-239/187.

10 Admiral Allan Smith, cited in Tamara Melia, *Damn the Torpedoes: A Short History of the U.S. Naval Mine Countermeasures* (Washington, DC: Naval Historical Center, 1991), 76.

11 Jason Menarchik, *North Korean Protective Mine Warfare: An Analysis of the Naval Minefields at Wonsan, Chinnampo and Hungnam during the Korean War* (Montgomery, AB: USAF Air Command and Staff College, 2010).

12 C.S. Forester, *Hornblower and the Hotspur* (New York: Little, Brown, 1962).

13 The destroyers' main armament varied over the duration of the war. Most featured four-inch guns, but *Sioux* and *Nootka* (on her first tour) had 4.7-inch while *Crusader* had 4.5-inch. Secondary armament was either 40 mm or 3-inch/50 weapons.

14 *Cayuga*, ROP, August 1950, 1; and Thor Thorgrimsson and E.C Russell, *Canadian Naval Operations in Korean Waters, 1950–1955* (Ottawa: Queen's Printer, 1965), 13.

15 Brock, "Korean War Report."

16 Flag Officer Second in Command Far Eastern Station (FO2C), "Korean War: ROP No 15," 30 August 1950, United Kingdom National Archives (UKNA), ADM 116/5794. Presumably, Brock uttered, "Just for the hell of it."

17 Interview with Vice-Admiral A.L. Collier, 37–38, DHH, BIOG file.

18 Jeffry Brock, *The Dark Broad Seas,* vol. 1 (Toronto: McClelland and Stewart, 1981), 217.
19 Michael Isenberg, *Shield of the Republic: The US Navy in an Era of Cold War and Violent Peace, 1945–62* (New York: St Martin's Press, 1993), 190.
20 Thorgrimsson and Russell, *Canadian Naval Operations in Korean Waters,* 17.
21 *Cayuga,* "Patrol Report – 20th November to 6th December, 1950," Library and Archives Canada (LAC), RG 24, Department of National Defence, vol. 11383, file 1926-355/30. Brock quoted Kelly's signal in his report but did not attach a copy. A US Navy history says that Brock "offered" to make the passage at night, failing to mention Kelly's signals about a deteriorating situation: see James A. Field Jr., *History of United States Naval Operations: Korea* (Washington, DC: Defense Department, 1962), 273.
22 *Athabaskan,* ROP, 5 January 1951, 1.
23 Michael Whitby, "A Letter from Korea by Lieutenant L.A. 'Andy' Collier," *Canadian Naval Review* 6, 2 (2010): 23, https://www.navalreview.ca/wp-content/uploads/CNR_pdf_full/cnr_vol6_2.pdf .
24 Interview with Vice-Admiral A.L. Collier, 42.
25 *Cayuga,* ROP, quoted in Thorgrimsson and Russell, *Canadian Naval Operations in Korean Waters,* 34–35.
26 FO2C to Commander-in-Chief, 22 January 1951, LAC, RG 24, Acc. 83-84/167), box 695, file 1926-DDE-218; and "The Chinnampo Affair," *The Crowsnest* (February 1951): 4.
27 *Sioux,* ROP, 18 October 1950; and *Athabaskan,* ROP, 8 December 1950, 3.
28 CDR (S) R.G. Harris to Flag Officer Pacific Coast, 14 May 1951, DHH, 92/79.
29 Brock, "Korean War Report," 8.
30 *Iroquois* to NSHQ, 19 November 1952, DHH, 92/79.
31 See Edward C. Meyers, *Thunder in the Morning Calm: The RCN in Korea, 1950–1953* (St. Catharines, ON: Vanwell, 1992), 137–38.
32 Meyers, *Thunder in the Morning Calm,* 167–74.
33 *The Crowsnest* (February 1951): 12.
34 Meyers, *Thunder in the Morning Calm,* 109.
35 Meyers, *Thunder in the Morning Calm,* 35.
36 For the rotation details, see Thorgrimsson and Russell, *Canadian Naval Operations in Korean Waters,* App. C, 141.
37 Director Naval Plans and Operations (DNPO) to Vice-Chief of Naval Staff (VCNS), "Reduction of RCN Korean Commitment," 20 February 1952, DHH, 81/520/1650-239/187.
38 DNPO to VCNS, 15 December 1950, DHH, 1650-1, vol. 3; and Naval Staff Minutes, 18 January 1952, DHH.
39 Author interview with Vice-Admiral H. DeWolf, Ottawa, 4 July 2000.
40 Peter T. Haydon, "Canada's Naval Commitment to the Korean War: Prudent Employment or Opportunism?" in *Canada's Pacific Presence: Purposeful or Peripheral,* ed. Peter T. Haydon and Ann Lynn Griffiths (Halifax: Centre for Foreign Policy Studies, Dalhousie, 1998), 126.
41 DNPO, "Employment of HMC Ships in Korea: HMCS *Magnificent,*" 5 September 1952, DHH, 81/520/1650-239/187.
42 Admiralty, Correspondence on Commonwealth and Foreign Navies, January-February 1953, UKNA, ADM 205/88; and VF-871 ROP, July 1953, LAC, RG 24, vol. 11, 615, 1926-219/871, vol 1. Lieutenant J.J. MacBrien, RCN, carried out an operational tour in jet aircraft as an exchange pilot with US Navy fighter squadron VF-781 flying Grumman Panthers. In a six-month Korean deployment, he flew sixty-six sorties and was awarded the US Distinguished Flying Cross for his "courageous leadership and outstanding demonstration of pilot skill." Two other naval aviators, Lieutenants R. Heath and W.J. Walton, flew Corsair F4U-5N night fighters with the US Navy's VC-3 but saw no action.

43 Commodore J.C. Hibbard, "Report on Korean Tour," 20 June 1952, p. 7, LAC, RG 24, 1983–1984 Acc/167, vol 465, file 1650-40.
44 Commander J. Plomer, "Korean War Report: Part One," 10, DHH, 81/520 1650-239/187. See also Jerry Proc's website on Canadian naval radar, http://jproc.ca/sari/sarrad2.html.
45 *Cayuga,* ROP, 13 August 1951, App. A.
46 *Cayuga,* ROP, 13 August 1951, App. A.
47 Commander J. Plomer, "Korean War Report: Part Two," DHH, 81/520 1650-239/187. See also Corbin Williamson, "Fighting with Friends: Coalition Warfare in Korean Waters, 1950–1953," *Joint Forces Quarterly* 83, 4 (2016): 99–104.
48 Hibbard, "Report on Korean Tour."
49 Plomer, "Korean War Report: Part Two."
50 FO2C, "Report of Experience in Korean Operations, July 1952–April, 1953," 15 July 1953, 1, DHH, 81/520 1650-239/187.
51 Lieutenant-Commander John Bovey in *Crusader,* ROP, 18 November 1952, 3.
52 Thorgrimsson and Russell, *Canadian Naval Operations in Korean Waters,* 359–60.
53 *Iroquois,* ROP, 5 November 1952, 1; John Bovey, "HMCS *Crusader*'s Report on Operations in Korean Waters, 18 June 1952 to 19 June 1953," 19 June 1953, DHH, 81/520, HMCS Crusader 8000; and John Bovey, "The Destroyers' War in Korea," in *RCN in Retrospect,* ed. James Boutilier (Vancouver: UBC Press, 1982), 254–62.
54 Malcolm W. Cagle and Frank A. Manson, *The Sea War in Korea* (Annapolis; US Navy Institute, 1957), 350; Great Britain Ministry of Defence, Naval Historical Branch, *British Commonwealth Naval Operations Korea, 1950–1953* (London: Author, 1967), 243.
55 *Crusader,* ROP, 18 November 1952, 5–6.
56 *Crusader,* ROP, 18 November 1952, 4–5.
57 *The Crowsnest* (July 1953): 5.
58 *Crusader,* ROP, 1 May 1953, 4.
59 "Ace of Train Busters," *The Crowsnest* (July 1953): 5.
60 For *Huron*'s grounding, see Meyers, *Thunder in the Morning Calm,* 224–30. Unfortunately, given the superb navigation record established by the other RCN ships, *Huron*'s grounding was the result of carelessness, not circumstance.
61 Naval Board minutes, 23 August 1950, DHH 81/520.

5

Cut and Thrust: The Canadian Army in Korea, June 1950–October 1951

William Johnston

ALTHOUGH THE FINAL two years of the Korean War were characterized by stalemated fighting along what would eventually become the Demilitarized Zone that now divides the Korean peninsula, the war's first year was dominated by a wildly shifting battlefield. The initial North Korean assault on the Republic of Korea in June 1950 quickly drove the Republic of Korea Army (ROKA) south of the capital of Seoul. Despite being reinforced by US Army units, the Communists forced the combined ROK and US forces into a defensive perimeter around the southern city of Busan by mid-July. While other UN countries – most notably Britain, Turkey, and Australia – committed to sending troops to Korea as the situation deteriorated throughout July, the Canadian government was initially reluctant to deploy ground forces. It was not until the evening of 7 August 1950 that Prime Minister Louis St. Laurent announced the country would recruit an infantry brigade for service in the Far East. Canadian Army Headquarters planned to reduce the time required to train the new formation by drawing on the large number of experienced Second World War veterans who had returned to civilian life in 1945. Enlistment in the "Special Force" brigade – designated the 25th Canadian Infantry Brigade Group – quickly exceeded expectations, and three new infantry battalions, created as 2nd Battalions of the regular army's existing infantry units, were filled by month's end.

Command of the new formation was given to a battle-experienced brigade commander, John Rockingham, who, like most of the men he was to lead, had also returned to civilian life after the Second World War. Although Rockingham was given the difficult task of building a combat-ready force from scratch, he was uniquely placed in being able to select his officers and non-commissioned officers from the largest pool of battle-tested veterans ever available to a Canadian general. This chapter argues that this combat-experienced leadership allowed the Special Force units – as exemplified by the performance of the 2nd Battalion, Princess Patricia's Canadian Light Infantry (PPCLI), at Kap'yong in April 1951 –

to demonstrate a high level of professionalism in their conduct of both offensive and defensive operations on the Korean battlefield.[1]

While the Special Force units were still engaged in their initial training at various bases across Canada, the need to send the Canadian brigade to Korea appeared to have been overtaken by events on the battlefield. In mid-September, the UN commander in the Far East, US General Douglas MacArthur, launched a daring amphibious assault on the port city of Inchon, forty kilometres west of Seoul. Combined with a simultaneous breakout by Eighth Army from the Busan perimeter, the North Korean forces were quickly routed and driven north across the thirty-eighth parallel. With a triumphant MacArthur in Seoul and UN forces preparing to cross the parallel to mop up the defeated Communists by month's end, it appeared the war would be over before any Canadian troops were sufficiently trained to take part. When it was suggested that Canada might at least offer one infantry battalion to "show the flag" as part of a UN occupation force, Ottawa agreed to send 2 PPCLI from Calgary. Commanded by a decorated Second World War battalion commander, Lieutenant-Colonel J.R. Stone, 2 PPCLI was chosen because of the proximity of its training base to the West Coast. Since the Patricias were not expected to see combat, the fact that they had not conducted any meaningful unit training prior to embarking for the Far East on 25 November 1950 did not appear to be a serious handicap.[2]

Even as the Patricias were on their way across the Pacific, however, the scope of the conflict was transformed yet again. Having decided to intervene in the conflict when UN forces pressed north across the thirty-eighth parallel, the Beijing government unleashed a surprise offensive by 300,000 Chinese troops at the beginning of December 1950. Overwhelmed by masses of infantry moving along ridgelines in the northern mountains, MacArthur's forces were badly routed as they tried to escape the onslaught. By the time the lone Canadian battalion had landed at Busan later that month, the UN forces had been driven out of North Korea and had only managed to stabilize the front some eighty kilometres south of Seoul.

Having been sent to the Far East before undergoing any unit-level training, 2 PPCLI was far from a cohesive, operational battalion when it arrived. Despite several attempts by Eighth Army headquarters to commit the Patricias to action immediately to help stem the latest Communist offensive, Lieutenant-Colonel Stone convinced his American superiors that his men needed to spend their first two months engaging in intensive company and unit training before being sent into battle. It was not until 18 February, then, that the battalion joined the 27th Commonwealth Brigade – composed of an Australian and two British infantry battalions and a New Zealand artillery regiment – to begin combat operations. As a result, the Canadians reached the battlefront just as Eighth Army's latest counteroffensive was launched to drive the Communists back to the thirty-eighth parallel.[3]

For the next several weeks, the Eighth Army forced the Communists north, and 2 PPCLI fought a series of actions against Chinese hilltop positions in central Korea. Often having to move along steep ridges that limited forward movement to single, eight-man sections, well-sited Chinese machine guns could hold up advancing troops until the enemy constructed its next defensive position farther north. The costliest of these ridgeline battles was a joint attack by the Patricias and the 3rd Battalion, the Royal Australian Regiment (3 RAR), on 7 March against a stubborn rearguard holding Hill 532. The day's fighting killed seven Canadians and wounded thirty-seven others while 3 RAR suffered twelve killed and twenty-four wounded in an unsuccessful assault. It was not until the following morning, after the enemy had withdrawn during the night, that the two battalions could occupy the feature. In all, 2 PPCLI's first three weeks of combat resulted in fourteen Canadians killed and forty-three wounded. As the enemy broke contact and retreated north in the face of the Eighth Army's general advance, the Commonwealth brigade reached its Albany Line objective, sixty kilometres east of Seoul, on 13 March before being moved into corps reserve to rest and refit.[4]

Assessing the initial performance of his battalion, Stone endorsed the army's decision to recruit a large proportion of Second World War veterans for the Special Force. As he informed Ottawa on 9 March, the Patricias were "fit, morale high, show lots of guts in close contact ... Troops are very well led and the aggressiveness they display in attack under difficult circumstances is a very great credit to the officers."[5] While Stone may have rued the altered circumstances of the war that had suddenly changed his battalion's role from occupation to combat, his comments reflect his satisfaction with the way combat-experienced senior officers and non-commissioned officers had been able to take a raw battalion and whip it into shape in a relatively short period. That level of experience was enhanced by the fact that the battalion was, in Stone's words, composed primarily of "adventurers: those who joined the army because there was a war to fight and they wanted to be there." The result was "a first-class, high-spirited group of soldiers."[6]

Continuing to pursue the retreating Chinese north throughout the last days of March, the 27th Commonwealth Brigade finally pushed across the thirty-eighth parallel on 8 April as they moved up the valley of the Kap'yong River. The ruggedness of the valley's hills, rising some 750 to 1,000 metres above the river, allowed the enemy to use a smaller force to delay the Commonwealth troops in that particular sector of central Korea rather than in the wider valleys to the east and west. Just how difficult it was to capture a hilltop position from even a relatively small group of entrenched infantrymen was demonstrated once again on 14 April when D Company attacked the battalion's final ridgeline objectives. According to the Patricia war diarist: "At 1655 hours the company attack went in [and] ... was successful in reaching [Hill 795] but the position was untenable ... Lieutenant M.G. Levy led the attack with great spirit and succeeded in reaching the well-held Chinese bunker on [Hill 795] with his platoon. However, the company withdrew on the commanding officer's orders."[7] Although the company suffered only five wounded in the attack, it was not until the morning of 16 April, after the Chinese rearguard had withdrawn, that the feature was finally secured.[8]

After turning over their Utah Line positions to the 6th ROK Division on 18 April, the 27th Brigade (less the New Zealand artillery regiment, which remained in place to support the South Koreans) moved into IX Corps reserve just north of the village of Kap'yong. The stiffening Chinese resistance that the brigade had encountered after crossing the thirty-eighth parallel on 8 April was reflective of a larger buildup of forces in preparation for yet another Communist offensive aimed at recapturing Seoul. The arrival of three fresh armies from China in February and the reinforcement of depleted formations gave the Communist command 630,000 soldiers across the entire front, the majority of them massed above Seoul. Although UN forces totalled only 418,000 personnel, including 11,500 Commonwealth troops divided between the 27th Commonwealth and 29th British Brigades, Eighth Army headquarters believed it could use its superior air and artillery assets to defeat the anticipated offensive. While the Americans were not particularly confident in the fighting abilities of the ROK divisions, the US formations were expected to stem the Chinese onslaught as the entire Eighth Army braced for an attack.[9]

The Chinese opened their Fifth Phase Offensive at 2000 hours on 22 April with an assault on the 6th ROK Division in the mountains north of the Kap'yong Valley. Attacked by the 60th and 118th Chinese Divisions, the South Korean formation was quickly overwhelmed. The survivors streamed south down the valley. As Xiaobing Li argues elsewhere in this volume, the main thrusts of the Chinese offensive were aimed towards Seoul, fifty kilometres to the west of Kap'yong, and at the important hydro dams above Ch'unch'on east of the valley. Nonetheless, the 118th Chinese Division closely followed the retreating remnants of the 6th ROK Division, hoping to sever the important east-west Route 17 highway just south of the village of Kap'yong. To block the Chinese attempt to cut the road to Ch'unch'on, the American IX Corps commander, Major-General William Hoge, ordered the 27th Commonwealth Brigade to establish a blocking position in the valley north of Kap'yong on the morning of 23 April while he tried to organize a new defence line along the Pukhan (now Bukhan) River with the 24th US Infantry Division to the west and the 1st US Marine Division to the east. With only two battalions immediately available, the British brigade commander, Brigadier B.A. Burke, deployed 3 RAR on Hill 504 to the east of the Kap'yong River and 2 PPCLI on Hill 677 to its west. As the remnants of the 6th ROK Division streamed past the Australian and Canadian positions through the afternoon of 23 April, 27 Brigade was reinforced by two American mortar companies and a fifteen-tank company of the 72nd US Tank Battalion. These reinforcements were joined that evening by the returning New Zealand artillery and a detachment of the 1st Battalion, the Middlesex Regiment, which had been sent north to help the South Korean division.[10]

The first elements of the Chinese 118th Division to make contact with the Commonwealth Brigade were two battalions moving down a tributary valley road to the east of the Kap'yong River. After brushing aside five US tanks positioned to the northeast of Hill 504, the Chinese became heavily engaged with 3 RAR's A Company on a northern spur of the feature. Throughout the night of 23–24 April, the Chinese launched successive human-wave attacks against the Australians but were unable to force 3 RAR from its hillside entrenchments. The RAR headquarters was driven from its position in the Kap'yong Valley between Hills 504 and 677 by a third enemy battalion and fell back on the Middlesex positions blocking the valley road to the south. Despite their stout defence – the twenty-four-hour battle cost the Australians thirty-two killed, fifty-nine wounded, and three captured – by early afternoon on 24 April, it was evident that 3 RAR would have to withdraw. Such was the deteriorating situation in the valley that several American Shermans, engaged in evacuating Australian wounded, fired on the Canadian entrenchments above Naech'on in the belief that they were Chinese troops (fortunately, only one Patricia was slightly wounded). As light faded from the battlefield on 24 April, D Company, dug in around the summit of Hill 677, also reported increased enemy movement to the north of its position. But the Australians' stout defence had inflicted heavy casualties on the Chinese, virtually halting their advance against the brigade's right flank and requiring them to reorganize their depleted ranks before finally turning their attention to the Canadian-held hill across the river.[11]

The Australians' successful retreat left 2 PPCLI as the forward battalion among the UN forces holding the Kap'yong Valley. Having listened to the battle for Hill 504 throughout the night, the Canadians spent the daylight hours of 24 April preparing for a similar onslaught on Hill 677. In view of the battalion's exposed location, Lieutenant-Colonel Stone positioned his four companies in a west-to-east arc, with D Company holding Point 677, C and A Companies on the descending ridgeline to the east, and B Company on a hilltop immediately west

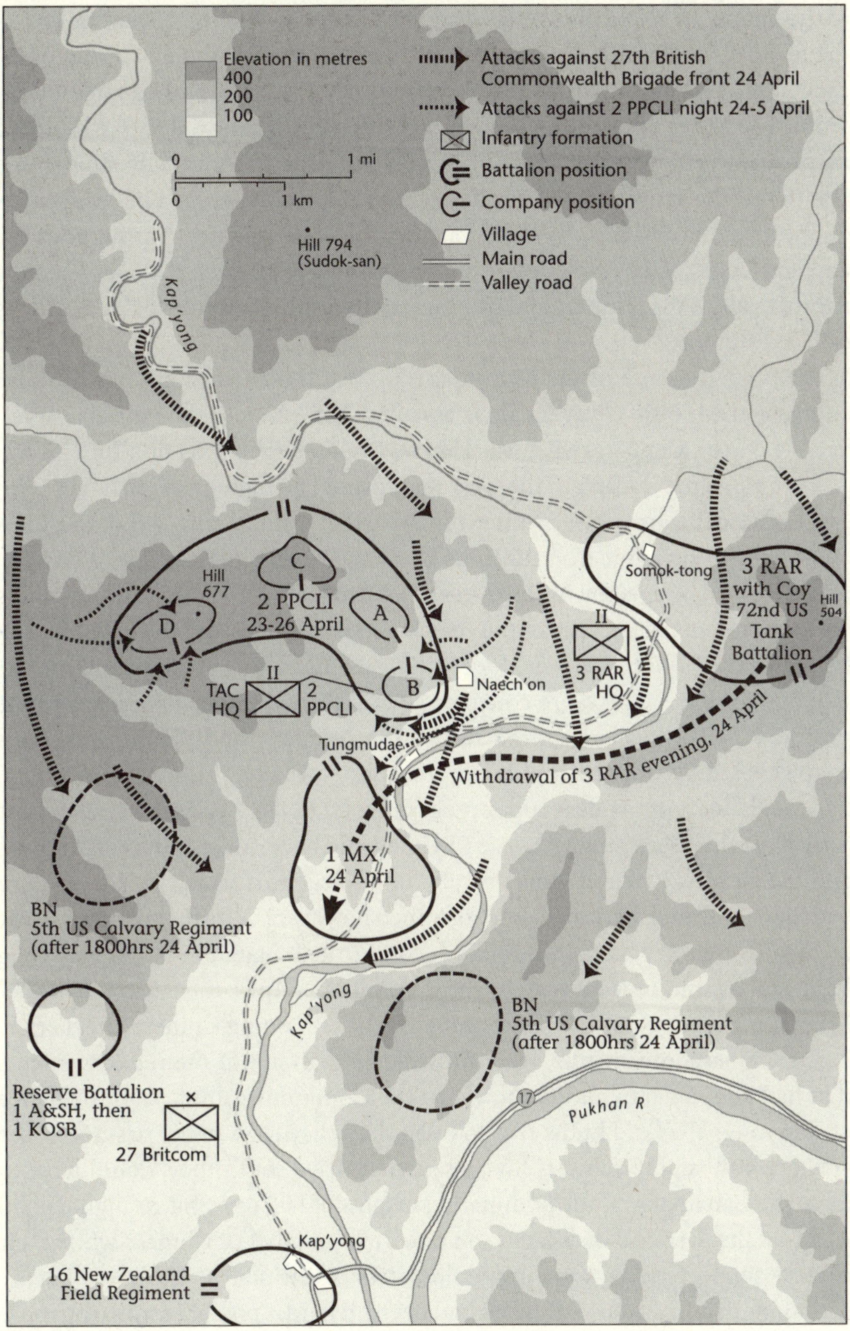

Map 2 The action at Kap'yong, 24–25 April 1951

Cartography by Eric Leinberger. Reprinted from William Johnston, *A War of Patrols: Canadian Army Operations in Korea* (Vancouver: UBC Press, 2003).

of the hamlet of Naech'on overlooking the valley road below. Given the size of the feature, the Patricia companies were arranged as individual strongpoints, each some two hundred to four hundred metres across and capable of all-around defence. With companies spread some three hundred to five hundred metres apart, however, it was not possible to organize mutually supporting positions. The ground between the company positions and all likely avenues of approach had to be covered by artillery and mortar fire. Throughout the daylight hours of 24 April, defensive fire tasks were registered and given code names to allow the gunners and mortarmen to respond rapidly to the infantry's calls for support.[12]

The rugged nature of the terrain also limited the enemy's approach routes and gave them little cover for their assaults. According to the Patricias' intelligence officer, Captain A.P.P. Mackenzie, D Company's "position on Hill 677 and the ridgeline leading to the west was covered by high grass" that had been crushed under the previous winter's snow so that it stood only "a foot to a foot-and-a-half in height ... The summits of all the small ring contours along the ridgeline were topped by isolated trees ... A direct north-south movement was hard for the enemy because of the steepness of the slopes and the type of cover found on the [forested] lower slopes ... For the most part artillery and mortar D[efensive] F[ire] fires were concentrated on the ridgeline approaches to the positions ... The steeper approaches to the company and platoon positions were covered by rifle fire and hand grenades."[13] Unlike the Australians, who had fought without artillery support because of the New Zealanders' night-time arrival north of Kap'yong village, 2 PPCLI would have not only its own mortars and the 24 New Zealand guns on call but also support from two US artillery battalions and an American battery of 8-inch howitzers. A further reinforcement of two US infantry battalions and a second British battalion in the Kap'yong Valley to the south meant that, by the evening of 24 April, the UN forces under Brigadier Burke's command outnumbered the remaining Chinese attackers.[14]

The Chinese, meanwhile, were most likely unaware of the reinforcements that had added depth and firepower to the Commonwealth brigade's defence of Kap'yong. They did know that to open the valley road to the passage of the artillery and supply vehicles for any further drive south they would have to force the Canadians off the dominating heights of Hill 677. Still, as night fell on April 24, the Patricias were facing an uncertain number of Chinese while their nearest supports were some two kilometres to the south. The three enemy battalions that had attacked 3 RAR had been hit hard – probably suffering more than one thousand casualties – but were reinforced by a second regiment from the 118th Division that had moved south through the main Kap'yong Valley with at least a battalion of Chinese occupying Hill 865 to the west of D Company on Point 677. In their rush to reach Route 17, the enemy left their artillery far behind and, as they had against the Australians the night before, the Chinese would have to make their attacks against the Canadians with only limited mortar fire for support.

In the clear night conditions, the Patricias were able to observe several hundred Chinese forming up at the base of B Company's position above the valley road at 2130 hours. The company commander, Major C.V. Lilley, quickly called for artillery and mortar support. Despite heavy defensive fire that disrupted the cohesion of the attack, the size of the enemy force allowed them to press up the slope to the Canadian entrenchments with, in Lilley's words, "the usual accompaniment of bugle calls, mortaring and red directional tracer. The attack overran a section of 6 Platoon on the left spine but the remainder held fast and retook the position."[15] The 6 Platoon commander, Lieutenant Harold Ross, later recalled that "the Chinese fight with a fanatical determination even though their tactics of massing men and sacrificing torrents of charging troops is archaic ... The Chinese do not easily give up their ground, but when they see the Patricias are not to be denied they turn and run, firing wildly."[16] Although one platoon position was temporarily overrun, the company was able to push the attackers back.

A somewhat larger number of Chinese renewed the attack up the steep slopes towards 5 and 6 Platoons one hour later. Although two sections of the more-exposed 6 Platoon were overrun, "the remainder of the company stood fast." Lilley recalled that "confused fighting followed. No. 6 Platoon headquarters and the section that remained ran out of ammunition and were ordered to fix bayonets and stand their ground. Wireless communications with the platoon broke down and the platoon commander decided to break out."[17] Despite some desperate fighting during 6 Platoon's withdrawal, the battalion war diary recorded that by 2300 hours "the greater part of the over-run platoon had managed to return to the co[mpan]y defensive perimeter."[18]

A second attack by one hundred to two hundred Chinese soldiers along a draw that led into the battalion's tactical headquarters immediately south of B Company was driven off by the battalion's mortars and the machine guns on the Patricias' half-tracks. Lieutenant-Colonel Stone recalled the devastating effect of the mortar platoon's defensive fire:

> The mortar platoon in those days was mounted for travelling on twelve half-tracks, six of which were deployed in the vicinity of battalion headquarters. Each half-track was equipped with one .50 and one .30 Browning machine-gun ... We held

fire until the Chinamen broke through the trees about 200 yards away, and then twelve machine-guns cut loose together. What with the rattle of the guns and the mortars firing at their shortest range, the enemy never had a chance.[19]

As the moon rose at 0100 hours, subsequent Chinese attacks were broken up by artillery and mortar fire before they could close with the Canadian positions. The ability of the defenders to spot and engage enemy formations in the river valley also brought an end to the sustained attacks being made against B Company. Although A and C Companies, occupying the battalion's centre, were left undisturbed, they had the nerve-wracking experience of listening to the fighting rage around them while being unaware of the outcome of the various attacks. One A Company soldier recalled, "We were surrounded by battles but we never fired a shot."[20]

As the attacks on 2 PPCLI's eastern flank petered out, the fighting shifted to D Company's positions around the summit of Hill 677. The Chinese on Hill 865 had to attack eastward along the ridgeline that connected their feature to Point 677 and were subject to prearranged artillery and mortar fire in reaching the Canadian positions. Its three platoons were dug in from west to east with 10 Platoon on the western slope of the summit facing the ridgeline that led off towards Hill 865 to the west. No. 12 Platoon's entrenchments were northeast of the summit although one of its sections was dug in seventy-five metres to the west covering an important Vickers medium machine-gun position northeast of 10 Platoon. No. 11 Platoon was to the east of 12 Platoon while the acting company commander, Captain J.G.W. Mills, and company headquarters were situated on the reverse slope behind the feature's summit. Beginning around 0130 hours on 25 April, the enemy mounted a series of attacks along the ridgeline leading to 10 Platoon but were driven off by small arms and mortar fire and by the Vickers machine-gun skillfully located in an enfilade position to the northeast of the platoon.

According to 10 Platoon's commander, Lieutenant Mike Levy, the Vickers fire forced the attackers to hesitate in their assaults. Levy, a Second World War veteran who had served with the British Special Operations Executive in Malaya, was fluent in Chinese and easily understood the shouted commands being directed at the wavering Chinese as they attacked his position. During a lull in the action, Levy exchanged insults in Chinese with the enemy commander.

This infuriates the Chinese officer, who orders his troops to "Press harder! Press harder! Kill! Kill! Kill the Imperialist Pigs!" I reply: "We are Canadian soldiers. Come to us, we have lots of food and medicine, and you will be well treated." The

> Chinese officer screams: "Don't listen to that Son of a Turtle!" ... a terrible insult in Chinese." [After one of my] exchanges with the Chinese commander, one of my men shouts "Tell the bloody platoon commander to Shut Up!" Each time our verbal exchange takes place the Chinese intensify their attacks.[21]

Despite being urged to press their attacks, the Chinese were held at bay by the effective artillery, mortar, and machine-gun fire of the defenders. It was not until the Chinese had circled to the north and killed the Vickers crew that they were able to mount more determined attacks on 10 Platoon. Mills subsequently reported that

> the machine-gun continued firing until the crew was completely overrun. Four men from the 12 Platoon section which were protecting the MMG post were able to disengage and make their way over to 10 Platoon positions where they carried on the firefight. They reported that the two machine gunners [Privates Maurice Carr and Bruce MacDonald] had been killed at their post.[22]

No longer having to contend with the devastating fire of the medium machine gun, by 0300 hours, the Chinese were able to mount more aggressive attacks on Levy's men. With the enemy pressing towards his position, the 10 Platoon commander made the courageous decision to ask Mills to have the New Zealanders direct their fire "to impact within 10–15 metres of our position." Levy was able to "direct the artillery up or down, left or right, depending on where I see the Chinese massing, and again upon their charging our position." Even so, the enemy were able to press their attacks to within seven metres of 10 Platoon's slit trenches, sufficiently close to effectively cut the platoon off from the rest of the company.[23] At tactical headquarters, Lieutenant-Colonel Stone recalled Mills's call "over the telephone (the line was miraculously intact) that his position was over-run and that the enemy had infiltrated everywhere. After some conversation, in which he assured me that the company was well dug in, he asked for an artillery concentration right on top of his position. I obliged."[24]

Levy's decision to shift the supporting fire on top of his own entrenchments finally had the desired effect. The battalion diarist recorded that "the Chinese continued to attempt an infiltration of the battalion area through D Co[mpan]y despite the art[iller]y and mortar fire. Each time art[iller]y engaged them they were forced to withdraw, but continued to engage D Co[mpan]y with accurately sighted MMG and mortar fire."[25] One of the 10 Platoon soldiers remembered hugging the bottom of his slit trench during each of the defensive bombardments:

> Our slit trenches were within hollering distance, when we got the word, we all crouched down in the trench. The artillery dropped a ten-minute barrage on top of us. It stopped that attack, but the Chinese came at us again. They were about to over run us, when another ten-minute barrage came in. Later, we were hard pressed and called in a third ten-minute barrage. We were convinced the artillery would kill us all, but there were no direct hits on any of the slit trenches. The Chinese, caught out in the open, were stopped cold.[26]

Although the enemy continued to probe D Company's entrenchments for the rest of the night, by 0600 hours they had largely broken off close contact.

While daylight brought an end to the direct attacks, Chinese patrols had infiltrated south of Hill 677, temporarily interrupting contact with the rest of the Commonwealth Brigade. Anticipating the possibility of being cut off from resupply, Stone had arranged for an airdrop for mid-morning when four US Air Force C-119s parachuted food and ammunition onto Hill 677. By the afternoon of 25 April, the Chinese had withdrawn from south of the Patricias, allowing the battalion to re-establish its supply lines, while the 72nd US Tank Battalion assisted the Canadians in clearing the northern slopes of the feature. By nightfall, all reports of enemy sightings had ceased. At a cost of ten killed and twenty-three wounded, the Patricias had successfully held the point position in the Kap'yong Valley, a defence that prevented the Chinese from reaching the Route 17 supply line as quickly as planned. Together with 3 RAR, the two battalions had been attacked by the equivalent of two regiments of the 118th Division totalling some six thousand men. The Patricias themselves estimated that the fighting on 24–25 April had killed some three hundred Chinese soldiers, a total suggesting that the 118th Division suffered over two thousand casualties during the three-day battle.[27]

For their determined stand at Kap'yong, the American high command awarded a US Presidential Unit Citation to each of 2 PPCLI, 3 RAR, and Company A, 72nd US Tank Battalion, the only occasion a Canadian Army unit has received such an award. The Patricias' impressive defence was aided by the battle experience of their commanding officer. Although the extent of the ground to be covered meant the companies were too far apart to provide one another with supporting fire, Stone had positioned them on terrain "that was vital to the defence of the area." The presence of so many Second World War veterans among its officers and non-commissioned officers also helped to steady the men under fire and provided them with battle-proven leadership. "The success of Kap'yong was due mainly to high morale and to good company, platoon and section commanders," Stone later explained:

> In their isolated defence areas, they kept their heads down, the morale of their troops up, and their weapons firing ... No one panicked, even when we knew we were surrounded and that there was some infiltration of the position by the enemy ... We stayed, fought and withdrew on orders in a soldierly fashion. This, in itself, was unique in Korea where "bug-outs" were the normal manner of withdrawing. In the circumstances, I say that the award [of the US Presidential Unit Citation] was well earned and the battalion deserved the public recognition of its actions of April 24/25, 1951.[28]

The Canadian battalion continued to hold its positions on Hill 677 until the evening of 26 April, when the Commonwealth brigade was pulled back into IX Corps reserve. Although the Fifth Phase Offensive had failed to breach the UN line, it had been penetrated at several points, and the Eighth Army commander, Lieutenant-General James Van Fleet, decided to give his forces some breathing space by pulling them back to a new line running from just north of Seoul and curving northeast across the peninsula to the East Coast. In so doing, Eighth Army abandoned the Kap'yong Valley to the Chinese, a move that did not sit well with the Patricias' commanding officer. It was Stone's opinion that "the withdrawal had been unnecessary. After breaking contact and falling back twenty miles, it was found there were no Chinese within eighteen miles."[29]

The Patricias ceased to be the only Canadian battalion in Korea on 4 May when the ships carrying the remaining units of the 25th Brigade anchored in Busan Harbour. Following an official welcoming ceremony, 260 officers and 5,056 men disembarked on 5 May. The brigade's historical officer remarked that the arrival was lacklustre: "The local government officials were at hand to present [battalion commanding officer] Lieutenant-Colonel Dextraze and the [troopship's] captain with a large bouquet of flowers. It was obvious that the welcoming committee had done this many times before and look[ed] thoroughly bored with the whole affair."[30] Rockingham immediately sent his two infantry battalions, the 2nd Battalion, Royal 22e Régiment (R22eR) and the 2nd Battalion, the Royal Canadian Regiment, north of Busan for two weeks of vigorous hill-climbing exercises. The Royals judged the physical exhaustion worthwhile "since it was reported that the hills around here are said to be small compared to the mountains in the north of Korea."[31] The group's artillery, armour, engineer, signals, transport, and other subunits meanwhile organized their equipment and prepared to join them. Most notably, C Squadron, Lord Strathcona's Horse (Royal Canadians) replaced the open-turret M10 tank destroyers they had trained on at Fort Lewis with readily available – and reliable – M4A3 Sherman tanks. The 2nd Field Regiment, Royal Canadian Horse Artillery, equipped with

25-pounder howitzers, was the first newly arrived unit to deploy when they moved their twenty-four guns north to support the Commonwealth brigade – which still included 2 PPCLI – holding its position south of the Han River following its withdrawal from the Kap'yong area.[32]

After completing their acclimatization training at Busan, the Canadian brigade moved into the front line on 20 May. They occupied their positions on the Han River just as the Chinese halted their offensive in the face of overwhelming UN artillery fire and air support. After being assigned to the 25th US Infantry Division on 22 May, the 25th Brigade joined in the Eighth Army counterattack to pursue the retreating enemy. As the Canadians moved up the Hant'an River Valley east of Seoul in late May, it became evident that the Chinese had pulled their main forces beyond the reach of the UN advance. Unfortunately, I Corps' decision to attach an underperforming Philippine battalion to the 25th Brigade further reduced the formation's combat power by forcing 2 R22eR to remain in close support of the attached unit. Despite the Canadian brigade already being four kilometres ahead of their flanking formations, divisional headquarters ordered Rockingham to penetrate farther north to the village of Chail-li while assuring him of US support on his flanks. With 2 R22eR keeping a close watch over the Filipino battalion, the Canadian commander would have only 2 RCR available for the operation.[33]

Despite deteriorating weather conditions, a reluctant Rockingham ordered the Royals to make the advance at first light on 30 May. The battalion mounted A Company in half-tracks, supported by a troop of Lord Strathcona's Horse (LdSH) Shermans, two Wasp flamethrowers, 75 mm recoilless rifles, and Vickers machine guns mounted on Jeeps, to drive up the valley road while the other three companies occupied high ground on either flank. Unfortunately, the Chinese had inserted a fresh regiment at Chail-li to organize a major defensive position in the valley and stall the UN's northern progress. Advancing in torrential rain that further hampered the operation, the Canadian column entered Chail-li before they were strongly attacked from both sides of the village by Chinese soldiers moving through the rice paddies. The mounted company was subjected to "increasingly heavy small arms, mortar, artillery and high velocity, low-trajectory fire" and was eventually forced to withdraw behind a supporting artillery barrage, using the hulls of the tanks to protect their wounded in the retreat down the road. C and D Companies on the slopes of Hill 467, to the southeast and overlooking Chail-li, held off further Chinese reinforcements as the enemy attempted to encircle the retreating Canadians. In their first engagement of the war, the Royals managed to escape a disaster but suffered six men killed and twenty-five wounded. Most of the casualties were incurred by C and D Companies defending Hill 467.[34]

At the beginning of 2 June, 2 PPCLI rejoined the 25th Brigade as the Canadian formation moved into I Corps reserve near the confluence of the Hant'an and Imjin Rivers in anticipation of the creation of the 1st Commonwealth Division under the command of British Major-General A.J.H. Cassels. After several weeks patrolling west of the Imjin, the entire Canadian brigade made their way northeast to the city of Ch'orwon (now Cheorwon) at the base of the important Iron Triangle region where they held a seven-kilometre front along the UN's Wyoming Line. The Chinese, still recovering from the heavy losses of their Fifth Phase Offensive, were content to remain eight to ten kilometres north of the UN positions. Throughout June and July, the Canadians mounted a series of tank-infantry patrols across the kilometres-wide no man's land to engage the Chinese outposts and maintain contact with the enemy. The Ch'orwon operations – conducted in exhausting summer heat – gave the Canadians a valuable opportunity to hone their military skills and develop an aggressive attitude while incurring minimal casualties. The long distances covered under tough Korean conditions further hardened the Special Force men, preparing them both physically and mentally to meet Rockingham's demands for more routine patrolling on other fronts.[35]

The creation of the Commonwealth Division on 28 July 1951 reduced both the size of Rockingham's immediate command and some of his responsibilities. While the infantry battalions and armoured squadron remained under his operational control, the supporting arms of the former brigade group were integrated into the divisional organization. Even then, they generally continued to be employed in support of the Canadian brigade, which also remained administratively responsible for their discipline and promotion. While the permanence of a divisional artillery organization allowed for better coordination of fire tasks by its seventy-two guns, perhaps the greatest advantage of the Commonwealth Division was the ability of its headquarters staff to shield the Canadians from some of the less militarily sound orders – such as maintaining outposts at all costs or overly aggressive patrolling demands – that occasionally emanated from higher American headquarters.[36]

As Cassels worked to integrate the Commonwealth Division into I Corps' operations, the Canadian brigade shifted south in mid-July to take up positions on the east bank of the sweeping curve formed by the Imjin River's junction with the Hant'an. For the next eight weeks, the three Commonwealth brigades launched battalion-sized probes up to ten kilometres west of the Imjin to determine the enemy's reaction and to establish the location of its main positions. The primary Canadian contributions were Operation Dirk, carried out by 2 RCR from 13 to 15 August, and a larger Operation Claymore, which was conducted by both 2 R22eR and 2 PPCLI from 22 to 24 August. These operations demonstrated

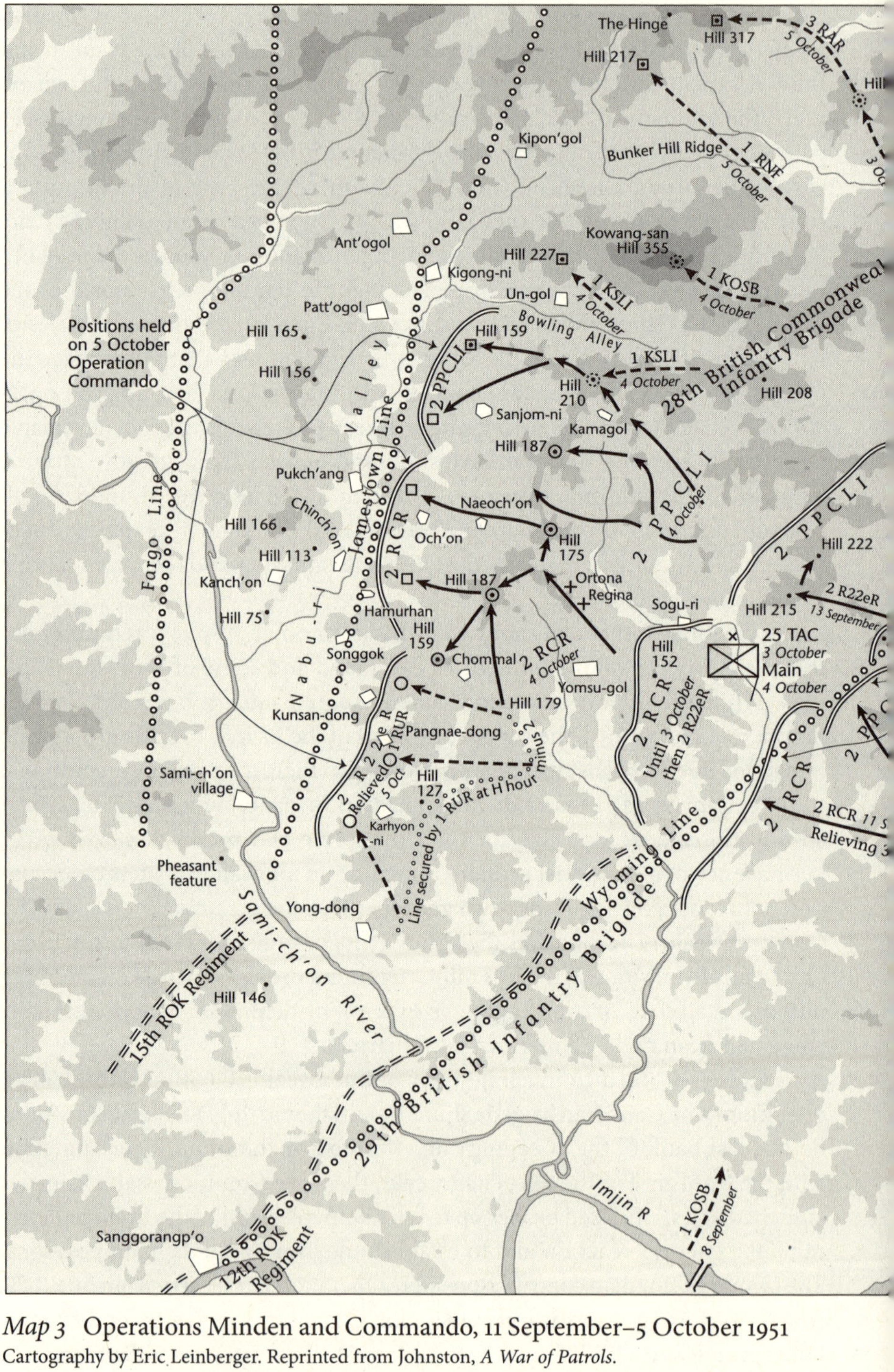

Map 3 Operations Minden and Commando, 11 September–5 October 1951
Cartography by Eric Leinberger. Reprinted from Johnston, *A War of Patrols*.

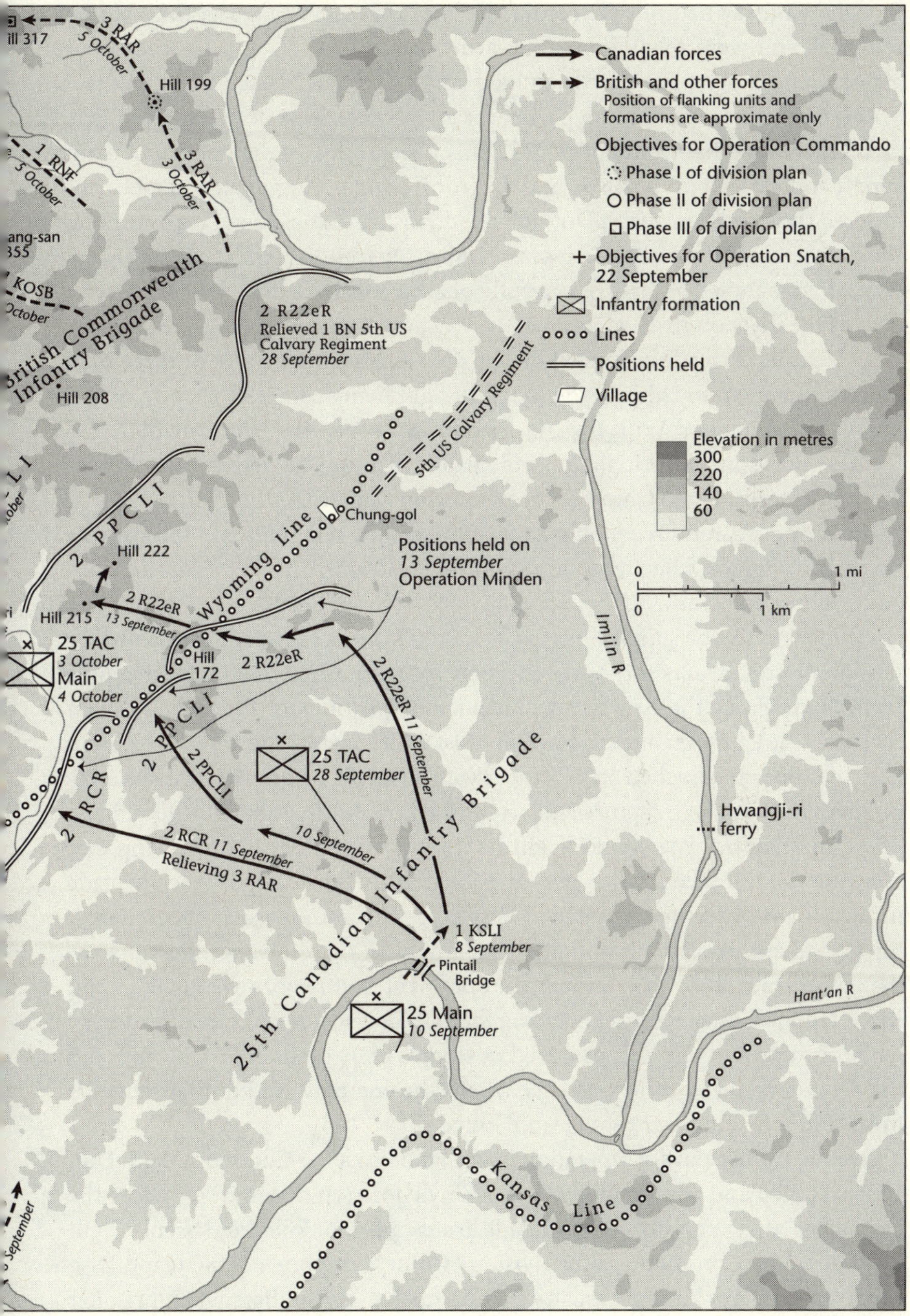

Canadian forces
British and other forces
Position of flanking units and formations are approximate only
Objectives for Operation Commando
Phase I of division plan
Phase II of division plan
Phase III of division plan
Objectives for Operation Snatch, 22 September
Infantry formation
Lines
Positions held
Village
Elevation in metres
300
220
140
60
0
1 mi
0
1 km
3 RAR 5 October
Hill 199
3 RAR 3 October
1 RNF 3 October
KOSB
British Commonwealth Infantry Brigade
Hill 208
2 R22eR
Relieved 1 BN 5th US Calvary Regiment
28 September
5th US Calvary Regiment
Chung-gol
2 PPCLI
Hill 222
Wyoming Line
Positions held on
13 September
Operation Minden
2 R22eR
13 September
Hill 215
25 TAC
3 October
Main
4 October
Hill 172
2 R22eR
2 R22eR 11 September
2 PPCLI
2 PPCLI
25 TAC
28 September
10 September
2 RCR
2 RCR 11 September
Relieving 3 RAR
25th Canadian Infantry Brigade
1 KSLI
8 September
Pintail Bridge
25 Main
10 September
Imjin R
Hwangji-ri ferry
Hant'an R
Kansas Line

that the Chinese had not yet recovered from the heavy losses of their spring offensive and were relying on small-arms fire to fend off attacks since their artillery and mortar fire were both inadequate and inaccurate.[37]

The August patrols were preparing for an advance west of the Imjin to take up a secure line that would prevent enemy observation of the important main supply route north to Ch'orwon and the Iron Triangle. On 7 September, I Corps ordered the Commonwealth Division to establish an extension of the Wyoming Line some five kilometres north of the Imjin. Operation Minden, as this effort was called, entailed a series of carefully phased advances over the next several days as the division reached its objectives against minimal enemy interference. The Canadian brigade advanced on the division's right at a cost of three men killed and ten wounded with the toughest fight being 2 R22eR's capture of Hill 172 on 12 September. With the Imjin no longer separating the Canadian and Chinese positions, Rockingham immediately instituted a vigorous patrol program to determine the Chinese forces' locations and intentions. His belief that maintaining a careful reconnaissance of the enemy positions was the key to a successful, vigilant defence remained one of the dominant features of Rockingham's tenure in command.[38]

To fully secure the supply lines to Ch'orwon, I Corps then proposed a further ten-kilometre advance on a five-division front to a new UN defensive line, Jamestown. Since the new line would include portions of the enemy's main defences, the Chinese were expected to resist with considerable force. Operation Commando was launched on 3 October with an attack by the 28th British Commonwealth Brigade to capture Hills 355 and 317 on the division's northern flank. The Canadian brigade would begin its assault on the left the following day, allowing the full seventy-two-gun divisional artillery to support each brigade in turn. In view of the stout enemy resistance the 28th Brigade encountered, the Canadians expected a similarly tough fight in their advance. Fortunately, the capture of Hill 355 on 3 October, the dominant feature northwest of the Imjin River, led the Chinese regiment facing the 25th Brigade to make an unexpected withdrawal from their well-prepared positions. Only on the 2 PPCLI front did the defenders put up stiff resistance when "the enemy stayed in their dugouts firing and refusing to surrender until killed."[39]

Overall, the five days of Operation Commando cost the Commonwealth Division 58 killed and 262 wounded. The enemy's decision to withdraw before the Canadians' attack resulted in the brigade losing only four killed and twenty-eight wounded. The Commonwealth Division's Chinese opponents, the 192nd Division, suffered 935 known casualties and a further 119 soldiers taken prisoner and was soon replaced in the line by two fresh divisions. American historian Allan Millett concluded that the Commonwealth Division "had made itself a formidable killer of Chinese soldiers. [Its] professionalism impressed ... Van Fleet, who had no complaints about the performance of the division and no desire to challenge its new reputation for operational success."[40] By comparison, the 1st US Cavalry Division, attacking on the Commonwealth Division's right flank, suffered 2,900 casualties in penetrating the strong fortifications on the Chinese 47th Army's main line of resistance that protected its main supply base at Sangnyong-ni. In making their sixteen-day assault, the cavalry division inflicted an estimated sixteen thousand casualties on the 47th Army and reduced its strength by half. In total, Eighth Army headquarters believed that Operation Commando had resulted in over twenty-one thousand enemy casualties.[41]

The UN advance to the Jamestown Line largely brought an end to the war of movement across the Korean peninsula. This was particularly true for the Commonwealth Division, which would continue to hold the same series of hilltop positions it had first occupied in October 1951 until an armistice was finally signed in July 1953. Although Canadian troops did not join in the cut-and-thrust operations of the war's opening phase until February 1951, 2 PPCLI quickly established a reputation for professional competence, a recognition exemplified by the award of a Presidential Unit Citation for its actions at Kap'yong. Led by officers and non-commissioned officers with invaluable Second World War combat experience, the 25th Brigade demonstrated a similarly high level of professionalism during its first six months on the fluid Korean battlefield. It was a standard that Rockingham's men would have to maintain as the war entered a prolonged period of static operations.

Notes

1 In this volume, the editors have chosen to use "Kap'yong" rather than its more recent spelling in revised romanization, "Gapyeong," owing to the former term's familiarity and reference to a specific battle.

2 For a more detailed discussion of the circumstances surrounding the recruiting and training of the Special Force, see William Johnston, *A War of Patrols: Canadian Army Operations in Korea* (Vancouver: UBC Press, 2003), 11–54.

3 William Johnston, "The Battle of Kap'yong, 23–26 April 1951," in *Fortune Favours the Brave: Tales of Courage and Tenacity in Canadian Military History,* ed. Bernd Horn (Toronto: Dundurn Press, 2009), 234–35; and Johnston, *A War of Patrols,* 55–67.

4 Johnston, *A War of Patrols,* 72–76.

5 Stone to Chief of General Staff, 9 March 1951, Department of National Defence, Directorate of History and Heritage (DHH) 112.009 (D87).

6 Colonel J.R. Stone, "Memoir: Kapyong," *Infantry Journal* (Autumn 1992): 12.

7 2 PPCLI War Diary (hereafter WD), 14 April 1951, Library and Archives Canada (LAC), RG 24, Department of National Defence, vol. 18,318.

8 Johnston, "The Battle of Kap'yong," 236.

9 Johnston, *A War of Patrols,* 85–87.

10 Johnston, "The Battle of Kap'yong," 237–38; and Johnston, *A War of Patrols,* 93–96.

11 Robert O'Neill, *Australia in the Korean War, 1950–53*, vol. 2, *Combat Operations* (Canberra: Australian Government Publishing Service, 1985), 140–41; Anthony Farrar-Hockley, *The British Part in the Korean War*, vol. 2, *An Honourable Discharge* (London: Her Majesty's Stationery Office, 1995), 156–57; Johnston, *A War of Patrols*, 96–97; Lieutenant-Colonel Herbert Fairlie Wood, *Strange Battleground: The Operations in Korea and Their Effects on the Defence Policy of Canada* (Ottawa: Queen's Printer, 1966), 76; and Captain A.P.P. Mckenzie, "2 PPCLI Action Kapyong Area – 23 to 26 Apr 51," 26 November 1954, 10–11, DHH 145.2P7.013 (D5).
12 Stone, "Memoir: Kapyong,'" 13–14.
13 Mckenzie, "2 PPCLI Action Kapyong Area."
14 Johnston, *A War of Patrols*, 99.
15 Lilley, report on action, quoted in G.R. Stevens, *Princess Patricia's Canadian Light Infantry, 1919–1957* (Griesbach, AB: Historical Committee of the Regiment, 1957), 3:301; and Mckenzie, "2 PPCLI Action Kapyong."
16 Lieutenant H. Ross, quoted in Hub Gray, *Beyond the Danger Close: The Korean Experience Revealed, 2nd Battalion Princess Patricia's Canadian Light Infantry* (Calgary, AB: Bunker to Bunker, 2003), 89.
17 Lilley, report on action, 3:301.
18 2 PPCLI WD, 24 April 1951, LAC, RG 24, vol. 18,318.
19 Stone, "Memoir: Kapyong," 14.
20 2 PPCLI WD, 24 April 1951; and Private Dan Johnson, quoted in Robert Hepenstall, *Find the Dragon: The Canadian Army in Korea, 1950–1953* (Edmonton, AB: Four Winds, 1995), 93.
21 Gray, *Beyond the Danger Close*, 4–5, 101.
22 Mills's report, quoted in Johnston, *A War of Patrols*, 102–3.
23 Johnston, "The Battle of Kap'yong," 254; and Gray, *Beyond the Danger Close*, 110, 114.
24 Stone, "Memoir: Kapyong," 14.
25 2 PPCLI WD, 25 April 1951.
26 Campbell, quoted in Hepenstall, *Find the Dragon*, 96.
27 Johnston, *A War of Patrols*, 103–4.
28 Stone, "Memoir: Kapyong," 15.
29 "Notes on Talk Given by Lt-Col J.R. Stone at AHQ, 0900 Hours 5 Jun 51," n.d., DHH 681.011 (D3).
30 Capt. G.D. Corry, 25th Canadian Field Historical Detachment WD, 4 May 1951, LAC, RG 24, vol. 18,434.
31 2 RCR WD, 10 May 1951, LAC, RG 24, vol. 18,341.
32 Wood, *Strange Battleground*, 88–94; and Johnston, *A War of Patrols*, 52–54, 108–12.
33 Xiaobing Li, *China's Battle for Korea: The 1951 Spring Offensive* (Indianapolis: Indiana University Press, 2014), 166–71; Allan R. Millett, *Allies of a Kind: Canadian Army – US Army Relations and the Korean War, 1950–1953* (Fort Leavenworth, KS: Combat Studies Institute Press, US Army Combined Arms Center, 2015), 31; and Johnston, *A War of Patrols*, 116–18.
34 Historical Officer, 25 Brigade, "The Battle of Chail-li, 2 RCR, 30 May 1951," n.d., DHH 145.2R13.013 (D2); 2 RCR WD, 30 May 1951, LAC, RG 24, vol. 18,341; and Wood, *Strange Battleground*, 101–6.
35 25 Brigade WD, 1–31 July 1951, LAC, RG 24, vol. 18,239; and Wood, *Strange Battleground*, 108–12. The attached Philippine battalion was reassigned away from the brigade as 2 PPCLI joined.
36 J.M. Rockingham, "Recollections of Korea," August 1975, LAC, MG 31 G12, 27–30; Millett, *Allies of a Kind*, 31–32; and Johnston, *A War of Patrols*, 138–43.

37 Maj. C.H. Lithgow, "Report on Operation 'Dirk,'" n.d., DHH 410B25.016 (D8); and Lt.-Col. J.A. Dextraze, "2 Bn R22eR Patrol Report, Operation 'Claymore,'" 29 August 1951, DHH 410B25.016 (D7).
38 Wood, *Strange Battleground,* 126–27; Farrar-Hockley, *The British Part in the Korean War,* 2:215–16; and Johnston, *A War of Patrols,* 153–56.
39 2 PPCLI WD, 4 October 1951, LAC, RG 24, vol. 18,319; and Maj.-Gen. A.J.H. Cassels, "1 Commonwealth Division Periodic Report, 2 May-15 Oct. 1951," n.d., United Kingdom National Archives, WO 308/27.
40 Millett, *Allies of a Kind,* 33; Farrar-Hockley, *British Part in the Korean War,* 2:229; and Wood, *Strange Battleground,* 132.
41 Walter G. Hermes, *Truce Tent and Fighting Front* (Washington, DC: Office of the Chief of Military History, US Army, 1966), 102; and Farrar-Hockley, *The British Part in the Korean War,* 2:230.

6

Canada's Defensive Battle, 1951–53

William Johnston

THE CUT AND THRUST of the first sixteen months of the Korean War contrasts sharply with the stalemate that developed on the ground after Operation Commando in October 1951. For the remainder of the war, the Commonwealth Division would continue to hold its Jamestown Line positions while negotiations with the Chinese and North Koreans dragged on at Panmunjom, often in a seemingly aimless and irrational manner. As discussed in the previous chapter, many of the 2nd Battalion's senior officers and non-commissioned officers – men who are the backbone of any combat unit and provide its direction and operational effectiveness – were veterans of the Second World War. Their combat-experienced leadership had been on full display during the war's mobile operations, not least by the energetic example set by the brigade commander, John Rockingham. Once the formation settled into its Jamestown Line entrenchments, the 25th Brigade would have to continue to perform at a high standard to effectively defend its static positions.

Over the next twenty-one months, the Canadian brigade would also undergo two full rotations of units and formation commanders before an armistice was finally signed in July 1953. The original Special Force units were replaced by regular army battalions in the spring of 1952 and, a year later, by more recently raised units of the expanding Canadian Army. This annual rotation of units and commanders gave each iteration of the brigade a very different character and approach to military operations. This chapter argues that the officers of the Special Force units exhibited a more thorough professionalism on the Korean battlefield than the regular officers of the 1st battalions that replaced them. The 2nd battalions were fortunate to have been led by John Rockingham, one of the more dynamic brigade commanders the Canadian Army has ever produced. His forward style of combat leadership in 1951–52 ensured that his officers kept on top of the tactical situations confronting them. The problems the Canadians encountered under Rockingham's successor, Brigadier M.P. Bogert, on the other hand, resulted from poor leadership at both the unit and formation levels, when the brigade seemed content to adopt a more passive attitude in defending their entrenchments. While Second World War veterans themselves, the regular officers of the 1st battalions had volunteered for peacetime service and were posted to Korea as part of their job. At that stage of their careers, some of them may not have been as highly motivated for combat duty as they needed to be. The 3rd battalions that arrived in Korea in the spring of 1953 do not offer the same contrast as the Special Force and regular units do. While these units had a leavening of veteran officers, they were very much products of the postwar army and were filled with more recent recruits. The 3rd battalions were also fortunate in having a good brigade commander, Brigadier J.V. Allard, who was willing to recognize – and take action to address – the formation's greatest weaknesses. From a Canadian Army perspective, the differences in the 25th Brigade's performance under each of its commanders make the Korean War an interesting study of the impact that battlefield leadership has on the conduct of successful combat operations.[1]

The portion of the Jamestown Line occupied by the division following Commando (3–12 October) ran diagonally across the Imjin salient from northeast to southwest and encompassed its highest feature, Hill 355. The Commonwealth positions were separated from the Chinese by a valley that followed the course of an unnamed tributary of the Sami-ch'on River running north past Hill 159 before turning east between Hills 227 and 355 to the north and Hills 159 and 210 to the south. The north-south section of this valley was often referred to by its area name, *Nabu-ri,* while the east-west section was called simply the "Bowling Alley" since its entire length was under enemy observation from the west and subject to direct fire. Typical of the Korean landscape, the valley was lined by a series of hills connected by ridgelines, with numerous gullies cutting into the Commonwealth positions. Under Rockingham's watchful eye, the company and platoon positions of each battalion were carefully laid out to allow for an all-around defence against attack from any direction. Acutely aware of just how thin on the ground each division was given the extent of front to be covered in Korea, the forward company positions were generally located on the ridges that ran into the valley from the higher hilltops while the reserve companies and their supporting armour were dug in on the main line of hills. Even as the 2nd battalions dug in and wired their new entrenchments, they were already sending out nightly reconnaissance patrols – small four- or five-man units that were meant to acquire information rather than engage the Chinese – to ascertain the enemy's new positions across the valley.[2]

As the war of movement came to an end, the brigade underwent its first rotation of units when the soldiers of 2 Princess Patricia's Canadian Light Infantry (PPCLI) reached the end of their year-long tour of duty. Having arrived at Busan in December 1950, the 2nd Battalion began to be replaced by the regiment's 1st Battalion in late October. The selection of 1 PPCLI also meant that the Special Force volunteers were replaced by regular force soldiers. As part of the rotation plan, the 1st Battalion – whose strength on 31 March 1951 had been 34 officers and 873 other ranks – was required to leave 280 parachute-trained Patricias in Calgary temporarily until they could be replaced by returning volunteers from 2 PPCLI. Nonetheless, some 360 1st Battalion men managed to transfer to fill the spots available while another 190 were placed on the unit's noneffective list. Such details contradict the official history's claim that the hasty recruiting process of the Special Force produced an inordinate number of unfit soldiers since a far larger proportion of the regular battalion's strength – some 550 men – were left behind in Canada when it received the call to serve.

The net result was that over five hundred inexperienced 3 PPCLI men who were undergoing their training at Camp Wainwright had to be transferred to Calgary. One of the young 3 PPCLI soldiers was Ted McNamara who, like most of his fellow recruits at Wainwright, had joined the army to fight in Korea. They were surprised, however, when they were asked to volunteer for an immediate posting to the Far East after only six weeks of basic training. Although the rumour circulating through Wainwright that three-quarters of 1 PPCLI had deserted rather than fight in Korea was untrue – the regulars had simply volunteered to remain in Canada – McNamara and his untrained buddies felt it was their duty to fill the breach left by the veteran Patricias and stepped forward to volunteer. Most of the inexperienced 3rd Battalion soldiers went into the ranks of the four rifle companies, meaning that the first two companies to depart for the Far East in late September, A and C, did so with "few experienced private soldiers, although the officers and NCOs were all Regulars." With little training under his belt when he left Canada, McNamara remembered feeling very green and unready when he filed into the entrenchments of the Jamestown Line a few weeks later.[3]

The inexperience of the 1st Battalion men was displayed soon after A and C Companies took their place in the line facing the Nabu-ri Valley. Although the Commonwealth Division had prepared their Jamestown Line positions for a long stay, a successful defence meant that they would not be allowed to simply sit tight in their dugouts. As part of an active defence, the Canadian brigade launched a three-company raid on the Chinese-held hills across from their positions on 23 October. Each battalion supplied one of the raiding companies. The raid, codenamed Pepperpot, was made in daylight, and the divisional artillery fired a covering barrage to create the appearance of a major attack along the entire Commonwealth front. For 2 PPCLI's part in the operation, Lieutenant-Colonel Jim Stone selected 1 PPCLI's newly arrived A Company rather than using one of the 2 PPCLI companies that were holding the forward positions.

Information about the enemy's strength and dispositions had been gathered over the preceding nights by a series of reconnaissance patrols, one of which resulted in the capture of a talkative Chinese medical orderly. Two nights before the raid, each of the battalions was ordered "to send out patrols to recce their start lines across the valley."[4] The Royal 22e Régiment (R22eR) company would assault the highest feature across the valley, Hill 166, on the left while the 1 PPCLI company attacked Hill 156 on the right and the Royal Canadian Regiment (RCR) occupied the ridgeline between the two features.

Jumping off from their start lines "behind a heavy and very accurate barrage," the PPCLI and RCR companies were able to secure their objectives by 1000 hours while the R22eR company, despite repeated efforts, could not capture the more heavily defended Hill 166. As a result, Rockingham ordered the withdrawal of all three companies commencing at 1315 hours, covered by an artillery barrage on the hills ahead of the objectives to deceive the enemy into thinking the Canadians would advance farther while a smoke screen would cover the withdrawal. The veterans of the RCR and R22eR companies did not delay in their return, and both companies reported their men back in their lines by 1402 hours. The inexperienced Patricias, who up to this point had performed well in the raid, did not fully appreciate the importance of a prompt withdrawal and did not report themselves as beginning to cross the valley until 1407 hours. Their hesitation cost the company a further ten casualties when they were caught in the valley by both the Chinese counterbarrage and the Commonwealth artillery's covering fire. Having suffered fourteen of the raid's twenty-six casualties, the 1 PPLCI company received Stone's "critical comments ... on the loss of an LMG, the failure to bring out the body of one of the dead, and the slowness with which the company withdrew."[5]

By the time the remainder of 1 PPCLI arrived on 5 November, the Chinese had begun to adopt a more aggressive posture across the division's front. The summer's peace talks had resumed on 25 October 1951 in a tented conference centre in no man's land near Panmunjom, but neither side was prepared to agree on a ceasefire while negotiations continued. By early November, the Chinese had recaptured Hill 317 from the 28th Commonwealth Brigade and launched several smaller attacks against the Canadian positions. Given the enemy's combativeness, Rockingham ordered his battalions "to send out nightly recce patrols forward of their FDLs [forward defended localities] to obtain information concerning the enemy's dispositions" and to remain vigilant for any sign of unusual activity in the Chinese defences.[6] By insisting that his men routinely leave the relative safety of their entrenchments and move across the valley, the Canadian commander ensured that the brigade's aggressive attitude would not fade during the stalemate on the ground. Smaller reconnaissance patrols could reconnoitre

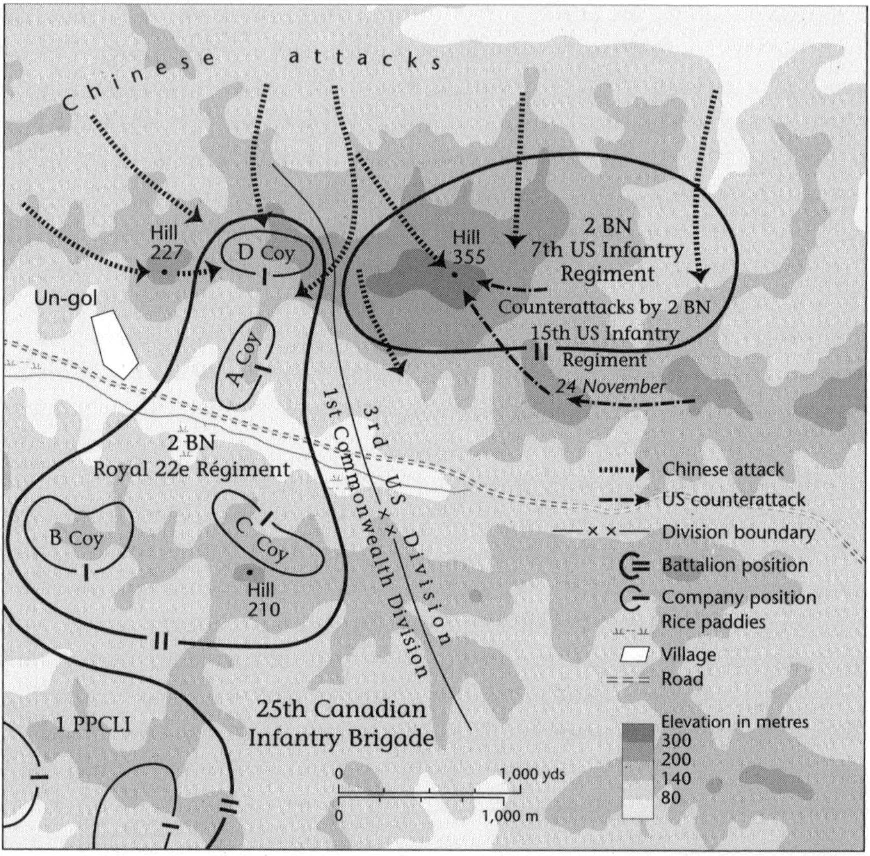

Map 4 Defence of Hill 355, 23–25 November 1951
Cartography by Eric Leinberger. Reprinted from William Johnston, *A War of Patrols: Canadian Army Operations in Korea* (Vancouver: UBC Press, 2003).

the enemy's day-to-day activities across the valley – rather than engage them directly – allowing the Canadians to maintain the initiative and prevent surprise. Less frequent were larger fighting patrols of twenty to thirty men that were intended to engage the enemy directly and, if possible, capture a prisoner. The brigade's vigilance reflected the nature of Rockingham's command and his attention to the tactical details of a successful defence. Aware of how difficult it was to take best advantage of the steep Korean hillsides in laying out field defences, Rockingham frequently visited the forward positions to correct faults in the positioning of entrenchments or the siting of weapons. Together with the vigorous patrol program, the formation commander's forward leadership ensured that the 25th Brigade would maintain an active defence.

On 22 November, I Corps adjusted the divisional boundaries, allowing the Commonwealth Division to move the 28th Brigade into reserve while shifting the Canadian brigade to the right. In its new position, the brigade's northern battalion had to locate two companies on the lower slopes of Hill 355, sandwiched between that feature and the Chinese-occupied Hill 227, and its other two companies across the Bowling Alley on Hill 210. The summit of Hill 355 and the ground to the east was now held by the 2nd Battalion, 7th US Infantry Regiment of the 3rd US Division. Rockingham chose Lieutenant-Colonel Jacques Dextraze's 2 R22eR to handle the difficult assignment on Hills 355 and 210. The most exposed entrenchments were given to the battalion's D Company on the low ridgeline west of 355 and directly below 227. Soon after occupying their new positions on the night of 21–22 November, Dextraze and Rockingham toured D Company's defences with the R22eR's commander, who took the time to site his men's automatic weapons to ensure the best defence possible. After continuous shelling, a Chinese battalion attacked Hill 355 at 1630 on November 23, forcing the Americans to withdraw and leaving D Company exposed to enemy attack from the heights to the east and the west. When a D Company corporal was later asked if the Americans "had moved off their position quickly or had just trickled off, he replied, 'Did they move fast? They moved so fast that their cigarettes looked like tracer bullets going down the hill!'"[7] As a result, the two R22eR companies north of the Bowling Alley spent an anxious night fending off Chinese attacks while they waited for the Americans to launch a promised counterattack to recapture the feature.

The 2 R22eR defence was aided by heavy supporting fire, including the seventy-two guns of the Commonwealth Division's artillery, direct fire from Strathcona tanks dug in on the Hill 159-210 ridgeline, and the 81 mm mortars of the 2 R22eR and 1 PPCLI mortar platoons. Although the US division had largely regained most of Hill 355 by mid-morning on 24 November, the largest attack on D Company came that evening when one of its platoon positions was temporarily overrun at the same time that the Americans above them were also heavily engaged. A second attack by three hundred Chinese moving down from Hill 227 at 0130 on 25 November was dispersed by a devastating mortar and artillery barrage before it reached the R22eR positions. By the time the beleaguered D Company was relieved by B Company on 26 November, the company had eleven men killed and thirteen wounded while the rest of the battalion had five killed and thirty-one wounded, most of the latter by Chinese artillery fire. By tenaciously holding on to their entrenchments despite being virtually surrounded, D Company's four-day defence of the saddle position provided a firm shoulder for the Americans to retake Hill 355 and prevented the Chinese from penetrating behind the feature, thus making the US counterattacks a more straightforward proposition.

By any measure, 2 R22eR's stout resistance compares favourably with the better-known defence of Hill 677 by 2 PPCLI at Kap'yong. While the Chinese attack on the Patricias was over within twenty-four hours, D Company had to remain ready for action for four days under direct enemy observation and machine-gun fire. The Patricias at Kap'yong also did not have to contend with Chinese artillery fire while 2 R22eR was subjected to the heavy and accurate fire of both Chinese artillery and self-propelled guns.[8]

Seeking progress in the Panmunjom truce talks, both sides agreed to halt offensive operations across the Korean front for one month beginning on 27 November. The ceasefire did not result in any discernable change for Canadian frontline units as Rockingham directed "that artillery and air activity would revert to normal, that infantry on recce patrols could direct artillery on[to] observed enemy, and that in general the brigade could attack 'with everything but infantry.'"[9] As in the past, Canadian recce patrols were sent out to scout the enemy's positions. The information reported by each patrol – the best routes across the valley, concealed approaches to the Chinese positions, the presence of machine guns, the position of mortar pits and dugouts – was assembled by the brigade's intelligence staff into an up-to-date picture of the far side of the valley to provide patrollers with an accurate briefing of the enemy's routine, the nature of the ground to be covered, places to avoid, and what they might encounter in any given area. For the next several weeks, the Canadians maintained their aggressive patrolling even as Major-General A.J.H. Cassels came under pressure from the US corps commander to launch company and battalion-sized raids against the Chinese. In response to American insistence, 1 PPCLI mounted a company raid against Hill 227 on the night of 10–11 December while 2 RCR sent a fighting patrol to Hill 166. While neither operation succeeded in capturing a prisoner, the Canadians at least demonstrated to higher command that the Commonwealth Division would remain aggressive during the developing stalemate on the ground.[10]

Until the brigade moved into divisional reserve on 18 January 1952, Rockingham's men maintained "a very strict vigilance" with any enemy activity being "reported promptly" and with battalion commanders making "every effort" to keep "their men on their toes."[11] Fearing the Eighth Army would lose its fighting edge during the protracted peace talks, the American command continued to insist that UN forces engage the enemy and inflict casualties to the point that, as the Commonwealth divisional staff explained to the brigades on 21 January, I Corps had "issued a horrid order saying every patrol WILL make contact."[12]

Unlike their American superiors, Commonwealth officers recognized that operating on the far side of the valley to observe the enemy's routine did not require a firefight as confirmation of aggressiveness. While Rockingham's men would maintain a vigilant defence, the demand that all patrols make contact meant that recce reports had to be adjusted to include some mention of the enemy even when no actual engagement had occurred. Even while in reserve, the 25th Brigade was still required to carry out one fighting patrol each week to satisfy the US command's misguided need for an exchange of fire.

When the Canadians returned to the line on 10 March 1952, they occupied positions on the division's left astride the wide Sami'ch-on river valley. The entrenchments on the hills to the west of the Sami'ch-on, known as the "Hook" position, were occupied by 1 PPCLI and 2 RCR. The Canadians quickly resumed sending out a mix of recce, ambush, and fighting patrols and quickly discovered that the Chinese had become more active across the Commonwealth front. Although most Canadian casualties during March and April were the result of enemy mortar and artillery fire, the Chinese efforts culminated in a company-sized attack on the Patricia platoon occupying Hill 132 on the night of 25–26 March, which killed eight Canadians and wounded another thirteen. A captured Chinese indicated that the enemy had thought they were attacking a British battalion of the 29th Brigade, a sign that divisional headquarters noted as being "indicative of our measure of control over the forward slopes thus rendering enemy observation ineffective."[13] Fortunately for the remaining Special Force battalions, the next month proved rather quiet, allowing 2 R22eR and 2 RCR to be replaced by their respective 1st battalions as Rockingham relinquished brigade command to Brigadier M.P. Bogert on 27 April 1952.

In contrast to Rockingham's militia background, Bogert was a regular officer who had served in the Canadian Army since graduating from the Royal Military College in 1930. His Second World War service included command of the West Nova Scotia Regiment in Sicily and Italy in 1943 and of the 2nd Brigade from October 1944 to the end of the war. The Canadian senior staff officer at Commonwealth Division headquarters thought that of the Canadian brigade commanders, "perhaps Brigadier Bogert, the eldest of the three, was less charismatic than the other two [Rockingham and Jean Allard] but nonetheless [was] a solid, unflighty and competent commander."[14] Although he was a combat-experienced officer, Bogert's success or failure would depend on his ability to instill in his battalion officers the energy and determination to keep the troops from developing a lethargic attitude towards operations during a static ground war. The arrival of the Canadian Army's regular battalions also brought a marked change in the character of the 25th Brigade. As the official historian remarked, the professional soldiers had a morale that was "more of the 'stiff upper lip' brand. Troops shined their kit in positions, kept themselves clean in spite of the difficulties, stressed orderliness, neatness, calmness, 'form.'"[15]

Unfortunately, the professionalism of the Canadian regulars was more readily visible in matters of appearance than in their battlefield performance. While up to half of the rifle company strength was made up of holdovers from the 2nd battalions who had not yet completed their tour or newer recruits from the 3rd battalion training pools, the officers and senior non-commissioned officers of the 1st battalions were all career regular force personnel. During their year-long defence of the Jamestown Line, many of the officers of the 1st battalions did not exhibit the same drive and initiative that had characterized the more thorough – and professional – operations of the Special Force units under Rockingham's command.

After only a week of acclimatization training behind the front, 1 RCR and 1 R22eR took up their positions on the Jamestown Line at the end of April. Following the aggressive patrols and raids the enemy had launched against the Commonwealth Division in March and early April, the Chinese lapsed into several months of relative passivity, giving the incoming Canadian units a grace period in which to adjust to Korean conditions without much in the way of enemy interference. Eighth Army headquarters, meanwhile, continued to insist on an aggressive patrolling and raiding policy across the entire UN front. Under Bogert's command, the 1st battalions quickly demonstrated a different operational approach than Rockingham's men. In May, the Canadian brigade conducted only twenty-two patrols that ventured beyond the middle of the Nabu-ri Valley of which twenty were larger fighting patrols and only two were reconnaissance patrols. While a fighting patrol of twenty to thirty men could gather some information about the Chinese positions as it moved across no man's land in search of a firefight, it was also more easily detected – and avoided – by a vigilant enemy. A recce patrol, on the other hand, could gain greater information by stealth, observing the enemy's routine without necessarily betraying its presence. The Canadian brigade's patrol tasking in June was little better than it had been in May, with only two reconnaissances being listed in its patrol task tables for early June and none in the last half of the month.

The virtual absence of Canadian recce patrols is particularly surprising given that two of the three battalions were completely unfamiliar with the terrain in front of their entrenchments while the enemy's relative inactivity would have allowed the incoming troops to conduct nightly recces against only limited opposition. Not only did the lack of information about the enemy's entrenchments and routine make the planning of fighting and ambush patrols ineffective, but it also stood in stark contrast to the full slate of reconnaissance patrols that had been conducted by the 2nd battalions.[16]

Without the up-to-date picture of no man's land that nightly reconnaissances could have provided, the large fighting patrols the Canadians conducted in May and June proved predictably disappointing. In keeping with I Corps directives to maintain an aggressive posture, the Canadian brigade ordered each battalion to conduct one strong fighting patrol each week. Those fighting patrols that did contact the enemy usually bumped into a similar Chinese patrol that had been set up to intercept them. Although a 1 RCR patrol that raided Hill 113 on the night of 31 May–1 June was praised by the divisional commander as "specially daring," any information gathered by larger patrols could have been gained by recce patrols with fewer casualties.[17] Unfortunately, most 1st Battalion officers appeared content to plan and brief their fighting patrols from secure observation posts on the hills behind the forward positions, restricting knowledge of the ground to be covered to what could be observed through the officer's binoculars and ability to read a map. One of the harshest critics of the 1st Battalions' performance was a company commander with 1 R22eR, Major W.H. Pope. A Second World War veteran, Pope lamented that the Canadians "ended up with higher casualties because of the 'sit-tight' mentality." Commenting on his fellow 1st Battalion officers, Pope believed that "many majors and lieutenant-colonels with Second [World] War experience were most concerned not to get themselves killed in a sideshow like Korea."[18] Unlike the Special Force officers who had returned to the army specifically to fight in Korea, many regular force officers had remained in the postwar military to serve in a peacetime army. A posting to Korea was simply part of their general service and did not necessarily stem from any desire to see more fighting at that stage of their career.[19]

A variation in the brigade's routine was introduced at the end of May – the "jitter" patrol – an effort to determine the Chinese dispositions by spraying their entrenchments with automatic fire from the valley floor. Since the information gathered depended on the enemy's inclination to return fire, the jitter technique was of dubious value and could not replace the absence of a serious Canadian reconnaissance program.

When the Commonwealth Division was again ordered by I Corps to capture prisoners in early June, each Canadian battalion was required to mount one large raid on the enemy positions in the hope of taking a Chinese captive. With the enemy easily able to escape into their extensive tunnel system whenever their opponents reached their entrenchments, the company-sized raids resulted mainly in Canadian casualties: six dead and eighteen wounded Patricias on the night of 20–21 June and one dead and twenty-four wounded Royals the next night (the large discrepancy between killed and wounded is partly explained by the low lethality of Chinese grenades).[20] While the 25th Brigade's results would undoubtedly have been improved by a more thorough understanding of the enemy's routine, none of the division's fighting patrols managed to capture a prisoner during this period, and the I Corps order to do so was suspended by Cassels at the beginning of July.[21] After their two-month initiation in the front line facing a mostly passive enemy, the Canadians spent the next six weeks in divisional reserve.

By the time the 25th Brigade returned to the forward positions in mid-August, they were confronted by a more aggressive enemy, one that was willing to probe the Commonwealth Division's forward defences on a nightly basis. The brigade's new positions were on the division's right with 1 R22eR occupying the Hill 159-210 ridgeline south of the Bowling Alley, 1 RCR holding Hill 355, and 1 PPCLI holding the less-exposed ground east of that feature. Once again, despite occupying a new sector of the front that was unfamiliar to them, the Canadians did not send out a single reconnaissance patrol in August to scout approaches to enemy positions, the location of old minefields, or wire entanglements in no man's land. In contrast, the Chinese reconnoitred their opponent's positions nightly, noting the location of Canadian standing patrols, cutting their wire, and scouting avenues leading to their entrenchments. As a result, those offensive patrols that the Canadians did mount were usually intercepted by the Chinese soon after leaving their own wire, which meant they were forced to fight on ground chosen by their enemy. Emboldened by the lack of a Canadian presence in no man's land, the enemy operated right up to the Canadian wire on a nightly basis, even throwing stones at Canadian standing patrols to draw small-arms fire. To an ever-increasing extent, the "sit-tight" mentality of the Canadians meant that they relied almost exclusively on artillery and mortar fire to drive off intruders.[22]

A notable exception to the Canadian patrol malaise was a lay-up reconnaissance made by 1 RCR's Lieutenant H.R. Gardner and Corporal K.E. Fowler in mid-September. From a concealed position some eight hundred yards north of Hill 227, the two Royals made notes on the enemy's activity around a field kitchen on its northern slope over a forty-eight-hour period. Based on his first-hand intelligence, Gardner devised a daring scheme to capture a Chinese soldier in a dawn raid. Taking five Royals with him, the lieutenant and his men returned to the kitchen area they had previously scouted and successfully captured a prisoner after cutting a telephone wire and waiting for a repairman to show up. For carrying out such a daring and well-planned patrol, Gardner and Fowler were awarded the Military Cross and Military Medal, respectively.[23] Although Gardner's raid had clearly demonstrated the benefits of making a proper reconnaissance, his success had little impact on subsequent Canadian patrols. In fact, the Canadians reduced their patrol activity even further in October despite the greater enemy presence in no man's land and their increasing focus on the RCR positions on Hill 355.[24]

Although the RCR's wire was "continually being probed by small numbers of enemy" and increased daily shell fire indicated a coming Chinese attack, Lieutenant-Colonel Peter Bingham proceeded on leave on 11 October, turning over the battalion to his second-in-command. As an indication of the enemy's dominance of no man's land, a 1 RCR raid on the enemy-held Hill 227 on the night of 12–13 October failed miserably when the Royals were ambushed soon after leaving their entrenchments. Enemy fire on the battalion reached a total of 2,246 artillery and mortar rounds on 22 October when B Company took over the exposed position on Hill 355's northwest shoulder. With the battalion failing to control the ground in front of their positions, the soldiers of B Company could only sit in their weapons pits and listen to the Chinese preparations. Finally, at last light on 23 October, the RCR positions were hit by an intense thirty-minute bombardment. The concentrations lasted for eight to ten minutes then moved onto the neighbouring positions, effectively sealing B Company off from support. Once their artillery had shifted, the Chinese quickly moved onto the position before most of the Commonwealth artillery's defensive fire tasks could hit them. Overrunning the Canadian entrenchments, the enemy raiders killed eighteen, wounded thirty-five, and captured fourteen Royals before withdrawing behind a covering barrage at 2100 hours.[25] Lieutenant Gardner later recalled the chaos in B Company's entrenchments as platoons retreated or were driven back.

> They were being heavily grenaded; some of the explosions could have been rifle grenades. Light mortar bombs were landing just behind them. Gardner saw someone he thought to be Lance Corporal Bawdin get an almost direct hit from a mortar. The officer himself must have received one of his wounds at this time. (He was hit by shrapnel in the right forearm and in both legs, and was superficially wounded in the right upper-arm by a bullet.) With Private Perry of 5 Platoon, who also had been wounded in the legs, he played dead. Meanwhile, the Chinese were milling about, shouting and blowing horns.[26]

The 23 October raid was the second costliest action for Canadian troops in Korea with sixty-seven 1 RCR casualties. This was twice as many losses as 2 PPCLI had suffered at Kap'yong. Because the Royals failed to control the ground immediately in front of their entrenchments, the Chinese exploited the terrain to dig caves from which they could mount a close-in assault. This resulted in the divisional artillery being denied the opportunity to decimate the attackers before they reached the Canadians' wire. As the R22eR's Harry Pope later commented, "The enemy's ability to raid successfully our strongest platoon and even company positions adversely affected our morale ... If the men become aware that the enemy can successfully raid any forward company position along the entire divisional front, the troops will 'take off,' 'bug out,' when the enemy hits. Defeat breeds defeat." Brigadier Bogert and his senior officers, however, viewed the raid as "a fine defence by 1 RCR." So long as the entrenchments were reoccupied after a raid, Canadian commanders were willing to tolerate the temporary loss of a company position and the resulting casualties.[27]

At month's end, the 25th Brigade moved into divisional reserve as part of the regular rotation of formations in the front line. Taking over the 1 RCR positions on Hill 355 was the 1st Battalion, the Royal Australian Regiment (RAR), which had to deal with the consequences of the Canadians' passive defence. According to their official history, the Australians quickly instituted "a heavy patrol program and hard fighting was necessary until the Chinese were forced to relinquish their grip ... The Canadians had not maintained concealment of their defences and advertised their presence by throwing empty food cans around their pits."[28] Beyond betraying defensive locations, this lax field discipline also meant that the Australians had to send out working parties to clean up the positions. While a certain amount of grumbling is inevitable whenever one military unit replaces another, there can be little doubt that the Australians were most unhappy at the situation left behind by the 25th Brigade's combined traits of timidity and sloth. There are no indications that the Australians had similar complaints when 3 RAR relieved the Canadian 2nd battalions in January 1952. Moreover, such tactically damaging behaviour would not have been tolerated by Rockingham during his frequent inspections of the battalions' foremost positions.[29]

When the Canadians returned to action at the end of November, they did so on the division's left flank astride the Sami-ch'on River, including the Hook position the brigade had occupied the previous March. The redeployment also coincided with the arrival of 3 PPCLI in Korea (commanded by Lieutenant-Colonel H.F. Wood, who later wrote the Canadian official history of the war, as well as a novel about the experience) to replace the outgoing 1 PPCLI. Back in the line, brigade headquarters finally – and rather belatedly – altered its patrol schemes by instructing its battalions to institute mobile, two-man listening posts in place of the previously ineffective standing patrols and place more emphasis on smaller reconnaissance patrols to gather information rather than large fighting patrols.[30] The brigade also benefited from a general lull in operations across the entire Korean peninsula during the winter months, even though the peace talks at Panmunjom had stalled over the issue of forcibly repatriating prisoners of war. At the end of January 1953, the Commonwealth Division was itself moved into I Corps reserve south of the Imjin River for a two-month period, the first time the division had been out of the line since its formation in July 1951. When the Commonwealth troops reoccupied their Jamestown entrenchments on 8 April, division headquarters assigned the 25th Brigade to the division's least vulnerable central sector, a decision influenced by the annual rotation of Canadian units as 3 RCR and 3 R22eR arrived in Korea to replace their 1st battalions.

The day after Brigadier J.V. Allard assumed brigade command on 25 April 1953, the armistice talks resumed after a six-month recess. Allard was a combat veteran of the Second World War, having successfully commanded the R22eR through much of the Italian campaign before being given command of the 2nd Division's 6th Brigade during the closing months of fighting in northwest Europe. The renewed optimism that a final ceasefire agreement might be within reach did not lessen either the increasingly aggressive Chinese activity across the front or the challenges facing Allard. Recognizing that defensive warfare was foreign to the offensive ethos of the Canadian Army's Second World War experience, the new commander emphasized to his officers the importance of weapons siting and frequent visits to the forward positions. Before Allard's reforms could take hold, however, the enemy launched a well-planned, battalion-sized raid on 3 RCR's C Company holding positions on the spur running into the valley from Hill 187. After repeatedly shelling the targeted positions on Hills 97 and 123 for several days, the Chinese raiders moved "gapping groups" into the valley after dark on 2 May to cut paths through the Canadian wire for the assault groups to overrun B Company's 7 and 8 Platoon entrenchments. The divisional artillery inflicted heavy losses on the well-organized raiders, but the Royals suffered eighty-two casualties, including eleven captured, the largest losses suffered during the war by any Canadian unit in a single engagement. According to the senior Canadian staff officer at division headquarters, "It came as rather a rude shock that the Chinese were able to move across such a wide no man's land and get in position for the attack without being spotted. 3 RCR could not have had an adequate screen of patrols out in front of their positions."[31]

In contrast to the lethargy that characterized Bogert's command, Allard not only acknowledged his brigade's tactical shortcomings but was also willing to take corrective action. In emphasizing forward leadership among his officers, the new brigade commander had to relieve several officers of their company commands. He also established a patrol school under the direction of the R22eR's Major Pope to provide week-long instruction to junior officers and non-commissioned officers on fieldcraft, recce patrols and outposts, stalking by day, and night-fighting patrols. The dissemination of such basic knowledge allowed Allard to mount a program of reconnaissance patrols – not seen in the

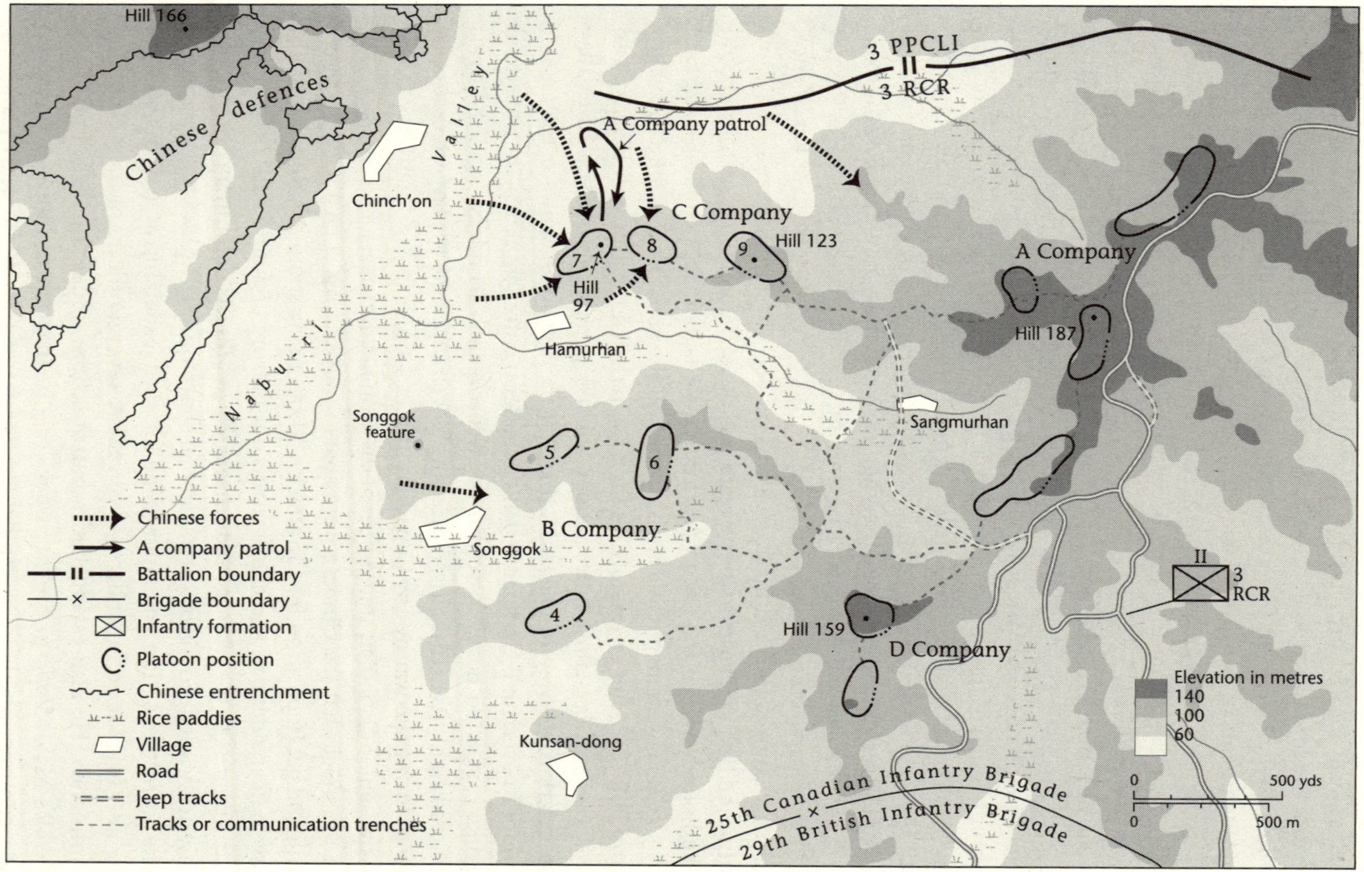

Map 5 Attack on C Company, 3 RCR, 2–3 May 1953
Cartography by Eric Leinberger. Reprinted from Johnston, *A War of Patrols*.

Canadian brigade since Rockingham's command – using numerous, two-man, wireless-equipped teams to cover the approaches in no man's land. He also strengthened the brigade's field defences, primarily by digging more tunnels and strengthening the overhead cover and fields of fire of light machine-gun positions to enable gunners to continue firing during a bombardment. In addition, Allard had a proportion of the brigade's Sherman tanks move into the valley floor at first light to engage in destruction shoots of the Chinese entrenchments. As the official history stated, "This special effort, combined with vigorous and aggressive patrolling, kept the Chinese on the far side of the river."[32]

The improved Canadian performance was noticed by division headquarters. When the brigade positions were rearranged on 27 June, the 25th Brigade was assigned to the division's right flank covering the exposed Hill 355-159 sector. Although the Canadians maintained a vigorous patrol schedule during the war's final month, the Chinese remained largely inactive on the Commonwealth Division's front as they concentrated their attacks on ROK (Republic of Korea) divisions. Hoping to be able to claim victory before signing an armistice, a large Chinese offensive in mid-June targeting the five ROK divisions holding the Eighth Army's centre inflicted over 7,300 South Korean casualties before it was halted on 18 June. The ROK government's decision that same day to release some 25,000 North Korean anti-Communist prisoners into the South Korean countryside prompted the Communists to renew large-scale attacks against ROK formations. As the fighting raged through the first half of July, the South Korean front was eventually penetrated to a depth of ten kilometres as the Eighth Army employed nine ROK and US divisions to stem the offensive and regain some of the lost ground. In a final act of war before the armistice was signed on 27 July, the Chinese fired a record 44,000 artillery rounds into the UN positions – but none against the Commonwealth Division.[33]

An examination of the 25th Brigade's operations under each of its three commanders provides valuable insight into the nature of successful battlefield command, with the Canadian Army's involvement in Korea demonstrating both how and how not to conduct military operations. The brigade's experience holding a static front during the last twenty-one months of the war proved to be every bit as challenging as the more fluid fighting of the opening months of 1951. Under Rockingham's dynamic leadership, the 25th Brigade demonstrated a thorough approach to its operations, both offensive and defensive. By their continual use of reconnaissance patrols roaming to the far side of no man's land, the 2nd battalions were able to build up a reasonable picture of the enemy's dispositions and routines, knowledge that was essential to planning both offensive and defensive operations. The small size of a recce patrol, moreover, allowed it to avoid enemy contact so that information could be gained with few casualties. Their vigorous patrol program also gave Rockingham's men a familiarity with the ground over which they had to operate and the confidence that they were more than a match for their Chinese opponents.

The problems the brigade encountered in 1952–53 under Bogert's command were primarily the result of risk-averse leadership and a "dug-out" mindset throughout the formation. While most soldiers agreed there were no new lessons to be learned in Korea, it is clear from their lethargic performance that the 1st battalions' officers either did not clearly understand the old ones or, more likely, lacked the drive and initiative that is so necessary for success in combat. The absence of reconnaissance patrols from the 1st battalions' task tables was a major shortcoming of the brigade while its "sit-tight" mentality produced a perceptible fear of the enemy's abilities and an overreliance on the divisional artillery to protect the defenders from serious attack. In Brigadier Jean Allard, the formation once again had a commander who both recognized that Canadian problems existed and was willing to take corrective action. Allard's emphasis on setting up a patrol school and instituting a vigorous patrol program was meant to overcome his men's lack of confidence when operating in no man's land. While the Korean conflict might be seen as Canada's "forgotten war," it provides valuable lessons on the importance of battlefield leadership to the success of a unit's combat operations.

Notes

1 For a more detailed discussion of the performance of the Canadian brigade in Korea, see William Johnston, *A War of Patrols: Canadian Army Operations in Korea* (Vancouver: UBC Press, 2003).

2 Johnston, *A War of Patrols,* 167–71.

3 T. McNamara, telephone interview with author, January 1995; Lieutenant-Colonel Herbert Fairlie Wood, *Strange Battleground: The Operations in Korea and Their Effects on the Defence Policy of Canada* (Ottawa: Queen's Printer, 1966), 163; and Johnston, *A War of Patrols,* 172–80.

4 25 Brigade War Diary (hereafter WD), 22 October 1951, Library and Archives Canada (LAC), RG 24, Department of National Defence, vol. 18, 240.

5 1 PPCLI WD, 24 October 1951, LAC, RG 24, vol. 18,312.

6 25 Brigade WD, 27 October 1951, RG 24, vol. 18,240.

7 J.M. Rockingham, "Recollections of Korea," August 1975, LAC, MG 31 G12, 33; and 1 PPCLI WD, 23 November 1951, LAC, RG 24, vol. 18,312.

8 2 R22eR WD, 21–23 November 1951, LAC, RG 24, vol. 18,357; 25 Brigade WD, 20–24 November 1951, LAC, RG 24, vol. 18,240; Wood, *Strange Battleground,* 153–60; and Johnston, *A War of Patrols,* 223–24.

9 "Weekly Summary No. 59," 5 December 1951, Department of National Defence, Directorate of History and Heritage (DHH) 410B25.013 (D99).

10 1 PPCLI WD, 10 December 1951, LAC, RG 24, vol. 18313; 2 RCR WD, 11 December 1951, LAC, RG 24, vol. 18,344; and 25 Brigade WD, 10–11 December 1951, LAC, RG 24, vol. 18,240.

11 25 Brigade WD, 23 December 1951, LAC, RG 24, vol. 18,240.

12 GSO(2) to Maj. D.H. George, 21 January 1952, DHH 410B25.019 (D19).

13 Maj.-Gen. A.J.H. Cassels, "1 Commonwealth Division Periodic Report, 15 February–30 June 1952," 5 July 1952, App. B, United Kingdom National Archives (UKNA), WO 308/27.

14 E.A.C. Amy, letter to author, 6 August 1999.

15 Wood, *Strange Battleground,* 184.

16 Johnston, *A War of Patrols,* 262–68.

17 Cassels, quoted in Wood, *Strange Battleground,* 190.

18 Pope, quoted in John Gardham, *Korea Volunteer: An Oral History from Those Who Were There* (Burnstown, ON: General Store Publishing, 1994), 130–31.

19 Johnston, *A War of Patrols,* 268–74.

20 1 PPCLI WD, 21 June 1952, App. 45, "Report on Fighting Patrol, 20/21 June," LAC, RG 24, vol. 18315; 1 RCR WD, 22 June 1952, LAC, RG 24, vol. 18,337; and Wood, *Strange Battleground,* 188.

21 C.N. Barclay, *The First Commonwealth Division: The Story of British Commonwealth Land Forces in Korea, 1950–1953* (Aldershot, UK: Gage and Polden, 1954), 127; and Maj.-Gen. A.J.H. Cassels, "1 Commonwealth Division Periodic Report, 15 February–30 June 1952," 5 July 1952, UKNA, WO 308/27.

22 25 Brigade Ops Log, September 1952, DHH 410B25.019 (D22).

23 "RCR Fighting Patrol," n.d., DHH 410B25. 013 (D17); and Wood, *Strange Battleground,* 204.

24 Johnston, *A War of Patrols,* 299–306.

25 Captain F.R. McGuire, "Enemy Action against PT 355," 30 October 1952, DHH 410B25.013 (D26); and Wood, *Strange Battleground,* 208–10.

26 Capt. F.R. McGuire, "Acct of Interview with Lt H.R. Gardner," 30 October 1952, DHH 410B25.013 (D26).

27 Major W.H. Pope, "Infantry Defences in Korea," 19 September 1953, DHH 681.009 (D11); 25 Brigade WD, 31 October 1952, LAC, RG 24, vol. 18,245; and Johnston, *A War of Patrols,* 306–15.

28 Robert O'Neill, *Australia in the Korean War, 1950–53,* vol. 2, *Combat Operations* (Canberra: Australian Government Publishing Service, 1985), 253; and Jeffery Grey, *The Commonwealth Armies and the Korean War: An Alliance Study* (Manchester, UK: Manchester University Press, 1988), 150–51.

29 Johnston, *A War of Patrols,* 316–18.

30 Major J.E. Leach, "Patrol Policy - 25 Cdn Inf Bde," 2 December 1952, 25 Brigade WD, December 1952, App. 14, LAC, RG 24, vol. 18,246.

31 E.A.C. Amy interview, 12 June 1953, DHH 410B25.013 (D9); and Maj.-Gen. M.M.A.R. West, "Periodic Report," 1 August 1953, annex 1 to App. B, UKNA, WO 308/27.

32 Wood, *Strange Battleground,* 239; and Allard interview, 10 June 1953, DHH 410B25.013 (D51).

33 Johnston, *A War of Patrols,* 368–70.

7

The Commonwealth Division

S.P. MacKenzie

From its establishment in the summer of 1951 down through to its disbandment in late 1954, the 1st Commonwealth Division was held up in Great Britain and elsewhere as an unparalleled example of the United Kingdom, its dominions, and former dominions linked together "as free and equal members of the Commonwealth of Nations." Participating countries were "freely co-operating" in the effort to restore "peace, liberty and progress" to war-ravaged Korea under the auspices of the United Nations.[1] As one of its senior staff officers put it, the division, incorporating as it did contingents from Australia, Canada, India, New Zealand, and the United Kingdom, was a way of "signifying to the whole world the unity and determination of the Commonwealth" to step up in Korea.[2] As the staged photograph that appears as Figure 14 in this volume suggests, the division thereby served, in the words of a former minister of state for Commonwealth relations, as "a most valuable example of Commonwealth co-operation."[3]

To be sure, troops from the various countries involved had served together previously, most recently in the Second World War.[4] In most cases, however, their participation had been at or above the divisional level and far from frictionless; various dominion commanders suspected that senior British Army officers viewed them as colonial subordinates rather than true partners in arms.[5] The creation of a Commonwealth Division, involving the operational integration of contingents on a more extensive yet more intimate scale than had been common in the past – units from no less than five countries functioning within a single fifty-thousand-man formation – offered London the opportunity to demonstrate in a military context that declarations of freedom and equality among Commonwealth member-states did not preclude collaboration among the parties involved based not just on complementary strategic interest but also on what the UK minister of defence termed "the spirit of the Commonwealth."[6]

What this phrase meant in the middle of the twentieth century was never precisely defined, but it was certainly designed to convey the idea of member-states associating and collaborating for the betterment of all concerned through a process of consensus and cooperation rather than deference or coercion.[7] In relation to the division, the Commonwealth spirit was thought to have manifested itself in an atmosphere of mutual comprehension and respect based on common values and a shared military heritage, which in turn produced a formation in which the various contingents operated together harmoniously, thereby generating consistent military success. Their united achievement in turn produced pride in the whole and what it represented for the Commonwealth of Nations. The purpose of this chapter is to explore how all this was, and was not, the case for the officers and other ranks of the Commonwealth Division.[8]

Satisfaction could certainly be taken in public acknowledgment of the division's military record in Korea, not least when expressed by senior Americans. In a 1952 ceremony to mark its first anniversary, Major-General Paul W. Kendall, the commander of its US Army parent formation, I Corps, stated that the "Commonwealth Division stands without peer among the troops of the Allied nations which make up the Eighth Army." Further accolades were provided by his superior, the commander of the US Eighth Army, Lieutenant General James Van Fleet, who praised the "high courage, unwavering determination and all-encompassing combat excellence" of "this great and gallant division."[9] From the First Battle of Maryang-san in October 1951 to the Third Battle of the Hook in May 1953, the deeds of units from the Commonwealth Division became the subject of successive celebratory volumes in the postwar decades.[10]

Jim Cassels, the British major-general who led the Commonwealth Division as general officer commanding for the first thirteen months of its existence, stated not long afterwards that his had been an "extremely good" command in which he took great pride: it was at his instigation, among other things, that photographs of representatives from the different national contingents were taken at the end of his time in command to provide him with a visual memento.[11] His successor, Mike West, another British Army major-general, who led the division for the remainder of the war, afterwards discussed his command with the semi-official historian, helping the latter determine that "the Commonwealth spirit was maintained throughout."[12] The commanders of the three infantry brigades that made up the bulk of the division tended to agree that friendly rivalry between contingents (within the context of a shared military heritage) had boosted a sense of common purpose and pride. John MacDonald, for instance, who served as acting brigadier of 28th Commonwealth Brigade for eight months in the second year of the war, later opined that the Commonwealth combination had "produced a remarkable *esprit de corps* and standard of efficiency."[13] His successor, Brigadier Thomas Daly from the Australian Army, concurred: "There was, not unnaturally, a friendly rivalry between units of different nationalities which kept everyone on their toes." He later reflected, "But the comradeship which developed ensured that units from widely varying [national] backgrounds came together as a homogenous whole, close-knit and mutually supportive."[14] The first commander of the 25th Canadian Infantry Brigade, John Rockingham, meanwhile, had already stated in his memoirs that "relations within the Commonwealth Division were, on the whole, tremendous."[15]

There were plenty of lesser divisional figures willing to echo such sentiments. "People were proud to belong to the Commonwealth Division," argued David Butler of the Australian Army, who in Korea served first as personal assistant to Cassels and later as commander of one of the Royal Australian Regiment battalions (1 RAR).[16] Lieutenant-Colonel Frank Hassett, the commanding officer of 3 RAR when it initially came under divisional control, later wrote that the "Commonwealth Division soon became a first-class fighting formation," adding that it was a clear demonstration of "the capacity of different nations to work together closely and efficiently in combat."[17] Colonel Geoffrey Anderton, the first assistant director of medical services, after his return to the United Kingdom at the end of his tour in Korea, in an address to his fellow Royal Army Medical Corps doctors, paid homage to "that great experiment in integration – the Commonwealth Division."[18]

Junior personnel also felt a sense of shared community. The entire division was "permeated" with the Commonwealth spirit, according to John Cormack, a young British officer serving in Korea with 12 Field Squadron of the Royal Engineers.[19] "At first, there was pride in the battalion and the Canadian Brigade," explained Sergeant John Richardson of the 1st Battalion, Princess Patricia's Canadian Light Infantry (1 PPCLI); but then, "when we saw more of the Brits and Aussies, we became proud to be in the Commonwealth Division and wear their shoulder patch."[20] Meanwhile Private John Larby of the Royal Corps of Signals, who had worked with 14 Field Regiment, Royal Artillery, in support of the British 29th Infantry Brigade, quite unknowingly echoed the commander of 25th Canadian Infantry Brigade in writing that the "comradeship of the Commonwealth troops was tremendous."[21]

Effort had gone into developing a command structure that could foster such perceptions. Since the bulk of the division's fighting manpower came from the United Kingdom, it was natural enough that its commanding officer should come from the British Army.[22] But it was no accident that Jim Cassels and then Mike West were chosen to lead it. Before taking command, Cassels had been a success with his hosts as a senior British liaison officer in Australia; at one point in the closing stages of the Second World War he had led a British brigade across the Rhine River linked to a Canadian brigade commanded by none other than

John Rockingham. He was fluent in French and could converse with members of the Indian field ambulance. Known as "Gentleman Jim," Cassels was admired by officers of the various Commonwealth nations for being capable and impartial.[23] His successor, Mike West, had served in the previous war as deputy commander of a brigade composed of British and Indian battalions and had a reputation for being both energetic and opinionated, which in practice meant that he, too, was admired by Commonwealth unit commanders for challenging unreasonable American tactical demands emanating from the corps level or above.[24]

It was also not coincidental that the next most senior administrative position at divisional headquarters, general staff officer, Grade 1, was held by successive representatives from the Canadian Army since Canada fielded the second-largest Commonwealth contingent.[25] More junior staff appointments were also divvied up more or less proportionately, so that at the time of its formation, Commonwealth Division headquarters and attached staff, with varying fields and levels of responsibility, included thirty-seven officers from the British Army, eleven officers from the Canadian Army, four officers from the Australian Army, three officers from the New Zealand Army, and a liaison officer from the Indian Army.[26]

According to the general staff officer, Grade 2, Major R.C.W. Thomas of the British Army, "the integration of Divisional Headquarters and the supporting Army and Services was accomplished smoothly."[27] His superior, the Canadian general staff officer, Grade 1, Lieutenant-Colonel E.D. Danby, concurred: "Whether due to careful selection of personnel or by good fortune," he reported, "no misunderstandings or clashes have occurred among the various nationalities at Div HQ."[28] It is also worth noting that while the British 29th Infantry Brigade was always led by a British brigadier and the 25th Canadian Infantry Brigade by a Canadian brigadier, it was possible to switch nationality at the top of the Anglo-Antipodean 28th Commonwealth Infantry Brigade. When Australia added a second battalion to its order of battle nearly a year after the Commonwealth Division was formed, command of this brigade passed from the British Army to the Australian Army.[29]

All this suggests that the various nationalities operated successfully and harmoniously in a spirit of shared heritage and friendship. Furthermore, looking back to their time in Korea, junior personnel of the division often expressed appreciation of and admiration for their Commonwealth comrades. The Indians of the 60th (Para) Field Ambulance were universally praised for their professionalism and the excellence of the medical care they provided.[30] The medical unit's culinary skills, moreover, were fondly recalled by those who enjoyed Indian cuisine.[31] The fire support given by the New Zealand gunners of 16th

Field Regiment was very much appreciated by frontline infantry – as an English private wrote, it "gave one a feeling of security to know that those chaps were behind us."[32] Individual 28th Commonwealth Brigade battalions in particular developed an almost familial bond with specific battery crews.[33] The gunners along with the drivers of 10 Company, Royal New Zealand Transport Corps, engaged in brotherly competition with Aussie and sometimes also Canadian personnel on and off the roads, exchanging creative insults with – and occasionally hurling nonlethal objects at – one another as they passed while keeping score as to which side had been able to appropriate the most jeeps or other vehicles from unauthorized sources.[34] Friendly banter between Aussies and Poms as their battalions relieved one another in the line aside, high regard for the fighting qualities of both Australian and Canadian troops was later expressed by a variety of soldiers from the United Kingdom; and British officers and men were commended individually or collectively by their Commonwealth cousins for their military professionalism.[35] Personnel of the various contingents enjoyed trading with one another for wanted items, while their commissioned officers in particular liked to play host or guest with their Commonwealth counterparts at invitation-only meals and parties of varying formality and scale.[36]

Despite all this, it would be wrong to conclude that amicability and cooperation were always the rule within the division. There is plenty of evidence that history and culture could encourage chauvinism and fractiousness as much as commonality and consensus of the kind the Commonwealth of Nations was supposed to represent. It also would be a mistake to imagine that most ordinary soldiers, even in the British case, necessarily felt much affinity to the organization.[37]

Celebrating the creation of the division as an unalloyed Commonwealth success airbrushes out the preceding lengthy and difficult negotiations over forms of commitment and spheres of responsibility that significantly delayed its birth. Uniting the various Commonwealth ground forces dispatched to Korea into a division made a good deal of sense given structural commonalities and strength in numbers. Yet while elements of various brigades arrived from Commonwealth countries and fought in Korea between the summer of 1950 and the spring of 1951, it took a full year for an actual Commonwealth division to take to the field.[38] Moreover, a rose-tinted view overlooks the fact that once the armistice had been signed in late July 1953, despite all the talk of it embodying the Commonwealth spirit, a proposal emanating from London that the division might remain in some permanent postwar form ran up against a fervent desire in other capitals – Ottawa in particular – to end the commitment as soon as the Americans would allow. Thus, the Commonwealth Division was formally deactivated in 1954 and never revived, as national interests and military equipment continued to diverge. The division was reduced to a brigade in 1954, to a Commonwealth contingent in 1956, and wound up the next year.[39]

Commonwealth *esprit de corps*, moreover, did not preclude various forms and degrees of friction between national contingents. The staff of 25th Canadian Infantry Brigade initially felt that some of their British divisional counterparts treated them as "small fry," in the words of Brigadier Rockingham.[40] This, in turn, led the staff of the brigade to appear standoffish enough for non-Canadians at division headquarters to use only the attached Canadian liaison officers in their dealings with them.[41] Nor were Australian-British relations within 28th Commonwealth Brigade necessarily always smooth. "I was relieved to learn, towards the end of my [1951–52] tour," the commanding officer of 3 RAR, Frank Hassett, wrote, "that an Australian brigadier was to command the brigade [in place of a Briton]. I make this perhaps uncharitable remark simply to illustrate that there were problems and that personality clashes are likely to be more prevalent in a multinational force."[42] After taking over command of 25th Canadian Infantry Brigade in the spring of 1953, Brigadier Jean Allard pushed back against various efforts at greater harmonization within the division because "it risked making the troops too uniform," that is, too much like the British Army. "At another time," he went on to recall in his memoirs, "it was suggested that our tank squadron be placed under British control. Under such an arrangement, the tank support for my infantry might have been provided by the Australians, whereas the Canadians might have supported the British. Here again, I gave my outright refusal."[43]

Interunit distrust involving different nationalities also sometimes developed despite relative isolation. Problems arose when Australian or British battalions took over positions from PPCLI, the Royal Canadian Regiment, and especially the Royal 22e Régiment's battalions. Incoming soldiers held the perspective that the Royal 22e Régiment did not pay enough attention to trench sanitation. According to the commanding officer of 1 RAR, Bunny Austin, in an interview conducted three decades later, the experience was like moving into a dunghill, a sentiment echoed by lower-ranking Australians and some British officers and men.[44] Of even greater concern, especially to Australian commanding officers, was a perceived Canadian tendency to limit patrolling, neglect the maintenance of minefields and other defences, and throw trash over trench walls, giving away their location.[45] In the retrospective opinion of the New Zealander adjutant of 16th Field Regiment, the Canadian troops had been "unpredictable in their behaviour, sloppy in their fieldwork, and generally arrogant about their abilities."[46] Canadians, for their part, could point to occasions such as when 2 Royal 22e Régiment had been expected to defend badly sited and poorly constructed British positions, and found some of the officers hailing from other

Commonwealth armies – especially those from the United Kingdom – irritatingly supercilious in manner.[47]

Much of the problem was solved when Mike West decreed a major change in deployment in November 1952. Instead of two brigades holding the line with one in reserve on a rotating basis, all three brigades would deploy at the front next to one another, and three battalions in each brigade would rotate to allow the brigadier to have two on the line and one as a backup. Whether the general officer commanding was responding to Australian or other complaints about the Canadians is unclear. Either way, this move meant the removal of most opportunities for intra-Commonwealth frontline alienation.[48]

At the same time, West's new structure may have diminished the likelihood of the fabled Commonwealth spirit being generated. The world of the infantrymen who occupied trenches, bunkers, and weapon pits tended to revolve around sections and platoons of fellow countrymen; contact with battalion or even company commanders, let alone other Commonwealth nationals, was a rarity or absent.[49] If single-nation brigades such as the British 29th and the Canadian 25th no longer exchanged places in the line, then troops in their units were much less likely to interact with other Commonwealth servicemen.[50] Even in the mixed 28th Commonwealth Brigade, the focus of allegiance, especially at the front in potentially life-or-death situations, could remain the unit or subunit. As an RAR soldier commented, "We were part of the Commonwealth Division, but for the average Dig like myself we were in one battalion commanded by an Australian, the company commander was Australian."[51]

Opportunities for contact among troops of different nationalities located behind the lines in support roles or among combat units held in reserve or rest camps remained more common. But both before and after the deployment shift, such encounters were not entirely positive, not least in situations when differences in pay rates became most apparent.[52]

The reputation of the Canadians remained problematic in the eyes of troops from other countries because of the widespread belief that members of the Canadian Army Provost Corps had acted with undue brutality in the running of the Commonwealth detention barracks located in the Seoul area, to which transgressors from the division could be sentenced to varying terms, according to the severity of their crime.[53] Robert Peacock, a young Canadian officer who served in Korea with both 1 PPCLI and 3 PPCLI, argued that extreme harshness yielded better soldiers: "Some of our very best NCOs got religion serving a term before they became corporals."[54] This particular officer's view was not shared by a visiting Indian Army doctor or, for that matter, the average Canadian soldier.[55] Meanwhile, the zealousness of a UK Royal Military Police sergeant in tracking down a trio of soldiers from 2 PPCLI for the sexual assault and murder of a group of Korean civilians near their camp had not made him very popular among some elements of the regimental family, notwithstanding the soldiers' horrific crimes.[56]

It was not only the Canucks, however, who sometimes found the Brits to be rather standoffish and, in the case of commissioned officers, as leaving the impression they viewed their Commonwealth brethren as rustics from the back of beyond.[57] British Army officers, for their part, probably did not appreciate having their accents parodied by Canucks or Aussies and sometimes had trouble adjusting to the more relaxed attitude to deportment and hierarchy among the Antipodean rank and file.[58]

Nevertheless, the Canadians were more culturally distinct than the rest of the Commonwealth fighting family in Korea, which in turn imposed a greater degree of separation.[59] Attachment postings aside, while it was fairly common to find Brits and Kiwis serving in Australian units in Korea and vice versa, it was comparatively rare to find Canadians serving in the British Army or the other way round.[60] While out of the line, soccer and cricket brought the other contingents together, but generally speaking, only Canadians could play ice hockey.[61] In addition, there was a language barrier in the case of soldiers from the Royal 22e Régiment.[62]

In conclusion, it is important to place in perspective the centrifugal-versus-centripetal forces at work within the Commonwealth Division. While the problems sketched out above indicate that some of the paeans to divisional *esprit de corps* and the "Commonwealth spirit" quoted earlier oversimplified a much more nuanced reality, and diverging interests meant the division was *sui generis* rather than a harbinger of the future, the fact remains that what drew the Commonwealth contingents together proved stronger over the lifetime of the division than what divided them.[63] All else aside, the divisional commander down to the ordinary private soldier agreed that their operational structures and methods, mostly of British origin, were more effective and certainly less risky than those employed by the US Army. Going it alone, even in brigade strength, would not only boost the odds of Commonwealth troops being mis-employed but also ultimately increase the likelihood of having to adopt American administrative procedures and tactical methods as well as equipment to work effectively as parts of American divisions. Nobody within the Commonwealth contingents wanted their unit to become a semi-integrated component of a US Army regiment or division. It often proved possible to work around cultural divides by, for example, producing multiple editions of *Crown News,* the division's newspaper, each edition designed to appeal to a particular national or even linguistic group. While the soldiers who assembled for group snapshots depicting a united Commonwealth Division were strangers to one another, they fully understood what the photographs were meant to represent.[64]

Notes

1 H. Duncan Hall, *Commonwealth: A History of the British Commonwealth of Nations* (London: Van Nostrand Reinhold, 1971), 859.

2 R.C.W. Thomas, "First Commonwealth Division in Korea," *Army Quarterly* 67 (April 1953): 33. Thomas was the general staff officer, Grade 2, at division headquarters in 1951–52.

3 *House of Commons Debates*, UK Parl., 5th Sess., vol. 523 (2 February 1954) (Arthur Henderson), 198.

4 See, e.g., Jonathan Fennell, *Fighting the People's War: The British and Commonwealth Armies and the Second World War* (Cambridge: Cambridge University Press, 2019).

5 It's worth noting that the consequences of such friction can be overstated: see, e.g., Douglas E. Delaney, "Cooperation in the Anglo-Canadian Armies, 1939–1945," in *The British Way in Warfare: Power and the International System, 1856–1956; Essays in Honour of David French*, ed. Greg Kennedy and Keith Neilson (Farnham, UK: Ashgate, 2010), 197–217.

6 Lord Alexander, in C.N. Barclay, *The First Commonwealth Division: The Story of British Commonwealth Land Forces in Korea, 1950–1953* (Aldershot, UK: Gale and Polden, 1954), vii.

7 This lack of definition – thereby avoiding potential clashes between members, especially between the old settler dominions and the new Asian states – extended even to the organization's name, allowing for the use of everything from *British Commonwealth of Nations* or *Commonwealth of Nations* to plain *Commonwealth*, depending on national preference. Britain regarded the organization as a means of preserving its global influence in a postimperial world. See Krishnan Srinivasan, *The Rise, Decline and Future of the British Commonwealth* (Basingstoke, UK: Palgrave, 2005), 22.

8 For references to the Commonwealth spirit and the division, see Terence Airey, "Review of *The First Commonwealth Division: The Story of British Land Forces in Korea 1950–3* by C.N. Barclay," *International Affairs* 31, 4 (1955): 506; and Barclay, *The First Commonwealth Division*, 86.

9 *New York Times*, 26 July 1952, 2; and see *Manchester Guardian*, 29 July 1952, 8.

10 See, e.g., A.J. Barker, *Fortune Favours the Brave: The Battle of the Hook Korea, 1953* (London: Cooper, 1974); Bob Breen, *The Battle of Maryang San: 3rd Battalion, the Royal Australian Regiment, Korea 2–8 October 1951*, 2nd ed. (Georges Heights, NSW: Headquarters Training Command, 1994); G.R. Stevens, *The Royal Canadian Regiment*, vol. 2, *1933–1966* (London, ON: London Printing and Lithographing, 1967), 219–68; and see also War Compilation Committee, *The History of the United Nations Forces in the Korean War*, vol. 2 (Seoul: Ministry of National Defense, 1973), 182–206. Later revisionist analyses suggest some of these accounts can be problematic: see, e.g., Nigel Steel, "Conquering Kowang San, Assaulting United: Myth and Misunderstanding in the Shade of Maryang San, October 1951," in *In From the Cold: Reflections on Australia's Korean War*, ed. John Blaxland, Michael Kelly, and Liam Brewin Higgins (Canberra: ANU Press, 2019), 217–34; and William Johnston, *A War of Patrols: Canadian Army Operations in Korea* (Vancouver: UBC Press, 2003), 283–345.

11 James H. Cassels, "The Commonwealth Division in Korea," *RUSI Journal* 98, 591 (1953): 365. On Cassels and the photographs, see Neville Williams, *A Conscript in Korea* (Barnsley, UK: Pen and Sword, 2009), 3–6.
12 Barclay, *The First Commonwealth Division*, 86, xvi.
13 J.F.M. MacDonald, in H.B. Eaton, *Something Extra: 28 Commonwealth Brigade, 1951 to 1974* (Edinburgh: Pentland, 1993), 89.
14 Thomas Daly, in Eaton, *Something Extra*, 122.
15 John Rockingham, in Johnston, *A War of Patrols*, 141.
16 David Butler, interview, Part 3, S0277, Australian War Memorial (AWM).
17 Francis Hassett, "Commanding a Battalion in Korea," in *Duty First: The First Australian Regiment in War and Peace*, ed. David Horner (Sydney, AU: Allen and Unwin, 1990), 384.
18 Geoffrey Anderton, "The Birth of the Commonwealth Division, Korea," *Journal of the Royal Army Medical Corps* 99, 2 (1953): 53.
19 John Cormack, interview, 21564/5, Imperial War Museum, Lambeth (IWM); see also Michael McBain, interview, 11105/10, IWM.
20 John Richardson, in Robert Heppenstall, *Find the Dragon: The Canadian Army in Korea, 1950–1953* (Edmonton, AB: Four Winds, 1995), 117.
21 Ron Larby, *Signals to the Right, Armoured Corps to the Left* (Leamington Spa, UK: Korvet, 1993), 154; see also, e.g., Geoff Holland, in Stephen F. Kelly, *British Soldiers of the Korean War* (Stroud: History Press, 2013), 77; and John F. Hatchard, *A Squaddy's Tale: Memories of the Forgotten War – Korea, December 1951 to October 1952* (Paihia, NZ: ColCom, 2006), 254.
22 At any one time, the British Army contributed to the Commonwealth Division three infantry battalions for the 29th Brigade, two for the 28th Commonwealth Brigade, a field artillery regiment to support the former along with tank squadrons, engineers, and signallers for the division, plus much of the logistical support and a field ambulance. The Canadian Army provided three infantry battalions for 25th Canadian Infantry Brigade with a supporting field artillery regiment, a squadron of tanks, plus various logistical and medical units. The Australian Army contributed one, and eventually two, infantry battalions to the 28th Commonwealth Brigade, which was supported by a field artillery regiment and transport unit from the New Zealand Army. The Indian Army contributed a field ambulance. See Barclay, *The First Commonwealth Division*, App. A and B.
23 See, e.g., on the Australian side, David Butler, interview, reel 4, S0277, AWM, https://www.awm.gov.au/collection/C989221; Hassett, "Commanding an Australian Battalion," 383; for the British, see, e.g., David Rose, *Off the Record: The Life and Letters of a Black Watch Officer* (Staplehurst, UK: Spellmount, 1996), 87, 91; and for the Canadians, see Rockingham's comment on Cassels in Johnston, *A War of Patrols*, 141.
24 See, e.g., Thomas Daly's comments in Garth Patten and Glyn Harper, *Still the Same: Reflections on Active Service from Bardia to Baidoa* (Georges Heights, NSW: Army Doctrine Centre, 1996), 34; see also Rose, *Off the Record*, 118, 134; and Horatius Murray, in John Donovan, ed., *"A Very Fine Commander": The Memoirs of General Sir Horatius Murray* (Barnsley, UK: Pen and Sword, 2010), 238.
25 The Canadian general staff officers, Grade 1, all lieutenant-colonels, were, successively, E.D. Danby, N.G. Wilson-Smith, and E.A.C. Amy.
26 Barclay, *The First Commonwealth Division*, App. C, 213–15.
27 Thomas, "First Commonwealth Division in Korea," 34.
28 E.D. Danby, in Johnston, *A War of Patrols*, 141.
29 Acting Brigadier G.F.M. MacDonald (British Army) handed over command of 28th Commonwealth Brigade to Brigadier Thomas Daly (Australian Army) in June 1952.

30 See, e.g., Jack Coley, interview, 20802/9, IWM; Hub Gray, with Grania Litwin, *Beyond the Danger Close: The Korean Experience Revealed – 2nd Battalion Princess Patricia's Canadian Light Infantry* (Calgary, AB: Bunker to Bunker, 2003), 19; Thomas Henson, interview, 22138/2, IWM; and F. Kingsley Norris, *No Memory for Pain: An Autobiography* (Melbourne: Heinemann, 1970), 296.

31 See, e.g., Anthony Bale, interview, 18497/4, IWM: Eric Burini, interview, 19630/14, IWM; Ian McGibbon, *New Zealand and the Korean War*, vol. 2, *Combat Operations* (Auckland, NZ: Oxford University Press, 1996), 158; Robert S. Peacock, *Kim-chi, Asahi and Rum: A Platoon Commander Remembers Korea, 1952–53* (Toronto: Lugus, 1994), 115; Dan Raschen, *Send Port and Pyjamas!* (London: Buckland, 1987), 215–16; Bob Ringma, *M*L*B*U: Full Monty in Korea* (Burnstown, ON: General Store Publishing, 2004), 93; John Teague, interview, 17278/1, IWM; see also Tim Carew, *Korea: The Commonwealth at War* (London: Cassell, 1967), 235; and Andrew C. Moffat, *Korea Memories: A Canadian Gunner's Experiences in the "Forgotten War"* (Ottawa: Keshet, 2006), 53–55.

32 Julian Tunstall, *I Fought in Korea* (London: Lawrence and Wishart, 1953), 78.

33 See Eaton, *Something Extra*, 32–33; see also, e.g., Gray, *Beyond the Danger Close*, 19; Douglas H. Mancktelow, *Atsuko and the Aussie* (North Vancouver: DMA, 1991), 54–55; and McGibbon, *New Zealand and the Korean War*, 2:158.

34 See Des Vinten, in Pip Desmond, *The War That Never Ended: New Zealand Veterans Remember Korea* (Auckland: Penguin, 2013), 200; Eaton, *Something Extra*, 89; McGibbon, *New Zealand and the Korean War*, 2:155–56, 158; William Hedges, interview, 18455/3, IWM; John Smith, in Kelly, *British Soldiers*, 85; Raschen, *Send Port and Pyjamas*, 77, 214; Ron Walker, "Last Days on the 'Hook,'" in *Korea Remembered: The RAN, ARA, and RAAF in the Korean War of 1950–1953*, ed. Maurice Pears and Fred Kirkland (Georges Heights, NSW: Combined Arms Training and Development Centre, 1998), 168. Other Commonwealth contingents might also engage in vehicle theft (see, e.g., Harold Pullen, interview, 18018/3, IWM), sometimes leading to serious embarrassment if the source was not American: see, e.g., J. Charles Forbes, *Fantassin: Pour mon pay, la gloire et ... des prunes* (Sillery, QB: Septentrion, 1994), 335–36.

35 On positive comments, see, e.g., Jean V. Allard, with Serge Bernier, *The Memoirs of General Jean V. Allard* (Vancouver: UBC Press, 1988), 175; Eric Burini, interview, 19630/18, IWM; Francis Cheeseman, interview, 20364/1, IWM; John Cormack, 21564/5, interview, IWM; Gray, *Beyond the Danger Close*, 19; Gerald Kingsland, *In Quest of Glory: Korean War Memoires* (London: New English Library, 1989), 132; Moffatt, *Korea Memories*, 55; and Thomas Nicol, interview, 26560/8, IWM; Bryan Webster, interview, 13451/2, IWM. On Aussie-Brit banter, see, e.g., Brian Hough, in Kelly, *British Soldiers*, 83; Mancktelow, *Atsuko and the Aussie*, 54, 71; and John Scott, interview, 19633/5, IWM.

36 On unit officers socializing over food and drink with officers from different Commonwealth countries, see, e.g., Anthony Firth, interview, 19853/3, IWM; Forbes, *Fantassin*, 331; Peacock, *Kim-chi, Asahi and Rum*, 87; Raschen, *Send Port and Pyjamas*, 75–77; and Rose, *Off the Record*, 95, 123, 158, 162, 163. On other-rank social visitations, see, e.g., John Fuller, interview, 17647/2, IWM; Leo Lacroix, in William Horrocks, *In Their Own Words* (Ottawa: Rideau Veterans Home Residents Council, 1993), 238. On intra-Commonwealth trading, see, e.g., John Fuller, interview, 17647/2, IWM; John Richardson, in Heppenstall, *Find the Dragon*, 151; Jim Jacobs, *From the Imjin to the Hook: A National Service Gunner in the Korean War* (Barnsley, UK: Pen and Sword, 2013), 124–25; Peacock, *Kim-chi, Asahi and Rum*, 38; and Drew James Ryder, "'Don't Forget the Boys in Korea': British Soldiers' Experience of the Korean War" (PhD diss., University of Northumbria at Newcastle, 2020), 177.

37 See Grace Huxford, *The Korean War in Britain* (Manchester, UK: Manchester University Press, 2018), 9.

38 On the negotiations surrounding commitments and responsibilities, see Jeffrey Grey, *The Commonwealth Armies and the Korean War* (Manchester, UK: Manchester University Press, 1988), 31–132.

39 Long-standing fears of being drawn into British imperial defence schemes rendered the idea of maintaining the Commonwealth Division in Asia "as welcome to the Canadian Government as haemorrhagic fever": David J. Bercuson, *Blood on the Hills: The Canadian Army in the Korean War* (Toronto: University of Toronto Press, 1999), 221; see also Grey, *Commonwealth Armies,* 183; and John C. Blaxland, *Strategic Cousins: Australian and Canadian Expeditionary Forces and the British and American Empires* (Montreal/Kingston: McGill-Queen's University Press, 2006), 138.

40 John Rockingham, in Johnston, *A War of Patrols,* 141.

41 Grey, *Commonwealth Armies,* 150.

42 Hassett, "Commanding an Australian Battalion," 384.

43 Allard, *Memoirs,* 179. Canadian resistance to integration attempts apparently included even such nonoperational matters as bathing and laundry: see Ringma, *M*L*B*U,* 103–4. A pattern of resistance among Canadian commanders to merging Canadian and British units dated back to the world wars. There was also strong resistance to surrendering dominion authority to the British from an Antipodean quarter in the form of Australian Lieutenant General Sir Horace Robertson, the nonoperational head of British Commonwealth Forces, Korea, based in Japan. See Grey, *Commonwealth Armies,* 64–121; and Jeffrey Grey, *Australian Brass: The Career of Lieutenant General Sir Horace Robertson* (Oakleigh, Australia: Cambridge University Press, 1992), 179–92.

44 Maurice Austin, in Grey, *Commonwealth Armies,* 150, 229*n*49; see Robert O'Neill, *Australia in the Korean War, 1950–53,* vol. 2, *Combat Operations* (Canberra: Australian War Memorial/ Australian Government Publishing Service, 1985), 286; see also Ronald Cashman, 19389/3, IWM; Hatchard, *Squaddy's Tale,* 171; Desmond Gunton, interview, 18333/2, IWM; Patrick Knowles, 19388/3, IWM; Bob Maslen-Jones, *Outrageous Fortune* (Dunbeath, UK: Whittles, 2006), 193, 219; Williams, *Conscript in Korea,* 63; and Ron Walker, "Last Days on the 'Hook,'" 160. See also Andrew Burtch's contribution to this volume concerning the high incidence of improper explosives/weapons handling within the Canadian lines. British units taking over from other British units could find their new home in a terrible state (see Rose, *Off the Record,* 154) while New Zealand gunners were known to question British standards of personal hygiene (see Des Vinten, in Desmond, *The War That Never Ended,* 205). Royal 22e Régiment believed they'd improved positions taken over from the British, not least in terms of personal comfort: see Forbes, *Fantassin,* 301.

45 Grey, *Commonwealth Armies,* 151–52; O'Neill, *Australia in the Korean War,* 2:286; see Ron Hughes, "The Static War," in Pears and Kirkland, *Korea Remembered,* 191; Rose, *Off the Record,* 176; and John Teague, interview, 17278/1, IWM. William Johnston makes a strong case that problems arose mostly with the regimental first battalions (1952–53) rather than the initial second battalions (1950–51) or later third battalions (1953). Johnston, *A War of Patrols,* 316–17.

46 McGibbon, *New Zealand in the Korean War,* 2:158; see also, e.g., D.J. Holland's *roman à clef, The Dead, the Dying and the Damned* (London: Cassell, 1956), 54.

47 See, e.g., Gray, *Beyond the Danger Close,* 20–21; Moffatt, *Korea Memories,* 75–76; and Peacock, *Kim-chi, Asahi and Rum,* 35–36. On the French Canadians having to take over poorly built and badly sited British positions, see Serge Bernier, *Le Royal 22e Régiment* (Montreal: Art Global, 2000), 212–13; and Johnston, *A War of Patrols,* 215.

48 See Johnston, *A War of Patrols,* 317–19. There were still, however, occasional situations where Canadian and other Commonwealth officers might encounter one another at the front and be privately critical of the others' manners or actions: see William Henry Pope, *Leading from the Front: The War Memoirs of Harry Pope* (Waterloo, ON: Laurier Centre, 2002), 175–76, 178–79.

49 On subunit isolation in the line, see, e.g., I.E. Bridge, interview, 17349/5, IWM; Allan Mavin, interview, 1992/14, IWM; Peacock, *Kim-chi, Asahi and Rum,* 39; and Robert Woollcombe, *All the Blue Bonnets: The History of the King's Own Scottish Borderers* (London: Arms and Armour, 1980), 131. There was, to be sure, regular contact with the noncombatant Korean porters of the Korean Service Corps who supported the frontline effort, plus, in the last months of the war, Korean Augmentation Troops, Commonwealth, a pair of whom were allocated per infantry section. But these Koreans, along with the refugees officially or unofficially attached to divisional units, were not considered part of the Commonwealth mix.

50 See, e.g., Leslie Pike, video interview, Veterans Affairs, https://www.veterans.gc.ca/eng/video-gallery/video/6085.

51 Des Guilfoyle, interview, AS01909, AWM, https://www.awm.gov.au/collection/C372914.

52 McGibbon, *New Zealand and the Korean War,* 2:155. Australian, Canadian, and New Zealand soldiers were known to be paid significantly more than their British counterparts, though relative estimates varied: see, e.g., Smyttan Common, in Tom Hickman, *The Call-Up: A History of National Service* (London: Headline, 2005), 84; Francis Dean, interview transcript, 20, S02295, AWM, https://www.awm.gov.au/collection/C969363; William Hedges, interview, 18455/2, IWM; and Peter Saunders, interview, 18748/3, IWM. On the effects of the pay differential in terms of intra-Commonwealth socializing, see, e.g., Leo Lacroix, in Horrocks, *In Their Own Words,* 238.

53 See, e.g., William Bushby, interview, 19658/2, IWM; John Fuller, interview, 17647/2, IWM; Larby, *Signals to the Right,* 119; Terence Lyon, interview, 20338/1, IWM; Roy Painter, interview, 20279/2, IWM; Vinten, in Desmond, *The War That Never Ended,* 197; see also Brent Byron Watson, *Far Eastern Tour: The Canadian Infantry in Korea, 1950–1953* (Montreal/Kingston: McGill-Queen's University Press, 2002), 171.

54 Peacock, *Kim-chi, Ashi and Rum,* 119.

55 See, e.g., Bob Douglas, in Ted Barris, *Deadlock in Korea: Canadians at War, 1950–1953* (Toronto: Thomas Allen, 2010), 127; and Watson, *Far Eastern Tour,* 171.

56 On the sergeant, see Gray, *Beyond the Danger Close,* 208–12. On this case, see Brian Munro, in Heppenstall, *Find the Dragon,* 264; and Chris Madsen, *Another Kind of Justice: Canadian Military Law from Confederation to Somalia* (Vancouver: UBC Press, 1999), 109–10, 185*n*70. While one of the soldiers received a life sentence for throwing a grenade into the Korean house to kill the occupants, another was released from custody on his return home to Canada. See also John Price, "Racism, Canadian War Crimes, and the Korean War: Shin Hyun-Chan's Quest for Justice," *Asia-Pacific Journal: Japan Focus* 10, 3 (2012): https://apjjf.org/2012/10/3/John-Price/3678/article.html.

57 See, e.g., William Bushby, interview, 19658/1, IWM; Bruce Matthews, *Wild Knights in No-Man's Land* (Wellington: Transpress, 2003), 145; and Moffat, *Korea Memories,* 31, 75–76. On the spread of "Canuck," see John Bishop, *The King's Bishop: A Canadian Corporal in Korea, 1950–51* (Duncan, BC: Fir Grove, 2000), 96.

58 On parodying British accents, see, e.g., Ringma, *M*L*B*U,* 104; and Eaton, *Something Extra,* 14. On evident British officer shock at more relaxed Australian and New Zealand concepts of officer-man relations, see, e.g., Allan Cull, in Desmond, *The War That Never Ended,* 151; and Larby, *Signals to the Right,* 155. Suspicion that French Canadian soldiers

only feigned lack of comprehension when addressed by Anglos did not help their reputation: see, e.g., Eric Burini, interview, 19630/18, IWM; Walter Robins, interview, 19865/3, IWM; and Carew, *Korea,* 235. Although, in many cases, only the Royal 22e Régiment officers were fluent in English: see, e.g., Canadian War Museum, Gerald Bowen interview, 31D 4 Bowen, 2–4, https://www.warmuseum.ca/collections/archive/3153465; John Cormack, interview, 21564/4, IWM; see also Raschen, *Send Port and Pyjamas,* 79. While some rank-and-file British solders seemed to have envied laidback Australian ways (see, e.g., James Murray, interview, 19060/2, IWM), cases of violent and criminal behaviour by Aussies against British servicemen in rear areas were not appreciated: see George C. Pagan, *A National Serviceman in Korea* (Swanage, UK: Finial, 2003), 51–52.

59 See, e.g., Michael Hickey, *The Korean War: The West Confronts Communism* (London: Murray, 1999), 282–83.

60 There was a noticeable number of transplanted Britons serving in 1 RAR. Colin Kahn, "The Reliving of Minor Tactics: Reflections of a Platoon Commander's War in Korea," in Blaxland, Kelly, and Higgins, *In From the Cold,* 184; Colin Chadwick, interview, 16593/23, IWM; Michael McBain, interview, 11105/10, IWM; Roy Painter, 20279/2, IWM; Frederick Todd, interview, 18623/3, IWM; and Williams, *Conscript in Korea,* 180. For comparatively rare examples of Canadians serving in rather than attached to British units and vice versa, see Bishop, *King's Bishop,* 46, 148; and George Cooper, *Fight, Dig and Live: The Story of the Royal Engineers in the Korean War* (Barnsley, UK: Pen and Sword, 2016), 13.

61 For an exceptional example of Canadians playing cricket, and New Zealanders playing ice hockey, see Moffat, *Korea Memories,* 183–85. On soccer as a uniting element between other contingents, see John Smith, in Kelly, *British Soldiers,* 86.

62 Keith Nutter, interview, 23349/6, IWM; see also Carew, *Korea,* 235; and O'Neill, *Australia in the Korean War,* 2:286.

63 On appreciation of American rations – especially as compared to British rations – and trading opportunities, see William Bushby, interview, 19658/1, IWM; John Cormack, interview, 21565/5, IWM; James Goulty, *Eyewitness Korea: The Experience of British and American Soldiers in the Korean War, 1950–1953* (Barnsley, UK: Pen and Sword, 2018), 166; Kelly, *British Soldiers,* 61, 65, 122; McGibbon, *New Zealand and the Korea War,* 2:169; Kenneth Phipps, interview, 19860/2, IWM; Ringma, *M*L*B*U,* 90–91; and Moffat, *Korea Memories,* 108. On Commonwealth personnel being dubious about the US Army, see Hickman, *Call-Up,* 77, 80; Kelly, *British Soldiers,* 61; Patrick Knowles, interview, 19388/4, IWM; McGibbon, *New Zealand and the Korea War,* 2:169–70; Moffat, *Korea Memories,* 92; Kenneth Phipps, 19860/2, IWM; and Alberic Stacpoole, interview, 12498/2, IWM. On the dangers of American command misemployment, see Carew, *Korea,* 236.

64 On a similar publicity photograph, see Williams, *Conscript in Korea,* 3–6. On *Crown News,* see David Fisher, interview, 18338/2, IWM.

8

The Royal Canadian Air Force in the Korean War

Richard Mayne

When the Korean War began in June 1950, the Royal Canadian Air Force's (RCAF) 426 "Thunderbird" air transport squadron sprang into action. It was the only unit in the RCAF that could. Half a decade of retrenchment following the Second World War had taken its toll on the air force and its capabilities. The force reached a peak strength of approximately 215,000 personnel in 1944 – the fourth-largest air force in the world – but fell to a mere fraction of that size after the war.[1] Yet in addition to 426 Squadron, the RCAF provided Canadian exchange fighter pilots who flew with United States Air Force (USAF) F-86 Sabre fighter squadrons engaged in operations against their North Korean and Chinese counterparts. The RCAF was also involved in the UN's electronic warfare efforts over the combat area.

This chapter is designed to focus on the RCAF's operational capabilities and explain why it could not do more. As such, it will not address other areas of interest, such as the role of air force nurses, ground crew, or the aviation experiences of the Canadian Army, Royal Canadian Navy, or the civilian assistance to the airlift provided through Canadian Pacific Airlines, although it should be noted that these topics are worthy of further exploration.[2] That said, the historiography of the Canadian air operational contribution to Korea is rich with various studies that range from chapters in commemorative official histories to numerous articles and monograph segments from journalists and historians.[3] Yet this chapter's uniqueness rests in an approach that looks at how five years of painful postwar government cuts left the RCAF unprepared to provide a sizable force to deal with the geopolitical shock of the Korean War and, perhaps more importantly, how air force leadership used this emergency to build a modern and sizable force that could respond to future threats from the Communist world in Europe.

Given that 426 Squadron was the only dedicated unit to provide direct support to the war, it is understandable that the RCAF's contribution has, at various times, been interpreted as somewhat less significant when compared to that of the Canadian Army and the Royal Canadian Navy. Even Brooke Claxton, the minister of national defence, implied this when he noted that while the navy had made a "great account of itself," the air force had made "a notable" effort.[4] Yet the shape of Canada's aerial contribution was a product of the Canadian government's fundamental attitude towards military spending, air power, and the country's role in international politics; as a result, it is necessary to lay the context to explain why the RCAF was unable to provide more operational resources to the war.

The demobilization of the RCAF after the Second World War occurred rapidly. By June 1946, all overseas RCAF squadrons had either been deactivated or returned to Canada.[5] In 1947, the RCAF continued to ebb; the service had a recorded strength of only 12,200 personnel (of all ranks), including an auxiliary force of 650.[6] These reductions would have important implications for the service's ability to respond to Cold War crises, but for Prime Minister William Lyon Mackenzie King's government, military spending was simply not a priority after the costly and painful war years. The government's focus reverted to domestic priorities and greater social spending alongside the demobilization effort.[7] The hoped-for peace and stability wilted in the face of East-West acrimony and aggressive Soviet manoeuvres such as the Czechoslovakia coup and similar consolidations of power across the emerging Eastern Bloc. The Soviet Union's June 1948 blockade of all land access to the Western-controlled portions of Berlin, an effort to force the West to abandon West Berlin or make concessions to the Soviets concerning planned reforms in West Germany, cemented the West's realization that the days of working with its former ally during the Second World War had come to an end.[8] Fearing a Third World War, the Americans and the British, in particular, turned to air power as a means to resolve the Berlin Crisis, by airlifting the necessities of life to the citizens in the isolated city.[9] Unlike its closest allies, however, the Canadian government reacted with extreme caution.

The effort to support such a massive airlift was considerable, and it was only a matter of time before a request was made for Canada to contribute aircraft and personnel.[10] King and his Cabinet's reaction helps explain why the RCAF could not provide a larger contribution to the Korean conflict two years later. The government was conflicted: some ministers believed that such active involvement in the crisis would threaten the government's desire for Canada to serve as a key negotiator on the world stage through the UN.[11] The result of deliberations within the RCAF was a decision to provide a squadron of ten Dakotas along with 219 air and ground crew, which could be deployed on a moment's notice.[12] But even Cabinet understood that such a force would only "be of a token character," that it was designed simply "for the purpose of giving the impression of Imperial solidarity," and that any request for transport support from Canada "would be a great embarrassment to us."[13] In the end, while the RCAF was ready to support the Berlin Airlift, the government made it clear that participation would not be required. For King's Liberals, it would be a contradiction to participate in running the blockade with military assets while presenting the country as a semineutral party to help settle the crisis diplomatically. Participation would raise the distinct possibility that Canada's "position as Peacemaker might be impaired."[14]

Although the RCAF did not participate in the Berlin Airlift, this crisis had an impact on the government's attitude towards military spending and preparedness. Beginning in December 1948 (roughly five months before the blockade ended in the West's favour), Claxton announced increases to the defence budget. The RCAF received funds for additional recruitment, infrastructure improvements, and equipment with a desire to develop a Canadian-designed and -built jet fighter.[15] When Prime Minister Louis St. Laurent replaced the cautious King in November 1948, there was a stronger desire for Canada to be internationalist. As Hector Mackenzie and Norman Hillmer discuss in this volume, these external pressures and the possibility of confrontation with the Soviets persuaded Canada to take a more active role in mobilizing the emerging Western alliance, most notably with the 1949 NATO alliance negotiations.[16]

Though the Canadian government had allocated new funds to the hollowed-out RCAF, rebuilding the RCAF's capabilities after five years of neglect was not easy. The overall policy was to focus on areas where Canada "was best suited and in which the greatest possible contribution could be made with the least cost in the shortest possible time."[17] For the RCAF, this translated into creating a suitable force to support NATO in the defence of western Europe and North America. The plans prepared for these tasks were ambitious.[18] But they were still realistic, as early discussions had led to a baseline for operational forces composed of

> five fighter squadrons ... and a Maritime squadron for anti-submarine duties, three transport squadrons, a photo reconnaissance squadron and a medium bomber squadron ... an auxiliary force of 14,500, which would include ten fighter squadrons ... In order to implement this program, 204 Type F.86 aircraft would be required. In addition, provisions would have to be made for 112 Type F.100 all-weather fighters as well as 26 Type C.19 military transport craft and 16 Maritime type aircraft.[19]

Realizing that governments often made commitments that they would claw back once international tensions subsided, the chief of the air staff, Air Marshal

Wilf Curtis, emphasized the necessity of increasing the pace of this plan by suggesting that "all indications pointed to the need of accelerating, rather than retarding, defence preparations. In a future emergency, air defence would be required immediately if war broke out."[20] The main problem for the air force was that procuring modern aircraft, raising squadrons, training personnel, and developing logistical networks to support such efforts could not be achieved overnight given the highly technical nature of the RCAF's work. The Korean War would illustrate his point particularly well.

St. Laurent used the Cabinet meeting of 19 July 1950 for a frank discussion on what Canada with its limited military resources could contribute to the UN's war effort. Aside from the RCAF's air transport role, Cabinet also considered the provision of acquiring further F-51 Mustang fighters from the United States that could then be sent to Korea. Fortunately, it was noted that the Americans "already had in the area all the fighter aircraft that could be usefully employed," and it was doubtful the Mustangs would have been of much help outside of a limited tactical strike role. Put more directly, this Second World War propeller-powered aircraft would have been outmatched and overpowered during the jet battles that were about to rage over Korea.

The Canadian decision to send an air transport squadron was much easier to make. After the Berlin Airlift strained the USAF's Military Air Transport Service (MATS), the Americans were anxious for logistical airlift support. The USAF let it be known that their planners would gladly accept 426 Squadron.[21] The squadron's senior officers, anticipating the request, had instructed 426 to prepare for operations even before official orders from either the government or senior RCAF leadership had reached it. At the time of North Korea's invasion, 426 Squadron was based out of Dorval Airport in Montreal and equipped with the Canadair North Star transport aircraft. The North Star, a modified version of the Douglas DC-4/C-54 Skymaster, boasted four powerful British-made Merlin engines that gave it a greater load, power, and speed advantage than the original American design. It was a robust machine. With a crew of five (pilot, copilot, navigator, radio operator, and flight engineer), its only significant drawback was that it was not pressurized – which meant it was unable to fly above harsh weather.[22] For the RCAF personnel who flew in the North Star, it was also notoriously loud.[23]

Thanks to the commander of 426 Squadron's foresight weeks earlier, the unit was ready, on 25 July 1950, to send six North Star aircraft to McChord Air Force Base near Tacoma, Washington, where they would be placed under the operational control of MATS.[24] The RCAF's airlift, Operation Hawk, soon took to the air. It would involve roughly eight hundred of the approximately one thousand RCAF personnel who served in the war.[25]

Only thirty-six hours after 426 arrived at McChord, three of their aircraft deployed on their maiden trip, bound for Haneda Airport near Tokyo, Japan. Over their eighty-one-hour round-trip route, these aircraft blazed a familiar pattern that aircrews who followed would come to know all too well. Called the "Northern great circle route," 426 Squadron, with some variations depending on weather, flew 2,398 kilometres from McChord Air Force Base to Elmendorf Field (near Anchorage, Alaska), then 2,474 kilometres onwards to Shemya (at the end of the Aleutian Chain), followed by the last 3,386-kilometre leg to their final stop at Haneda. From there, passengers or supplies were off-loaded before being sent by other means to South Korea. Backup airfields included Adak on the Alaska Panhandle and Misawa, Japan.

More often than not, 426 would fly the northern route in reverse to get home, but at times it would use a southern path across the mid-Pacific, which consisted of stops at Wake Island; Hickam Air Force Base in Honolulu, Hawaii; San Francisco's Travis Air Force Base; and then home to McChord.[26] This southern route offered many benefits, including warmer temperatures, but as one observer noted, it "was slightly beyond our safe range." Looking for tiny islands in a vast ocean was another worry, and the fear of engine failure along these expanses "heightened your sense of vulnerability."[27] The mid-Pacific routes were therefore generally reserved for critical medical evacuations, as the speed advantage of the RCAF North Star got them stateside two or three hours earlier than the USAF's C-54s.[28]

Both routes had their challenges. Navigation was always difficult. According to Flight Lieutenant Donald Connolly, a North Star navigator, the McChord-to-Elmendorf leg was considered "relatively straight-forward" and "quite adequate" as aircraft could make good use of radio beacons as well as long-range navigation system (LORAN), which determined an aircraft's position through cross bearings of radio signals. However, the farther the receiver got from the signal's source, the less accurate it was, to the point where it was useless in remote areas.[29] In these instances, such as the leg between Alaska and Japan, navigation became more of an art than a science, relying on astro fixes on the stars as well as the archaic technique of "pressure pattern navigation," which compared changes in pressure and radar altimeter readings to determine which way the aircraft was drifting. And finally, there was dead reckoning, also known among aircrew as "guess-timation," which determined the aircraft's position simply from its course and speed. Each of these navigation methods was difficult over the North Pacific as constant cloud cover prevented star shots with astro-navigation. Aircraft approaching Japan also had to fly within ninety-six kilometres of Soviet territory, where they were barraged by Russian jamming that greatly reduced the effectiveness of radio aides, homing beacons, and voice channels.[30] The southern route, on the other hand, had some, but not all, of these difficulties; yet it required even more precise navigation to deal with the greater length of time spent over open water.[31]

Weather was by far the greatest foe facing 426's air and ground crew. As one member of the squadron noted, navigation was difficult, but landing and taking off were the real threats. Using Shemya as an example, it was observed that this Alaskan airfield "may have been invented to separate boy pilots from men pilots."[32] Using the descriptive prose expected of a top-notch author, Pierre Berton, on assignment for *Maclean's* to cover the airlift, reflected on the northern weather:

> If any place merits the designation, "end of the earth," it is this tiny island of Shemya, a pinprick on the map, a piece of volcanic rock erupting from the cold northern ocean, treeless and cheerless as the grave and chill with clinging mist and sifting snows. We hit the tarmac with a forty-knot crosswind which threatened to blow us off the runway. Down at the other end lay the smashed wreckage of a four-engine B-17, blown right over the bank by a similar crosswind.[33]

The rest of the northern route was equally unforgiving as 426 aircraft faced icing as well as high and unpredictable winds throughout its journey, particularly the winds that flowed across the Kamchatka Peninsula.

Alongside the considerable navigation challenges, it was a remarkable achievement that no RCAF crews were lost during the war. Aside from the aircrew's skills, a great deal of credit was also given to the ground-controlled approach system, or GCA, operated by the Americans by which trained personnel on the ground helped direct landings similar to modern air traffic towers. Comedian Bob Hope after his Alaska tour quipped that GCA stood for "Greeting – Congratulations – Alive!," a nod to the navigation system and personnel without which the Korean airlift would have been "a virtual impossibility."[34]

After conducting its first mission, 426 carried on with the task of getting settled at McChord throughout August and September 1950. Still short of crews and aircraft, 426 air personnel flew 155 hours per month during this early part of the operation. Not only was this considered "excessive" (it was double what was allowed by any civilian airline); but it was also observed in a unit report, with some joyful pride, that this Canadian squadron was operating on an average of seven hours per aircraft per day – one hour more than its US counterparts in MATS. It was maintaining a schedule of one round trip every three and a half days. Squadron leadership therefore felt justified in telling Ottawa that the squadron was "standing up very satisfactorily."[35]

With such a frenzied pace, maintenance of the aircraft became an issue. The heavy workload and low pay allowances (extra money to subsidize additional costs related to deploying) also began to attrite morale, especially among the ground crew.[36] Moreover, living conditions were observed as being "far from satisfactory," so much so, in fact, that Claxton reported in a fall 1950 trip to Korea: "I had had complaints from here because transportation was not allowed for families to join the airmen ... Some of the men had brought out their families at their own expense and were finding the cost of living around Seattle to be beyond their means. Despite the fine work it was doing, the morale of the Squadron was not too good."[37] A pay raise quelled some of the personnel's worries, while the arrival of additional aircraft from 426's home station at Lachine (Dorval), Quebec, also relieved pressure as there were now twelve aircraft at the ready.[38]

Despite initial difficulties, the maintenance section continued with its work; in the words of an aircrew member, "The ground crews' efforts established a record that had our USAF counterparts quite amazed; and it did us all proud."[39] The squadron had, indeed, done well, and while its contribution to the airlift would continue, 426 was relocated to its home station at Lachine on 1 June 1951. The move was a result of crowding at McChord and "because of a decrease in Pacific airlift requirements."[40] The squadron would revert to MATS control when conducting airlift requirements for Korea, and by the end of Hawk, on 9 June 1954, it had flown some 34,000 flying hours, carried approximately 13,000 personnel, and airlifted 3,500 tons of freight.[41] The actual number of final sorties, often quoted at 599, is contested, as recent research suggests that the end tally may have been 584 sorties. However, the most important statistic is that Operation Hawk was carried out without a single casualty. This is even more remarkable because 426 flew directly into South Korea several times and therefore entered the combat zone.[42]

During its impressive effort during Operation Hawk, the squadron had a number of life-threatening close calls. An incident on 15 September 1950, in which 426's commanding officer was at the controls, almost led to disaster when an overloaded North Star filled with US troops and tank ammunition suffered mechanical failure but nevertheless managed to make a difficult emergency landing. Another time, on 2 October 1950, a North Star narrowly escaped catastrophe when the aircraft, flown by Flying Officer Donald M. Payne, DFC, had an engine spin out of control some 1,120 kilometres out of Shemya. It limped back to base due only to the skill of the pilot and aircrew. There was also another near crash in April 1951, when a North Star was accidentally directed to descend into a hill near Ashiya that did not appear on the air tower charts. This aircraft hit the treetops, incurring severe damage, but miraculously managed to land.[43] Other hair-raising incidents illustrate the same point; namely, that the airlift was a dangerous assignment regardless of whether the squadron flew in the combat area.

Citations were issued for acts of bravery during all these occurrences and for other contributions to Operation Hawk. Unfortunately, the citations did not always capture the hair-raising experience of landing a stricken aircraft as was illustrated by Payne's experience:

> When approximately 700 miles South-west of Shemya the number three engine of the aircraft he was flying suddenly went out of control; attempts to feather it proved useless and the only means of reducing the RPM [revolutions per minute] was by decreasing speed. When it became apparent that either the propeller or complete engine assembly might break loose at any moment Flight Officer Payne sent out a distress signal and prepared his crew for ditching. However, as a result of his outstanding ability he was able to keep the aircraft airborne without further damage allowing him to return to Shemya.[44]

In the end, and to cite a specific report, these distinctions included one "Officer of the Order of the British Empire (OBE), one Member of the Order of the British Empire (MBE), four Air Force Crosses, two Air Force Medals and thirteen Queen's Commendations."[45] This was suitable recognition to all those who contributed to Canada's primary air power contribution, which was achieved without the loss of cargo or, more importantly, life.

In addition to the airlift, the RCAF's other significant contribution was to loan fighter pilots to the USAF. To prepare the RCAF to fly the F-86s that the government ordered in 1949 for domestic air defence needs, as well as the NATO air superiority mission in Europe, several Canadian pilots were integrated into USAF fighter squadrons to gain an appreciation for this new aircraft and its flight characteristics. One such member of the RCAF was Omer Levesque, already serving with the American 334th Squadron of 4th Fighter Interceptor Wing, who would fight in Korea after that unit was sent overseas in late fall 1950. Levesque was an experienced Second World War pilot, but his first involvement with the F-86 made it clear that he was about to fight in a new type of aerial war; he recorded that this aircraft "was like being on a bucking bronco – I didn't ride it, I just hung on! It had lots of power and could turn on a dime."[46]

At the beginning of the war, UN forces easily gained air superiority over an inexperienced North Korean air force that flew outmoded Second World War aircraft, but the Americans faced a pressing challenge once China entered the conflict in October 1950. On 1 November 1950, the first group of MiG-15s made their appearance in a combat role over the skies of Korea. These fighters easily picked off formations of US B-29 Superfortress bombers on missions over targets in North Korea. Mounting losses of these heavy bombers led American president Harry Truman to authorize the deployment of F-86 jet fighters to the Korean theatre.[47]

The MiG-15 and the F-86 made for strange adversaries in the sense that both had strengths and weaknesses that produced a balance between the two aircraft; even though they were technically quite different, they were nevertheless well matched. For instance, the lightweight MiG could fly higher and had a quicker rate of climb, but its roll rate was lower. And while its 37 mm cannon packed a powerful punch, it, along with its two 23 mm machine guns, had a slow rate of fire. Moreover, the MiG-15 experienced some loss of control at high speeds. On the other side of the ledger, the heavier F-86 enjoyed a small speed advantage in level flight, was much faster in a dive, and was more stable, particularly in high-speed turns, and had a much greater rate of fire from its six .50 calibre machine guns. Yet the defining factor that gave the UN forces an advantage was the experience and training of their pilots over their North Korean and Chinese counterparts.[48]

As a result, with the introduction of the F-86, the air war changed yet again as the MiG-15 pilots, who were already limited by the short range of their fighters (approximately 1,120 kilometres), took refuge at Chinese bases just behind the border with North Korea. UN pilots, who were under strict orders not to penetrate Chinese airspace for fear of triggering a global war, therefore faced a geographical and political red line.[49] The MiGs' safe haven in China resulted in an operational area where they were most active, a roughly rectangular block of airspace that famously became known as "MiG alley."[50] It was in this area where the UN relied on fighter sweeps and screens to maintain localized air superiority to support tactical and strategic strikes.

Omer Levesque loved piloting fighters, and his fellow squadron mates nicknamed him "Throttle" because of his thirst for speed. The F-86 did not disappoint in this regard. Levesque recalled breaking the sound barrier in a dive while pursuing a MiG-15: "You don't look at the speed when you're in hot pursuit like that." He continued, "The G-force was terrific, it was like having the weight of a piano on your shoulder."[51] Levesque received an American Air Force medal for flying twenty missions (sorties) over four days between 17 and 21 December 1950. This remarkable average of five sorties in twenty hours was evidence of his squadron's intense operational tempo.[52] Yet his most memorable moment of the war was when he shot down a MiG-15 over the Yalu River on 31 March 1951 while escorting a large formation of B-29s during a daylight bombing mission.

The UN's tactical and strategic bombing of North Korea was significant. In all, some 635,000 tons of bombs (as well as additional tonnage of napalm) were used to suppress Communist ground forces, communication centres, and railways and other transportation infrastructure hubs, as well as a strategic campaign to neutralize certain North Korean cities and destroy industrial targets.[53] During one of these missions, Levesque was flying circuits around the much slower B-29s when he suddenly heard another pilot call out "Bandits!" – the term for incoming hostile aircraft. At that point, the Sabres dropped their external fuel tanks (a standard procedure when engaging in a dogfight). With his flight, Levesque turned towards two MiGs that had separated from the other attackers. In some measure, this action did not come as a surprise to Levesque since the B-29s had just dropped their bombs on the target (a bridge), and "once we hit [it] that sure got the goddam MiGs up."[54] Levesque closed on one of these MiGs that was climbing in the direction of the sun in an effort to blind and lose his pursuer in the glare. When Levesque kept up the pursuit, the MiG changed tack, entering a steep dive. Following the MiG in a downward spiral, Levesque's F-86 dropped 23,000 feet in seconds. Levesque finally opened up with his six .50 calibre guns. The recoil slowed his jet by some sixty-five kilometres per hour. Now at an altitude of 15,000 feet, his rounds hit their mark and tore into the MiG-15. Levesque recounted:

> We kept diving. There was no time to think. I remember looking back a couple of times. You've got to do that. You look back twice every time you look forward. If you don't you can be sure there'll be another one on your tail ... I was right with him; he didn't even try to pull up. I saw him splatter, then it blew up ... You feel all drained out and terribly tired and alone. You're 200 miles from the nearest Allied lines.[55]

It was all over in a matter of two minutes, but Levesque faced an unexpected threat while climbing to rejoin the action. The rattled B-29 gunners mistook him for a MiG – not an uncommon occurrence given the similarity in appearance between the Sabre and its main adversary – and opened fire. After waggling his wings to indicate he was a friend, they stopped, but not before "lots of shells had just missed me." Levesque would make it home with only ten minutes of fuel remaining. Ground crews prepared his Sabre for another sortie, which he flew later that same day.[56]

After flying seventy-one missions during his tour and receiving the American Distinguished Flying Cross for his aerial victory, Levesque returned to Canada in late spring 1951. Lieutenant General G.E. Stratemeyer, commander of the US's Far East Air Force, wanted more pilots like Levesque. He approached the Canadian Military Mission Far East in Tokyo to inform them he was "prepared to rotate Canadian jet pilots through USAF formations in Korea to enable the RCAF to gain operational experience in the field." Much to his chagrin, RCAF Air Marshal Wilf Curtis felt that the RCAF was in no position to contribute to the USAF's F-86 force with RCAF aircraft, although he did instruct the Canadian air member (Washington), Air Commodore M.M. Hendrick, to begin laying the foundation for a potential exchange program of pilots.[57]

Curtis and the RCAF were pulled in multiple directions, trying to rebuild neglected capabilities amid a global crisis. Potential Communist aggression had to be confronted in Korea, but the more pressing threat was to Europe. Unable to deal with both the conflict in Korea and developing an air division to support NATO in Europe – one that would grow to four wings of twelve squadrons – Curtis felt he could not send aircraft to Korea. His program required accelerated production timelines for Canadair's F-86 manufacturing and the addition of Canadian-designed and built Avro CF-100 Canuck fighters to the RCAF fleet for continental defence. Both of these ambitious programs required dedicated logistical support and a training regime to produce new RCAF pilots.[58] It was a daunting task that years of neglect had made more desperate, revealing once again the challenge of rebuilding the RCAF to meet multiple threats within a short timeline.[59]

By 1952, growing air combat losses in Korea led to another formal American appeal for more F-86s and pilots to fly them. In a move that historian Hugh Halliday has described as Canada's most significant contribution to the Korean War's air battles, sixty Sabres built by Canadair intended for service with the Air Division in Europe were redirected to augment the USAF in Korea.[60] While Curtis originally believed that the RCAF needed all its trained pilots to remain in Canada to help shape and instruct the influx of recruits brought on board to support the Air Division, the USAF's renewed appeal for RCAF pilots gave him cause to reconsider the value of an exchange program. Additional pilots would assist the USAF's war effort, and the Canadians would receive invaluable jet-age combat experience that could be passed on through the RCAF. This, in turn, would assist the RCAF's readiness for the key NATO mission in central Europe.[61]

Curtis was in a bind. He did not have enough resources to support both the demand for Korea and the defence requirement to protect Western Europe from a possible Soviet invasion. These competing interests were also felt keenly at the squadron level. In 1952, 426 Squadron found itself committed to supporting Operation Hawk even as its aircraft were tasked with taking resources overseas to build up the Air Division, first in North Luffenham, England, and then in Metz, Marville, and Grostenquin, France, as well as in Zweibrücken, Baden-Soellingen, West Germany.[62] As a result, when it came to assisting the air superiority effort in Korea, Curtis did what he could to establish an exchange program that would see two pilots sent immediately in March 1952, Flying

Officers S.B. Fleming and G.W. Nixon, who would be followed by others with at least fifty hours' flight time on Sabres. Once in Korea, their tour would consist of either fifty missions or six months in the theatre, whichever came first.[63]

As one of the first to follow in Levesque's footsteps, Fleming managed to impress his American supervisors who characterized him as "a capable, courageous and aggressive jet fighter pilot ... [who] served as a flight commander and his leadership was most commendable. The confidence and experience gained by Flying Officer Fleming should make his a valuable asset to the Royal Canadian Air Force."[64] These remarks were backed by his solid combat record. On one sortie in late spring 1952, escorting RF-80 reconnaissance aircraft over the Sui-ho reservoir area, his tactics appeared to literally scare some of his enemies out of the sky, as the MiGs retreated from potential combat.[65] Fleming was an aggressive fighter. He flew eighty-two missions before being recalled to Canada, where he shared his knowledge and experience with airmen in training.[66]

Other pilots proved their mettle in Korea, such as Flight Officer Claude LaFrance, who was sent to Korea after complaining to the senior echelons that those being picked for combat were governed by "an old boys net" of ex-Second World War veterans. Individuals who had joined the RCAF after 1945, he argued, were not getting a chance to test their training in battle, which seemed to defeat the purpose of the program. His bold gambit worked. At twenty-two years old – the youngest of the RCAF F-86 pilots who flew in Korea – LaFrance reported to the USAF's 4th Fighter Interceptor Wing on 28 May 1952. In reality, his claim of favouritism towards combat-experienced pilots was unjustified, as the RCAF had a logical reason for its policy, which had been explained at an Air Council meeting only six days after LaFrance arrived in Korea:

> Some of these positions were being filled by newly graduated pilots who, of course, were inexperienced and required considerable training by the USAF before they could fly in combat. Furthermore, it was not considered that they could impart the knowledge gained on return to Canada as well as a more experienced pilot. The CAS felt that ... these exchange positions ... should be drawn from the fighter wings as much as possible.[67]

LaFrance proved a capable fighter pilot. On 5 August 1952, he shot down a MiG during a pitched air battle, forcing the pilot of the downed jet to eject, then he hounded a second MiG that raced for the safety of Chinese territory north of the Yalu River.[68]

While LaFrance represented the youngest RCAF fighter pilot to serve in Korea, Group Captain E.B. Hale was the oldest, at the age of thirty-eight. As the commanding officer of 1 Fighter Wing at North Luffenham, England, Hale was key in developing the RCAF's new presence in Europe. He made a convincing argument that he should be sent to Korea, where the USAF took his presence seriously, for experience that could be passed on to others. In fact, Hale was quartered with the United States' most celebrated and top-scoring pilot from the Second World War, Colonel F.S. Gabreski, who commanded the 51st Fighter Wing.[69] Hale's successful service in Korea achieved the exchange program's aim of gathering information for the future Air Division in Europe.[70] Drawing from his experience, Hale made many recommendations about crew training, writing that he "planned on using a similar system in his Fighter Wing." The CAS seconded his recommendations, which subsequently informed the Air Division's doctrine and training.[71]

Although the exact number of RCAF pilots flying in American squadrons varies in the records, ranging from twenty to twenty-five pilots, the official number cited from RCAF documents is usually twenty-two personnel.[72] While not all of these RCAF pilots can be described, some had experiences that could be considered outside the "norm" for an RCAF fighter tour in Korea. Flight Lieutenant E.A. Glover, a native of Niagara Falls, Ontario, was credited with three confirmed victories and at least three probable kills.[73] His efforts resulted in an American Distinguished Flying Cross, but he was also presented with the more coveted Commonwealth Distinguished Flying Cross. Glover became the only RCAF member to get this particular distinction at a time when Canada was technically at peace.[74] The second highest-rated RCAF fighter pilot was J.D. Lindsay, who was known in his USAF squadron as "MiG-magnet."[75] He was credited with two victories during his time in theatre as well as damaging two others, and he was decorated for these achievements through an American Distinguished Flying Cross. Attesting to the easy integration of RCAF pilots into US squadrons, Lindsay also received a letter of commendation from the USAF, noting that his elevation to element leader after only four missions "appears, at present, to be the most rapid promotion of the RCAF pilots involved."[76] Squadron Leader A.R. Mackenzie's experience was perhaps the most extreme because he had the unfortunate distinction of being taken prisoner by the North Koreans (and then transferred to the Chinese) after he was shot down on his thirteenth mission.[77] His time as a prisoner of war was a horrible psychological ordeal, but he also kept a secret that was not revealed until the 1980s: he had, in fact, been shot down by friendly fire.

According to the best sources available, RCAF fighter pilots accounted for a total of nine kills and ten damaged, as well as two probable victories.[78] The exchange program further resulted in indispensable combat experience that was passed on to the Canadian Air Division in Europe.[79] Yet there was at least one other small operational commitment provided by the RCAF that is not fully understood because much of the information is still classified. As an electronics expert, a term used to describe individuals who studied Russian radio and communications jamming as well as their ability to track Western aircraft, Group Captain K.R. Patrick's talents were in high demand due to his knowledge of "the most secret devices"[80] Patrick was appointed to a five-week deployment to Korea so he could study the Communist radar as well as electronic countermeasure systems for the US and Canadian governments by flying in special B-29 missions that resulted in him being recognized with United Nations and Canadian Korea medals as well as the Legion of Merit (Officer) by the American government for his work in electronic warfare.[81]

In the early 1950s, much was asked from the RCAF, and it did what it could after five years of deep cuts to its funding and establishment. The work of 426 Squadron was inspiring because of the hectic operational tempo of Operation Hawk but also because this unit simultaneously had to contend with domestic missions and the supply requirements needed to build up the Air Division in Europe. Although few could have predicted the geopolitical shock of the Korean War, the fact remains that the Canadian government was completely unprepared. Lack of air power poignantly illustrated how difficult it was to suddenly recreate capabilities after years of neglect.

The historical lesson, therefore, is that the technical nature of the RCAF's capabilities meant that it was in no position to send its own fighter squadrons to Korea once the MiG-15 air superiority fighter made its appearance. The Vampire and Mustangs in the RCAF's inventory at that time would have been no match against this advanced Soviet-built aircraft, although the training and experience of Canadian pilots may have mitigated some of this disadvantage. In an example of institutional agility, the RCAF used the fighter-pilot exchange program to highlight the skills of its aviators once they were put in the seats of the powerful and modern F-86 Sabres. The lessons they learned were passed on to new airmen recruited to serve in Canada's other two major Cold War commitments: NATO and the defence of North America.

As their Korea experience so clearly demonstrated, it was only the skill, flexibility, and determination of the RCAF's personnel in 1950 that allowed Canada to contribute to the UN's air war. Moreover, if history is to show its relevance to modern decision-makers as a guide and teacher, the Korean War underlines that strategic shocks cannot be predicted and that having a rapid-response capability to these crises requires time to build and train highly technical air power capabilities. The Korean War presented the government of Canada and the RCAF with stark choices and competing priorities. It also profoundly informed Canada's decision to focus on the development of the Air Division in

Europe. This decision had important implications for the service's growth, development, and credibility. It enhanced Canada's and NATO's security, but it came at the expense of making a larger contribution to the defence of democracy in Korea.

Notes

1 Leslie Roberts, *There Shall Be Wings: A History of the Royal Canadian Air Force* (Toronto: Clarke, Irwin, 1959), 237; and Randall Wakelam, *Cold War Fighters: Canadian Aircraft Procurement, 1945–54* (Vancouver: UBC Press, 2012), 29–30.

2 Excellent sources on these topics include Nancy Power Shiner, "In the Best Interest of the Service: RCAF Flight Nurse as the New Woman, 1945–1959" (master's thesis, Dalhousie University, 1988), 11–12, 71–82, 102–4; and G.W.L. Nicholson, *Canada's Nursing Sisters* (Toronto: A.M. Hakkert, 1975), 214–21. For the army's aviation role, see D.W. Francis, "The Air Observation Post," *Canadian Army Journal* 9, 3 (1951): 48–58; Hugh Halliday, "Khaki in the Blue," *CAHS Journal* 1, 4 (1963): 73, 89; Donald G. MacLeod, "The Canadian Army Contingent 1647th Tactical Control Group US Air Force Korean War 1950 to 1956," circa June 2014, Department of National Defence, Directorate of History and Heritage (DHH), Donald G. MacLeod Collection, 2014/6. For the Royal Canadian Navy (RCN), please see J.D.F. Kealy and E.C. Russell, *A History of Canadian Naval Aviation, 1918–1962* (Ottawa: Queens Printer, 1965), 124. For the role of Canadian Pacific Airlines, see file "Korean Airlift – Canadian Pacific Airlines, Copies of Correspondence from Deputy Minister Files on Cost of Korean Airlift, Various Dates," DHH, file 111.21.01, and DHH, Raymont Collection, 73/1223, series 3, file 1324.

3 Department of National Defence, *Canada and the Korean War* (Ottawa: Art Global, 2002); Brereton Greenhous and Hugh A. Halliday, *Canada's Air Forces, 1914–1999* (Ottawa: National Defence, 1999); James Eayrs, *In Defence of Canada: Growing Up Allied* (Toronto: University of Toronto Press, 1980); and Larry Milberry, *Canada's Air Force at War and Peace*, vol. 3 (Toronto: CANAV Books, 2001).

4 Claxton memoir, Library and Archives Canada (LAC), MG 32 B5, Brooke Claxton Fonds, vol. 227, 1142; and Department of National Defence, *Canada and the Korean War,* 15.

5 Roberts, *There Shall Be Wings,* 238; and Greenhous and Halliday, *Canada's Air Forces,* 122.

6 Greenhous and Halliday, *Canada's Air Forces,* 122; and "Plan H for the Royal Canadian Air Force," 1 April 1951, DHH, 181.004 (D 48).

7 Eayrs, *In Defence of Canada,* 196.

8 Robert Bothwell, *Alliance and Illusion: Canada and the World, 1945–1984* (Vancouver: UBC Press, 2007), 67; and Tony Judt, *Postwar: A History of Europe since 1945* (New York: Penguin, 2005), 146–47.

9 For more on the Berlin airlift, see John M. Schuessler, Adam R. Seipp, and Thomas D. Sullivan, eds., *The Berlin Airlift and the Making of the Cold War* (Houston: Texas A&M University Press, 2022).

10 "Berlin Airlift: Canadian Participation, Berlin, 30 March 1949," DHH, Raymont Collection, 73/1223, series 3, file 1324.

11 Eayrs, *In Defence of Canada,* 42–43, 50.

12 Cabinet Conclusions, 9 and 25 September 1950, LAC, RG 2, Privy Council Office, series A-5-a, vol. 2646.

13 Eayrs, *In Defence of Canada,* 43, 46.

14 Eayrs, *In Defence of Canada,* 50.

15 Roberts, *There Shall Be Wings,* 238.

16 Timothy Andrews Sayle, *Enduring Alliance: A History of NATO and the Postwar Global Order* (Ithaca, NY: Cornell University Press, 2019).

17 "Berlin Airlift."

18 "Plan H for the Royal Canadian Air Force." For an excellent account of this period, see Bertram Frandsen, "The Rise and Fall of Cold War Air Force, 1948–1968" (PhD diss., Wilfrid Laurier University, 2015), chaps. 1 and 2.

19 Cabinet Defence Committee, 22 December 1949, DHH, 12/1223, box 66, file 1374.

20 Cabinet Defence Committee, 22 December 1949, DHH, 12/1223, box 66, file 1374.

21 Hugh A. Halliday, "Operation Hawk: The Korean Airlift," *Legion: Canada's Military History Magazine,* 7 August 2013, https://legionmagazine.com/operation-hawk-the-korean-airlift-2/.

22 Department of National Defence, *The Insignia and Linages of the Canadian Forces,* vol. 4, *Operational Squadrons* (Ottawa: Canadian Forces Heritage Publications, 2000), 2–163; Larry Milberry, *Canadair North Star* (Toronto: CANAV Books, 1982), 140–94; and Donald Connolly, "Remembering the Korean Airlift," *Air Force Magazine,* December 1983, 18.

23 "Report on 426 (T) SQN Activities from 25 Jun to 25 July 50," DHH, Operational Reports, 74/337, 31; Connolly, "Remembering the Korean Airlift," 4; and "Report on 426 (T) SQN," DHH, Operational Reports, 74/337.

24 "Pacific Airlift 426 Sqn RCAF in Korean War 19 Jul 50/23 Jul 50/23 Jun 51," DHH, Operational Reports, 74/337; and Laurence Motiuk, *Thunderbirds for Peace: A Diary of a Transport Squadron* (Ottawa: Larmot Associates, 2004), 184.

25 Carl Mills, "The RCAF in the Korean War," *Maple Leaf,* 25 June 2020, https://www.canada.ca/en/department-national-defence/maple-leaf/rcaf/2020/06/the-rcaf-in-the-korean-war.html.

26 Department of National Defence, *Canada and the Korean War,* 129; Greenhous and Halliday, *Canada's Air Forces,* 128; and Halliday, "Operation Hawk," 3.

27 Connolly, "Remembering the Korean Airlift."

28 Pierre Berton, "Milk Run to Korea," *Maclean's Magazine,* 15 May 1951, 15.

29 "Report on 426 (T) SQN," DHH, Operational Reports, 74/337.

30 "Reds Jam Radio Waves to Confuse RCAF Planes," press clipping, Annual Historical Report, 1952, DHH.

31 Connolly, "Remembering the Korean Airlift," 5; and Berton, "Milk Run to Korea," 6.

32 Connolly, "Remembering the Korean Airlift," 5.

33 Berton, "Milk Run to Korea," 12.

34 "Report on 426 (T) SQN," DHH, Operational Reports, 74/337; and Pierre Berton, "Milk Run to Korea."

35 Roberts, *There Shall Be Wings,* 240; "Report on 426 (Transport) Squadron, 8 September 1950," DHH, Operational Reports, 74/337, file "Operational Reports Korean Air Lift 426 (T) Squadron Lachine."

36 "Report on 426 (Transport)."

37 Claxton memoir, 1157–58.

38 "Report on 426 (Transport)."

39 Connolly, "Remembering the Korean Airlift," 18.

40 "Pacific Airlift Report 19 Jul 50/23 Jul 50/23 Jun 51," DHH, Operational Reports, 74/337, file "Operational Reports Korean Air Lift 426 (T) Squadron Lachine."

41 Greenhous and Halliday, *Canada's Air Forces,* 128, 130.

42 Mills, "Operation Hawk." Mills claims that 599 sorties is a "discrepancy" as "there were only 584 missions; for some unknown reason the numbered listing of flights had jumped

from '439' on Nov. 26, 1952, to '455' on Nov. 28, 1952." Motiuk's book, on the other hand, appears to have a sortie-to-sortie account that confirms the number at 599: Motiuk, *Thunderbirds for Peace*, 761–77.

43 Connolly, "Remembering the Korean Airlift," 17.

44 Citation for D.M. Payne, n.d., DHH, Biog P (Payne).

45 Press release, 4 June 1952, DHH, 181.003 D5423; and Mills, "Operation Hawk," 4.

46 Department of National Defence, *Canada and the Korean War*, 132; and Herb Kugel, "From Spitfires to Saberjets: The Making of an Ace," *Aviation History*, May 2010, reproduced on HistoryNet, 3 March 2018, https://historynet.com/the-making-of-an-ace/.

47 Hugh Halliday, "In Korean Skies," *CAHS Journal* 2, 4 (1986): 9–10.

48 Department of National Defence, *Canada and the Korean War*, 134.

49 Terry Leversedge, *Canadian Eagles in Crimson Skies: Canadian Fighter Pilots in the Korean War, 1950–1954* (Ottawa: Kestrel Publications, 2020), D-1/2.

50 Department of National Defence, *Canada and the Korean War*, 134; and Leversedge, *Canadian Eagles*, 6–9.

51 "Fly Boys Look Back as Men," *Ottawa Citizen*, 10 November 1984; and Levesque, DHH, Biog L (Levesque).

52 Halliday, "In Korean Skies," 10.

53 For details on the UN bombing campaign of North Korea, see Bruce Cumings, *The Korean War: A History* (New York: Modern Library, 2010).

54 "Armistice Anniversary: Former Fighter Pilot Recalls Sabre Jet's Baptism by Fire in Korea," *Ottawa Citizen*, 27 July 2018.

55 "Armistice Anniversary."

56 Halliday, "In Korean Skies," 12. See also Kugel, "From Spitfires to Saberjets."

57 Air Marshal Wilf Curtis to Combined Joint Staff (Washington), 10 February 1951, DHH, 181.0003, D5423.

58 For one of the best accounts on the development of the Canadian Air Division in Europe, see Ray Stouffer, *Swords, Clunks and Widowmakers: The Tumultuous Life of the RCAF's Original 1 Canadian Air Division* (Ottawa: Royal Canadian Air Force, 2015). For continental defence, see Richard Goette, *Sovereignty and Command in Canada-US Continental Air Defence, 1940–57* (Vancouver: UBC Press, 2018).

59 Eayrs, *In Defence of Canada*, 224.

60 Greenhous and Halliday, *Canada's Air Forces*, 130.

61 "Address by Minister of National Defence," 17–18 January 1952, AOC Conference, DHH, 73/1223, Raymont Collection, file 2000.

62 Operational records on supporting the establishment of the Air Division can be found in LAC, R112, RG 24-E-1-c, vol. 42061, file 960, "Leap Frog 3," pt. 1.

63 Halliday, "In Korean Skies," 123; and Department of National Defence, *Canada and the Korean War*, 135.

64 "336th Ftr Intep Sq – APO 970, Subj; Flying Officer Sanford B Fleming, RCAF," 15 June 1952, DHH, Biog F (Fleming).

65 S.B. Fleming, "Report of Korean Duty with United States Air Force," 1 October 1952, DHH, Biog F (Fleming).

66 Memo to CAS, F/O S.B. Fleming, 14 May 1952, DHH, Biog F (Fleming); and Department of National Defence, *Canada and the Korean War*, 135.

67 Minutes of the 157th Meeting, 4 June 1952, DHH, 73/1223, Raymont Collection, series 3, file 1823.

68 "Loretteville Airman Bags MiG in Korea," *Quebec Chronicle-Telegraph,* 5 August 1952; and "Combat Record, 39th Fighter Interceptor Squadron, 26 September 1952, LaFrance," DHH, Biog L (LaFrance).
69 National Defence College, 10 July 1963; and Headquarters, 9 June 1952, 51st Fighter Interceptor Wing, DHH, Biog H (Hale).
70 Headquarters, 9 June 1952, 51st Fighter Interceptor Wing, DHH, Biog H (Hale).
71 Minutes of the 157th Meeting.
72 "RCAF Combat Pilots," DHH, 181.003 D5423.
73 Arthur Bishop, *True Canadian Heroes in the Air* (Toronto: Key Porter Books, 1992), 289.
74 Please see copy of the following article located on file Biog G (Glover): Neil MacArthur, "In Memoriam: S/L Ernest (Ernie) Glover, DFC, 1922–1991," *CAHS Journal* 1 (1992): 35; Glover, Award of the Distinguished Flying Cross, no date, DHH 181.003 D5423.
75 Halliday, "In Korea Skies," 128.
76 James Douglas Lindsay, DFC, CD, DHH, Biog L (Lindsay), Reference, 8 May 1953; Correspondence, 15 August 1963, Lindsay; RCAF, 1 Air Division HQ-Metz France, Lindsay, T72; 20361 S/L J.D Lindsay DFC, CD, DHH, Biog L.
77 "The Andy MacKenzie Story," National Air Force Museum of Canada Archives, file 2012.13.27. Also see "I Was a Prisoner of the Chinese Reds," n.d., DHH, 2004/16, Mackenzie Papers.
78 Milberry, *Canada's Air Force at War and Peace,* 87.
79 RCAF Air Intelligence Summary, June 1951, DHH, 181.003 (D3235); and Wing Commander Merifield, "Sabre v MiG," 8 May 1953, DHH, 181.003 (D5423).
80 Biography developed by Edith Baker, 2 January 1973, DHH, Biog P (Patrick).
81 "Group Captain Kenneth R. Patrick Retires from the RCAF," 29 February 1960; and Patrick, G/C K.R, RCAF press release, n.d., DHH, Biog file P (Patrick).

9

China's Battles for Korea

Xiaobing Li

In 1950–53, the People's Republic of China sent more than 3 million troops to Korea. The conflict became a war between China and UN forces (UNF) from the United States, Britain, Canada, Australia, and other countries. The international coalition forced the Chinese army to engage in different ways of war, for which the Chinese People's Volunteers Force (CPVF) was not fully prepared. While Marshal Peng Dehuai associated US forces with firepower and speed, the CPVF commander observed that the British and Canadian troops' battle preparation, flexibility, and counterattacks were different in addition to their firepower. Based on recently available Chinese Communist sources, this chapter offers a perspective on "the other side of the hill" by summarizing the CPVF's war effort in Korea, analyzing their operational tactics, and discussing engagements and setbacks against Canadian troops.

Confronted by UNF air and naval superiority, the CPVF suffered heavy casualties (totalling 1.05 million) in the Korean War, including 183,000 dead, 383,000 wounded, 455,000 hospitalized, 21,400 taken as prisoners of war, and 4,200 missing in action.[1] Among the Chinese prisoners of war, 7,110 were repatriated back to China, and another 14,200 Chinese prisoners opted for transport to the Republic of China (Taiwan).[2] China did not withdraw its forces from Korea until 1958. The CPVF remained in Korea for eight years since its first entry in October 1950 – two years and nine months of actual combat and five years and three months after the Korean Armistice was signed on 27 July 1953. The People's Republic of China spent about 10 billion yuan (renminbi) during the war.[3] In terms of war materials and supplies, the Chinese government transported 5.6 million tons of goods and supplies during the Korean intervention. Between 1950 and 1953, China's military spending represented 41, 43, 33, and 34 percent of its government's annual budget.[4] It was the largest single expenditure of resources for China in any single war during the Cold War.

Strategic Objectives and Offensive Campaigns, October 1950–April 1951

Before Chinese armies entered Korea, Mao Zedong, president and chairman of the Chinese Communist Party, actively supported North Korea's invasion plan since he considered Korea China's security "buffer zone" against a pro-American Japan. In April 1950, the Chinese Army transferred to North Korea 70,000 Korean Chinese soldiers, who were seasoned troops who not only fought in the Chinese Civil War but also provided valuable artillery and engineering support. In early August, when the northern invasion was halted, Mao began preparation for China's intervention in Korea. However, in early October, he devised a defensive plan to position the CPVF around the fortieth parallel between the Yalu River and Pyongyang and then awaited the UNF's advance.[5] The initial strategy would build defensive lines in mountainous areas north of Pyongyang and Wonsan, more than 190 kilometres south of the Yalu, to stop an invading force. To carry out Mao's defensive strategy, Peng Dehuai rushed to Shenyang (Manchuria) and met with army and division commanders on 14 October 1950. He clarified that the CPVF's task was to protect North Korea by taking up positions in the northern terrain, which had not been occupied by the UNF.[6]

On 19 October, the CPVF 40th Army crossed the Yalu by train and then marched south to meet the UNF six days later.[7] Five more armies, consisting of eighteen infantry divisions and three artillery divisions totalling 260,000 men, joined the first echelon and initiated the CPVF's first battle in Korea from 25 October to 7 November. Chinese officers were told they faced the US and ROK (Republic of Korea) forces, but many were unaware they fought an international military coalition. The CPVF used the same combat tactics it had perfected during the Chinese Civil War (1946–49), such as surprise attacks, roadblocks to separate enemy units, and night attacks to negate superior enemy firepower. When they ambushed the UNF in the first encounter, Chinese troops tried to avoid US troops, preferring to target ROK forces to better their chances of winning the first battle.[8] However, due to misinformation, the CPVF's 116th Division engaged the US 1st Cavalry's 8th Regiment. The 39th Army thought a ROK regiment held Unson and ordered its 116th to attack on 1 November. The Chinese did not know the Americans had taken over the positions from the ROK's 15th Regiment the day before. After engaging the Americans, officers of the 39th Army noted some weaknesses of US troops, namely, their dependence on roads for their trucks, artillery, and uninterrupted supplies, and that they only operated during daytime under air cover.[9] Although the CPVF suffered 10,000 casualties, their intervention blunted the UNF's northward advance and stabilized the military situation in North Korea. The Chinese troops established defensive lines, and Peng reported the first battle as a victory to Mao.[10] Emboldened by the victory, Mao shifted China's war objective from defending North Korea to winning a glorious victory and driving the UNF out of Korea. As a result, Beijing rejected a UN request in early December for a negotiated peace.

To achieve a total victory, Peng deployed 240,000 Chinese troops on the western front against the 130,000 soldiers of US Eighth Army's I and IX Corps and 150,000 men in the east against 90,000 troops of US X Corps. The CPVF endeavoured to "divide, encircle, and annihilate" the US IX Corps from behind and envelop the UNF at the Chongchon River.[11] Peng launched an all-out counterattack over a 160-kilometre-wide front from 25 November to 24 December as the Second Campaign against General Douglas MacArthur's "Home by Christmas" offensive. Under massive Chinese attacks, the UNF began an overall retreat in the west on 29 November to allow the Eighth Army to withdraw back into South Korea. In the east, the US 1st Marine Division broke through the Chinese encirclement and retreated to the south on 1 December. The Second Campaign was a major victory for the CPVF since it pushed the front line back to the thirty-eighth parallel and recaptured Pyongyang, the capital city of North Korea. Among the 80,000 Chinese casualties were 40,000 soldiers lost in the Battle of Chosin Reservoir, where the US X Corps managed to withdraw most of its strength south, notwithstanding its more than 17,800 battle and nonbattle casualties. Mao Anying, one of Mao Zedong's sons, was among those killed on 25 November in an air raid against the CPVF HQ.[12]

Encouraged by the CPVF's early success, Mao declined Peng's request on 8 December to pause CPVF offensives until next spring and defend the areas north of the thirty-eighth parallel. Mao cabled the marshal: "At present, America, Britain, Canada, and other countries are asking our army to stop north of the 38th Parallel so they can re-organize their troops to continue the war. Thus, our army must cross the 38th Parallel. It will be most unfavorable in political terms if [our forces] reach the 38th Parallel and stop north of it." Mao planned for the CPVF to reunite Korea and placed his own political considerations and ambition over Peng's military calculation. On 13 December, the chairman instructed Peng to "continue your southward march, look for opportunities to wipe out several enemy units, hopefully in the areas south or north of Kaesong, or the area not far from Seoul."[13] He emphasized to Peng on 26 December that "We should understand that the Korean problem cannot be settled without experiencing a serious struggle, without eliminating all or at least most of the puppet forces, and without eliminating at least 40,000 or 50,000 more of the American and British forces."[14] In the same telegram, Mao also set forth a new rule for the CPVF: "Not to come back to the motherland until the enemy forces in Korea have been eliminated."[15] Mao wanted a total victory to demonstrate Chinese proficiency in arms. From 30 December 1950 to 8 January 1951, Peng launched the Third Campaign against UNF defences along the thirty-eighth parallel. Over eight days, the CPVF crossed the thirty-eighth parallel, moved into South Korea, recaptured Seoul, South Korea's capital, and pushed the UNF 130 kilometres south to the thirty-eight parallel.[16] The CPVF and the North Korean People's Army (NKPA) lost 8,500 men during the campaign, including 5,800 Chinese and 2,700 North Korean soldiers.[17] Beijing organized parades and parties with fireworks after taking Seoul in the clear-cut victory.

Chinese, Russian, and North Korean leaders increasingly pressured Peng for a quick victory in Korea. The general launched the CPVF's Fourth Campaign from 25 January to 21 April. However, it was disrupted along the Hangang River in late January, when General Matthew Ridgway led four US divisions and two British-led brigades (the 27th and 29th Commonwealth Brigades) in an offensive towards Seoul. To reduce pressure on the Hangang, three Chinese divisions, totalling 25,000 men, attacked Chip'yong-ni, a small town defended by 6,000 UNF troops. UNF units formed a defensive perimeter around the town, refusing to yield the strategic road junction. For two days, the Chinese mounted attack after attack against UNF positions, but the defenders, with sufficient air and artillery support, refused to surrender. On 17 February, the US 1st Cavalry Division arrived to reinforce Chip'yong-ni. From 22 February to 6 March, the 2nd Battalion, Princess Patricia's Canadian Light Infantry (2 PPCLI), swept aside Chinese rearguard positions on the surrounding hills. Facing attrition from the withering battle, the Chinese could not organize another effective attack.[18]

Some historians consider the battle of Chip'yong-ni a turning point in the Chinese intervention. The setback exposed the CPVF's weaknesses and convinced the UN Command that the UNF could stop Chinese offensives. The impact was also felt in Beijing, which changed its strategic objective from a quick victory (driving the UNF out of Korea) to a prolonged war for a UNF withdrawal after the Americans suffered irreplaceable losses. On 1 March, Mao explained to Stalin that he was prepared for a war of attrition as it would "take several years to inflict casualties of hundreds of thousands of American troops to make them beat a retreat in the face of difficulties."[19] China sent additional reinforcements to Korea to offset losses and to achieve the new objective.[20] By mid-April, Chinese forces in Korea increased to 950,000 troops, including forty-two infantry divisions, eight artillery divisions, four antiaircraft artillery divisions, and four tank regiments.

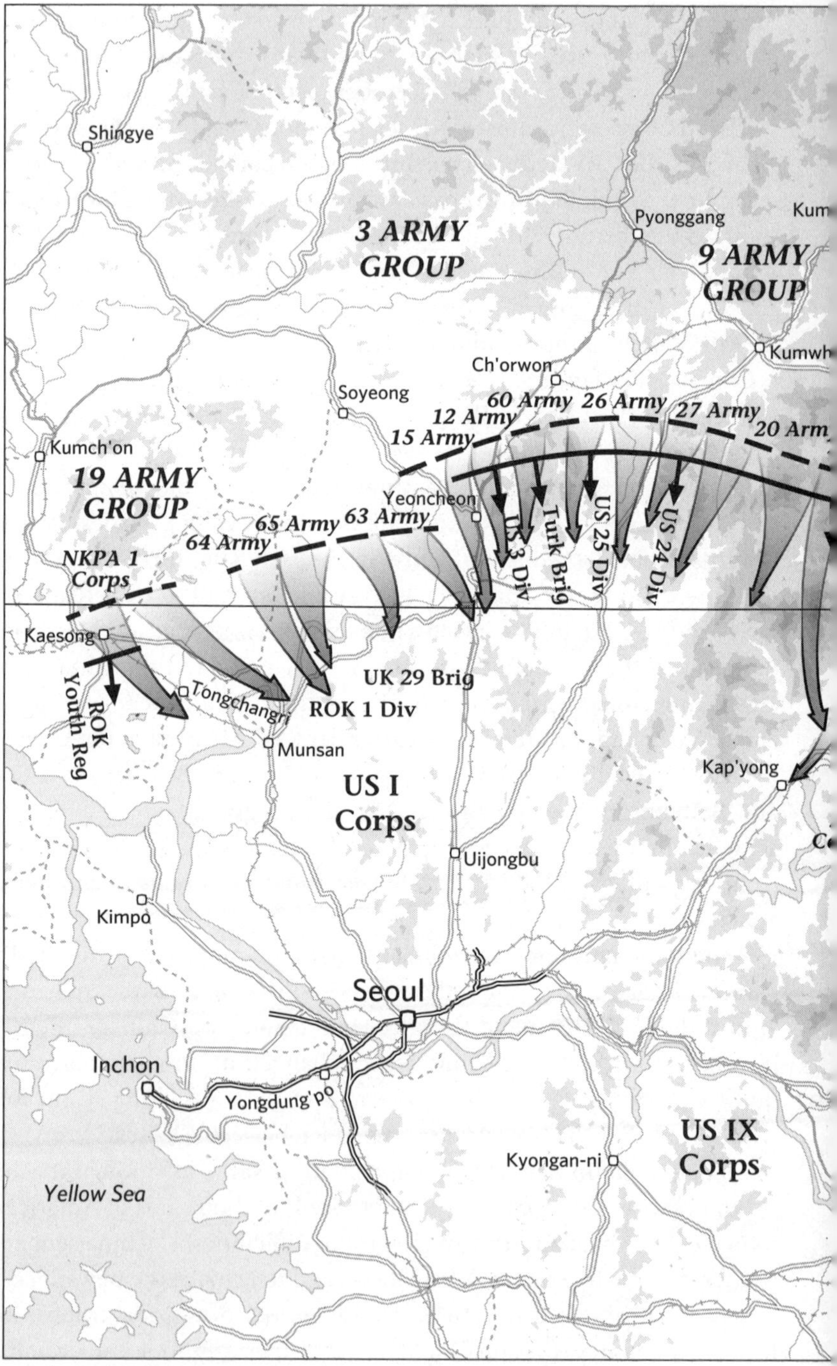

Map 6 Operations in the Fifth Campaign, 22–24 April 1951
Cartography by Eric Leinberger.

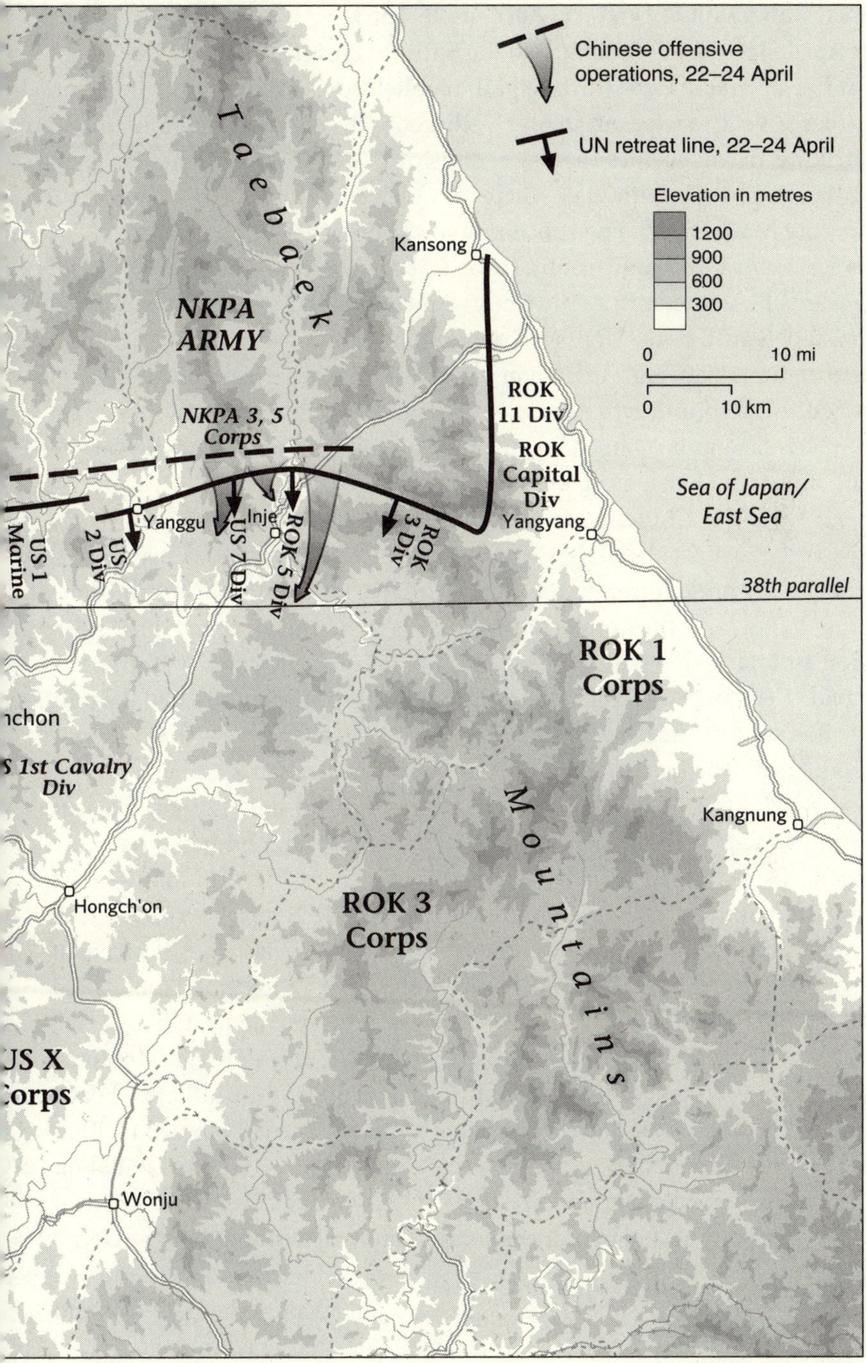

Chinese offensive operations, 22–24 April
UN retreat line, 22–24 April
Elevation in metres
1200
900
600
300
0
10 mi
0
10 km
Taebaek Mountains
NKPA ARMY
NKPA 3, 5 Corps
Kansong
ROK 11 Div
ROK Capital Div
Yangyang
Sea of Japan/ East Sea
38th parallel
Yanggu
Inje
US 1 Marine
US 2 Div
US 7 Div
ROK 5 Div
ROK 3 Div
ROK 1 Corps
ROK 3 Corps
nchon
S 1st Cavalry Div
Kangnung
Hongch'on
US X Corps
Wonju

The Last Campaign for Victory, April–June 1951

On 22 April 1951, the CPVF launched the Fifth (or Spring) Offensive Campaign against the UNF across the thirty-eighth parallel along a sixty-kilometre front. Mao ordered Peng to wipe out 50,000 UNF troops by "concentrating your forces and striking hard" against three US divisions, and British, Canadian, and Australian brigades to "eliminate [them] as much as possible in this campaign." To carry out Mao's order, Peng concentrated 548,000 CPVF and 150,000 NKPA troops against 320,000 UNF troops. He believed it would be "the decisive battle" of the war.[21] First, the 40th Army would attack the UNF's centre at Kap'yong, which was defended by the UNF's 27th Commonwealth Infantry Brigade, including British, Canadian, and Australian battalions, to open a gap in UNF lines.[22] Then the 20th, 26th, and 27th Armies would quickly bypass Kap'yong, penetrate south, reach Chenpongchon (Chenpeongchon) east of Seoul, and cut off the US 24th and 25th Divisions before destroying them.[23]

On 22 April, the Chinese opened the Fifth Campaign with the 9th Army Group's strike against the UNF's twenty-five-kilometre-wide defensive lines. The 40th Army broke through the ROK 6th Division's positions north of the Kap'yong Valley, and the 40th's commander, Wen Yucheng, ordered his 118th Division to attack the 27th Commonwealth Infantry Brigade at Kap'yong's crossroad.[24] The 3rd Battalion of the division's 354th Regiment reached the hills outside Kap'yong the next evening and faced a strong defence by 27th Commonwealth Infantry Brigade's 3rd Battalion, the Royal Australian Regiment, on Hill 504 and 2 PPCLI on Hill 677. The 354th Regiment's 3rd Battalion of 520 men was commanded by the 354th's chief of staff, Liu Yuzhu, and battalion commander Li Dezhang. To launch their night attacks on the Commonwealth's positions, dug into the hills, Liu ordered several hundred men into each attack to charge the 27th Commonwealth Infantry Brigade's defensive positions again and again and to engage in hand-to-hand combat. The Chinese battalion failed to take the hills and dug into the valley to await reinforcements. On 24 April, the US 72nd Heavy Tank Battalion, attached to 27th Commonwealth Infantry Brigade, counterattacked with several Sherman tanks and inflicted heavy casualties on the Chinese battalion, among them regimental officer Liu. That night, Li Dezhang pulled the sixty men remaining of the 354th's 3rd Battalion out of the Kap'yong Valley and retreated north.[25] Meanwhile, Lieutenant-General James Van Fleet dispatched reinforcements to Kap'yong to strengthen the UNF's defences.

The CPVF's 118th Division reached the Kap'yong Valley the next day and struck the defenders on the two hills hard with constant massed wave attacks at night. The Canadians and Australians defended their positions with fire support from several US tanks and New Zealand gun positions, inflicting heavy casualties on the Chinese division. According to Lieutenant Kenneth Koch of the US 72nd Tank Battalion, on the night of 24 April, Koch's tanks fired

> 162 rounds of 76mm main armament ammunition, 32,000 rounds of .30 caliber machine-gun and over 11,000 rounds of .50 caliber ... Between 2:00 am and first light, the tanks had been fighting at ranges from 15 feet to 75 yards and at times the crews were obliged to repel Chinese attacks by hurling grenades from their turrets and using their "grease guns" [M3 submachine gun] on their assailants.[26]

Koch estimated that his tanks killed between 100 and 150 Chinese attacking troops that night.

It was not until 28 April, and after 27th Commonwealth Infantry Brigade's withdrawal, that the 118th took Kap'yong. But it was too late, as the 40th Army had failed to penetrate and encircle UNF lines as planned. Because of the delayed seizure of Kap'yong, the entire front developed into an attritional battle along contiguous defensive lines, with much lower UNF casualties than expected and much higher Chinese casualties than hoped for – between 35,000 and 60,000, or about 5,000 to 8,000 men each day.[27] The CPVF's resources were soon exhausted, and the offensive ground to a halt. The first step in the Spring Offensive failed to achieve the campaign objective of annihilating UNF divisions and brigades; instead, Chinese forces suffered heavy losses, and Peng called off the first phase of the attacks on 29 April.[28]

From 16 to 21 May, Peng launched the second phase of the Spring Campaign by attacking four ROK divisions in the east. The CPVF-NKPA Joint Command, however, did not reach its goal of annihilating three ROK divisions in the second phase; the joint attack merely destroyed some elements of the ROK 3rd and 9th Divisions. The Communists failed to achieve their strategic goal because of tactical miscalculations, unfamiliarity with the terrain, unexpected weather, and both old and new challenges. Supply shortages, lack of artillery firepower, and heavy casualties had plagued the Chinese since the beginning of the war; new problems started in May with breakdowns in the chain of command, slow troop movement, and communication difficulties within the NKPA. On 21 May, Peng was forced to call off the second phase of the campaign and withdraw his armies.

After receiving Peng's withdrawal order, Yang Dezhi, commander of the 19th Army Group, ordered his armies to pull back north on 22 May. However, the 63rd Army – the 19th's elite force – advanced much farther south than the other two armies in the group during the second step of the campaign. Although 63rd's commander, Fu Chongbi, knew his army needed to withdraw immediately, he received an order on 28 May to protect Ch'orwon (Cheorwon), a key point for CPVF transportation and supply.[29] "Even if the entire 63rd Army loses all of its troops in the defense," Peng instructed Yang Dezhi, "Cheorwon must be held for fifteen to twenty days."[30] The 19th Army Group reinforced Fu Chongbi with two artillery regiments. Fu deployed his 189th Division on the left of the defensive line against the US 25th Division and the 25th Canadian Infantry Brigade. The 189th deployed its 566th Regiment to defend the peaks of and the nearby village of Chail-li.[31]

On 30 May, soldiers of the 2nd Battalion, the Royal Canadian Regiment, charged positions held by the 566th's Second Battalion on Kakhul-bong but faced a strong defence. The Chinese concentrated their machine guns from their well-constructed trenches. The battalion deployed only one company to the forward line while holding the remainder in reserve to avoid casualties by UNF air bombing and artillery shelling. Having decided to shift from static defence to mobile defensive manoeuvres, the battalion commander launched a surprise counterattack against the Canadian troops that afternoon.[32] To hold the 189th's defensive positions, the 63rd Army was obliged to throw its reserve force, the 188th Division, into action.[33] Fu ordered all artillery units to provide fire support to the 189th's positions the next day. Peng was so concerned about the 63rd Army's situation that he called Fu directly three times asking for complete battlefield assessments, while repeatedly stressing the importance of holding back the UNF attacks.[34] By the morning of 2 June, the 189th Division had withdrawn. Three days later, the CPVF Command ordered the 63rd Army to fall back. Although it suffered more than 10,000 casualties, the army bought time for the CPVF main forces to establish the next lines of defence along Kansong (Kanseong), Samcheon-ri, and Konangpo-ri, about 100 kilometres north of the thirty-eighth parallel.[35]

The CPVF Spring Offensive, from 22 April to 10 June, was the longest Communist operation of the war and the largest battle since the Second World War. Yet the campaign failed. The UNF put up an effective defence, and an immediate counteroffensive drove the CPVF and NKPA north of the thirty-eighth parallel while inflicting 90,000 casualties. Thereafter, Communist forces never came close to Seoul or launched another major incursion southward. The CPVF's failure forced Mao to reconsider both his political and military goals in Korea, and Beijing looked to a negotiated settlement rather than a victory that would reunite Korea under North Korean rule.

Strategic Defence and Tactical Offences, July 1951–July 1953

After the CPVF's failed Spring Campaign, the war degenerated into a stalemate, leading to the truce negotiations on July 10. The fighting, however, continued during negotiations. The stalemate became the most forgotten phase of the "forgotten war," even though about 45 percent of all UNF casualties occurred between July 1951 and July 1953. During this period, Chinese forces in Korea increased to a record high of 1.45 million soldiers, including fifty-nine infantry divisions and fifteen artillery divisions. Soviet leaders accepted Mao's new strategy for waging a prolonged war, and Stalin agreed to deliver arms for sixty Chinese infantry divisions from fall 1951 to 1952. During the stalemate, twelve Soviet Air Force divisions engaged in the air war, including 72,000 Russian pilots, technicians, ground service personnel, and antiair defence troops.[36]

As part of the new phase of warfighting, the CPVF made important strategic and tactical changes to defend their positions along the thirty-eighth parallel and placed a greater emphasis on the war of trenches, outposts, and aggressive raids. The trench warfare that ensued between the CPVF and UNF matched that of the First World War in Europe in scale, intensity, and destructiveness. Positional defence and short frontal counterattacks were new to the Chinese, so mounting an effective defence against a technically and logistically superior UNF was a challenge. The eastern section of their defensive line near the Haean Basin (the Punchbowl) failed in August 1951 when the US 2nd Division attacked the CPVF-held hills during the Battle of Bloody Ridge. The US X Corps continued the UNF offensives, fighting the Battles of Bloody Ridge and Heartbreak Ridge from 13 September to 15 October and occupying 179 square kilometres of CPVF-NKPA territory.[37]

In the aftermath of this costly combat, Peng warned Mao that the CPVF was unaccustomed to fighting trench warfare. Worried that an unfavourable battleground situation might undermine the Communist bargaining positions at the truce talks, Peng ordered the 19th and 20th Army Groups on 16 October to conduct small-scale, tactical counterattacks against the UNF in the west and middle fronts. On 24 October, the 47th Army commenced counterattacks by sending one battalion to charge US positions on the hills north of Sangok-dong. The next day, the 67th Army deployed several companies to attack US positions at Hill 690 at Kuam-san and Hill 1089 east of Pukhan-gang (Bukhan) River. Starting on 3 November, the 64th and 68th Armies initiated counterattacks against twenty-six UNF positions. The 191st Division of the 64th attacked Hills 355 and 187 around Maryang-san, which had been taken and guarded by one British battalion and Canadian troops from the Royal Canadian Regiment. The Chinese division sent three battalions to attack these positions with the support of fifty-seven artillery guns and ten tanks. The Chinese almost took the hill with a heavy artillery barrage but were later forced to retreat by the resolute Canadian defenders. With US assistance, the Canadians and British eventually drove the Chinese division off from the Maryang-san area. By late November, the 64th and 68th Armies recovered twenty-one of the twenty-six positions, but

Maryang-san was not one of them, as the Chinese forces had recaptured it in see-saw battles.[38]

To avoid further loss of territory, the CPVF and NKPA constructed an artillery-fire-proof underground tunnel system along the front line, totalling more than 1,250 kilometres. Additional surface entrenchment and communication lines ran along nearly 6,300 kilometres of the front. An army of workers also constructed defensive barriers and a tunnel system along the western and eastern coasts against a possible UNF landing in North Korea. By early 1953, the completed antilanding defence system comprised 3,150 kilometres of trenches and 725 kilometres of tunnels.[39] With the new system, the Chinese moved from large-scale offensives to the more limited targeting of a regiment or even a battalion in each attack. The UNF tested the Chinese tunnels when the US 45th Division attacked Hill 275, or Old Baldy, about 40 kilometres northeast of Panmunjom near the thirty-eighth parallel, on 26 June 1952. The Chinese defenders and defences held out against the heavy American firepower. For nine months, each side took turns launching assaults, taking the hill, and then defending it. After losing Old Baldy to the other side, the combatants would repeat the sequence all over again. The People's Liberation Army viewed the see-saw battle on the hills as a Chinese victory because the CPVF's tunnel defence stopped UNF attacks.

One of the heaviest trench battles took place from 13 October to 8 November 1952 at two hills in the Iron Triangle that the UNF named Triangle Hill and CPVF called Shangganling (Tall Hill). In early October, the CPVF staged an attack on a critical point known as White Horse Hill. To counter this offensive, Lieutenant-General James Van Fleet conducted Operation Showdown to seize Communist positions in the Iron Triangle area. On 13 October, US 7th and ROK 2nd Divisions attacked the hills and forced Chinese troops off the ridge and, after several days of fierce combat, into their well-constructed tunnels. Then, for nearly a month, the CPVF's 29th and 45th Divisions of the 15th Army and the 31st Division of the 12th Army, totalling 43,000 troops, fought a see-saw action.[40] During the day, UNF forces drove Chinese troops into the tunnels, but at night the Chinese counterattacked and recovered their surface positions, only to lose them again when daylight returned. While the UNF held the advantage of air power and artillery support, the CPVF reinforced its defences with two artillery divisions, shelling the UNF with 400,000 rounds during the battle. This prolonged battle was one of the war's bloodiest engagements.[41] Although the 15th Army lost more than 15,000 men, the battle was described as a victory and became a well-known story in China due to the soldiers' resilience.

The CPVF continued their piecemeal offensives throughout winter 1952 and spring 1953 by attacking UNF outposts scattered across the main line of resistance.

In March 1953, an armistice became more likely when Chinese and North Korean negotiators agreed to an exchange of sick and wounded prisoners of war. Fighting thereafter intensified, in part because the Chinese tried to strengthen their negotiating position. By April, the fighting remained fierce on Pork Chop Hill, 50 kilometres north of Seoul. On 30 April, Deng Hua, acting CPVF commander, conducted new attacks on the UNF-held hills along the front, including Hill 187, held by the 3rd Battalion, the Royal Canadian Regiment. The Chinese hit Hill 187 hard on 2–3 May since Deng emphasized the need for attacks on "American and other foreign forces."[42] By 25 May, the CPVF had launched twenty-nine attacks on twenty enemy positions. Chinese troops believed their operations helped China's positions at the truce talks.

The largest Chinese campaign since the 1951 Spring Offensive took place just two weeks before the armistice was signed. On 13 July, the CPVF concentrated two army groups, including eight infantry armies and eight artillery divisions, totalling 240,000 troops and 1,110 artillery pieces, for an attack against the UNF positions at Kumsong. During the ten-day offensive, the Chinese artillery fired 700,000 rounds against the ROK 3rd, 7th, 8th, and Capital Divisions.[43] After the ROK fell back, the CPVF armies built up defences against anticipated UNF counterattacks. From the Chinese military viewpoint, the Kumsong Campaign demonstrated a significant improvement in the CPVF's combat capabilities and strength.

On 27 July, the Korean armistice was signed at Panmunjom. On 5 August, in accordance with agreements reached during the negotiations, the prisoner exchange began. Mao Zedong judged China's intervention a victory because it saved North Korea's Communist regime, improved China's relations with the Soviet Union, and secured a newly established people's republic from being invaded or threatened by a Western power like the United States. Peng Dehuai stated that the Korean War began the transformation of the Chinese military into a modern force.[44] From the conclusion of the 1951 Fifth Offensive Campaign until the end of the war, the CPVF adopted more cautious and realistic strategies, including maintaining a relatively stable front line; increasing CPVF air force, artillery, and tank units; and bolstering logistical support. Indeed, the CPVF increasingly became a mirror image of its American, British, and Canadian counterparts in its prosecution of the war, with a much more professional fighting force that engaged in combined arms warfare and heavy concentrations of artillery fire. In this respect, the UNF turned out to be a "useful adversary" in the Korean War.[45]

The military intervention in Korea permanently ensured China's brooding influence in East Asia. Chinese military involvement in Korea promoted the Chinese Communist Party's international status and projected a powerful image of China as the vanguard of the Communist countries against the United States.[46] China's increasing political ambition and rising international position demanded a strong, modern military to enhance "China's prestige and influence in the international arena."[47] Throughout the Cold War and beyond, international relations in Northeast Asia had to include China. This is the legacy of China's war for Korea. China's political position changed from peripheral to central. Xi Jinping, chairman of the Chinese Communist Party, emphasized this in his 2010 speech at the "Celebration of the CPVF's Participation in the War to Resist America and Aid Korea" when he stated that the tremendous impact and historical significance of the war "will never fade away with time."[48] Even if forgotten in the West, the Korean War is by no means forgotten in China.

Notes

1 Chen Hui, "Tracing the 180,000 Martyrs of the War to Resist the US and Aid Korea," in *Kangmei yuanchao: 60 nianhou de huimou* [Resisting the US and aiding Korea: Retrospective after sixty years], ed. Zhang Xingxing (Beijing: Contemporary China Publishing House, 2011), 127; Xu Yan, "Chinese Forces and Their Casualties in the Korean War," trans. Xiaobing Li, *Chinese Historians* 6, 2 (1993): 56–57; and Shuang Shi, *Kaiguo diyi zhan: Kangmei yuanchao zhanzheng quanjing jishi* [The first war since the founding of the state: The complete story of the War to Resist the US and Aid Korea] (Beijing: CCP Party History Press, 2004), 2:836–37. The UNF intelligence statisticians put Chinese losses far higher: 1.5 million casualties in all categories, including killed in action, died of wounds and disease, missing in action, and wounded in action. Walter G. Hermes, *Truce Tent and Fighting Front* (Washington, DC: Office of the Chief of Military History, US Army, 1988), 477–78.

2 Xu Yan, *Diyici jiaoliang: Kangmei yuanchao zhanzheng de lishi huigu yu fansi* [The first encounter: A historical retrospective of the War to Resist the US and Aid Korea] (Beijing: China's Broadcasting and Television Press, 1990), 308–10.

3 This amounts to about RMB$475 billion or CAD$94 billion, in 2023.

4 Military History Research Division, PLA Academy of Military Science, *Zhongguo renmin zhiyuanjun kangmei yuanchao zhanshi* [Combat experience of the CPVF in the War to Resist the US and Aid Korea] (Beijing: Military Science Press, 1990), 233–34.

5 Mao's telegram to Zhou Enlai, 14 October 1950, in *Mao Zedong junshi wenxun: Neibuben* [Selected military papers of Mao Zedong: Internal edition] (Beijing: PLA Press, 1981), 2:649–50; and Xiaobing Li and Glenn Tracy, trans. and eds., "Mao's Telegrams during the Korean War, October-December 1950," *Chinese Historians* 5, 2 (1992): 73–74.

6 Peng Dehuai, "Speech at the CPVF Army and Division Commanders Meeting, October 14, 1950," in *Peng Dehuai junshi wenxuan* [Selected military papers of Peng Dehuai] (Beijing: CCP Central Archival and Manuscript Press, 1988), 325 (hereafter *Peng's Military Papers*).

7 Hong Xuezhi, *Hong Xuezhi Huiyilu* [Memoirs of Hong Xuezhi] (Beijing: PLA Press, 2007), 376.

8 The CMC document, "The Central Military Commission's Circular on the Combat Characteristics of South Korean Troops, October 30, 1950," drafted by Mao Zedong, in *Jianguo yilai Mao Zedong wengao* [Mao Zedong's manuscripts since the founding of the

state] (Beijing: CCP Central Archival and Manuscript Press, 1993), 1:630–31 (hereafter *Mao's Manuscripts since 1949*); Li and Tracy trans. and eds., "Mao's Telegrams during the Korean War," 66–67.

9 Li Qingshan, *Zhiyuanjun yuanchao jishi* [The CPVF's records of aiding Korea] (Beijing: CCP Party History Press, 2008), 142.

10 Peng, "The General Report on the First Campaign after [the CPVF] Entering Korea and Operational Plan for the Next Step," 13 November 1950, speech at the First Enlarged Meeting of the CPVF Party Committee, *Peng's Military Papers,* 335.

11 Peng, "My Story of the Korean War," in *Mao's Generals Remember Korea,* trans. and eds. Xiaobing Li, Allan Millett, and Bin Yu (Lawrence: University Press of Kansas, 2000), 33.

12 Mao Anying was Peng's Russian interpreter and secretary at the CPVF General HQ. For his death, see Hong Xuezhi, "The CPVF's Combat and Logistics," in Li, Millett, and Yu, *Mao's Generals Remember Korea,* 118–21; and Du Ping, *Zai zhiyuanjun zongbu: Du Ping huiyilu* [At the CPVF General HQ: Memoirs of Du Ping] (Beijing: PLA Press, 1989), 94–98.

13 Mao's telegram to Peng, "The CPVF Must Cross the 38th Parallel for Engagements, December 13, 1950," in *Mao Zedong junshi wenji* [Collected military papers of Mao Zedong] (Beijing: Military Science Press, 1993), 6:239; and *Mao's Manuscripts since 1949,* 1:408–9.

14 Mao's telegram to Peng and Pak Il-yu, 26 December 1950, in *Mao's Manuscripts since 1949,* 1:420–22, 734–36. Since the Second World War, or China's War to Resist Japanese Invasion (1937–45), Mao Zedong had emphasized the "body count," or eliminating more enemy troops. It became part of his "people's war" doctrine, a Chinese military doctrine in which Chinese leaders and generals believe they can eventually win a war by killing a superior number of the enemy. Ho Chi Minh applied it to the Vietnam War in the 1960s.

15 Mao used the slogan to boost the CPVF's morale: "After finishing this campaign, all main armies should ... strengthen political mobilization of the troops (not to go back to the motherland until the enemy forces in Korea have been eliminated)." Mao's telegram to Peng and Pak, 26 December 1950, *Mao's Manuscripts since 1949,* 1:734–36; and Shuguang Zhang and Chen Jian, trans. and eds., *Chinese Communist Foreign Policy and the Cold War in Asia: New Documentary Evidence, 1944–1950* (Chicago: Imprint Publications, 1996), 219.

16 Xiaobing Li, "China's Intervention and the CPVF Experience in the Korean War," in *The Korean War at Fifty: International Perspectives,* ed. Mark F. Wilkinson (Lexington: Virginia Military Institute Press, 2004), 144–45.

17 The Communist forces claimed an annihilation of nineteen thousand enemy troops during the campaign, most of whom were Republic of Korea Army troops. Xu, *Diyici jiaoliang,* 67.

18 Yang Di, *Zai zhiyuanjun silingbu de suiyueli: Xianwei renzhi de zhenshi qingkuang* [My years at the CPVF General HQ: Untold true stories] (Beijing: PLA Press, 1998), 106–9, 111–13.

19 Mao's conversation in Peng, "My Story of the Korean War," 35; and Xu Yan, *Mao Zedong yu kangmei yuanchao zhanzheng* [Mao Zedong and the War to Resist the US and Aid Korea], 2nd ed. (Beijing: PLA Press, 2006), 208.

20 Liaoning Provincial Government, work reports and meeting minutes, January–May 1951, in "Liaoning shengzhengfu dang'anshi, 1948–1968" [Liaoning Provincial Government Archives, 1948–68], Shenyang, Liaoning; and Xu, "Chinese Forces and Their Casualties in the Korean War," 49, 51.

21 Peng, "Speech at the CPVF Enlarged Fifth Party Committee Conference, April 6, 1951," in *Peng's Military Papers,* 386–87.

22 The British 27th Brigade was made up of one British infantry battalion, a New Zealand artillery regiment, and one Canadian and one Australian infantry battalion. Lt. Maurie Pears, interviews with the author, Australian War Memorial, Canberra, Australia, October 6–7, 2011. Lt. Pears served in the Australian infantry battalion of the British 27th Brigade. See also Brian Catchpole, *The Korean War, 1950–1953* (New York: Carroll and Graf, 2000), 129–34.

23 Hong, *Hong Xuezhi Huiyilu,* 465; and Chu Yun, *Chaoxian zhanzheng neimu quangongkai* [Declassifying the Korean War] (Beijing: Current Affairs Publishing, 2005), 289.

24 Tan Jingjiao et al., *Kangmei yuanchao zhanzheng* [The War to Resist the US and Aid Korea] (Beijing: China Social Science Press, 1990), 138–39.

25 Li Ying et al., *40 jun zai chaoxian* [The 40th Army in Korea] (Shenyang: Liaoning People's Press, 2010), 189–91.

26 Michael Hickey, *The Korean War: The West Confronts Communism* (New York: Overlook Press, 1999), 216.

27 Peng planned to annihilate 60,000 UNF troops with estimated casualties of 50,000 to 60,000 CPVF troops in the Fifth Offensive Campaign. See Peng's telegram to the CMC and all the CPVF armies, 18 April 1951, in *Peng's Military Papers,* 390–92; Military History Research Division, PLA-AMS, *Zhongguo renmin zhiyuanjun kangmei yuanchao zhanshi* [Combat experience of the CPVF in the War to Resist the US and Aid Korea] (Beijing: Junshi kexue chubanshe, 1990), 137, 157.

28 Peng's telegram to Mao and the CMC, copied to Kim Il Sung, 26 April 1951, quoted in Wang Yan et al., *Peng Dehuai zhuan* [Biography of Peng Dehuai] (Beijing: Contemporary China Press, 1993), 466.

29 When Fu withdrew the 63rd Army without an order from the army group command, the army's party committee decided to protect their commander. For more details, see Shuang, *Kaiguo diyi zhan,* 1:401.

30 The CPVF Command's telegram to the 19th Army Group and 63rd Army Commands at 1700, 28 May 1951, quoted in PLA Academy of Military Science (PLA-AMS), "The Unforgotten Korean War: Chinese Perspective and Appraisals," 2:462. "The Unforgotten Korean War" is an unpublished manuscript written by PLA retired officers and officer-historians and sponsored by the Office of Net Assessment, Office of the US Secretary of Defense, in 2006.

31 Zhao Jianli and Liang Yuhong, *Fenghuo 38 xian: Diwuci zhanyi zhanshi baogao* [The flames of battle raging across the thirty-eighth parallel: Combat report on the Fifth Campaign] (Beijing: Military Science Press, 2007), 289–90.

32 The CPVF Command's telegram to the 19th Army Group and 63rd Army Commands at 0000, 3 June 1951, quoted in PLA-AMS, "The Unforgotten Korean War," 2:463.

33 Composition Committee, ed., *38 xian shang de jiaofeng: Kangmei yuanchao zhanzheng jishi* [The fight over the thirty-eighth parallel: The recorded truth of the War to Resist the US and Aid Korea] (Beijing: PLA Literature Press, 2010), 355–58; and Luo Xuanyou, *Chaoxian zhanzheng: Zhengzhan jishi* [The Korean War: The battle records] (Beijing: PLA Literature Press, 2007), 335–37.

34 PLA-AMS, "The Unforgotten Korean War," 2:463–64.

35 Yang Dezhi, *Yang Dezhi huiyilu* [Memoir of Yang Dezhi] (Beijing: PLA Press, 1992), 566, 568.

36 Their active engagements threatened the UNF air raids and aerial bombing north of the thirty-eighth parallel during Operation Strangle in 1951 and created an airspace near the Chinese border that Soviet aircraft could contest, known among UNF pilots as "MiG Alley."

37 Peng's telegram to Kim Un, quoted in PLA-AMS, "The Unforgotten Korean War," 2:549.
38 Military History Research Division, PLA-AMS, *Kangmei yuanchao zhanzhengshi* [History of the War to Resist the US and Aid Korea] (Beijing: Military Science Press, 2000), 3:391–402.
39 Statistics from the Memorial Museum of the War to Resist the US and Aid Korea, Section Four, Group Seven, "Gouzhu dixia changcheng" [Building the Underground Great Wall], Dandong, Liaoning Province. See also Xu, *Diyici jiaoliang,* 123–24.
40 Zheng Yanman, interview with author, Harbin, Heilongjiang, August 2002. Also see Zheng, "The Chinese Go Underground," in *Voices of the Korean War: Personal Stories of American, Korean, and Chinese Soldiers,* ed. Richard Peters and Xiaobing Li (Lexington: University Press of Kentucky, 2003), 173–84.
41 Du, *Zai zhiyuanjun zongbu* [At the CPVF General HQ] (Beijing: Jiefangjun chubanshe, 1989), 544, 552, 556.
42 The battle directives issued by Deng Hua, to all CPVF armies in May 1953, quoted in PLA-AMS, "The Unforgotten Korean War," 3:686–87.
43 Yang, *Yang Dezhi huiyilu,* 742–43; and Luan, *Xue yu huo de jiaoliang* [The contest: Blood versus fire] (Beijing: Huayi chubanshe, 2008), 345.
44 Peng, "China's Military Experience in the Past Four Years and the Fundamental Issues for Our Future Military Development," speech at an enlarged CMC meeting in December 1953, in *Peng's Military Papers,* 468–69.
45 I borrow *useful adversary* from Thomas J. Christensen in his research on grand strategy and Sino-American relations. But *useful adversary* here describes the CPVF's learning curve in Korea through its engagements with the UN/US forces. See Christensen, *Useful Adversaries: Grand Strategy, Domestic Mobilization, and Sino-American Conflict, 1947–1958* (Princeton, NJ: Princeton University Press, 1996), 1–2.
46 For example, Mao's conclusion at the Second Plenary Session of the CCP Seventh Central Committee, 13 March 1949, and Mao's speech, "Address to the Preparatory Meeting of the New Political Consultative Conference," in *Selected Works of Mao Tse-tung* (Beijing: Foreign Languages Press, 1977), 4:1464, 1470.
47 Ellis Joffe, *The Chinese Army after Mao* (Cambridge, MA: Harvard University Press, 1987), 1.
48 Xi Jinping's speech at the "Sixtieth Anniversary Celebration of the CPVF's Participation in the War to Resist the US and Aid Korea," *Renmin Ribao* [People's Daily], 26 October 2010, http://paper.people.com.cn/rmrb/html/2010-10/26.

10

Flesh and Blood: The Commonwealth Division and Medical Care in the Korean War

Meghan Fitzpatrick

> *The Korean conflict may have been a localized war, but it was a dirty and difficult one. It served as a training and testing ground and [as] in the case of all wars, medical knowledge was advanced.*[1]

THERE IS NO MORE brutal way to understand the cost of war than to look at its sick, wounded, injured, and ill. The story of battlefield medicine during the Korean War provides insights into the hardship combatants faced and the difficulties medical providers had to surmount to preserve life. The 1st Commonwealth Division brought together a team of doctors, nurses, and medical personnel from four nations, who worked together under numerous pressures, from staff shortages to cultural differences, lack of resources, logistical obstacles, and a hostile landscape. Nonetheless, they were expected to safeguard the well-being of each individual who came under their care. This chapter examines the scale of that challenge by looking at how the division's medical services were pieced together – the role their national contingents played and how they interacted. It considers the nature of the casualties by reviewing the common conditions patients suffered and how they were treated through various phases of the medical chain from front to rear. I conclude by reflecting on why Korea remains a pivotal moment in the history of the medical services at war.

The Medical Team

War rarely arrives at a time of one's choice, and Korea was no exception. When North Korea invaded South Korea on 25 June 1950, the United States and its allies were not prepared for the scale of what followed and rushed forces from Japan and Hong Kong. They had precious time to build up the necessary manpower through conscription and hurried recruitment. The 27th Commonwealth Brigade arrived in the South Korean city of Busan in late August. Over the subsequent months, it was followed by additional British personnel and contingents from Australia, Canada, and New Zealand.

Medical support was patchwork in those early days. The 26th British Field Ambulance was the first unit of any appreciable size. It arrived aboard the troopship *Empire Pride* on 5 November 1950. Led by Captain W.J. James of the Royal Army Medical Corps, it had 13 officers and 125 other ranks on strength and was supported by 22 Field Surgical Team, 9 Transfusion Team, and 223 and 224 Mobile Dental Teams.[2] That same month, 29 British General Hospital opened in Kure, Japan, about a day's journey by ship from the Korean coast.[3] The 60th Indian Field Ambulance and Surgical Unit joined its British counterparts in the field in December. Commanded by Lieutenant-Colonel A.G. Rangeraja, the unit represented India's sole contribution to the fighting and rapidly acquired a reputation for professionalism and, as one historian noted, treating "friend and foe alike."[4] It was not until summer 1951 that medics from the Royal Canadian Army Medical Corps streamed into theatre, with the arrival of 25th Canadian Field Ambulance and 25th Canadian Field Dressing Station (25 FDS) in May and July, respectively. Around the same time, a new two-hundred-bed Convalescent Depot opened, in which British medical service personnel cared for the wounded as they recuperated.[5] Prior to the creation of the Commonwealth Division on 28 July 1951, these units operated largely independently of one another.[6]

Understrength and overwhelmed, Commonwealth contingents often relied on the generosity of the US Army Medical Corps for everything from casualty evacuation to specialty care. In a little under a year, the UN coalition fighting in Korea had grown to include more than twenty countries, the majority of which were incapable of fielding their own medical services.[7] This put a strain on the United States, which provided manpower and resources. As a result, senior leaders in Washington pressured their Commonwealth counterparts to take greater responsibility for their own medical support services, contributing to the formation of a division.[8] The vast American military medical system in Korea made it difficult to locate troops until they had been evacuated or repatriated entirely. In turn, it could take months to return that individual or replace him with someone else. This made it difficult to generate the appropriate number of replacements to ensure that the Commonwealth units were up to strength. Each of the Commonwealth nations was already struggling to sustain its commitment to the war, so inefficencies in casualty administration were unsupportable.[9]

Stitched together by necessity, the division's medical services were an exercise in integration. Led by a command team of Australian, British, and Canadian officers, the medical services were primarily composed of units from the latter two nations.[10] Initially designed to treat only the minor sick and wounded, 25 FDS became the de facto nerve centre of Commonwealth health care in the field.[11] A hospital in all but name, the Canadian dressing station consisted of over two hundred beds divided into surgical, medical, psychiatric, and venereal disease sections. At any time, it was supported by three field ambulances, which were composed of a headquarters and forward units that collected casualties from regimental aid posts.[12] Each field ambulance accepted patients from any Commonwealth country, but only two had a fully multinational staff. Stood up in September 1952, the British Communications Zone Medical Unit was an assemblage of British, Canadian, and Australian doctors and nurses. Cannibalized from other units, it took control of evacuations through Seoul. The unit also served as a transit point for patients from 25 FDS who were en route to the 1,200-bed British Commonwealth General Hospital in Kure, Japan. Composed of staff from each nation, the hospital was built on top of what was originally a British unit (29 British General Hospital) and supported the entire division.[13]

The level of integration between Commonwealth units in Korea and Japan was unparalleled, even when compared with the First and Second World Wars. So it is not surprising that it resulted in complications. Everything from mundane tasks like record keeping to critical life-saving care was complicated by national differences. What is more, Ottawa imposed a rule that Canadian troops receive treatment from Canadian units alone. Popular domestically, this was a logistical pain for the rest of the division.[14] Commonwealth units did not enjoy uniform deployments, which led to irregular unit handovers, loss of unit memory and clinical experience, and bureaucratic complications.[15] Canadian and Indian personnel were volunteers, and many of them were veterans of the Second World War. The same was initially true of British medics, but as the war dragged on, they were replaced with younger men conscripted through National Service. By the latter stages of the conflict, more than 50 percent of British doctors were conscripts, fresh from medical school. The United Kingdom's overextended global commitments helped account for the shortage of experienced clinicians in Korea. In turn, the shortage put pressure on the remaining Commonwealth countries to absorb the impact.[16]

Surviving Korea: Medical Care in Action

Tensions among the nations' senior military and political leadership were real and had an impact on how care was delivered. However, evidence suggests these complications were manageable rather than terminal. Indeed, scholars widely consider the Korean War to be a seminal moment in the history of medicine on the modern battlefield. Mortality rates dropped from 66 per 1,000 wounded during the Second World War to 34 per 1,000 five years later in Korea.[17] From 1950 to 1953, 4,817 Commonwealth troops were wounded, and 1,263 were killed in action.[18] The death-to-wounding rate was roughly 20 percent of all Commonwealth Division casualties, which is comparable to American figures and significantly lower than rates recorded during the Second World War, which hovered around 40 percent.[19] These figures demonstrate that within a few short years, battlefield survivability had increased substantially. Korea has been described as a "war of patrols" and the fighting was less mobile than much of the fighting during the Second World War, which may account for some of the differences.[20] A stalemate at the front for nearly two years meant that there was time and space to remove the wounded and transport them for medical care because medical services were not overrun by attacks and counterattacks.

In addition, medics in Korea benefited from other distinct innovations in care. Many of these improvements lay in the field of surgery, including the introduction of specialized units as close to the front lines as possible. Known as mobile army surgical hospitals, or MASH units, by the US Army, they aimed to maximize a patient's chances of survival in the immediate aftermath of trauma. According to medical historian Darryl Tong, their development "represented a paradigm shift away from damage control surgery." In fact, these hospitals were often the "highest echelon surgical facility available in country" and could conduct more sophisticated surgeries closer to the front lines than ever before. Experiences in Korea helped to validate the concept of the MASH, which went on to be used during subsequent operations, including in Vietnam and during the first Gulf War.[21] The 60th Indian Field Ambulance functioned as a MASH and, according to one historian, impressively had a "reputation of having the lowest loss of casualties of all front-line medical services in Korea."[22] From December 1950 to February 1954, it admitted more than 200,000 patients and conducted over 2,300 surgeries.[23] The remaining Commonwealth field ambulances also had their own specialized surgical and transfusion teams. Thanks to close relations with allies, they were able to send patients who required more extensive and specialized care to nearby American, Norwegian, and Swedish units.[24]

Surgical and other medical units in Korea were also better equipped to address the common complications of recovery from combat injuries than their predecessors had been less than a decade before. Life-saving antibiotics such as penicillin were not produced on an industrial scale until the latter phases of the Second World War. This made Korea the first time these drugs were systematically available to treat infection, rather than being rationed as they had been during the Second World War.[25] Casualties in the Korean War also benefited from revolutionary innovations in casualty transport. From 1950 to 1953, most wounded and ill soldiers were moved by hand stretcher and then evacuated using jeep ambulances. However, Korean roads were infamously bad, which meant that it could take an ambulance between eight to twelve hours to move a patient forty to sixty kilometres.[26] During the rainy season, roads were often washed away or could become impassable with mud. All year long, collisions along main supply routes were common. The commander of the US Eighth Army, General Walton Walker, died in one such traffic accident in December 1950.[27]

Presented with such obstacles, medical units began using search and rescue helicopters in medical evacuation (MEDEVAC) roles. Territory that took hours to traverse by road took minutes in the air. Easily identifiable by its large plexiglass bubble canopy, the Bell H13D was the primary helicopter used by the US military and relied upon by units from all nations.[28] Primitive by today's standards, it was equipped with open-air litters attached to its sides, in which stretchers carrying the seriously wounded could be stowed. Helicopters transported only around 4 percent of UN coalition casualties, including Commonwealth troops.[29] This underwhelming number did not, however, diminish the helicopter's positive impact on morale and did much to enhance its role as an emerging critical MEDEVAC platform.

Improved frontline surgical treatment saved thousands of lives in Korea, including those of Commonwealth troops. Besides innovations in surgical care, it was preventative measures and high hygiene standards that proved to be key to most patients' swift recovery. Most patients admitted to Commonwealth medical units suffered from illnesses and injuries incurred from the daily grind of an unrelenting environment, and they were, in most cases, not life-threatening. The chief causes of admission were respiratory, gastrointestinal, and dermatological conditions.[30] Cramped living conditions, a diet of ration packs, and lengthy periods of stress presented a challenging mix of circumstances that produced a steady flow of patients. And the local wildlife, particularly rodents and snakes rife in the forward entrenchments, proved to be more than just a passing irritant.

During the Korean War, UN forces were confronted with an unidentified condition, now known as epidemic hemorrhagic fever (EHF). The first cases were recorded in spring 1951 along the thirty-eighth parallel and spread to over 3,200 troops over the next two years.[31] With a mortality rate of between 5 to 7 percent, the US Military Academy described EHF as being "characterized by the acute onset of headache and nausea that progressed to blood leakage, neurological impairment and kidney failure."[32] Hemorrhage typically began on the third day after infection and could last up to eight days, necessitating the use of transfusion. Medical teams discovered patients could go into severe shock if care was delayed. Troops who contracted EHF were typically evacuated to the British Commonwealth General Hospital in Kure, Japan, which was equipped with an isolation wing for the treatment of contagious diseases. Contemporaneous reports suggest there was little doctors could do other than manage symptoms. Treatment involved sedation, bed rest, aspirin, cold sponging, controlling body temperature, and careful restriction of fluids.[33]

Both the United States military and the Commonwealth Division launched intensive studies to discover the etiology of EHF. Several teams were dispatched to investigate, but the results were disappointingly limited. Researchers discovered EHF had first been described by the Japanese army decades earlier in Manchuria.[34] Peaking in spring and autumn, it did not seem to spread directly from person to person, and doctors at the US Army's 8228th MASH unit postulated "rodent-born mites" were the vector.[35] This theory was widely accepted at the time. Consequently, UN forces implemented preventative measures, including, as one Canadian medical study noted, the "impregnation of clothing with miticidal and repellent materials."[36] However, this had a negligible impact. The true origin of the disease remained unknown and was only revealed in 1976 when the real culprit was identified as a type of striped field mouse.[37] The disease was transferred to humans through contact with fecal matter, urine, and saliva. There was little protection for those living in rough-hewn trenches. Modern medicine had taken transformational leaps by the mid-twentieth century, but the threat of communicable disease remained an ever-present drain on frontline units.

The arrival of winter brought no relief. This was especially true in the first winter, when more than 8,000 UN soldiers suffered some form of cold injury.[38] Similar to the Western Front during the First World War, conditions like trench foot and frostbite took a toll, and officers were warned, "CONTEMPT of the WINTER means a CERTAIN CASUALTY."[39] Like EHF, the cold wreaked such havoc that it merited a special inquiry. Teams from the United States and Canada were dispatched to investigate every possible contributing factor from the quality of winter gear to how disciplined the average soldier was in changing his socks. This study eventually contributed to improvements in the design of clothing as well as the widespread enforcement of preventative hygienic measures.[40] In an April 1954 article, Captain P.M. Bretland (Royal Army Medical Corps) recalled the challenge of soldiering in winter:

> Each man ... is brought into a warm place and removes his boots and socks. The inspecting officer asks him if he has any foot trouble, checks his boots, socks, and insoles, and examines his feet. Any deterioration in the condition ... is noticed and the man referred to the Medical Officer. The man then washes his feet in warm water, dries them carefully, powders them and puts on a clean dry pair (or two pairs) of socks. Insoles are also changed.[41]

Cold injuries were a major drain on resources. Discipline was not a panacea, but it did bring cases to manageable levels for the remainder of the war.

Wintertime accidents were not as easy to prevent and remained a perennial concern. Each year, there was always an increase in burn cases when the temperatures started to drop. Frontline troops were issued kerosene-fuelled stoves to heat bunkers and trenches. But it often proved difficult to secure needed supplies of fuel. As a result, troops would adapt equipment to use gasoline, often with deadly results. In Brent Byron Watson's study of the Canadian Army in Korea, he notes that field stoves malfunctioned, creating a pool of gasoline in the stove's base that eventually exploded.[42] Such fires caused painful burns, and if the heat was intense enough, nylon parkas could fuse to skin. In 1952, the No. 1 Canadian Army Operational Research Team reported over half of the 1,500 stoves issued to troops had been adapted in some way. Used in enclosed spaces, they could easily spark fires or cause carbon monoxide poisoning.[43] Lieutenant Charles Belzile, future commander of the Canadian Army, narrowly escaped a blaze after the armistice that destroyed his Quonset hut and killed Lieutenant Milton Vipond.[44] Without major improvements to the kit issued, the threat of injury was always possible for something as simple as trying to stay warm.

Doctors and nurses could treat or control the majority of medical complaints admitted on a daily basis. Venereal disease, or VD, was another problem entirely. Within the UN coalition, the division had the highest rates of infection for common sexually transmitted conditions. British forces in nearby countries such as Burma, Singapore, and Malaya reported similarly heightened rates of infection (144.3 cases per 1,000) in 1951.[45] But these numbers paled in comparison to VD rates recorded in the Korean-Japanese theatre. By 1952, there were nearly 10,000 cases in the Commonwealth Division alone, which amounted to well over 300 men per 1,000. This was ten times the rate reported during the Second World War.[46] Most infections originated in Japan, where soldiers spent time in cities such as Kure or Tokyo. Sex workers were common in guest houses and taverns, and their services were easily affordable to relatively affluent Western troops.[47]

The division once again turned to preventative measures to dampen escalating rates.[48] Routine instructions showed that prophylactics were freely available. Every unit issued condoms and was ordered to establish a prophylactic ablution centre where troops could anonymously secure further hygienic care. But later studies suggest these measures relied too heavily on the motivation of servicemen to either abstain from sex altogether or engage in exceptionally diligent measures to prevent infection afterwards. The British military abolished the centres altogether in 1957.[49]

For those infected, oral penicillin was the treatment of choice for the ease with which it could be administered without impacting operational effectiveness. Like other aspects of battlefield medicine, the use of antibiotics had a sweeping impact on the length and nature of treatment. These drugs made care for VD shorter and less painful.[50] For the division's leaders, it unfortunately did nothing to rein in rates of infection, which remained the highest in theatre. But this was arguably not a problem to be solved by doctors and nurses. Instead, it owed more to issues beyond the purview of a field medical unit, such as discipline. During previous wars, the United Kingdom, Canada, Australia, and New Zealand had all punished servicemen who contracted venereal disease with a combination of fines and imposed confinement in hospital.[51] By the 1950s, only the British Army continued to maintain some form of penalty and did not actually pursue this policy in Korea because of continual shortages of manpower.[52] From April 1952 until the end of the war, the Canadian contingent attempted to reverse its position by insisting that men who contracted VD in the last three months of their tour remain on duty until they tested negative for infection. This only encouraged greater secrecy among those who found themselves so afflicted.[53] In other words, punishment was not a realistic fear, and it was something that could be avoided.

The war in Korea left a lasting mark on the bodies of all who fought there, from bomb blast burns to fever to frostbite. There is also no doubt it left a permanent imprint on their minds. As Canadian veteran Robert Turner explained in his memoirs, "Before you're at the front long, you see buddies getting killed and wounded. The longer you remain in the line the harder it becomes. You carry the fear with you every day and as your tour of duty gets longer the fear becomes stronger."[54] Overall, psychological casualties represented between 5 and 9 percent of admissions to division medical units. During the Second World War, the number of these cases could range dramatically depending on the theatre and the nature of the fighting involved.[55] Consequently, it is difficult to make a direct comparison on numbers alone. The diagnostic trends established during previous wars remained unchanged. More than 50 percent of patients suffered from some form of anxiety-related condition, widely known as "psychoneuroses," and acute stress reactions to combat rose along with the number of overall battle casualties.[56] Typified by many of the same behavioural and emotional symptoms as psychoneuroses, "battle exhaustion" was loosely defined as a condition connected to direct experience of combat and typified by "weariness, apathy, jumpiness [and] disinterestedness."[57] The term *exhaustion* was intended to imply the patient's state was a temporary one, from which it was possible to recover.[58] It shares similarities with what the medical community has now termed post-traumatic stress disorder (PTSD), which generally results from "direct personal experience of an event that involves actual or threatened death or serious injury, or other threat to one's personal physical integrity; or witnessing an event that involve[s] death, injury or threat to the physical integrity of another person."[59]

Mental health care was not widely available to Commonwealth soldiers at the war's outset. Stitched together like a quilt, Commonwealth medical services were not fully assembled in those early months. In the Second World War, battle-exhaustion cases were treated close to the front lines to ensure prompt care and the swift return of soldiers to combat. Commonwealth medical units failed to adopt this approach and lessons learned; instead, they opened in November 1950 a small thirty-bed psychiatric unit not in Korea but in Japan, hundreds of kilometres from the front. High psychological evacuations continued into summer 1951 as a result. Divisional authorities subsequently appointed a psychiatrist to run a thirty-bed ward out of 25 FDS. Based in the field, this doctor periodically toured frontline field ambulances to evaluate affected soldiers and decide whether their cases required extended care or hospitalization.[60]

This chapter demonstrates that Korea was an inflection point in the modernization of some aspects of battlefield care. This is unquestionably true for trauma surgery, which benefited from specialized units and innovations in evacuation. But the same cannot be said of psychiatry, which would have to wait for revolutionary changes. Doctors in Korea were effective in delivering short-term treatment to soldiers suffering from psychological distress, returning up to 83 percent to their units.[61] But this does not mean soldiers were necessarily restored to their previous state of mental health. Military psychiatrists focused on relieving symptoms that undermined a soldier's ability to live and work safely on the front lines. This meant treatment was conservative and relied on regimes with a longer track record, including sedation and basic talk therapy.[62] To be fair, doctors also had few pharmaceutical options. Drugs created for the treatment of psychological disorders remained rare. The world's first antipsychotic medication, chlorpromazine, was only created in 1950 and not released on the market until 1953. Some of the earliest antidepressants were also manufactured during this decade but remained experimental.

The absence of such medication should also be kept in mind when we consider the misuse of alcohol and drugs. Individuals suffering with anxiety, depression, and other psychological problems often attempt to regulate distress through substance abuse. This was likely true in Korea, but existing archival records do not present historians with a clear picture of alcohol and drug consumption within the division. Nevertheless, the United Kingdom, Australia, Canada, and New Zealand all had a heavy-drinking culture. In line with previous wars, each maintained a daily rum ration, despite growing evidence that alcohol had a negative impact on an overtaxed body.[63] The Canadian Army's director general of medical services, Brigadier-General W.L. Coke, even defended the practice in a three-page briefing that argued in favour of alcohol's morale-enhancing qualities. Beer was cheap and commonly available, with over 10,000 cases shipped each week. Officers could purchase hard liquor, and there was little control over consumption.[64]

The war diarist for the 1st Battalion, Princess Patricia's Canadian Light Infantry, acknowledged this permissive environment:

> The supply of liquor in Korea is a delight to alcoholics. It is plentiful and cheap ... An ounce of Canadian Club or Haig sells for ten cents in the [mess] and that gives the mess a respectable profit ... There [is] a tendency towards excessive drinking by both officers and sergeants ... probably a result of boredom and the newfound plenty.[65]

Local moonshine was another option, if a dangerous one. As Andrew Burtch notes in this volume, it even contributed to the deaths of some Canadian soldiers. But in an environment where alcohol was an accepted if deleterious part of life, consistent warnings seem to have deterred few. As historian Brent Byron Watson concludes in his 2002 book, *Far Eastern Tour,* "So long as alcohol achieved the broader objective of maintaining morale, field commanders appear to have accepted a certain amount of misuse."[66] Even if officials had recognized this as a problem, they may not have seen it as an issue worthy of medical attention. Influential groups such as the American Medical Association did not even recognize alcoholism as a disease until 1956.[67]

As for narcotics, there is nothing in the records to suggest addiction was a problem in Korea. Nor do any of the seminal American studies of the war highlight it. Indeed, there are only a handful of books and articles that suggest the need for further investigation. In the 1987 book *The Medic's War,* historian Albert Cowdrey makes a passing reference to heroin being readily available.[68] Lieutenant-Colonel Elspeth Cameron Ritchie of the US Army goes further. In a 2002 article for *Military Medicine,* she argues that "drug abuse was a major problem with [US] Army soldiers addicted to opiates in port towns such as Busan" and that "heroin use went from smoking to intravenous injections."[69] She claims almost half the soldiers were addicted in some units.[70]

And there is evidence to suggest this is a plausible scenario. During Japanese rule, Korea had been a producer of opium and other narcotics in the decades leading up to the war. Records from the division's provost marshal also acknowledge Busan as a site of crime, including black market activity.[71] According to E.C. Ritchie, US officials struggled to find a solution, but she does not explain whether this problem was ever resolved. If Ritchie is correct about the levels of drug abuse, this would represent a critical dimension of the war that has yet to be documented, one that would say a great deal about mental health. It is difficult to believe Commonwealth troops would not have fallen prey to some of the same patterns of drug use as their American counterparts. They operated in the same locations and had comparable purchasing power. And yet, to date, no historian has commented substantively on drug abuse within the division. The archives also seem devoid of direct reference. It is a curious omission and one still to be resolved.

Conclusion

Whether their wounds were physical or psychological, those Commonwealth soldiers who returned home from Korea did so through the same complex, painstakingly assembled evacuation system. Once patients reached hospital in Japan, medical staff evaluated whether repatriation would be necessary for further care.[72] To assemble the largest number of patients into the fewest flights, these longer-distance evacuations took place only once a month. The passenger-cargo planes were equipped to carry close to thirty patients. They leapfrogged across the Far East to refuel before conveying patients to the United Kingdom, Canada, Australia, and New Zealand.[73]

Doctors and nurses in Korea and Japan played a vital role in ensuring the survival of soldiers who returned to the battlefield and those who were evacuated. From field ambulance to general hospital, they played a key part in increasing rates of battlefield survivability through the application of new innovations. Working alongside allies, they managed to preserve life in the face of numerous obstacles and arguably contributed to Korea's status as a turning point in the annals of military medicine. This is a worthy legacy but not one without complications. A Canadian Senate investigation conducted in the 1990s examined higher-than-normal rates of mortality among Korean War veterans but came to inconclusive findings as to the reasons why.[74] Meanwhile, a 2005 study looking at the health of Australian veterans found that they similarly experienced an over 20 percent higher mortality rate than the general male population of comparable age and suffered from "excessive levels of anxiety, PTSD and depression."[75]

There are likely numerous reasons for this situation, from exposure to pesticides and other hazards in theatre to how health care was delivered on their return home. What is more, political leaders in all four Commonwealth countries generally portrayed the Korean War as a "police action," downplaying the severity of fighting to avoid the escalation of hostilities. This meant Korean War veterans returned home to domestic populations that understood little of the trauma they had endured. Consequently, these veterans received far less recognition than their Second World War predecessors, which may have contributed to a sense of isolation and negative health outcomes.[76] In any event, what happened in Korea and in subsequent years stands as a reminder that war does not end when the fighting stops but leaves behind marks that require a lifetime of vigilance and compassion.

Notes

1 "Royal Canadian Army Medical Corps (RCAMC) in the Korean War," Directorate of History and Heritage, Department of National Defence (DHH), file 147.013 (D4).

2 Meghan Fitzpatrick, *Invisible Scars: Mental Trauma and the Korean War* (Vancouver: UBC Press, 2017), 24; Franklin Cooling, "Allied Interoperability in the Korean War," *Military Review* 63, 6 (1983): 28; and C.N. Barclay, *First Commonwealth Division: The Story of British Commonwealth Land Forces in Korea, 1950–1953* (Aldershot, UK: Gale and Polden, 1954), 12.

3 "6 Convalescent Training Depot, RAMC, Jan-Dec 1953," National Archives at Kew (TNA), WO 281/908; and J.J. Flood, "Psychiatric Casualties in UK Elements of Korean Force: December 1950–November 1951," *Journal of the Royal Army Medical Corps* 100, 1 (1954): 41.

4 Darryl Tong, "The Management of Maxillofacial Trauma during the Korean War: A Coming of Age of a Speciality," *Journal of Military and Veterans Health* 19, 2 (2011): 10–11.

5 W.S. Stanbury, Canadian Red Cross Society, July 1952, Canadian War Museum (CWM), 58C 3 22.

6 Meghan Fitzpatrick, "Invisible Scars: Mental Trauma and the Korean War" (PhD diss., King's College London, 2014), 54; and Canadian Inter-service Medical Committee, 4 September 1946, Minutes, Library and Archives Canada (LAC), RG 24, Department of National Defence, 83-84/167, box 7717, file 20-1-1, pt. 1, quoted in Bill Rawling, *Myriad Challenges of Peace: Canadian Forces Medical Practitioners since the Second World War* (Ottawa: Government Publishing Office, 2004), 34.

7 The countries that contributed combat forces to the UN coalition included South Korea, the United States, Canada, Australia, the United Kingdom, Australia, New Zealand, France, Belgium, Netherlands, Luxembourg, Greece, South Africa, Colombia, the Philippines, Turkey, and Thailand.

8 Avinder Gobindpuri, *Forgotten War: Medicine in Korea* (London: University College London, 2005), 3; Commander-in-Chief, British Commonwealth Forces Korea (BCFK), H. Robertson to Chief of General Staff, Melbourne, Chief of General Staff, Wellington, Chief of Imperial General Staff, London, Cipher Message, 15 November 1950, National Archives of Australia, CRS A5954, box 1661, file 4.

9 B.L.P. Brosseau, "Notes from Korea," *Canadian Army Journal* 8, 1 (1953): 107.

10 Medical Services, BCFK, TNA, WO 308/21.

11 Bill Rawling, *Death Their Enemy: Canadian Medical Practitioners and War* (Quebec: AGMV, 2001), 68, 240, 250–51.

12 Director General of Medical Services, Royal Canadian Army Medical Corps Study Papers, vol. I-A/Cap-Capt., January 1952, CWM, 58C 3 22.1.

13 Adjutant General Branch, BCFK, Six Monthly Report, 1954, TNA, WO 308/7; Fitzpatrick, "Invisible Scars," 83; Darryl McIntyre, "Australian Army Medical Services in Korea," in *Australia in the Korean War 1950–1953*, Vol. 2, *Combat Operations*, by Robert J. O'Neill (Canberra: Australian War Memorial and the Australian Government Publication Service, 1985), 571; and Stanbury, Canadian Red Cross Society, July 1952, CWM, 58C 3 22.1.

14 While this was the policy imposed by Ottawa, it was not always followed by those in the field. As a result, there are records of Canadian admissions in other nation's medical units, including the 60th Indian Field Ambulance, the Norwegian Mobile Army Surgical Hospital, and the US 121 Evacuation Hospital. HQ BCFK, Historical Records, 1954, TNA, WO 32/21831; and Report of Assistant Director of Medical Services visit, 17–21 April 1951, TNA, WO 32/21831.

15 Fitzpatrick, *Invisible Scars,* 31; and "Discussion on Military Medical Problems in Korea," *Proceedings of the Royal Society of Medicine* 46 (10 June 1953): 1038.

16 Army Medical Advisory Board, Meetings, 1 July 1949–September 1954, 8 December 1950, 4, TNA, WO 32/13465.

17 Ted Barris, *Deadlock in Korea: Canadians at War, 1950–1953* (Toronto: Macmillan, 1999), 110; Eric Linklater, *Our Men in Korea* (London: HMSO, 1952), 66; and H.F. Wood, *Strange Battleground: Operations in Korea and Their Effects on the Defence Policy of Canada* (Ottawa: Queen's Printer, 1966), 258–59.

18 Max Hastings, *The Korean War,* Pan Grand Strategy Series (London: Macmillan, 2000), 407.

19 William Wiesmann, Nicole Draghic, and John A. Parrish, "Advances in Modern Combat Casualty Care with a Vision to the Future," in *War and Medicine,* ed. Melissa Larner, James Peto, and Nadine Monem (London: Black Dog Publishing, 2008), 228.

20 William Johnston, *A War of Patrols: Canadian Army Operations in Korea* (Vancouver: UBC Press, 2003).

21 Tong, "Management of Maxillofacial Trauma," 11.

22 Hub Gray, *Beyond the Danger Close: Korean Experience Revealed – 2nd Battalion Princess Patricia's Canadian Light Infantry* (Calgary, AB: Bunker to Bunker, 2003), 19–20.

23 Tong, "Management of Maxillofacial Trauma," 10.

24 "Allied Interoperability in the Korean War," *Military Review* 63, 6 (1983): 45.

25 Milton Lewis, *Thorns on the Rose: History of Sexually Transmitted Diseases in Australia in International Perspective* (Canberra: Australian Government Publishing, 1998), 242; and John Parascandola, *Sex, Sin and Science: A History of Syphilis in America,* Healing Society: Disease, Medicine and History (Westport, CT: Praeger, 2008), 21.

26 Early in the Korean War, the Commonwealth Division struggled to locate its medical units close to the front lines due to manpower and resource shortages. This included 25 FDS, which was nearly forty kilometres behind the front line in Seoul and responsible for controlling limited air evacuations from the Kimpo Airstrip. As a result, the unit was split into two sections in summer 1952, one of which moved forward to position itself only fifteen kilometres from the front. The British Commonwealth Communications Zone Medical Unit was opened in September 1952 to take over control of Kimpo Airstrip. This allowed the section of 25 FDS that had remained in Seoul to finally move forward and rejoin the other half of the unit. Lieutenant-Colonel A. MacLennan, Officer Commanding 26 FDS, 1 Commonwealth Division, "Questionnaire on Korean Campaign Answers, 1950–1952," Wellcome Library and Archives (WLA), Royal Army Medical Corps Muniments Collection, 761/4, box 158; and Brosseau, "Notes from Korea," 107–8, 111–15.

27 B.D. Jaffey, Casualty Evacuation in Korea, September 1952, RG 24, vol. 18,385; and Jack Gifford, "Invoking Force of Will to Move the Force," in Combat Studies Institute, ed., *Studies in Battle Command* (Washington, DC: US Army Command and General Staff College, 1995), 143.

28 Gobindpuri, *Forgotten War,* 29–33.

29 Tong, "Management of Maxillofacial Trauma," 11–12.

30 Edgar Jones and Simon Wessely, "Hearts, Guts and Minds: Somatisation in the Military from 1900," *Journal of Psychosomatic Research* 56, 4 (2004): 425–29; and War Office, "Report on Health of Army 1953," 31 July 1956, TNA, WO 279/614.

31 Seung-Hum Yu, "Epidemic Haemorrhagic Fever in Korea," *Yonsei Medical Journal* 22, 2 (1981): 127; Connie Schmaljohn and Brian Hjelle, "Hantaviruses: A Global Disease Problem," *Emerging Infectious Diseases* 3, 2 (1997): 95; and Ho Wang Lee, *Haemorrhagic Fever with Renal Syndrome (Korean Haemorrhagic Fever): Annual Summary Report* (Chongnoku, Seoul: University College of Medicine, 1989).

32 US Military Academy, *Lessons Learned from Experiences with Epidemic Hemorrhagic Fever during the Korean War* (New York: US Military Academy, n.d.).

33 Seung-Hum, "Epidemic Haemorrhagic Fever in Korea," 130.

34 Seung-Hum, "Epidemic Haemorrhagic Fever in Korea," 127.

35 US Military Academy, *Lessons Learned.*

36 Paul Sneath, *Survey of Sources of Supply, Professional Attainments and Wastage Medical Officers of the Canadian Forces,* 1960, LAC, Paul Alfred Turner Sneath Fonds, MG 31 J7, vol. 1.

37 US Military Academy, *Lessons Learned.*

38 Fitzpatrick, *Invisible Scars,* 71; Adrian Roberts, *Synopsis of Causation: Cold Injury* (London: Ministry of Defence, 2008), 3–4; and "Cold in Korea," *Lancet* 260, 6727 (1952): 233.

39 "Conquer the Korean Winter, Simple Rules for All," DHH, file 681.023 (D21).

40 J.M. Adam, Royal Army Medical Corps, and W.S.S. Ladell, Department of Scientific Advisor to Army Council, *Report of Field Studies on Troops of the Commonwealth Division in Korea,* Winter 1951–52, 28 June 1954, TNA, WO 348/117; and Samuel C. Bullock, Luther L. Mays, and Albert N. Berenberg, "A Study of the Personality Traits of Frostbite Casualties," in *Cold Injury: Korea 1951–1952,* ed. Army Medical Research Laboratory and Kenneth Dew Orr (Washington, DC: US Government Printing Office, 1953), 664–735.

41 P.M. Bretland, "Principles of Prevention of Cold Injuries: Notes on the Problem as Encountered, and the Methods Used, in Korea," *Journal of the Royal Army Medical Corps* 100, 2 (1954): 96.

42 Brent Byron Watson, *Far Eastern Tour: Canadian Infantry in Korea, 1950–1953* (Montreal/Kingston: McGill Queen's University Press, 2002), 120.

43 K.L. Campbell, "Sum of Experiences Korean Campaign," DHH, file 145.2R13019 (D1); and Canadian Army Operational Research Team, *Burns and Fires in the 25th Canadian Infantry Brigade,* LAC, RG 24-C-3, vol. 18247.

44 LAC, personnel file, Lieutenant Milton Cameron Vipond.

45 War Office, "Report on Health of the Army, 1946–1948," TNA, WO 279/610.

46 War Office, "Report of Health of the Army, 1951–1952," TNA, WO 279/610; Historical notes, BCFK, TNA,WO 308/21; Periodic Report, 1 November 1952–1 April 1953, TNA, WO 308/30; and "Extract from Minutes of 58th Meeting of Defence Council," LAC, RG 24, 83–84/167, box 7717, 20-1-1, pt. 4.

47 Albert E. Cowdrey, *The Medics' War* (Washington, DC: Centre of Military History, 1987), 146; Tom Hickman, *The Call-Up: A History of National Service* (London: Headline, 2005), 195; and Holly Sanders, "Panpan: Streetwalking in Occupied Japan," *Pacific Historical Review* 81, 3 (2012): 425.

48 Some historians, including scholar David Bercuson, have tied the Canadian contingent's higher VD rates to the failure of Canadian officials to provide sufficiently for the "physical and spiritual well-being" of troops. In contrast to their British and Australian counterparts, the Canadians did not open a dedicated recreation centre in Japan for troops on leave until late in the war. However, this does not sufficiently explain the difference in rates. It may have had more to do with how much disposable income soldiers had. For example, Canadian troops earned "$14.25 CAD more in basic pay every week" than the average British soldier. David Bercuson, *Blood on the Hills: The Canadian Army in the Korean War* (Toronto: University of Toronto Press, 1999), 174; and K. Meghan Fitzpatrick, "Prostitutes,

Penicillin and Prophylaxis: Fighting Venereal Disease in the Commonwealth Division during the Korean War, 1950–1953," *Social History of Medicine* 28, 3 (2015): 573.

49 ADMS War Diary, Monthly Liaison Letter, no. 14, July 1952, TNA, WO 281/887; AQ Branch, Commonwealth Division, June 1951, TNA, WO 281/25; and Director of Army Health, 5 June 1963, TNA, WO 32/17701.

50 ADMS, Monthly Liaison Letter, no. 14; D.K. Tucker, ADMS Conference, 22 December 1952, TNA, WO 281/887; ADMS, Monthly Liaison Letter, no. 22, March 1953, TNA, WO 281/888; "Report on Organisation and Work of HQ BCFK during Period 1 Oct. 1951–31 Mar. 1952," TNA, WO 308/5; and Fitzpatrick, "Prostitutes, Penicillin and Prophylaxis," 555–75.

51 Mark Harrison, "Sex and the Citizen Soldier: Health, Morals and Discipline in the British Army during the Second World War," in *Medicine and Modern Warfare,* ed. Roger Cooter, Mark Harrison, and Steve Sturdy (Amsterdam: Rodopi, 1999), 225–50.

52 General Sir Anthony Farrar-Hockley, *The British Part in Korean War,* vol. 2, *An Honourable Discharge* (London: Her Majesty's Stationery Office, 1995), 275.

53 "Extract from the Minutes of the 58th Meeting of the Defence Council," 27 May 1952, LAC, RG 24, 83-84/167, box 7718, 20-1-1, pt. 4; 1 Commonwealth Division Monthly Liaison Letter, September 1952, TNA, WO 281/887; Brigadier J.R. Rockingham, Recollections of Korea, LAC, MG 31-G12, John Meredith Rockingham Fonds; and Watson, *Far Eastern Tour,* 138.

54 Robert Turner, *Moments That Forever Haunt Me: An Account of One of the Worst Periods of the Korean War* (Kemptville, ON: Veterans Publications, 2005), 6–7.

55 Fitzpatrick, "Invisible Scars," 117; and 25 FDS War Diary, 1951–53, LAC, RG 24-C-3, vols. 18395–97; and Edgar Jones and Simon Wessely, *Shell Shock to PTSD: Military Psychiatry from 1900 to the Gulf War* (London: Taylor and Francis Group/Psychology Press, 2005), 121.

56 25 FDS War Diary, 1951–53.

57 Royal Canadian Army Medical Corps Study Papers, "Medical General Series – Psychiatric Casualties in Battle," CWM 19840049-035, Textual Records 58C 3 22.1.

58 "Medical General Series – Psychiatric Casualties in Battle."

59 Carol MacDonald, Kerry Chamberlain, and Nigel Long, "PTSD and Its Effects in Vietnam Veterans: The New Zealand Experience," *NZ Journal of Psychology* 24, 2 (1995): 63.

60 25 FDS War Diary, 1951–53; and H.F. Wood, *Strange Battleground,* 275.

61 25 FDS War Diary, 1951–53; ADMS War Diary, 1951–53, TNA, WO 281/886-88; Col. Anderton, ADMS, 1 Commonwealth Division, "Questionnaire on Korean Campaign, 1950–1952," RAMC Muniments Collection, RAMC/761/4; and J.S. McCannel, ADMS Monthly Liaison Letter, no. 26, July 1953, TNA, WO 281/888.

62 Flood, "Psychiatric Casualties," 45.

63 Watson, *Far Eastern Tour,* 161–64.

64 Watson, *Far Eastern Tour,* 161; and Howard N. Cole, *NAAFI in Uniform* (United Kingdom: London, NAAFI, 1982), 178.

65 Operation of the Officers' Mess in Korea, 1 PPCLI War Diary, App. 46, LAC, RG 24.

66 Watson, *Far Eastern Tour,* 169.

67 Kathy Bettinardi-Angres, "Understanding the Disease of Addiction," *Journal of Nursing Regulation* 1, 2 (2010): 31.

68 Cowdrey, *Medics' War,* 250.

69 E.C. Ritchie, "Psychiatry in the Korean War: Perils, PIES and Prisoners of War," *Military Medicine* 167, 11 (2002): 902.

70 Ritchie, "Psychiatry in the Korean War."

71 "Historical Notes: A Branch," TNA, WO 308/9.

72 For a patient to qualify for repatriation, they had to be incapable of return to duty for a

period of over 120 days. "Evacuation Policy: Korean Theatre of Operations," 23 May 1951, LAC, RG 24, 1983-1984/048, box 2153, file 5835-I, pt. I.

73 Fitzpatrick, *Invisible Scars,* 82; and David Oates, "Memories of Kure, Japan: A Personal Experience," Memories of Kure, Japan: A Medic in the Korean War, https://www.kurememories.com/page4.htm, accessed 10 June 2010; and Rawling, *Myriad Challenges,* 79.

74 House of Commons, Evidence to Subcommittee on Veterans Affairs of the Standing Committee on National Defence and Veterans Affairs, 37th Parl., 3rd Sess., No. 004 (5 May 2004) (Mr. David Cotter), https://www.ourcommons.ca/DocumentViewer/en/37-3/SVET/meeting-4/evidence#Int-923112

75 Jillian Ikin Sims and Dean McKenzie, *Health Study 2005: Australian Veterans of the Korean War* (Dept. of Epidemiology and Preventative Medicine, Faculty of Medicine, Nursing and Health Sciences, Monash University, 2005), 11–12.

76 Fitzpatrick, *Invisible Scars,* 91.

11
Canada's Korean War Dead

Andrew Burtch

Brigadier-General W.H.S. Macklin is an inescapable presence when studying the Canadian Army's response to the Korean War. He was a veteran of the Hundred Days campaign of the First World War, a staff officer and brigade commander during the Second World War, including a role preparing Canadians for the Aleutian campaign, and from 1949 until his retirement in 1954 the army's adjutant-general.[1] His views, especially on the nature of the volunteers who made up the Canadian Army Special Force, had an important influence on the writing of the official history of the Korean War.

If nothing else, Macklin was a stickler for details. One of the things that caught his eye in the days immediately following the Korean War's armistice in 1953 was a series of inaccuracies in reporting about Canada's war effort. Macklin wrote to the staff of the Directorate of Personnel Records: "I have seen two or three despatches which give the number of Canadians who died in Korea as 296." For example, he continued, an editorial that appeared in the *Ottawa Citizen* on 28 July stated: "Of the men who engaged on land 1500 were casualties of whom more than 200 were killed ... We might as well let the world know what the Army actually accomplished. It is most disappointing when an editorial uses the expression 'over 200' when they really mean about 380." He ordered the directorate to confirm the actual number of deaths linked to service in Korea so that the record could be set straight.[2]

Getting to the actual number was an act of some bureaucratic finesse between the armed forces and the Department of Veterans Affairs, and it led to a final number of 516, immortalized in *The Korean War Book of Remembrance*. That book covered all deaths linked to service in Korea between June 1950, when the war began, and December 1956, when the last Canadians left. Although the total number of those killed in action, who died of wounds, or who were missing in action was established early, a fuller accounting of the dead is in order.

Three hundred and twelve Canadians were killed in action, died of wounds, or were missing or presumed dead. A further 143 died from accidents in Korea,

Japan, Canada, and the United States or in transit. Forty-nine soldiers fell ill and died either during or after the war. Eight soldiers died by suicide during the war. And four died as the result of homicide or manslaughter. These figures, developed using archival materials related to the casualty administration and the personnel records of all Canadian soldiers and sailors who died in service during the Korean War, demonstrate that the official number produced to commemorate the war tells us a great deal about the way casualties were classified and recorded and which types of casualties went unrecorded and, as such, became unremembered casualties of the "forgotten war."

Personnel records reveal that fallen service personnel were more than statistics; they provide information about their background, motivations for enlisting, and how their deaths registered with the families. Their families' grief extended for decades beyond receiving the dreaded telegram. Within many of the files, we also see the investigations of boards of inquiry struck in the field that include interviews with the dead's closest friends, their commanding officers, and their chain of command. These records give us a better (if imperfect) picture of the circumstances of the death and the character of the dead.

Slightly fewer than half of the 516 Canadians listed in *The Korean War Book of Remembrance* – 256 soldiers – were killed in action. In the first phase of the Korean War, in winter and spring 1951, Canadian soldiers participating in UN counteroffensives encountered an enemy that, while numerous, was not as well armed with heavy weapons as the UN. From February to April 1951, a period that culminated with the Battle of Kap'yong, the main cause of death was Chinese small arms, primarily from medium machine guns, submachine guns, rifles, grenades, and light mortars.

In their first encounter with the enemy, C Company, 2nd Battalion, Princess Patricia's Canadian Light Infantry (PPCLI) crested Hill 444 and charged the objective. Corporal James Alvin Calkins of Rocky Mountain House, Alberta, fell with three other Canadians as the Chinese rearguard announced its presence with bursts from a concealed machine gun. Calkins, "an alert, vigorous lad who looks the picture of health," was struck with bullets in the chest and just below his right eye. He was killed instantly.[3] Also killed in the first salvo was Private Elliott Gordon Mackay of Charlottetown, Prince Edward Island, the youngest Canadian killed in Korea. He had signed up under his cousin's name and was underage.

Lieutenant-Colonel Jim Stone, the commanding officer of the 2nd Battalion, described the enemy's position succinctly: "In defence they sat tight in fox holes, allowing troops to approach within 15 yards before using their grenades. Machine guns to the rear gave covering protection."[4] Enemy armour and artillery were virtually absent from the battlefield, as was air cover, so fighting on the hills was close, dirty, and bloody. Those who fell were perforated with bullets or slashed open by shards of metal.

The number of deaths by artillery increased markedly as the fighting moved into the static phase. When armistice negotiations began in fall 1951, the Chinese forces dug in and sighted heavier concentrations of fire onto Canadian positions. During the ten weeks leading up to the October 1952 bombardment and raid of B Company, 2nd Battalion, Royal Canadian Regiment positions on Hill 355 (see William Johnston, Chapter 6 in this volume), the exposed Royals endured heavier and heavier bombardments, sometimes up to three hundred shells a day. This resulted in a trickle of fatal and nonfatal casualties as the shells cratered outposts and killed Canadians caught in the open.[5] Canadians on patrol were pinned down with machine-gun fire as Chinese forces and harried with mortar bombs until they could withdraw.

After a lull of a few days in October, the full raid was unleashed on the night of 23 October. A shattering bombardment claimed more than twenty Canadian soldiers. The terrible injuries inflicted by the shelling showed the fragility of the human body. Corporal William Joseph Ryan, a seminary student turned soldier from Montreal, was one of those caught in the open. The record of his injury is stark: "Traumatic amputation left thigh with deep penetration right thigh." After the battle, fellow soldiers recognized his remains only by his facial features. A catalogue of the fatal injuries suffered in this one bombardment chronicles the damage done to other soldiers throughout the night: "Penetration into brain through occipital," "deep penetration with massive destruction left upper lung," and "deep penetration, left mandible, right leg, right groin."[6]

The wounded survivors of the raid trickled into the advanced dressing station and mobile hospitals. A medic remarked of the injuries, "It's a wonder some of those guys were still alive."[7] In his memoir of the Battle of Kap'yong, Hub Gray reflects on "the agonies of remembering" that some survivors endured after Korea: "It is an evocative haunting that pursues one in the dark recesses of memory. Never to be spoken of. It is never shared, contained only within one's self."[8] In the immediate aftermath of the battle, however, the fallen, or what remained of them, were wrapped in tarps and sent south to be registered and interred in Busan. Telegrams raced home to send their families the terrible news.

After enemy action and vehicle accidents, one of the leading causes of death among soldiers deployed to Korea was accidental firearms discharges and so-called battle accidents – from fatigue, faulty equipment, friendly fire from divisional artillery and mortars, and errant landmines. Handling deadly weapons requires strict discipline to avoid unnecessary and avoidable deaths, which explains why contemporary soldiers face unforgiving charges and fines for negligent discharges. Contemporary disciplinary measures are the result of lessons learned in blood, but, in Korea, the rules were not uniformly enforced. For example, in March 1951, Private Herbert Peter Campbell, a Royal Canadian Army Service Corps driver attached to 2 PPCLI, lost his Sten submachine gun and had it replaced with a .38 calibre revolver, which he got into the habit of handling in his off hours. On 13 March, while sitting in his tent in the rear echelon chatting with other soldiers, Campbell's gun fired as he twirled it in his hand, an unfortunate habit. He was sent to hospital with a head wound and died the following day. A board of inquiry struck after his death ruled out suicide and found negligent weapons handling to be the cause of death. They suggested tamely, "It seems reasonable to state that NCOs present could have been more alert in restraining the unnecessary handling of firearms in tented accommodation."[9]

The weapons-handling problem did not go away with time. Two years after Campbell's death, Private Joseph Arthur Adelaide Deschenes, 1st Battalion, Royal 22e Régiment, again sitting in a tent playing with his pistol, joked that if any other soldiers of the regiment were killed, he would leave the front for B Echelon and kill anyone who tried to stop him. He pulled out his pistol to punctuate his decision. A lance corporal told Deschenes to stop fooling around with the weapon, prompting the young soldier to remove the magazine from the pistol. He then jokingly put the pistol to his temple and pulled the trigger, a pantomime of suicide he often would enact after cleaning his weapon. However, this time a bullet was in the chamber. Deschenes died before reaching the regimental aid station. The board of inquiry ruled "careless, but not deliberate, handling of a pistol."[10] Apart from these outlandish accidents, most of the deaths by negligent discharge took place as one might expect, in training accidents, from misfires during sidearm cleanings, or during inspections. In all, approximately twenty Canadian soldiers died because of accidental discharge of their own weapons or because of a weapons accident during the war or after the armistice.

While negligent discharges cleanly fall under the rubric of "accidental death," the circumstances surrounding deaths resulting from the Canadian soldier's proximity to explosive weapons and equipment are considerably more complex. Most of these fatal errors were clear-cut accidents. The first four Canadians to die during the Korean War never made it to the battlefield; all were killed in August 1950 while training at the Canadian Army base in Petawawa, Ontario. As soldiers from the 2nd Battalion, Royal Canadian Regiment, raced through drills at the base's mortar range, one of the bombs dropped down the two-inch mortar tube exploded prematurely, killing four soldiers instantly.[11] Similar incidents took place, such as when grenades exploded in bunkers because of faulty fuses or poor training, or when soldiers nonchalantly picked up and tossed unexploded shells during a patrol.

Other accidents that occurred in the heat of battle defied easy classification. Consider the case of Lance Corporal Frederick Morris. An engineer with 23 Field Squadron, Morris was arming landmines in the approach to Canadian positions when on 12 June 1952, apparently startled by nearby artillery fire in support of an infantry patrol, he slipped onto a buried mine. It exploded, throwing him into the air and landing him directly on an antitank mine laid outside Canadian lines. Little was found of him save for a portion of one arm and his spinal column.[12] Lance Bombardier Cyril Williams Richards arrived as part of A Battery, 1st Regiment, Royal Canadian Horse Artillery, in Korea in 1952. On 11 March 1953, during his troop's shoot against an enemy target, a shell fired by one of the troop's 25-pounder howitzer crews, located behind Richards' gun pit, exploded prematurely and directly above the gun pit. Richards and two other gunners were thrown to the ground. Richards was hit by shell splinters in the stomach and his legs. He received first aid at the site of the accident and was evacuated, first to the Regimental Aid Post and then to an American medical unit, but he died on arrival. A board of inquiry declared his death an accident, even though his death was difficult to distinguish from deaths in the heat of battle when "friendly fire" often claims lives.[13]

The classifications that determined how a death should be categorized were set by Canadian Army Headquarters. In Korea, the standards were set as the result of queries from No. 2 Canadian Administrative Unit, based out of Kure, Japan, shortly after the bulk of the Canadian brigade arrived in Busan in May 1951. The specific category that concerned the administrative unit, tasked with guiding how deployed units communicated and documented casualties, was that of the "battle accident."

The classification "battle accident" was initially adopted by the British. The Canadian Army adopted the term in 1944 during the Italian campaign. The goal of this change appears to have been to reduce administrative strain on units because a battle accident, unlike accidents, did not have to be investigated through a board of inquiry.[14] According to this definition, a battle accident included "accidental injuries sustained in forward areas, but not occurring during action, or in close proximity to the enemy" or "accidental injuries sustained in action or in close proximity to the enemy, but caused by or contributed to the culpable negligence or misconduct of the injured person."[15]

While seemingly clear, the Directorate of Personnel Records registered concern that messages to next of kin that contained this classification raised unnecessary questions about whether the army or the individual was at fault. Major

W.T. Chambers, director of personnel records, suggested the classification be amended to "injured in action," allowing for casualties incurred "while immediately engaged in, going to, or returning from, an engagement with the enemy, whether or not directly attributed to enemy action," as well as injuries in forward areas taking place outside of enemy action, and injuries sustained in action or in proximity to the enemy that are due to individual negligence. Chambers concluded his analysis of the issue by raising concerns about deaths resulting from landmines, which should be classified as "killed in action by mine explosion" rather than accidents, as some had been (and would continue to be) reported. He noted, however, that this classification applied only to enemy mines. "It is appreciated that death or injury could be attributed to one of our own mines, but it is not considered sound for this information to be provided to the next of kin."[16] In other words, the families of soldiers who had been killed by friendly fire would not be informed of the actual circumstances that led to their deaths.

Brigadier M.L. Brennan, director general of army personnel, issued his response to Chambers' findings in July, noting that in modern war the line between the "front" and "rear" areas was blurred. He explained that criteria governing the category "killed in action" or "battle accident" depended on the loose wording – *direct result of enemy action*. He latched on to Chambers' discussion of mine accidents and indicated that "there is nothing accidental about a mine casualty. The enemy placed the mine with deliberate intent. This was a result of enemy action and should be shown as such." But when it came to the question of other accidents – specifically, vehicle accidents, accidental explosions, and injuries due to falls – Brennan opined that *battle accidents* was too broad a term, mainly because it defined these accidents as battle-related because they took place in forward areas. Brennan determined that a new classification was needed to replace the 1944 model. So *battle casualties* would refer to casualties attributable to the enemy regardless of where they took place in a theatre of operations, allowing for mines, long-range artillery, and guerrilla activity to be included. *Nonbattle casualties* would refer to those casualties in the theatre of operations "not attributable to enemy action."[17] These directives, once adopted, were sent forward to No. 2 Canadian Administrative Unit in August 1951 and formed the basis for future classifications of casualties in Korea.

The way that deaths and injuries were interpreted by the forward units, and by the army as a whole, had a direct impact on whether casualties were counted as battle-related. This, in turn, affected how the cause of death was communicated to families. Although the nature of many of the casualties was reasonably evident – killed in action by artillery, death by gunfire wounds, and succumbing to illnesses in theatre – accidents left some considerable room for interpretation and misinterpretation. Take, for example, the case of Private Gerald Payton, 2nd Battalion, Royal Canadian Regiment. His death was classified as "killed in action," yet the regimental war diary for the date of his death, 25 July 1951, states: "A tragic accident occurred in the evening, when Private PAYTON of D Company stepped on a trip flare and was killed instantly."[18] Payton's death was fundamentally similar to the accidental death of Lance Corporal Morris, yet owing to the initial classification, he was deemed killed in action. Perhaps the trip flare was planted by the enemy, but the war diary suggests otherwise.

Take also the case of Cyril Richards, who was killed by an artillery shell that exploded prematurely during a troop shoot against the enemy. His death was considered accidental. In contrast, the death of Private Jean Berchmans Dumas, a soldier with the 2nd Battalion, Royal Canadian Regiment, was initially listed as accidental. When he heard movement in front of his position, he prepared to throw a grenade, and it exploded in his hand, killing him instantly. His death was later reclassified as "killed in action."[19] Apart from Dumas' closer proximity to the enemy, the circumstances of the two men's death were similar enough to indicate that the categories and classifications were malleable and subject to interpretation and debate.

Many of the accidental deaths were attributed, at least in part, to alcohol consumption. Historically, Canadian soldiers were impressive drinkers, in step with Canadian civilians who, as a whole, consumed beer, wine, and spirits in prodigious quantities.[20] Whether it was liquid courage, a taste of home, or a sleep aid, alcohol overseas was often a necessary evil, even if it was the root cause of countless courts martial.[21] Despite the hardships of life in the Korean hills, the relief of a stiff drink was never out of reach for the enterprising soldier. In fact, Canadian units received a regular issue of beer (one bottle of Japanese Asahi beer a day) and a shot of rum. Co-located with other national formations within the Commonwealth division, Canadians could also trade with ease. And following in the grand tradition of civilians having the misfortune of being located near an active warzone, brothels and off-limits bars thrived in villages and hamlets behind the front lines, catering to Korean and UN forces, who proved difficult to police.[22] So soldiers, much like their civilian counterparts, over-indulged, leading to accidents, as tragic as they were foreseeable.

Even when beer and rum were not readily available, or when the supply had been exhausted, enterprising soldiers improvised. On 17 March 1951, 2 PPCLI feted the birthday of Lady Patricia Ramsay, their honorary colonel and namesake. Food, sports, and drink were consumed. The festivities followed the Patricias' gruelling northward march during UN counteroffensives in February and early March. Each man received five beers that night, three from the battalion and two from Lady Patricia. When that issue ran out, some soldiers brought out illicit alcohol. Altogether, six men, including Private Kenneth Roger Monague, were evacuated to hospital for alcohol poisoning.

Monague had enlisted on 16 August 1950 in Toronto, two hundred kilometres south of his home in the Christian Island Reserve No. 30, part of Beausoleil First Nation, on the southern shore of Georgian Bay. Like most of Canada's Korean War recruits, he had an eighth-grade education and stopped school at age fourteen to work. In Korea, he fell ill shortly after drinking wood alcohol – "canned heat" – and died of respiratory failure on 21 March 1951 at the 60th Field Ambulance, a hospital managed by the Indian Army's medical corps. Monague and three others were listed as having died of "acute alcoholism." The sad news wound its way to Monague's mother, who still resided at Christian Island. The army notified the Ontario Provincial Police, who reached out to the Indian agent. On the morning of 22 March 1951, the police and the agent boarded a boat to travel to the reserve. They characterized his death as "self-inflicted." Monague's mother demanded to know what had transpired. She pleaded with the army and requested "full particulars ... I cannot believe that death would have been self-inflicted, as he had always in his letters home expressed his desire to be home again, someday." No additional details were forthcoming, save for notification of Monague's burial in Busan.[23] It was a cruel and unnecessary obfuscation of the nature of his death, making it appear to be a suicide instead of an accident.

In Korea, the PPCLI took the deaths of the four soldiers seriously. All stores of wood alcohol were confiscated and placed under the battalion's control. On the day of the evacuation, the battalion's commanding officer, Lieutenant-Colonel Jim Stone, assembled his men and addressed them about spiking their beer with canned heat. He "mentioned the case of the two men who died in A Coy as a direct result of doing so" and noted that "all canned heat is to be withdrawn from the battalion."[24] Though nothing so dramatic as the March 1951 mass poisoning recurred, six other Canadians listed in *The Korean War Book of Remembrance* died as a result of confirmed or suspected alcohol poisoning either in Canada, in Korea, or while on leave in Japan.[25]

Many other accidental deaths were linked to misadventure due to alcohol consumption or the search for alcohol in theatre. The most peculiar deaths by alcoholic misadventure were likely those of Privates Robert Allan Christie and Albert Clifford Earhart, members of the Black Watch who arrived in Korea after the armistice to supervise the Demilitarized Zone. In January 1954, both men disappeared after trying to cross the Imjin River in search of unlicensed bars found behind UN lines. The ice broke, and the men were heard screaming before they fell silent. Christie was recovered downriver in April 1954 and identified by a fellow soldier because of the tattoo on his left arm. Alarmingly, on closer examination, Christie's body was riddled with bullets in the head, chest, and lower extremities. The autopsy discovered bullets of American and British manufacture, leading the Board of Inquiry to conclude that perhaps, in death, Christie floated past a firing range facing the river. Earhart was not recovered until June 1954. The pair were reunited in the memorial cemetery in Busan.[26] If deaths by alcohol poisoning and misadventure were few among the Canadians who died overseas, alcohol played a supporting role in many accidental deaths and often figured in the final hours of deaths by suicide.

Four months after the Korean War armistice, Private Benoit Boutin was in crisis. The second of sixteen children who grew up on a farm in Sainte-Jeanne-d'Arc, Quebec, Boutin attended school until June 1945, when he completed his second year of classical training at the Rimouski seminary. He stopped because he lost interest. He chose to enlist in April 1951 and arrived in theatre the next year.

Originally scheduled to depart for Korea in July 1953, Boutin missed his draft, likely owing to poor behaviour since he was repeatedly absent without leave both during training and while overseas. He did not return home until October 1953. Like most soldiers returning from Korea, Boutin received thirty days' special disembarkation leave with pay. He returned to the family farm, where his father and siblings lived. He spent much of the following month drinking, despite interventions from his family and priest. On the day before he was scheduled to return to service, and after his younger siblings left for school, Benoit found a .22 rifle in his father's wardrobe. He went upstairs with the rifle and told his sister Hughette to watch out for a Chinese attack. Several minutes later, Hughette heard a shot. She heard the rifle fall to the floor. She did not want to go upstairs, so she went to see her neighbour. "J'avais peur qu'il me prenne pour une chinoise et qu'il me tire par le chassis." When she and her siblings returned, she told them that she thought Benoit had shot himself. They entered the house singing so that Benoit would not think they were Chinese and fire on them. She and her other brother went upstairs and found that Benoit had died as a result of a bullet through the temple.[27]

Eight soldiers who enlisted for Korean War service died by suicide in theatre and at home. Some did so before being issued their uniform; some while on the verge of returning home; one within a month of coming home. These men represent 1.5 percent of the total number of casualties (8 out of 516) resulting from Canada's participation in the Korean War. There is nothing exceptional about these men being included in *The Korean War Book of Remembrance* or being buried with military honours at home or overseas. The same was true of deaths by suicide in the world wars. But the true tally of deaths by suicide may never be known. To qualify for inclusion in *The Korean War Book of Remembrance,* a soldier had to meet clear criteria.

The eight suicides were those that could be considered service-related and included in *The Korean War Book of Remembrance.* A key element in the tally of official deaths was the question of whether a soldier was still on duty related to Korea. This was determined by the time they had enlisted for duty with the Canadian Army Special Forces (but before they actually deployed to the Korean theatre), and in many others had to do with postredeployment policies. Each soldier, upon his return from the Far East theatre, received a thirty-day disembarkation leave, after which he would report back to his unit either for continued service and a new posting or a discharge from the armed forces. In that month-long window, some soldiers drowned during boating outings with families, others died in road accidents, and, in one case, a man died while splitting wood at the family farm. All were counted as deaths related to Korean War service because the soldier was still considered part of the Canadian contingent for Korea.

Although counting soldiers who died by accident or misadventure after returning home may seem like an inflation of casualties, in the case of suicides, this thirty-day rule means that deaths resulting from traumas suffered in Korea have surely been undercounted. The choice was made to simplify the gathering of names for *The Korean War Book of Remembrance* and to alleviate the administrative burdens of the Canadian Army. The committee overseeing the book decided not to include deaths among veterans who continued to serve with the army after they returned to their units from their thirty-day leave block. Those who had Korea service on their record but died while still serving with the army would be considered deaths on strength in the regular forces as opposed to Korea deaths, even though a case could be made that their deaths were related to their earlier Korea service.[28] It would be impossible to determine how many Canadian veterans of Korea took their lives in the decades after the war. However unsatisfying, it appears that few countries have tracked veteran suicides in anything approaching a comprehensive manner. The United States did not begin formally tracking suicides until the early 2000s, for example.[29] In the same way, it may well be impossible to reach a convincing or satisfying conclusion about what motivated these suicides.

In discussing suicides in the Canadian Army during the Second World War, Department of National Defence historian Yves Tremblay points out that those soldiers who did die by suicide appear to have had many of the same motivations as people in civilian cases: "Broken hearts and schizophrenic conditions ... insoluble financial problems, marital problems, alcohol problems, and the expectation of a difficult life after the return to peace."[30] Indeed, in most of the cases cited above, bearing witness to traumatic events does not appear to have been a primary factor, but perhaps it was a contributing factor. Most of those who killed themselves in Korea were not frontline soldiers. Nor did most have direct combat experience. This phenomenon seems to have carried over from the First and Second World Wars. It is perhaps enough to conclude, as Tanya Navaneelan notes in her overview of Canadian suicide rates, "No single determinant, including mental illness, is enough on its own to cause a suicide. Rather, suicide typically results from the interaction of many factors."[31]

A close reading of the personnel files for the dead reveals how familial, economic, psychological, and professional pressures, from pre-existing dynamics to those imposed by the war, intersected and resulted in fatalities. Alcohol factored into military and civilian life, both as a stress reliever and as an aggravating risk for suicide. Based on testimonies offered at the courts of inquiry, the Canadian Army did not seem to offer many neuropsychological supports, but informal support networks – such as soldiers watching other soldiers, noticing when someone was off, and trying (and failing) to assist fellows in need of help – existed. In the aftermath of witnessing a suicide, soldiers struggled to understand what drove their colleagues to take their own lives. This question, more than any other, likely lingered long after the war's end.

For much of history, deaths by disease and illness were war's greatest killers until the widespread use of preventive medicine and effective antibiotics – within the military, at least – reduced these deaths to acceptable losses. Korea was the third war where this medical advantage played a key role in reducing the number of Canadian deaths and evacuations due to pathogens, infections, and other illnesses.[32] Of course, the coverage was not absolute, as even Colonel Jim Stone, 2 PPCLI's commanding officer, was evacuated for treatment for smallpox about a month before the triumph at Kap'yong.[33] This alarming incident, likely the result of contact with dead civilians in one of the villages the PPCLI passed through as part of their winter advance, led the entire battalion to be revaccinated out of a preponderance of caution.[34] Other diseases common to deployed military forces such as dysentery were debilitating and led to wastage as troops drank from unclean water in unsanitary conditions, but they were not usually fatal. In fact, only one Canadian soldier died of dysentery during the Korean War.[35] Careful attention to sanitation facilities during the more static phase of the war helped eliminate some of the risks of gastrointestinal afflictions.

Far more frightening for the Canadian soldiers and their medical establishment in Korea was the onset of tropical diseases spread by insects and other vermin. Malaria, historically one of humanity's most deadly afflictions, only claimed one Canadian soldier, no doubt a testament to the effective-if-unpleasant regime of antimalarial drugs the brigade's medical authorities administered to prevent the worst effects of the illness.[36] Far more worrying for Canadian soldiers and the medical establishment was the novel illness of hemorrhagic fever. United Nations forces began encountering this endemic illness in spring 1951.[37] Transmitted by contact with rodents, the fever caused vomiting, headache, and cough followed by internal and external bleeding. As historian Brent Byron Watson notes, the disease's terrible symptoms and the lack of effective treatment made the prospect of contracting the fever a frightful environmental threat and the source of rumours among soldiers in the line.[38] One soldier recalled the death of Sergeant Stuart Franklin Cowan from the fever: "The medical staff could do nothing for him, except watch him die, bleeding from every orifice of his body, including his navel and eyeballs; nothing would stop the hemorrhaging."[39]

Though some estimates for deaths among Canadians from this frightful disease range as high as twenty-six soldiers, a complete review of the personnel files reveals that only five deaths were linked to the fever, confirming Watson's hypothesis that ostensibly high rates of hemorrhagic fever in the Canadian brigade were due to misdiagnosis by doctors wary of this new and ominous illness and widespread fear by soldiers.[40]

Most of the forty-nine deaths resulting from illness or natural causes were caused by afflictions that were relatively commonplace in North America such as heart disease or cancer. For example, at least eighteen Canadian soldiers listed in *The Korean War Book of Remembrance* died as a result of heart disease or complications affecting the heart. The first to die from heart disease was Private William James Lewis Austin. On the morning of his death, 20 December 1950, Austin was discharged owing to his poor health. He had served in the Second World War with an antitank regiment, fighting in northwest Europe. At one point in his service, he was treated for battle exhaustion. His health suffered after the war, and he complained of chronic stomach and chest pains. Recruiters overlooked some of his health complaints when the call went out for the Canadian Army Special Force in August 1950 because of desperate conditions overseas and his prior experience. Poor health, anxiety, and post-traumatic stress led to his being discharged on 20 December. After having lunch with his mother, Austin fell ill and collapsed on the sidewalk in Kingston, Ontario. He was taken to hospital and pronounced dead. Owing to Canadian Army regulations, notwithstanding his discharge that morning, his paybook had been stamped, so he was paid up to and including that day.[41] Technically, he remained in the Canadian Army Special Force, and while his death had nothing to do with Korea service, he is nevertheless counted among Canada's Korean War dead.

If heart conditions manifested suddenly – claiming soldiers on the street, in their troopship berth, or in their tent – cancer, that dragon, manifested more insidiously over time. Of the twelve deaths caused by cancer (approximately a quarter of those who died by illness or natural causes), approximately half contracted it after their service in Korea. In some cases, the deaths were linked to service overseas, some as much as four years earlier. For example, in January 1951, Craftsman Ronald Harvey Taylor was serving in a workshop in Korea when he was struck in the shoulder by a flying flange from a truck differential. Pain from the injury persisted, and when doctors found a tumour in his humerus, he was evacuated from Korea in September 1951. The doctors opted to amputate his arm and shoulder. He was fitted with a shoulder prosthetic and discharged from the army. He died in April 1954 in London, Ontario, after the cancer, Ewing sarcoma, spread to his heart and brain.[42]

Other deaths were likewise recorded and added to *The Korean War Book of Remembrance* up to the December 1956 cut-off date for inclusion. If that date, instituted to recognize Canada's impending departure from Korea in 1957, were removed, surely the number of deaths related to illnesses contracted or discovered while in Korea would increase, much as in cases of deaths by suicide.

Given the high-stress situations soldiers found themselves in, it should come as no surprise that murder at home and overseas led to some deaths. Four Canadian soldiers died as the result of criminal acts: two of these soldiers died at home, two while deployed. The first death under questionable circumstances was that of Private Harry Blake MacEachron, one of the soldiers of 3 PPCLI training at Camp Wainwright, Alberta, in June 1951. After an evening of drinking and banter, MacEachron and another soldier, Frederick James Sabbatis, got into a dispute and went into the stores tent to fetch boxing gloves to settle it. Somehow Sabbatis and MacEachron ended up handling rifles instead, and Sabbatis shot MacEachron at close range. Jim Empey heard the shot, spotted Sabbatis running from the tent, and held him while he investigated the cries for help.

Empey witnessed MacEachron's death. He turned to Sabbatis.

> I asked him why he did it and he said he didn't do it, so I didn't say anything more. We just stood there. When MacEachron was crying for help, I thought I could help him but I was about 4 feet away from him and I could hear the blood gushing out, and I could see where the hole was blown in his back and I knew right then that an artery was cut through the chest, there was nothing I could do but stand there and watch.[43]

The military's board of inquiry and the RCMP investigation reveal that MacEachron's death bore some of the hallmarks of negligent weapons discharges elsewhere. Both parties had been drinking, and Sabbatis insisted the weapon went off accidentally. If the two had not been involved in an argument beforehand, one wonders whether the army would have marked off MacEachron's death simply as an accident stemming from negligence rather than a criminal affair.

The death of Private Emile Joseph Sanscartier, 1st Battalion, Royal 22e Régiment, likewise muddies the issue of classification. Major Guy D'Artois, a decorated veteran of the Second World War, was forced to shoot the soldier with his pistol after Sanscartier, apparently unstable, menaced his fellow troops with his rifle. Sanscartier was buried alongside other Canadian casualties. Officially, his cause of death was "accidentally killed."[44]

For many families, the greatest tragedies were cases where their loved ones were killed in Korea and their remains never recovered. Of the 516 official deaths listed, five Canadian soldiers died at sea in aircraft crashes or were swept overboard during naval operations. Another sixteen went missing in action during fighting on the peninsula. The next of kin didn't even have the small comfort of seeing a snapshot of a headstone in the Busan cemetery. For some families, the hope that their loved ones had somehow survived stretched on for decades.

Stories swirling around the death of an individual soldier could cause lasting harm to their loved ones at home. John Richard Toole, known as "Dickie" to his family, enlisted in the Canadian Army as part of the August 1950 recruiting effort for the Special Force for Korea. He embarked as a reinforcement for 2 PPCLI in mid-April 1951 and arrived in theatre in May. On the night of 11 October 1951, Corporal Toole was out with a wiring party when Chinese forces attacked 2 Platoon of A Company. The platoon managed to repel the attack with the battalion's first use of recoilless rifles in the field, but one soldier was killed by mortar fire. In the aftermath, Toole went missing.[45]

When the Chinese machine guns and mortars opened up, there were several ridges where Toole could have gone for cover and may not have heard the withdrawal order. The members of his platoon did not see him wounded during the fighting, and his platoon commander, Lieutenant A.W. Watt, thought he might have been captured because, Watt suggested, he tended to freeze up under enemy fire.[46] The family received notice that Toole was missing in action. But a month later, the waters were muddied when the *Toronto Telegram* reported that "frontline rumors persist that Toole's body was later found in a straw shack between the lines and that he had been murdered by Chinese Communists by being shot in the back." Major Vance Lilley, the officer in charge of the investigation into Toole's disappearance, denied the rumour. Army Public Affairs contacted the *Telegram* and the *Hamilton Spectator* to shut down further speculation.[47] In a March 1952 telegram, the army informed Toole's mother that her son might have been taken prisoner, but then the list of suspected prisoners was revised and Toole's name was removed. Nellie Toole wrote the army that summer to explain her concern that her son was no longer considered a prisoner. Major-General Macklin replied, expressing the army's frustration that all efforts to contact prisoners had failed and that "every possible effort is being made by the United Nations authorities to obtain some positive details."[48]

Two years after Toole's disappearance, when the armistice was signed and prisoner exchanges began, the Toole family was still waiting by their radios to hear the news that their son was among the Canadians filtering through the lines.[49] News finally came in October 1953, when Macklin wrote to Nellie Toole to inform her of the results of the Canadian Army's investigation: "In view of an article appearing in a Toronto newspaper over a year ago in which your son's name was mentioned, it was hoped that, if a fact, the interrogation of repatriated Prisoners of War would produce some evidence, but, to date, no word has been forthcoming." Macklin asked Toole's mother if she had any other correspondence or evidence that would provide proof of life.[50] When no further information was forthcoming, a review of the available evidence led the Canadian Army's Directorate of Records to conclude that Toole should be reclassified as killed in action on 11 October 1951. The Toole family was informed of this news in November 1953.

Toole's family did not give up hope that the military was mistaken. As late as 1985, when the government of Brian Mulroney was building diplomacy with the Chinese government, Toole's family wrote to Mulroney demanding that the matter of Toole's whereabouts be determined as part of the talks. In September 1985, Mulroney directed his office to launch an inquiry to locate records about Toole's disappearance. His deputy noted, "His family refuses to believe he is dead and that still, somewhere, he is a POW."[51] In June 1992, it's likely the family still held out hope. That month, Russian president Boris Yeltsin pledged during a visit to Canada to help investigate the case of a soldier who went missing in Korea in 1951, presumably the story of Toole's disappearance.[52]

In summer 2021, the Department of National Defence's Casualty Identification Program launched an effort in concert with the Republic of Korea's Ministry of Defence Agency for Killed in Action Recovery and Identification to renew the search for the fifteen Canadians who went missing during the war. The goal was to identify recovered human remains. The Department of National Defence put out a call to family members and descendants of the missing to aid in the forensic search. As of publication, the results of this research were not yet known.[53]

Surviving family members reflected on "Dickie's" long absence from their lives and revealed that their mother had been the primary force pushing for answers about his disappearance in the face of stories circulating that he had been killed, wounded, disappeared, murdered, and so on. The loss of her son had a physical and mental impact; according to her daughter, she died ten years after Toole disappeared, partly from grief.[54] Toole's father, oldest brother, and partner carried on the search, building a file of letters and accounts that could help bolster their case to find closure. While in later years they assumed the worst, stories still circulated in the family that perhaps he had suffered from a head wound, wandered off, and settled down and started a new life in Korea with a local family.

As unlikely as that outcome might have been, it was, nonetheless, a common narrative among families of those who lost someone in the world wars, and it was a hopeful narrative that allowed the missing to live fruitful lives, even if their families at home were left wondering about their fate. In the Toole family, though, Remembrance Day was particularly difficult. Memories of Dickie came closer to the surface, and his portrait, hanging in their homes, became a more marked presence. Even though family members are now too young to have memories of Dickie and his character, they still hope for answers.[55]

Research into the personnel files, casualty administration procedures, and the process by which *The Korean War Book of Remembrance* offers up the figure of 516 Canadian soldiers who died between 1950 and 1956. But this figure is a necessary tabulation, not one that captures the full cost of the Korean War. It doesn't capture the lives lost through illness or service-related physical or mental injury years after a soldier's deployment ended.

The number of Canadians lost in Korea is dwarfed by losses among their enemies and their allies in the United Nations Command during the war. During the opening phase of the Chinese offensive leading to Kap'yong in April 1951, hundreds of Chinese soldiers in a single regiment drowned in one hour when they misjudged the strength of the Imjin River's tides during a crossing.[56] The Canadian raid on Dieppe in August 1942 resulted in nearly double the total number of Canadian fatal casualties during the Korean War. Second World War veterans would later point to the comparatively lower death rates in Korea as a rationale to exclude Korean War veterans from local Legions or to call into question whether Korea was a war like the one they had fought. For historians, however, the number of dead is of less interest than what personnel records reveal about the dead, the nature of the losses, and how casualty administration and notifications were forced to change over the course of the war. These important records, and hopefully this exploration, reveal how these losses were also felt at home, and how, in some small measure, the Canadians who died as the result of service in Korea are remembered.

Notes

1 "Maj. Gen W.H.S. Macklin, Ex-Adjutant-General Defence Policy Critic," *Globe and Mail,* 26 November 1966.

2 Brigadier-General W.H.S. Macklin to Directorate of Personnel Records, 28 July 1953, Library and Archives Canada (LAC), Department of National Defence, RG 24, 1983-84/048, box 918, file 2590-1929/2, pt. 3.

3 Personnel file, James Alvin Calkins, M-80003, LAC.

4 "Notes on Talk by Lt-Col J.R. Stone at AHQ, 0900 Hours 5 Jun 1951," Department of National Defence, Directorate of History and Heritage (DHH), 681.011(D3) Operations.

5 Vince Courtenay, "New Recruit," unpublished manuscript in author's possession.

6 Personnel file, William Joseph Ryan, SD-4862, LAC. The other fatalities mentioned are Privates Edward Joseph Wright, Alexander Rowbotham, and Frederick Joseph Whiting.

7 Cosmo Kapitaniuk, as quoted in Ted Barris, *Deadlock in Korea: Canadians at War, 1950–1953* (Toronto: MacMillan, 1999), 204.

8 Hub Gray, *Beyond the Danger Close: The Korean Experience Revealed* (Toronto: Northwest Printing, 2003), 154.

9 Board of inquiry, personnel file, Herbert Peter Campbell, B-800627, LAC.

10 Board of inquiry, personnel file, Private Joseph Arthur Adelaide Deschenes, SD-4744, LAC.

11 The soldiers were Corporal Kenney Ray and Privates William James Brayley, Norman Hughes, and Danuiel Murphy. LAC, RG24-C-1-c, vol. 31838, file 1012-P90, pt. 1.

12 Statement of Captain K.J. Chisholm, 23rd Independent Field Squadron, personnel file, Lance Corporal Frederick Morris, SH-13071, LAC.

13 Board of Inquiry, personnel file, Lance Bombardier Cyril William Richards, SK-8468, LAC.

14 No. 2 Canadian Administrative Unit, ADM letter 25, 21 May 1951, LAC, RG 24 1983-84/048, box 918, file 2590-1929/2, pt. 1.

15 Memorandum, Directorate of Personnel Records, Major W.T. Chambers, 19 July 1951, LAC, RG 24 1983-84/048, box 918, file 2590-1929/2, pt. 1.

16 Memorandum, Major W.T. Chambers, 19 July 1951.

17 Memorandum, 26 July 1951, Brigadier W.L. Brennan, LAC, RG 24 1983-84/048, box 918, file 2590-1929/2, pt. 1.

18 2 RCR, war diary, 25 July 1951, LAC, RG 24-C-3, vol. 18,342.

19 Personnel file, Private Jean Berchmans Dumas, D-801455, LAC. See also 2 Royal 22e Régiment, war diary, 2 October 195, LAC, RG 24-C-3, vol. 18357.

20 Sales of beer in Canada averaged approximately ninety-five litres per person per year between 1949 and 1956, for example. That would roughly equal 3.5 pints a week for every Canadian of legal drinking age. Beer sales in Canada peaked in the mid-1970s, when each Canadian purchased approximately five pints a week. Statistics Canada, "Control and Sale of Alcoholic Beverages, Year Ending March 31, 2021," *The Daily,* https://www150.statcan.gc.ca/n1/daily-quotidien/210421/dq210421b-eng.htm.

21 Tim Cook, "'More Medicine Than a Beverage': 'Demon Rum' and the Canadian Trench Soldier in the Second World War," *Canadian Military History* 9, 1 (2000): 17, https://scholars.wlu.ca/cmh/vol9/iss1/2/. See also Alex Souchen, "Killing Time, Not Germans: Reserve Positions in the 3rd Canadian Infantry Division during the Battle of Normandy," *Canadian Military History* 30, 1 (2021): 22–25, https://scholars.wlu.ca/cmh/vol30/iss1/1/.

22 Meghan Fitzpatrick, "Prostitutes, Penicillin, and Prophylactics: Fighting Venereal Disease in the Commonwealth Division during the Korean War," *Social History of Medicine* 28, 3 (2015): 555–75.

23 Personnel file, Private Kenneth Monague, B-800846, LAC.

24 2 PPCLI, war diary, 20 March 1951, Princess Patricia's Canadian Light Infantry Regimental Museum and Archives (PPCLI Archives).
25 Alcohol poisoning or deaths from natural causes aggravated by alcohol were suspected in the case of John Akinam, Laurie Albert Canning, George Tremblay, William Earl Morrison, Michel Paul Chiasson, and Bennie Clements.
26 Personnel file, Private Robert Allan Christie, SM-18283, LAC.
27 Personnel file, Private Benoit Boutin, SE-6813, LAC.
28 "Books of Remembrance – Minutes of Second Meeting, 7 February 1959," LAC, MG 32 D252, Allan B. Beddoe Fonds, vol. 31, file 12.
29 John Bateson, *The Last and Greatest Battle: Finding the Will, Commitment, and Strategy to End Military Suicides* (New York: Oxford University Press, 2015), 20–21.
30 Tremblay reflects: "When you read files of Second World War soldiers who committed suicide, it is striking that so few seem related to actual combat or horrors of war or scenes of poverty or the liberation of death camps": Yves Tremblay, "Back from War," *Literary Review of Canada,* January-February 2012, http://reviewcanada.ca/magazine/2012/01/back-from-war/.
31 Tanya Navaneelan, "Suicide Rates: An Overview," Statistics Canada Catalogue 86-624-X, https://www150.statcan.gc.ca/n1/pub/82-624-x/2012001/article/11696-eng.htm.
32 See Tim Cook, *Lifesavers and Body Snatchers: Medical Care and the Struggle for Survival in the Great War* (Toronto: Penguin Random House, 2022), 397–420.
33 2 PPCLI, war diary, 24 March 1951, PPCLI Archives.
34 Brent Byron Watson, *Far Eastern Tour: The Canadian Infantry in Korea, 1950–1953* (Montreal/Kingston: McGill-Queen's University Press, 2002), 126.
35 Personnel file, Lance-Corporal Jean Charles Madore, SD-4881, LAC.
36 Watson, *Far Eastern Tour,* 128–29; and personnel file, Corporal Marc Henri Michaud, SE-103633, LAC.
37 John R. Paul and William W. McClure, "Epidemic Hemorrhagic Fever Attack Rates among United Nations Troops during the Korean War," *American Journal of Epidemiology* 68, 2 (1958): 126.
38 Watson, *Far Eastern Tour,* 131.
39 Earl Richardson, quoted in Watson, *Far Eastern Tour,* 131. Richardson misremembered Cowan's name as "Crowen" in his account.
40 Watson, *Far Eastern Tour,* 131–32.
41 "If Part II order entry and discharge certificate show Pte Austin as discharged effective 20 dec 50 and he was paid up to and including that date in accordance with P&A 67(3) he was still in the army at the time of his death": personnel file, Private William James Austin, C-9953, LAC.
42 Personnel file, Craftsman Ronald Harvey Taylor, SB-153603, LAC.
43 Trial transcript, *Frederick James Sabbatis,* Supreme Court, Provincial Archives of Alberta Accession 83.1 Box 68 File 11083-C.
44 In a clipping attached to the board of inquiry, the Canadian Press wire story was headlined "War-Famed Major Kills Gun-Blazing Rebel Private." An accompanying analysis contained a finding from the legal arm of the Canadian Army: "Army Shooting Called Legal If Defensive: 'Well Within Law' If No Other Way to Keep Order."
45 2 PPCLI, war diary, 11 October 1951, PPCLI Archives.
46 Questionnaire of a missing officer or soldier, 22 October 1951, personnel file, John Richard Toole, B-801850, LAC.
47 Lt-Col. H. Stewart to Director General Army Personnel, 23 November 1951, Toole personnel file.
48 Toole personnel file.

49 "Sarnia Kin Await News of Pte Toole," *Sarnia Canadian Observer*, 3 September 1953.
50 Macklin to Mrs. Charles Toole, 7 October 1953, Toole personnel file.
51 Patrick MacAdam to Hon. Harvie Andre, 12 September 1985, Toole personnel file.
52 *House of Commons Debates*, 34th Parl., 3rd Sess. (19 June 1992) (Sheila Maureen Copps), https://www.lipad.ca/full/permalink/3916946/. The request to Yeltsin emerged from an initiative from the Historic Sites and Monuments Board to locate missing soldiers, according to then MP Sheila Copps. Copps, private correspondence with author, 10 June 2022.
53 Canada, Department of National Defence, news release, "Seeking the Families of Canadian Army Soldiers Missing in Korea," 28 June 2021, https://www.canada.ca/en/department-national-defence/news/2021/06/seeking-the-families-of-canadian-army-soldiers-missing-in-korea.html.
54 Martin, phone conversation with author, 27 July 2022.
55 Martin, phone conversation with author, 27 July 2022.
56 Xiaobing Li, *China's Battle for Korea: The 1951 Spring Offensive* (Bloomington: Indiana University Press, 2014), 108–9.

Part 3
Korean War Memories and Legacies

12
The Korean War's Prisoners

Jonathan Vance

The story of captivity during the Korean War could have been one of kindness, decency, and forbearance. After all, the Second World War had just provided examples of every possible conduct to be deprecated in the care and maintenance of prisoners, and it had all been studied in fine detail since 1945. There had been millions of POWs and internees on all sides, armies of civil servants and volunteers working to lighten the burden of captivity, and countless diplomats and neutral officials monitoring and negotiating their treatment, guided by a dense web of international law and precedent. No government could claim ignorance of best practices or argue that it found itself in an unprecedented situation where POWs were concerned – because so soon after six years of war, nothing could be unprecedented. Furthermore, the leading nations of the world had just completed exhaustive discussions that produced the Geneva Convention Relative to the Treatment of Prisoners of War (1949), the newest iteration of international law as it applied to POWs. It was, in a very real sense, a user's manual for how to be a responsible detaining power.

It was all for nought. The Korean War is remembered not for the exemplary treatment of POWs by anyone but for the politicization of captives and the fact that both sides made them the targets of attempted indoctrination and psychological warfare. Both the UN Command and their Communist adversaries treated POWs with flagrant disregard for international law and humanitarian concerns alike. Prisoners became pawns of a much bigger game and suffered needlessly as their welfare was subjugated to the ideological demands of the Cold War.

Prisoners of war, as a collective, were of critical importance in Korea. The prisoner of war, as an individual with unique challenges, was not – not even, as was the case for Canada, when he was only one among dozens. Indeed, although the Canadian authorities did everything they could on behalf of their men in enemy hands – setting up a framework to protect them in captivity, monitoring and attempting to influence the negotiations that might bring them home, and preparing for their repatriation and eventual reintegration into civilian life – there was little Canada could control. Most of what the thirty-three Canadian POWs experienced can only be understood in an international context.

The ink was barely dry on the new Geneva Convention when the war in Korea began, and no government had yet ratified the agreement. China and North Korea were not even signatories. Nevertheless, all sides eventually announced they would, indeed, abide by the provisions of the convention. Still, there is little indication that either side had given much thought to what to do if it suddenly found itself with large numbers of enemy POWs to house, feed, and clothe – which is precisely what happened. Within weeks of entering the war, the US Army lost thousands of soldiers as POWs in the Battle of Taejeon. Before war's end, they would be joined in Communist captivity by another four thousand of their countrymen, as well as nearly one thousand British soldiers and thirty-three Canadians. Those numbers are far from firm, and it is quite likely that some of the thousands of men listed as missing in action were captured and disappeared at some point while in enemy hands.

The number of Chinese and (North and South) Korean POWs is even more difficult to pin down. Again, many of the missing might well have been captured and either executed or quickly inducted into whatever army had captured them. More problematic is the failure of either side to maintain adequate records of prisoners; even during the war, neither the Communists nor the UN Command seem to have had any definite idea of how many POWs they held. That reality, combined with the tendency of all detaining powers to reclassify, transfer, or simply "lose" captives (some were almost certainly executed, but many more seem to have taken advantage of lax guarding and simply wandered away) meant that an accurate accounting was never achieved, or perhaps even attempted. This, in itself, was not unheard of (neither the Germans nor the Russians on the Eastern Front in the Second World War made much of an effort to compile accurate records of POWs, and even the Western allies after VE-Day were less than scrupulous in their accounting of German prisoners), but it would become significant in Korea.

Even in the absence of accurate statistics, it is evident that the POW experience in the Korean War was painful, particularly for the United States. American servicemen died in droves in Korean POW camps, especially early in the war. The generally accepted figure is 2,730 POW deaths (out of 7,190 reported prisoners), although it is quite likely that some of the more than 8,000 Americans who were listed as missing died in captivity.[1] This represents a staggering 38 percent of the total reported American POWs in Communist hands, the highest

POW death rate in US history.[2] Hundreds of American POWs confessed to various kinds of collaboration with their captors (including the fourteen who were court-martialled after the war), and twenty-one US servicemen (as well as one British marine) elected to remain in Communist China after the war. These inconvenient truths, when combined with the dubious record of most combatants in dealing with POWs, mean that the captivity story of the Korean War was far more complex than it should have been.

The war was not yet a year old when discussions began in July 1951 for an armistice. The issues were many and varied, including the creation of a Demilitarized Zone and the establishment of a commission to discuss alleged ceasefire violations. But the POW issue was among the last to be resolved. As US negotiator Admiral Turner Joy observed in his diary, he spent nearly a year on the job and left the position with the POW matter still unresolved: "The wording of only one paragraph, in an armistice document containing sixty-two paragraphs, stood in the way of an honorable agreement ... After a bitter verbal battle lasting over ten months all paragraphs but that one had been agreed upon."[3] In the end, negotiators would meet on 158 separate occasions as they worked to hammer out a deal.

Everything hinged on Article 118 of the new Geneva Convention of 1949, which mandated the immediate repatriation of all POWs at the end of hostilities. The Western democracies had pushed for this provision to embarrass the Soviet Union, which had failed to repatriate countless German and Japanese POWs in 1945 and continued to use them as forced labour (the Western allies overlooked their own retention and similar use of POWs long after the war had ended while lobbying for the article). But if immediate repatriation was intended to help some captives, it certainly hurt others. Thousands of Russians who had been captured in German uniform were, as a sacrifice to relations between wartime allies, forcibly returned to the Soviet Union. Despite Stalin's promises, many of these unfortunate repatriates were executed or sentenced to long prison terms in the gulags.[4]

Regardless of the clarity of Article 118, as early as August 1950, the United States realized that the situation was far from simple. It was apparent that some of the Communist POWs in UN Command camps would not want to return home, either because they were unwilling conscripts or because (as the US government liked to think) they had reached the enlightened conclusion that capitalism was preferable to communism. Realizing that they held thousands of Chinese and North Korean POWs who did not want to return to their homes to live under Communism and that this could be used as a coup for propaganda purposes, the United States and the UN Command elected to ignore this new provision of the Geneva Convention. Mandatory repatriation was out; voluntary repatriation, whereby prisoners could decide if they wanted to return home or choose a new home, was in.

This position had a number of elements in its favour. It allowed US president Harry Truman's Democrats to avoid the unpleasant possibility of having to force POWs to return to living under a regime that it would come to regard as a mortal enemy. At the same time, forcible repatriation would be an admission of the legitimacy of the Democratic People's Republic of Korea and the People's Republic of China, rather than the anti-Communist regimes that the United States was backing in Taiwan and South Korea. Finally, with an election in the future and the Republicans sure to trumpet the accusation that the Democrats were soft on communism, it would give Truman a small victory to throw in the face of his political opponents.

But as the Joint Chiefs told Defense Secretary George Marshall on 8 August 1951, it was still contrary to the Geneva Convention, and the repudiation of a principle that they had pushed for in the international community just a couple of years earlier should not be done lightly.[5] Sadly, few decision-makers were sufficiently informed on the subject to deal with it effectively. It is perhaps symptomatic of the flawed decision making of the war that an issue that had obstructed a settlement for so long because of its practical and philosophical complexities was the very issue that senior commanders admitted they understood only vaguely.

That lack of awareness would prove to be crucial to the story, and it was a problem that the Americans had created for themselves. In September 1950, the US Army assumed control of all POWs on behalf of the UN Command to ensure that the POWs were treated according to the Geneva Convention. There was some concern that the South Koreans tended towards brutality in the treatment of prisoners, a fear that was heightened both by more recent killings of suspected Communists by Republic of Korea (ROK) police and other government operatives, and by rumours that numerous high-ranking ROK army officers had served in Japanese police and security units during the Second World War.

This enlightened decision was undermined by the fact that, in practical terms, the United States was ill-prepared to deal with the number of POWs that it soon found itself guarding. The camps quickly became overcrowded, and conditions deteriorated. More significantly, in the absence of sufficient manpower to administer the camps properly, the Americans turned over much of the day-to-day running of the camps to the prisoners themselves. This, in itself, was not unusual; during the Second World War, many detaining powers relied on the prisoners for internal camp administration at the lowest level.

What complicated the situation in Korea was that the POWs ran the gamut from hardcore Communists to hardcore anti-Communists, with a majority of peasant conscripts falling in the middle and simply wanting to get on with their lives. There had been no attempt to sort out the friends from the foes, so control of any given compound fell to whatever group was the strongest. And because the detaining power had given POW groups control over internal compound discipline and the distribution of food and supplies, the extremists had many weapons at their disposal. American soldiers rarely entered the compounds (prison-camp guard duty was often reserved for ineffective soldiers who seemed unable to handle the simplest of tasks), so US authorities did not grasp the depth of the divide nor the lengths to which extremists on both sides would go to win the mini-cold war in each compound. The prisoners who emerged as leaders in their camps were the most extreme, and they resorted to violence and compulsion to bring the mass of prisoners over to one side or the other. The longer the camps remained open, the more vicious and deeply entrenched became the two sides.[6]

The failure to understand the nature of captivity may well explain why the repatriation issue was mishandled so badly. General Mark Clark, head of UN Command, for instance, later recalled that the POW problem was the one matter on which he had not been properly briefed.[7] It may be that there was no one able to brief him. Although the Joint Chiefs accepted nonforcible repatriation in August 1951, General Omar Bradley, chair of the Joint Chiefs of Staff, was ambivalent. He was worried about the possibility of retaliation against UN Command prisoners and the likelihood that the Communists would see this breach of the convention as a precedent to be used to their advantage in the future. Dean Acheson, undersecretary at the US State Department, tried to argue for both sides of the debate at the same time; he said that UN Command prisoners were best served by standing by Article 118, but he did not want to force anyone to return home to be tried for collaboration.[8] For his part, the British foreign secretary, Anthony Eden, once the details of the matter were fully explained to him, admitted, "I did not know that our legal grounds were so poor." However, the British government decided that, whatever its feelings, it could not afford a break with Washington over the fate of a few thousand POWs. It rested its position on the language of international law, insisting that "released and repatriated" (the phrase used in the Geneva Convention) did not mean "forcibly repatriated."[9]

There seemed to be no way to protect the UN Command prisoners and the anti-Communists at the same time unless the Communists could be convinced to accept a one-for-one exchange. That had been the UN Command's preferred option as early as December 1950: because the UN Command held far more POWs than the Communists, an all-for-all exchange meant sending home thousands of Communist POWs to get back a few hundred in return (although there were thousands of UN Command and South Korean prisoners in Communist hands, most of those had not yet been officially confirmed as POWs – and so the UN could only count on getting back the men whose status has been confirmed). But the Communists had always rejected a one-for-one deal because they could only come out on top through an all-for-all agreement.[10]

An American official came up with an idea that was either brilliant or underhanded. It hinged on the fact that neither side had supplied a full list of prisoners. The UN Command could screen all the Chinese and North Koreans in their camps, remove from their lists the names of everyone who did not wish to be repatriated (thereby securing the principle of nonforcible repatriation), and then supply the shortened lists to the Communists and call it an all-for-all exchange.[11] Despite concerns that this was just the kind of sleight-of-hand that the United States consistently castigated its adversaries for, on 27 February 1952, the expedient was accepted.

Having steadfastly refused to specify how many UN Command prisoners they held, the Communists now demanded to know how many of its soldiers were in UN Command camps and how many were likely to want repatriation. At this point, UN Command's ignorance of conditions in their own camps came into play. There were over 130,000 POWs in the UN Command's hands (the majority of them were local conscripts who had been swept into uniform by advancing North Korean Forces and who happily surrendered to the UN Command when the opportunity presented itself), but officials had no idea how many of them wanted to be repatriated to China and North Korea. Eventually, they produced, apparently out of thin air, a number – 116,000 might agree to return home, or roughly 40 percent of the Chinese and 90 percent of the North Koreans. UN Command officials were confident that the Communists could live with that number.[12] To move from the rough estimate to actual names required that all Communist prisoners be individually screened to determine their wishes. As a demonstration of how little they understood the conditions in their own prison camps, officials believed this could be completed in a day.

The screening, unwisely dubbed Operation Scatter, was done in early April 1952 and, in keeping with its codename, was a haphazard affair. In total, 44,000 prisoners refused to be screened (or rather the POWs who controlled their compounds refused to allow them to be screened), and UN Command assumed they were all happy to return home. Even more alarming was that some 14,000 prisoners could not be accounted for at all.[13] Having lost more than 10 percent of its POWs should have set off alarm bells at UN Command, but it was quite in keeping with its detention practices. One young South Korean guard at a POW transit facility in Pyongyang in 1950 recalled telling his superior that he thought a number of recently captured North Koreans had escaped over the wire during the night. The squad leader did not seem to care, remarking that it was impossible to be sure how many men had escaped. "We did not keep an accurate count or list of prisoners," recalled the young guard. "There were just too many of them, and the number changed constantly."[14]

The results of the screening were an even greater embarrassment. Of the more than 100,000 prisoners who were screened, only 31,000 wanted to return home to North Korea or China, a fraction of what UN Command had predicted. Knowing that the Communists would never accept such a low number, UN Command struggled to find a way to make the best of a bad situation. They decided to add to the list any POW who had not been screened and then found a group of some 9,000 other prisoners who, in a murky piece of accounting, had been reclassified as civilians although they had been captured while in combatant roles. These expedients pushed the number up to 70,000 repatriates, likely still not enough to satisfy the other side.[15] Another screening operation, undertaken in July 1952, produced a list of 83,000 Communist prisoners willing to return home – probably still not enough.[16]

While the screening operation was underway, an episode that exemplified the UN Command's prisoner problems unfolded: the Koje Incident. Koje-do Island (now Geojedo), off the southwestern coast of the Korean peninsula, had been chosen as a detention centre for prisoners held by the UN Command, even though it was entirely inappropriate for the purpose. There were few water sources on the small, mountainous island, and the topography made it difficult to construct large compounds or to leave buffer zones between compounds. As Lieutenant General Matthew Ridgeway, in command of the US Eighth Army, tartly observed, Koje-do was "hardly the ground a sane man would have chosen to erect camp sites."[17] Nevertheless, as many as thirty-two compounds were eventually set up on the island to house close to 150,000 POWs, including diehards on each side of the political spectrum and everyone in between.

Violent encounters between rival groups of prisoners were virtually a daily occurrence, but the situation soon became more serious. In May 1952, Communist prisoners from one compound seized the camp commandant, Brigadier General Francis Dodd, and held him captive, demanding that the principle of nonforcible repatriation be rejected. Dodd and his successor, Brigadier General Charles Colson, quickly acceded to all demands and accepted responsibility for the violence. The US Army rewarded their capitulation by demoting both men to colonels. To show that Dodd (who had signed documents while in POW hands) and Colson had not spoken on behalf of the UN Command, the US Army moved quickly to relocate thousands of prisoners and sent in the 187th Airborne Regiment to make its point. On 10 June 1952, extremists in the camp armed with homemade weapons and Molotov cocktails faced off against the paratroopers in a skirmish that ended with 40 prisoners and 1 US soldier dead and more than 140 wounded on both sides.

Koje-do was a mess, and it left a bad taste in the mouth of everyone involved – except the governments of China and North Korea, for whom it was a propaganda windfall. The US military had been embarrassed, and Washington was infuriated with President Syngman Rhee's South Korean government, which had been meddling in camp affairs on the side of the hardline anti-Communists. Nor were its allies happy. In the aftermath of the violence, the United States requested assistance from other members of the coalition to rescue the situation at Koje-do. Units from different countries were posted to Koje-do, but no one bothered to consult the governments concerned – much to their annoyance.[18] When Ottawa learned that a company of the Royal Canadian Regiment had been deployed to Koje-do, Lester Pearson, secretary of state for external affairs, took the unusual step of issuing a public rebuke to the US government, reminding it that Canadian forces should remain under Canadian command and control: "No part of these forces should be detached therefrom except after consultation and with the agreement of the Canadian government."[19]

But not everyone took the same view. Pearson was called to task by Toronto MP George Hees for airing the subject in public rather than making private representations to Washington, something that only served to make Canada "look ridiculous in the eyes of our allies."[20] Canadian Second World War radio correspondent Willson Woodside suggested in an article in *Saturday Night*, a popular weekly Canadian periodical, that the Koje Incident was the result of Allied unseriousness: "We have been 'going easy' with enemy prisoners, giving them soft treatment in the hope of securing better treatment for our men in enemy hands and aiding the truce talks." The kid-glove treatment, Woodside argued, had achieved nothing beyond giving the enemy a propaganda victory.[21] The Royal Canadian Regiment's historian, for his part, thought the whole thing was a "tempest in a teapot." Its soldiers had no trouble moving prisoners without bloodshed and had developed excellent relations with the captives – to the point that the end of B Company's posting to Koje-do was marked with a celebratory sports meet that drew competitors and spectators from the POWs and the regiment.[22]

The Koje Incident might have been quickly forgotten had the results of the screening been as expected, but the realization of having badly misjudged the situation put Washington in a tight spot. Throughout the remainder of the negotiations, the Communists would continually remind UN Command delegates that they had promised 116,000 repatriates but could only deliver 83,000 – evidence of Western dishonesty and perfidy.

The UN Command felt it had no alternative but to shift its negotiating strategy and abandon everything it had been working towards. The endgame was no longer a commitment to bringing UN POWs home from behind barbed wire, even if it meant giving up huge numbers of Communist POWs. Now, it would offer shelter to huge numbers of Communist prisoners who were unwilling to be repatriated. These prisoners would be held up as champions of democracy and symbols of the triumph of Western values in Asia.[23] With that about-face, Communist POWs in UN hands were prioritized over UN POWs in Communist hands.

To complicate matters further, it was in the best interests of the US government to say as little about the POW situation as possible. Even the use of brainwashing by the Communists had to be downplayed, for fear it would bring a public reaction against delays in the peace process.[24] Few Americans could be expected to support a policy that allowed UN Command prisoners to languish in captivity while efforts were made to safeguard nonrepatriates, especially after reports surfaced of appalling conditions for American POWs over winter 1950–51.[25] Admiral Turner Joy made no secret of his opinion: "We should not sacrifice our men for a bunch of Chinese and North Koreans who were formerly our enemies and had shot at us." His successor, Major General William K. Harrison, reported receiving many letters from relatives asking the UN to concede the POW issues so their relatives could come home.[26] Letters to newspapers at that time suggested that Western publics had little general sympathy for the fate of captured enemy soldiers, regardless of the circumstances of their capture or their self-proclaimed desire to embrace the capitalist way of life.[27]

At least there was one piece of good news. In December 1952, the UN General Assembly voted overwhelmingly in favour of a resolution that prioritized the refugee provisions over the POW provisions of the Geneva Convention.[28] In practical terms, this was a vote in favour of nonforcible repatriation. The resolution had no legal standing, but the UN Command could claim it as an important endorsement.

As far as Canadians were concerned, these discussions were largely theoretical. The release of official casualty lists, as mandated by international law, had been a bone of contention since early in the war. For much of the war, only a small portion of the men in enemy hands were officially reported as such – because anyone officially reported as a POW had to be accounted for at the end of hostilities. This made it even more difficult for POWs to be dealt with as individuals rather than as a collective. UN Command constantly asked for the names and nationalities of POWs held in the north, but the Communists would say only that all POWs would be released by both sides after the armistice. Matthew Ridgeway, commander of the US Eighth Army, countered that it was impossible to negotiate without knowing the number of prisoners held by both sides. But it was not until 18 December 1951 that the first lists were exchanged, and even then, each side accused the other of incomplete reporting.[29]

That exchange provided the first official confirmation that Canadians had been captured: Casualty List No. 88, released by National Defence on 27 December 1951, reported that Orval Jenkins of the Royal Canadian Horse Artillery was a prisoner of war, having been captured in August 1951. He would be the only Canadian confirmed in captivity for over a year, until Casualty List No. 174 of 22 April 1953 included the name of Lance Corporal Paul Dugal of the Royal 22e Régiment, captured in June 1952. By that time, Dugal had already been released.

However, even with only one man in enemy hands, Canadian officials had already made a start on the administrative arrangements for safeguarding personnel in enemy hands. Mindful of the experience of the Second World War, when the task was much bigger and more complicated than anyone could have imagined, the Canadian Red Cross Society was quick to appoint Colonel Cuthbert Scott as its special liaison officer to the Canadian government.[30] Since the Red Cross was identified in international law as the official aid agency working on behalf of POWs, Scott was ready to become a critical resource on everything from the notification of capture to the regulations governing the sending of parcels to POWs. One member of Parliament asked the House of Commons about mail service to POWs, but the minister of national defence, Brooke Claxton, replied that, since only one Canadian was confirmed a prisoner, this was hardly likely to be an issue.[31] The *Daily Worker*, published by the Communist Party of Great Britain, a tireless critic of UN Command and the Rhee government, helpfully reported that prisoners would be allowed to send letters through the good offices of the Committee of the Chinese Congress of the Defenders of World Peace in Beijing.[32]

In hindsight, Jenkins and the other Canadians who followed him into captivity benefited from the Canadian brigade's late arrival to the Korean conflict. As a result, they missed that first winter of captivity, when conditions were at their worst and so many American POWs died from malnutrition, disease, neglect, and mistreatment.[33] More important, Canadian POWs enjoyed some protection by way of being regarded as very much junior partners of the great powers (particularly the United States, whose men probably suffered more in captivity because the North Koreans regarded Washington as the evil imperial puppet master). Ottawa might well have been infuriated to be cast as little more than an inconsequential pawn in a much bigger game, but Canadians in Communist hands benefited from this opinion.

In comparison to their American and British comrades, Canadian prisoners suffered little studied abuse. Attempts to indoctrinate or brainwash them seem to have been half-hearted at best, and minor infractions committed by Canadians were often overlooked by guards who would have punished US or other Commonwealth POWs severely for the same deeds. Their guards gave every indication of hating Americans but of not giving much thought to Canada. A number of francophone Canadian prisoners hid behind the language barrier, thereby convincing their captors to ignore any soldiers who did not speak English. The interrogators apparently did not know or care enough to test those claims.[34]

George Griffiths of the Royal Canadian Regiment, captured in October 1952, was shown crude pictures of Canadian and American flags. When he pointed to the Red Ensign to indicate he was Canadian, the soldiers pulled out their bayonets and gleefully began stabbing the Stars and Stripes.[35] Griffiths' captors later pressed him to admit he was only in Korea because his government had sent him there. Perhaps not wishing to offend anyone by saying there was no other reason for him to be in Korea, he was relieved when the matter was dropped.[36] Occasionally, Canadians felt something approaching pity from their captors. Len Badowich, also of the Royal Canadian Regiment but captured in May 1953, recalled being given history lessons about communism and capitalism but no concerted effort at indoctrination. More memorable was the guard who told him sadly that Canadians were nothing more than "running dogs for American warmongers."[37] Canadian soldiers were, as far as many Communist soldiers were concerned, just the kind of feckless drones that imperialist powers always took advantage of.

The Communists were keen to persuade UN Command pilots in captivity to confess to involvement in biological and chemical warfare operations, but they were not the only prisoners to be affected by the enemy's obsession with germ warfare. Len Badowich recalled camp staff announcing to his compound that the Americans were trying to spread disease as a weapon of war and that prisoners were required to catch flies to combat the spread. Each prisoner was solemnly presented with a fly swatter and a paper bag and given a quota of one hundred flies a day to catch. Boredom has historically been one of the defining characteristics of war captivity, so for the men in Len's camp, this was a most welcome diversion. They took to the hunt with gusto, so much so that flies grew scarce in the vicinity. Not to be deterred, the prisoners began playing poker at night, with the stakes consisting of caches of dead flies that could be presented to the staff to make up quota. When flies became even scarcer, they spent ages carefully pulling apart the bodies of flies so that a pile of fifty might pass for seventy. It might sound like a pointless waste of time, but the one thing that

POWs have in abundance is time, and this at least gave them something constructive to do.[38]

In general, the treatment of Canadians in Communist camps was probably best summed up by Thomas Rothwell of the Royal Canadian Regiment, captured in October 1952: "Our treatment was correct, certainly not severe."[39] They endured stints in solitary confinement (some of them quite long), plenty of instances of petty violence, half-hearted efforts at psychological warfare and indoctrination, dreadful living conditions, a near-complete absence of medical treatment, and isolation from their families and government.

But the historian must make two important qualifications. First, their treatment was nowhere near as severe as that endured by American and British POWs in Korea. They were in captivity for shorter periods than many UN Command prisoners, and some of them spent only a few weeks in a permanent prison camp, where more intense indoctrination or calculated abuse might have taken place. This is not to minimize the experience of Canadian POWs in Korea, but it is to say that things could have been much worse.

Second, it must be conceded that Canadian prisoners, especially those captured late in the war, frequently endured the same conditions as their captors. The typical Chinese or North Korean soldier lived a miserable life while on campaign, with brutal officers, inadequate food and medical supplies, and a general disregard for their well-being. All too frequently, captor and captive suffered together. James Gunn of Toronto was one of the members of the Royal Canadian Regiment captured in May 1953. Beginning at last light each day, the prisoners and their Chinese guards trudged together towards the north; they walked for a few hours and then slept on the floor of whatever abandoned hut they could find. They all subsisted on the same inadequate ration of rice, they all suffered the agonies of dysentery, and they probably even shared the same lice.[40] In such situations, for the Chinese to observe the provisions of international law would have meant, as Canada's official campaign historian observed, "actual preferment of prisoners over their own soldiers."[41]

The armistice negotiations ground on through winter and early spring 1953, with progress coming at a painfully slow pace. It took the death of Joseph Stalin on 5 March 1953 to break the logjam. The new Soviet leadership called for a quick conclusion to the war, and on 30 March 1953, the Chinese premier, Zhou Enlai, announced that his side was ready to discuss the exchange of sick and wounded prisoners. The UN Command pounced on this statement and suggested an immediate resumption of armistice negotiations.[42] The Communists still declined to give numbers, simply repeating that they were prepared to release all POWs who were entitled to repatriation to a neutral nation under

Articles 109 and 110 of the Geneva Convention.[43] It took less than two weeks to reach and sign an agreement. The position articulated by the Communists was interesting, given the nature of the discussions over the past eighteen months. They insisted that Article 118 of the Geneva Convention represented a principle that was "unshakable" and that nonforcible repatriation was a sham: "The Korean and Chinese side does not acknowledge that there are prisoners of war who are allegedly unwilling to be repatriated. Therefore, the question of the so-called forced repatriation or repatriation by force does not exist at all." However, if there were Communist POWs who were "filled with apprehensions and are afraid to return home as a result of having been subjected to intimidation and oppression," they could be turned over to a neutral state temporarily, "and through explanation given by our side, gradually freed from apprehensions." This, the Communists concluded, represented "a just solution to the question of repatriation."[44]

The exchange itself began just nine days later. In the hasty preparations for the repatriates' reception, Canada made a number of requests of British Commonwealth Forces Korea, especially regarding a speedy return of the men to Canada. However, Canada's mission commander, Brigadier R.E.A. Morton, admitted that everything was in the hands of the Eighth Army; Canada could not demand, only ask and hope its wishes were met.[45] On 20 April 1953, the first Commonwealth POW to cross over at Panmunjom as part of Operation Little Switch, the first scheduled prisoner exchange, was Lance Corporal Paul Dugal of the Royal 22e Régiment; Arthur Baker of Montreal, also of Royal 22e Régiment and a POW since November 1951, followed him a few days later. They brought out the first definite news of other Canadians in Communist captivity in the form of a list of the dozen members of the Royal Canadian Regiment who had been taken prisoner at Little Gibraltar in October 1952. For six months, their families and friends had been informed that they were missing in action.

About one hundred UN Command prisoners were returned in Little Switch, the majority in reasonably good physical condition. This provided great reassurance in the West, where next of kin of POWs could allow themselves to feel optimistic. "Though it only be for reasons of propaganda," observed the *Hamilton Spectator,* "the Communist enemy has demonstrated a certain humanity in the treatment of his prisoners which lessens the bitterness of our animosity and reassures our minds over the condition of prisoners not yet freed."[46]

The next day, the optimism faded as more was heard from the repatriates. There were accounts of physical and psychological abuse, disease, miserly rations, and brutal guards. The headlines screamed, "Atrocities against POWs," "Red Brutality to POWs," and "Death Trek Kills POWs."[47] It was enough for the *Hamilton Spectator* to issue a retraction of sorts: "The upsurge of relief and hope which greeted the first happy repatriates at the Panmunjom prisoner exchange camp has been dashed by the stories told by later arrivals."[48] Other journalists, however, noted that the horror stories emanated mostly from US and British prisoners, particularly prisoners captured in 1950 rather than later in the war.[49] Whether the repatriates' horror stories would apply to the Canadian POWs whose names had been brought out by Dugal and Baker remained to be seen.

The Communists insisted that all sick and wounded prisoners had been released at Panmunjom, but the UN Command retorted that it was aware of at least four hundred other POWs who were eligible for release but remained in captivity. It took another two months to reach an agreement for the release of all prisoners by both sides. One point at issue was whether nonrepatriates would remain in Korea to be interviewed by their own side or be moved elsewhere. The Communists were adamant that they should be moved because it would be impossible for those interviews to take place fairly within the jurisdiction of the detaining power.[50] The UN Command, for its part, suspected that the Communists were playing for time so their prisoners could be fattened up a little before they were released, a suspicion that may, indeed, have had some merit. There are many accounts from POWs of suspicious improvements in rations, liberties, and general treatment, improvements that could not be explained until they learned later that their release was imminent. Thomas Rothwell reported that at some point during the summer, their meagre rations were inexplicably supplemented by eggs, ham, powdered milk, pork, and beef.[51] James Gunn also recalled the prisoners' surprise when their captors doled out markedly better food, including small amounts of meat.[52]

This explains why the UN Command prisoners who were returned in Operation Big Switch in August 1953 were in generally better health than those who came back four months earlier. American troops received all repatriated POWs at Panmunjom and escorted them to the aptly named Freedom Village nearby for a quick medical exam, a new uniform, a light snack, a selection of Canadian magazines and newspapers, and some paperwork by officers from each national contingent. The next stop for the Canadians was Britannia Camp, run by British Commonwealth Forces Korea, for a more rigorous medical exam and a night's rest. The next day, the Canadians were moved to 38 Canadian Field Ambulance for debriefing, medical examinations, and an introduction to Canadian journalists. They were then flown to Japan to board a Canadian Pacific Airways flight to Vancouver.

That left one Canadian in enemy hands, Squadron Leader A.R. "Andy" MacKenzie, a Second World War fighter ace who was on a posting to the US 5th Air Force and was downed by friendly fire over North Korea in December

1952. The Chinese and North Koreans took a particular interest in aircrew, and many were bullied into admitting that they had been operating north of the Yalu River (this was the crime to which MacKenzie was forced to "confess"), in China proper, or that they had been engaged in chemical warfare raids. Some airmen who were known to have been captured never returned from Communist captivity. MacKenzie might have suffered the same fate had Canadian diplomat Chester Ronning, one of Ottawa's representatives at the Korean War talks and one of Canada's few long-serving China specialists, not made a direct and personal request to Zhou Enlai. In December 1954, two years to the day after being shot down, MacKenzie was taken to the Chinese border with Hong Kong and released.[53]

The Korean War POW experience reflects favourably on none of the major combatants, and the aftermath was, if anything, even less edifying – from the moment prisoners were released into friendly hands. Given the ideological nature of the war and the fear of POWs being brainwashed, armies (not to mention governments, journalists, and the public) seemed most concerned with how their men had withstood those pressures. The Canadian brigade's intelligence officer, Lieutenant W.J. "Bill" Beaman, was ordered to interview returning POWs to find out how the Canadian prisoners had behaved in captivity and to collect material for further study. However, he was inexperienced and had been given almost no guidance about what to look for.[54] At the same time, officers were directed to monitor all press interviews with prisoners to ensure that journalists did not ask anything that might embarrass or upset the repatriates.[55]

The outcome was frustrating for ex-POWs and journalists alike. James Gunn recalled that, after arriving in Freedom Village, he and his comrades were questioned by intelligence officers who seemed most interested in finding out if they had remained loyal. They were keen to know if POWs had resisted their captors by attempting escape, a question that struck Gunn as especially idiotic: "You're a white Anglo living in a country that's nothing but mountains, for Christ's sake."[56]

Journalists looking for good stories were equally frustrated. Canadian Press war correspondent Bill Boss wrote that returned Canadians had been so alarmed by their intelligence officers that they refused to answer questions:

> I have yet to get a straight answer from a Canadian prisoner on such questions as whether any of our men were subjected to atrocities or "brainwashing" by the Reds ... American correspondents ask such questions of their POWs and get answers ... Canadian POWs have been terrified by the briefing they received at

> Munsan. They are made to sign the Official Security Act, are informed they are bound to it and are subject to imprisonment if they violate it. They're so impressed by this briefing that even when they get home here, they're afraid to talk.[57]

Newspaper articles from the period after Big Switch bear out the suggestion that intelligence officers successfully created a nonnarrative for the returned POWs rather than allowing any narrative that reflected their individual experiences. Second Lieutenant C.G. Owen of the Royal Canadian Regiment, captured in May 1953, declined to speak about being held in solitary confinement, saying only that "that story will come out."[58] Thomas Rothwell admitted he had been locked alone in a hut for ninety-two days but said that he was not permitted to elaborate.[59] Even when pressed, he refused to budge, saying only that the treatment had been fair.[60] Orval Jenkins also declined to say much about his treatment. When asked if any Canadians had fallen prey to Communist propaganda and brainwashing, he glanced over at the army intelligence officer who was monitoring the interview and replied that he did not think he was supposed to talk about such things.[61]

This apparent refusal to allow returning POWs to speak for themselves may be behind some odd misinterpretations that appeared in press accounts. Shortly after his return to Canada, Len Badowich recalled seeing a newspaper headline that read something like, "POWs returning to Canada still suffering from the effects of their captivity." In fact, the ex-POWs in his group were all nursing bad hangovers when they faced Canadian journalists in Vancouver – they were feeling the effects not of captivity but of the copious amounts of alcohol available on the flight from Japan.[62]

But at least Canada declined to subject its returned POWs to a program of disindoctrination or re-education, holding instead to "the belief that the influence of their families and friends will go as far as anything to restore their political balance."[63] In contrast, more than seven thousand Chinese POWs returned home to face the wrath of the Communist government. They were expelled from the Communist Party, deprived of job opportunities, forced to divorce, sent to do hard labour in rural areas, and even executed. It was thirty years before the Chinese government allowed their reputations to be rehabilitated, but even then, the process was long and difficult.[64]

American prisoners were greeted at Freedom Village by medics and aid workers – but also by psychiatrists, intelligence officers, and lawyers. Interrogations began almost immediately and continued on the ships that carried them home, which had been retrofitted to create a series of interrogation booths below decks. There were courts martial and lengthy prison sentences for some, but those processes were plagued by problems. The fourteen accused were chosen arbitrarily (because hundreds of other ex-POWs admitted to similar kinds of collaboration on various levels), and there was no consistency in how the services treated their own men. Finally, a soldier who elected to stay behind in Communist China and later returned to the United States might escape punishment altogether – he could not be court-martialled, because the military had dishonourably discharged him and the army had no jurisdiction over men who were civilians.[65] Given the level of public outcry over how the repatriates were treated, is it a coincidence that in the wake of the courts martial, Stanley Kubrick made his first major cinematic release, *Paths of Glory*? Was he making a point with his story of the French Army mutinies of 1917 and the three soldiers who were chosen at random to face trial for the supposed crimes of their entire regiment? The entire situation reflected so poorly on the United States that it is impossible to miss a sense of smugness underlying one Canadian assessment of the situation. In *Canadian Forum*, Donald Hugh Gillis decried the American decision to hold ex-prisoners at Valley Forge Army Hospital to be "decommunized" after they were suspected of having fallen under the influence of propaganda in Korea. This, wrote Gillis, proved that the United States had lost faith in the healing power of democratic society.[66]

Despite the arduous negotiations that produced it, even the organization created to deal with nonrepatriates, the Neutral Nations Repatriation Commission, was a failure. One of its early supporters had been the Indian delegate to the UN, Krishna Menon, who found an ally in Lester Pearson, by then president of the UN General Assembly. But Menon struggled against what he believed to be the obstructiveness of the United States, and Pearson feared he was ready to wash his hands of the entire idea.[67] Dean Acheson, for his part, despised Menon, whom he took to be a meddlesome empire builder, and distrusted Pearson by association.[68] The repatriation commission was, by all accounts, conceived in acrimony and delivered in ill will. Its life course was entirely predictable.[69]

The five-member body was to take responsibility for the twenty-three POWs from both sides who had declined to be repatriated and provide a forum in which officials could speak to their nonrepatriates in the hopes of wooing them home again. In theory, it was a positive step; in practice, it functioned largely as the cynic might have expected. It began work on 23 September 1953 and soon revealed its true colours. Sweden and Switzerland invariably sided with the UN, while Czechoslovakia and Poland usually took the side of China and North Korea. Only India made genuine attempts at neutrality, attempts that were frequently drowned out by accusations of coercion and bad faith. On 20 January 1954, after four months of fruitless wrangling, the commission sent all of its charges back to the detaining powers and, a month later, dissolved itself.

On a more positive note, there was much commentary of a philosophical nature on what could or should be expected of soldiers who fell into enemy hands. The US Army quickly promulgated its new Code of Conduct in August 1955, placing emphasis directly on the POW to continue the fight. It was not enough simply to resist the blandishments of the enemy; the POW was expected to "make every effort to escape and to aid others to escape." Army lawyer George S. Prugh Jr. thought this was going too far and that the statement should be modified to account for what is reasonable under the conditions of captivity. He went on to note approvingly the position of Canada, Britain, and France, that certain conduct was forbidden but, beyond having a duty to return to the service of government as soon as possible, nothing active or specific was required of prisoners.[70] When he envisaged "the extension of the battlefield into the prisoner of war compound, to making the captive a prisoner at war rather than of war," he was thinking in two directions: that the POW might well continue to contribute to the war effort should circumstances allow; and that, contrary to the cliched declaration that German soldiers gave to new POWs during the Second World War ("For you, the war is over!"), the POWs' war was never really over, not even after he returned home.[71]

In 1966, the US Army published the second volume of its official history of the Korean War. It dealt with the last two years of the conflict, particularly the armistice negotiations. *Truce Tent and Fighting Front,* by Walter G. Hermes, is an impressive work, judicious and sensible, with a refreshing willingness to point fingers where they ought to be pointed. On the fate of prisoners of war, Hermes admitted that nonrepatriates had, indeed, been protected over the last fifteen months of the war and went on to tackle the cost directly. Safeguarding the North Korean and Chinese nonrepatriates had unquestionably prolonged the war. And during that prolongation, he argued, the UN Command sustained an additional 125,000 casualties, while the Chinese and North Koreans probably took more than twice that number.[72] The cost of defending a principle, then, was close to 400,000 casualties. As historian Charles Young observed, it was a heavy price to pay for a humanitarian notion that, as much as anything, was really a fig leaf for a struggle over political ideologies.[73]

Young goes on to make the case that Korea has become a forgotten war because its most intractable principle, the treatment and disposition of prisoners of war, could never be publicly discussed. Washington knew full well that if the American people ever learned that the only thing standing in the way of ending the war was the fate of a few thousand nonrepatriates, the Chinese and North Koreans who had once been the enemy, support for the war would have collapsed.[74] Even after the war, the subject could scarcely be mentioned.

Eisenhower's victory speech of 26 July 1953 did not refer to voluntary repatriation or the nonrepatriates: "Eisenhower could not proclaim victory on voluntary repatriation because no one knew that was what they had been fighting for ... America had not declared it as a war aim."[75] Even in this sense, the Canadian experience was subsumed into the international one. With the great powers determined to apply to the entire captivity narrative the old aphorism "least said, soonest mended," Canada's POWs had little hope of escaping the historical oblivion to which others wanted to consign their story.

Notes

1 Paul M. Cole, *POW/MIA Issues,* vol. 1, *The Korean War* (Santa Monica, CA: RAND, 1994), 21.
2 William Clark Latham Jr., *Cold Days in Hell: American POWs in Korea* (College Station: Texas A&M University Press, 2012), 241.
3 Allan E. Goodman, ed., *Negotiating while Fighting: The Diary of Admiral C. Turner Joy at the Korean Armistice Conference* (Stanford, CA: Hoover Institution Press, 1978), 3.
4 The classic account of the unfortunately named Operation Keelhaul is Nikolai Tolstoy, *Victims of Yalta* (London: Hodder and Stoughton, 1977). See also Nicholas Bethell, *The Last Secret: Forcible Repatriation to Russia, 1944–47* (London: Deutsch, 1974) and Mark R. Elliott, *Pawns of Yalta: Soviet Refugees and America's Role in Their Repatriation* (Urbana: University of Illinois Press, 1982).
5 Sydney D. Bailey, *The Korean Armistice* (Basingstoke, UK: MacMillan Academic, 1992), 87.
6 Callum A. MacDonald, "'Heroes behind Barbed Wire': The US, Britain and the POW Issue in the Korean War," in *The Korean War in History,* ed. James Cotton and Ian Neary (Manchester, UK: Manchester University Press, 1989), 138.
7 Bailey, *The Korean Armistice,* 88.
8 MacDonald, "Heroes behind Barbed Wire," 139.
9 Bailey, *The Korean Armistice,* 88.
10 Memorandum on Cease Fire Committee, 15 December 1950, Library and Archives Canada (LAC), MG26 N8, Lester B. Pearson Fonds, vol. 1, file 5.
11 MacDonald, "Heroes behind Barbed Wire," 140.
12 MacDonald, "Heroes behind Barbed Wire," 141–42.
13 Bailey, *The Korean Armistice,* 95.
14 H.K. Shin, *Remembering Korea 1950: A Boy Soldier's Story* (Reno: University of Nevada Press, 2001), 100.
15 MacDonald, "Heroes behind Barbed Wire," 142.
16 Rosemary Foot, *A Substitute for Victory: The Politics of Peacemaking at the Korean Armistice Talks* (Ithaca, NY: Cornell University Press, 1990), 160.
17 Bailey, *The Korean Armistice,* 96.
18 Kenneth K. Hanson, *Heroes behind Barbed Wire* (Toronto: D. Van Nostrand, 1957), 12.
19 *House of Commons Debates,* 21st Parl., 6th Sess., No. 3 (26 May 1952) (Lester B. Pearson), 2552.
20 *House of Commons Debates,* 21st Parl., 6th Sess., No. 4 (20 June 1952) (George Hees), 3481.
21 Willson Woodside, "The Meaning of Koje," *Saturday Night* 67 (14 June 1952): 16.
22 G.R. Stevens, *The Royal Canadian Regiment,* vol. 2, *1933–1966* (London, ON: The Regiment, 1967), 246.
23 MacDonald, "Heroes behind Barbed Wire," 144.

24 Charles S. Young, "POWs: The Hidden Reason for Forgetting Korea," *Journal of Strategic Studies* 33, 2 (2010): 330.
25 Foot, *A Substitute for Victory*, 121.
26 MacDonald, "Heroes behind Barbed Wire," 141; and Foot, *A Substitute for Victory*, 149.
27 William H. Vatcher, *Panmunjom: The Story of the Korean Military Armistice Negotiations* (New York: Praeger, 1958), 117.
28 United Nations, General Assembly res. 610(VII), 3 December 1952, https://digitallibrary.un.org/record/211409?ln=en#record-files-collapse-header.
29 Bailey, *The Korean Armistice*, 96.
30 W. Stuart Stanbury, National Commissioner, Canadian Red Cross Society, to G.E. Rinfret, Postmaster General, 24 February 1951, LAC, Post Office Department Fonds, RG 3, vol. 3424, file 36-26-2
31 *House of Commons Debates*, 22nd Parl., 1st Sess., No. 6 (27 March 1953) (Brooke Claxton), 6422.
32 High Commissioner, UK, to External Affairs, 27 March 1951, LAC, RG 3, vol. 3424, file 36-26-1.
33 Albert D. Biderman, *March to Calumny: The Story of American POWs in the Korean War* (New York: Macmillan, 1963), 111.
34 Bill Boss, "More Canadians Freed by Reds," *Brantford Expositor*, 25 August 1953, 1; and Herbert Fairlie Wood, *Strange Battleground: The Operations in Korea and Their Effects on the Defence Policy of Canada* (Ottawa: Queen's Printer, 1966), 250.
35 John Melady, *Korea: Canada's Forgotten War* (Toronto: Macmillan, 1983), 134.
36 Joyce Surman, "Brighton Korea Vet Reminisces," *POW Journal* (Summer 1988): 19.
37 Quoted in Boss, "More Canadians Freed," 2.
38 *The Memory Project*, Vol. 2: *Len Badowich's Cold War Timeline*, https://www.thememoryproject.com/wp-content/uploads/2021/09/Len-Badowichs-Cold-War-Timeline-EN.pdf, 8.
39 *Dundas Star*, 19 August 1953, 1.
40 Korea Veterans Association, Canada, Heritage Unit, newsletter, October 2016, https://www.kva27.ca/james-gunn-newsletter-pows.html.
41 Wood, *Strange Battleground*, 249.
42 Secretary of State, Commonwealth Relations, London, to British High Commission, Ottawa, 31 March 1953, LAC, RG 25, Department of External Affairs, acc 86-87/160, box 18, file 619-J-40.
43 Canadian Embassy, Washington, to External Affairs, 6 April 1953, LAC, RG 25, acc 86-87/160, box 18, file 619-J-40.
44 Canadian Embassy, Washington, to External Affairs, 10 April 1953, LAC, RG 25, acc 86-87/160, box 18, file 619-J-40.
45 Canadian Military Mission, Tokyo, to Chief of the General Staff, 6 April 1953, Department of National Defence, Directorate of History and Heritage (DHH), 112.009 (D98).
46 Editorial, "The First to Return," *Hamilton Spectator*, 21 April 1953, 6.
47 *Ottawa Evening Citizen*, 22 April 1953, 1; *Vancouver Province*, 22 April 1953, 1; and *Toronto Telegram*, 21 April 1953, 1.
48 Editorial, "Hopes Dashed," *Hamilton Spectator*, 22 April 1953, 6.
49 *Sherbrooke Daily Record*, 24 April 1953, 1.
50 Canadian Embassy, Washington, to External Affairs, 8 May 1953, LAC, RG 25, acc. 86-87/160, box 18, file 619-J-40.
51 *Dundas Star*, 19 August 1953, 1.
52 Korea Veterans Association, Canada, Heritage Unit, newsletter, October 2016.

53 See Andy MacKenzie, "Encounter over Korea," *Canadian Military History* 3, 1 (1994): 117–22.
54 Major S.R. Elliott, *Scarlet to Green: A History of Intelligence in the Canadian Army, 1903–63* (Toronto: Canadian Intelligence and Security Association, 1981), 550.
55 Instructions to No. 25 Canadian Public Relations Unit, 24 July 1953, DHH, 410 B25.059 (D1).
56 Korea Veterans Association Canada, Heritage Unit, newsletter, October 2016.
57 *Vancouver Sun*, 31 August 1953, 21.
58 *Vancouver Sun*, 31 August 1953, 21.
59 *Hamilton Spectator*, 21 August 1953, 1.
60 *Dundas Star*, 2 September 1953, 1.
61 *Hamilton Spectator*, 21 August 1953, 1.
62 *The Memory Project*, 2: 9.
63 Memo from Commonwealth Relations Office, 18 May 1953, LAC, RG 25, acc 86-87/160, box 18, file 619-J-40.
64 Pingchao Zhu, "Disgraced Soldiers: The Ordeal of the Repatriated POWs of the Chinese People's Volunteer Army from the Korean War," *Journal of Chinese Military History* 4, 2 (2015): 162–200.
65 Raymond B. Lech, *Broken Soldiers* (Urbana: University of Illinois Press, 2000), esp. chaps. 9–11.
66 Donald Hugh Gillis, "The Brave and the Free," *Canadian Forum* 33 (July 1953): 77.
67 Notes on Korean Discussions, 4 November 1952, LAC, MG 26 N8, vol. 1, file 6.
68 John English, *The Worldly Years: The Life of Lester Pearson*, vol. 2, *1949–1972* (Toronto: A.A. Knopf, 1992), 63.
69 For an excellent account of Canada's part in the creation of the commission, see Greg J. Donaghy, "Blessed Are the Peacemakers: Canada, the United Nations, and the Search for a Korean Armistice, 1952–53," *War and Society* 30 (2011): 134–46.
70 George S. Prugh Jr., "The Code of Conduct for the Armed Forces," *Columbia University Law Review* 56, 5 (1956): 678–707.
71 George S. Prugh Jr., "Prisoners at War: The POW Battleground," *Dickinson Law Review* 60 (October 1955–June 1956): 123–38.
72 Walter G. Hermes, *Truce Tent and Fighting Front* (Washington, DC: Office of the Chief of Military History, US Army, 1966), 500–1.
73 Young, "POWs," 327–28.
74 Young, "POWs," 328.
75 Young, "POWs," 330.

13

Returning Home: The Canadian Veterans' Experience

Ted Barris

ON 30 AUGUST 1953, just over a month after UN Command and North Korean officials signed the armistice at Panmunjom, Korea, eleven former captives in Communist Chinese prison camps stepped off the airplane that had brought them home to Canada. Canadian Press reporter Joe MacSween met the former POWs in Vancouver and asked questions. The story he filed described one of the men as "outwardly laconic." He witnessed another desperately "gather his family into his arms." They all shied away from publicity, especially photographs, because "their Communist captors had photographed them for propaganda purposes, leaving an unpleasant association with the men."[1]

Private Don Orson, a Royal Canadian Regiment rifleman captured when Hill 355 was overrun by Communist forces in October 1952, seemed less inhibited. He kibitzed with his comrades, reporters, and other family members outside the Sea Island Airport terminal. "Did it happen?" asked Orson, repeating MacSween's question about his Korean War experience. He didn't have the words. He swept his arm over the assembly, referring to the gaiety of the occasion.

"No, it never happened," said Private Ron Watson, another Royal Canadian Regiment infantryman who had made at least one attempt to escape Camp 3, deep in North Korea. "Let's forget it ever happened," he told the Canadian Press reporter.[2] That ended the interviews.

Watson's words were prescient because without encouragement, most Canadians did just that. They forgot or rarely acknowledged that the Korean War had happened. The country had plenty of other more newsworthy distractions to talk about. A national pipeline was in the works to bring Alberta oil to Sarnia, Ontario. The St. Lawrence Seaway would soon give ocean freighters access to international Great Lakes ports. The federal government had begun issuing a new series of old-age security cheques. Some hospitals were introducing a new radiation therapy, called Cobalt-60, for fighting cancer. The Stratford Festival, in its second year, announced an expanded nine-week season. And the newly minted CBC Television network began rehearsals for two of its former radio hosts who would star in *The Wayne and Shuster Show.*

Canadians had little time or interest in giving veterans back from Korea anything like a hero's welcome. No ticker tape parades. No brass bands. No civic receptions. No passionate embraces in the streets between returning troops and women they didn't know. There were a few exceptions. In late 1953, when the 1st Battalion of the Royal Canadian Regiment landed in Ottawa, its troops paraded through the capital and received a personal welcome from Prime Minister Louis St. Laurent on Parliament Hill. At the docks in Seattle, Washington, officials hired a band, and there were women in hula skirts to greet returning 2nd Battalion vets. But the ship held mostly homebound Americans, so by the time most Canadians arrived home in Saskatoon, Timmins, or Chicoutimi, nobody noticed or cared. In the words of one returning platoon commander, his men were considered little more than "an administrative problem to the processing staff."[3]

This chapter explores the nature of homecoming for Korean War veterans like Don Orson and Ron Watson. While every veteran had his own return to civvy street, what was common across the country was a general lack of awareness or understanding on the part of the Canadian public. The operations of Canada's Special Force to defend the UN Peace Charter in South Korea between 1950 and 1953 seemed to have escaped people's attention. Even historians overlooked the Korean War. This chapter is based on a library of first-hand interviews with Canadian servicemen I conducted in the 1990s.

Bill Jackson arrived home from the Korean War nine months before the armistice. By October 1952, he had served in Korea for a year with Princess Patricia's Canadian Light Infantry and had witnessed his share of warfare and war zones. On the way in, north from Busan, his troop train accidentally killed dozens of civilians on the tracks in Daegu (Taegu). On his first night on the Jamestown Line, Jackson had to bury dead Chinese soldiers before bedding down in his slit trench. During Operation Pepperpot, north of the Imjin River in October 1951, a Chinese mortar bomb explosion killed one of his friends. And many nights in his bunker, "I'd wake up with the nose of a rat inches from my face."[4]

When he came home to Brooks, Alberta, the train platform was empty. Nobody had notified his parents. He had to phone long-distance to the family farm for someone to pick him up. About a month later, Jackson attended a Remembrance Day observance and then joined an evening smoker at the local Legion Hall. No women. Just forty or fifty veterans sitting, drinking, and telling war stories.

At one point, a friend of the Jackson family rose to address the gathering. He and Jackson's father had served in the First World War together.

"Hold it. Hold it," the veteran called out. The chatter in the room quieted down. "We've got a guy just back from the trenches in Korea," he said. "And we'd like to welcome him."

Bill Jackson felt a little embarrassed.

"Go ahead," encouraged Jackson's father. "Stand up and say something."

Jackson slowly got to his feet. But before he could utter a word, a voice boomed from the back of the hall, "Sit down, you asshole. You were in Korea. So what?"

Don Flieger's reception proved even worse. While on duty at Kimpo Airport, near Seoul, in February 1952, the former bank clerk and semipro hockey player woke up one morning with bleeding blisters on his ankles and wrists. A quick-thinking doctor at a US MASH unit realized the Canadian Service Corps corporal had contracted hemorrhagic fever. The doctor pumped him full of penicillin and transfused his blood. En route home to Saint John, New Brunswick, Flieger underwent seven more transfusions. He recovered after months at Lancaster Military Hospital.

"When I got out of hospital," Flieger recalled, "I went back up to Fredericton, my home depot. That night, I went to the Legion. I was in uniform. But they wouldn't let me in. Said I wasn't a veteran. I told them my story, but they said, 'That doesn't cut it here. Korea was just a skirmish.'"[5]

These attitudes, however dismaying to the Korea veterans, represented the chauvinism that sometimes existed between generations of soldiers or different military units. A few years earlier, Legion members had witnessed friction between veterans of the First World War and the Second World War as new arrivals attempted to join Legion Halls. No Korea veterans disputed the scope and importance of the world wars compared to their own service. No Korea veterans ever claimed survival of the free world depended on them, although some believed the war was necessary to stem communism. Canadian shores and streets were never under threat of Chinese invasion. But the Royal Canadian Legion's initial rejection of more than thirty thousand Canadians who had served in Korea as volunteers still stung.

It is a fact that UN delegates, as well as political leaders of the sixteen member nations that contributed fighting forces, described Korea as a "police action." And in the strictest interpretation of the UN's "maintenance of international peace and security" principle, the soldiers sent to South Korea were, indeed, enforcing that concept. The label, concocted to avoid legal declarations of war, muddied the waters at home, even if the situation at the front had been clear. No one in the trenches north of the Imjin River from 1951 until the armistice considered fighting there anything less than a war of attrition. From the outset, the UN secretary-general, Trygve Lie, described North Korea's armed move across the thirty-eighth parallel as a "war against the United Nations."[6]

From as early as fall 1951, however, combat in Korea seemed an overlooked phenomenon. When he returned to Canada after a visit to the Korean front lines, the archbishop of Edmonton warned there was an "ominous danger" that Canadian troops might "become infected with the feeling that Canadians at home have relegated the Korean war to a position of unimportance." The Reverend W.F. Barfoot added that he feared their efforts amounted to little more than "a forgotten war."[7]

It was the early evening hours of New Year's Day, 1953, and Ted Zuber, a Royal Canadian Regiment sniper, had come in from a successful daytime mission. He'd taken out a Chinese sniper in front of the Hook. Most in his battalion felt it was tit for tat, since the night before, Corporal John Gill, a section leader bringing his patrol back through a UN defensive line, had been killed by a Chinese sniper. Private Zuber had then settled down in the tunnels beneath the Hook position to sleep.

Also in the tunnel that night were a combat engineer named Connors and two South Koreans who had been assigned to work with him. But, at that moment, the threesome was resting. Connors lit a candle and began reading a paperback. Meanwhile, a fourth man, a signaller named Doug Rainer, had permission to take a cigarette break in the tunnel. He sat next to the sleeping Zuber.

That same night, about twenty recruits arrived in the area as part of a reinforcement draft from Canada. The replacements had just begun preparing their weapons for the night's postings. One of the new men began priming a box of a dozen grenades in the tunnel. It was about midnight when one of the grenades he primed slipped from his hands. The grenade had a four-second fuse. Instead of shouting an alarm or tossing the grenade farther down the tunnel, the recruit ran out of the tunnel.

The explosion decapitated one of the Korean workers and severely wounded the other in the chest. Connors' leg was broken in two places. Part of the signaller's foot was blown off. Ted Zuber took shrapnel up and down his legs and in the buttocks. The regimental aid post was already busy when the wounded arrived. The medical officer was working over sawhorses, so Zuber – on a stretcher – was placed on the bunker floor next to the wounded South Korean labourer. A medical corporal approached and saw that Zuber's pants were bloodied. "What is it?" he asked.

"I think I'm okay," Zuber said. He pointed at the Korean. "What about him?"

"Oh Christ," the medic said. He knelt to investigate.

"Hey!" the medical officer shouted to the corporal. "Our own first!"

There was no argument. The corporal got up from the Korean and moved to Zuber. "Forgive me," he said.[8]

Zuber was conscious enough to be horrified, horrified for the dying South Korean, horrified for the dilemma facing the young corporal. The two Canadians heard the wheezing next to them end. The Korean labourer had taken his last breath.

Farther behind the lines, at a Norwegian MASH unit, Zuber remembered a doctor smirking as he probed the wounds in his buttocks. The surgeon took eighteen pieces of shrapnel from the bones in his legs and the flesh of his backside, but Zuber's greatest fear was not realized. His genitalia were intact. Not that lovemaking crossed his mind while at the Hook.

"Emotion was a luxury we learned to give up in the front lines," Zuber said. "I never heard a dirty joke the whole time I was in Korea. It just went completely out of your world. Emotion was something you just didn't tolerate."

On 26 January, sniper Ted Zuber was back in the line. That day, the regiment's war diary recorded that he "unleashed poetic justice today when he killed two Chinese [snipers,]" one of whom was carrying the identification tags of Corporal Gill, the soldier killed on New Year's morning. In the emotionless war of attrition at the front lines in Korea, killing the sniper was considered an evening of the score.

Zuber's tour of duty ended later in 1953. He'd scored his share of kills, and his talent for sketching had also been put to work. He made dozens of field drawings of Chinese positions and bunkers for the Canadian Intelligence Section. Then, for his own amusement, he drew sketches of soldiers washing, writing letters, or waiting and tucked them all away.

"Years later, when I decided to commit myself to putting my memoirs of the Korean War on canvas," Zuber said, in his art studio in Ontario, "I looked at the sketches and realized they were emotionless. They were about as interesting as a topographical map. Every single face was absolutely dead, lifeless, no expression whatsoever." He eventually began to paint from memory, and "the one thing I had to inject later was the emotion."

At first, Zuber refused to show his Korean War paintings to anyone. But when the Canadian War Museum began searching for a visual history of the war, a private buyer (who'd purchased Zuber's work) donated the paintings. The collection was revealed, and Zuber accepted his new role as artist for the Korean War.

Finding his way back into civilian life proved more complicated for Lance Bombardier Jim McKinny. When his outfit, the Royal Canadian Horse Artillery, disembarked the train at Winnipeg at the end of its tour in 1953, McKinny recalled being formed up with fellow gunners at the railway station and marched downtown to the cenotaph that marked the fallen of the two world wars. The young veteran felt genuine excitement knowing that his parents and girlfriend had come in from western Manitoba to welcome him home.

"But I couldn't face [my girlfriend] for nearly a month," McKinny said. "We only lived twenty-three miles apart, but I just couldn't handle people anymore. I had written to her every day I was away, but I just couldn't put my feelings into words. I was literally bushed. Korea made me a social misfit."[9] And while he eventually broke the ice with his girlfriend, Lee (whom he later married), McKinny locked away everything that had happened in Korea. He never spoke to family or friends about it. He made no effort to find fellow veterans. It was the chapter of his life he preferred to forget.

Then, in 1991, he and Lee decided to attend a Saskatoon Legion dance. When McKinny dropped by the branch to buy the tickets, he was asked to fill out a form, on which he included his overseas service in 1952–53.

"Oh," said the Legion official. "You're a Korea veteran?"

"Yeah," answered McKinny. He paused, thinking the worst, "Can't we join?"

"Oh, sure," the man said. "I was just curious because your group meets here once a month downstairs."

"What group?"

"The Korea Veterans Association," the man said.

The Korea Veterans Association of Canada had its beginnings in a small reunion at Camp Borden in summer 1973. About 130 veterans and their wives gathered for the initial event, and a year later, they formed the association with Clyde Bougie as its president. When Jim McKinny joined Unit 61, the Saskatoon branch, in 1991, he found kindred spirits among his fellow veterans. And finally – after nearly forty years – he began to address his memories of service in Korea. What's more, McKinny began campaigning to have local cenotaphs around Saskatchewan rededicated to include recognition of the Korean War and its veterans.

When he got home from his year-long tour of duty, medic Don Leier found out his service in Korea wasn't worth a single dollar. In 1950, he'd left the Saskatchewan family farm to make room for his eight brothers. He'd learned to administer needles, tourniquets, and first aid. And in 1952 he served with the Royal Canadian Army Medical Corps, attending to the wounded at an advanced dressing station. But in the early 1960s, back in Saskatoon, Leier went to a veterans' loans officer to get a down payment for his first house. The man refused. "Korea was no war, just a police action. Here's fifty cents. That's all you're getting."[10]

With that, Leier pretty much dismissed his Korea service for good. In 1982, Leier's ten-year-old daughter, Lisa, interviewed her dad for a social studies project on war. The Grade 6 student wrote some poetry and a short story based on her father's reminiscences. She borrowed his photographs, and she transcribed an interview with him.

"What unit did you serve in?" she asked.

"The 37th Field Ambulance, Royal Canadian Army Medical Corps," Leier said.

"What exactly was your job?"

"I worked in the advanced first-aid station."

It was the first time since the veterans' loan incident that Don Leier had thought about his service in Korea and the first time he cared to talk about it. The interview had both light and sobering moments, such as when Lisa asked him: "Is the TV show *M*A*S*H* realistic?"

"Just the medical stuff," Leier said. "Not the pranks they played."

"Were you ever scared?" she asked finally.

"Yup," Leier said. "I was scared."

On the night of 23 October 1952, thirty-four men in B Company of Royal Canadian Regiment infantry moved into one of the forward defensive positions in front of a mountain the Koreans called Kowang-san. But continuous Chinese artillery bombardment of Hill 355, as the Canadians knew it, left few of the field defences for protection. Minefields and protective barbed wire had been destroyed. Weapon pits that held ammunition had been buried by the shelling. Bunkers the troops used for shelter had caved in. And ground-laid telephone lines linking the forward positions to the company command post had been chopped to pieces.

A rifleman with No. 5 Platoon, Private George Griffiths, was one of those occupants posted to a trench near a weapon pit to protect a thirty-calibre machine-gun position in the B Company area. The twenty-two-year-old infantryman remembered, "It was just like the movies where we're ducking every time an enemy shell comes in ... the dirt hitting our helmets. Bang, rattle, rattle ... And all I could think of was that I had left a good job on Bay Street in Toronto to come to this."

At 1820, about an hour after sunset, Chinese gunners put down a tremendous concentration of artillery fire on B Company's position for eight or ten minutes. Then it focused fire on positions to the left and right of the Canadian position for another forty-five minutes. In what had been known as a "box barrage" during the First World War, the Chinese bombardment effectively cut off B Company on both flanks and the rear. Every soldier in those forward positions knew that a Chinese infantry attack was imminent.

Even before the last of the Chinese artillery shells exploded around their weapon pit, Griffiths and his trench mate, Art Bates, heard the bugles of the charging Chinese infantry. The Chinese sometimes sent a first wave of assault troops through their own artillery barrage to improve the element of surprise. This time it worked. Several of the Canadian weapon pits were soon facing heavy small-arms and mortar fire, which forced the surviving defenders to fall back. The No. 5 and 6 Platoon commanders were soon pinned down; in fact, the only reason one of them survived was that he played dead as the Chinese passed over him. Meanwhile, Griffiths and Bates, who didn't know about the general retreat, were cut off from the rest of their company. They ran for their lives through the decimated trench system.

At a crossroads in the trenches, Griffiths and Bates made a fateful mistake. They chose a trench that led deeper into the Chinese advance. To make things worse, a shell exploded close by and sent shrapnel into Griffiths's right foot. He put his head down and kept on going and was soon lagging behind Bates. But Griffiths was running out of time and space. The trench led to a bunker and a dead end. He could hear the Chinese troops on the ground above the trenches, all around him, so, one by one, he tossed his remaining four hand grenades into their midst. This brought down another Chinese concussion grenade, which caught him in the shoulder and left knee.

"I knew I was beat," Griffiths said. "I pulled aside the blanket in the doorway of the bunker and fell inside. There were three or four bodies there. Didn't know who they were. But I lay down and reloaded my rifle ... When two Chinese came in. One had a flashlight and a rifle, the other a burp gun which fires 450 rounds a minute. My single shot Lee-Enfield was good for nothing.

"Now in the heat of battle, when it comes to taking prisoners, they don't take your pulse to see if you're dead or alive. They stab you with a bayonet ... So they stabbed these other guys and they were dead. When they came to me, I went, 'Uh-uh!'"[11]

Behind the bunker in which George Griffiths surrendered, about a dozen members of his B Company had made it safely to A Company lines. A counter-attack was underway. And Commonwealth brigade artillery had already begun a heavy bombardment of the area that Griffiths and his comrades had tried to defend. By 0330 on the morning of 24 October, Hill 355 was completely back in the UN's hands. The action had killed eighteen Royal Canadian Regiment troops, wounded thirty-five more, and left fourteen prisoners of war, including Private George Griffiths.

For nearly ten months, Griffiths and 171 other UN POWs – men from Greece, Turkey, France, Australia, the United States, Puerto Rico, and Canada – sat through the daily interrogation and indoctrination. The prisoners were not given a change of clothes. They were not given medical attention. The mud and straw huts they ate and slept in had no tables, no chairs, no beds, no blankets, and no lights. Just dirt floors. The occupants called themselves the "Throwbacks" because they didn't accept the Chinese version of the truth. They refused to give the Communists the answers they wanted.

Even the letters POWs were allowed to write home had to reflect the correct attitude. Griffiths tried numerous times to write his wife, Barbara. As far as she knew, George was missing in action and presumed dead. He tried desperately to write prose that would pass the camp censors. But when he described his clothing as "a uniform that looked like a quilted blanket," they forced him to rewrite, and rewrite, because they felt he was complaining that all he had for warmth was a blanket. The letters never reached his wife.

But one letter he wrote in December 1952 did reach his friend Dick Ogden in Brighton, Ontario, in May 1953.[12] In it, he offered enough small talk about a Thanksgiving supper served by the Chinese Volunteer Army and the winter weather being similar to home that it passed both the Chinese and British censors. And that's how Barbara Griffiths discovered her husband was still alive half a year after his capture.

In June 1953, treatment suddenly improved in the camps. (Griffiths later found out that improvements coincided with peace talks at Panmunjom taking a positive turn.) The Chinese gave them each a hat, a pair of pants, socks, a pair of running shoes, and a tube of toothpaste. Griffiths had not received medical attention throughout his imprisonment, but all of a sudden, his health became a priority. Chinese doctors fed him five opium seeds as a general anesthetic for an operation. They put a pillowcase over his head because Chinese culture discourages watching surgery on the body. But Griffiths removed the hood and watched as they cut out the shrapnel that had been blown into his foot the night of the attack on Hill 355. When Griffiths was mobile again, the Chinese transported him and other POWs by truck to the rail terminus at Manp'ojin, North Korea, and by train to Freedom Village (Panmunjom) and across the Bridge of No Return to the south.

During his first hours of freedom, George Griffiths was deloused, given a new set of Australian-made clothes, and fed a big meal with Coca-Cola and beer. The food was so rich, he got sick. In hospital, they operated on his wounds again and examined his eyes and his teeth. And then they flew him home aboard a Canadian Pacific passenger plane. Aside from bits of shrapnel still in his body, the only mementoes of his imprisonment were a crucifix he'd fashioned from that tube of toothpaste and a tiny booklet. The booklet was made out of cigarette papers he'd hidden under his belt, and in it were all the names and addresses of the POWs he had been with. The Canadian government confiscated the booklet.

When Private George Griffiths finally arrived aboard the train in Toronto, his anxious wife, Barbara, his younger brother, Verdon (also a Korean War veteran), and his parents awaited him. So did a rude reception at the Kingston Veterans Affairs office a short time later. There, he requested a veteran's allowance of seven hundred dollars for a down payment on a house where he and Barbara could have a family and forget about the war and the imprisonment.

"You have no benefits." The civil servant shrugged.

"What do you mean?" Griffiths asked.

"No benefits. It wasn't a war ... Not officially, anyway."

Griffiths nearly throttled the man. When he calmed down and the circumstances were sorted out, the Royal Canadian Regiment veteran eventually got a down payment. But that wasn't the last outburst borne out of his experience in Korea. In 1982, when he worked as a prison guard at Ontario's Warkworth Institution, there was an attempted escape in his part of the facility.

"I had one prisoner ahead of me and another behind," Griffiths recalled. Suddenly, he was back in North Korea in 1952, and a prisoner himself. He remembered the ten months of deprivation and brainwashing and relived his own attempt to escape. "I fired three times at the prisoner going by me. I wanted him dead. I wanted him killed the same way [the Chinese] killed a Canadian soldier and walked over him in Korea. You see, in my mind, I was surrounded again. I was still a prisoner."

Beginning in January 1951, Canadians killed in the war were carried to a permanent cemetery near Busan. There, the Republic of Korea offered about fifteen hectares of land in tribute to the UN war dead. In 1992, Korean War veteran Bill Allan and his wife travelled to South Korea on a revisit. The entire trip proved to be an emotional roller coaster for the former private in the 3rd Battalion. But their visit to the UN cemetery in Busan affected him most of all. As he walked, Allan snapped pictures of the crosses and markers of some of his fallen comrades, including his Maritime friend, Bernard "Tunny" MacDonald, killed on patrol on 8 January 1953. Back in Canada, Allan turned the photographs over to fellow Royal Canadian Regiment veteran George Mannion, past president of Unit 57 of the Korea Veterans Association in Brampton, Ontario.

Coincidentally, the day Mannion was sorting through Allan's revisit shots, the phone rang. A soft-spoken female identified herself as Mary Robertson of Don Mills, Ontario. "I'm looking for someone who may have known my brother in Korea."[13]

"What's your brother's name?" Mannion asked.

"Tunny MacDonald," she said, in a whispery voice. "He was killed over there."

Mannion held the photograph Bill Allan had taken of MacDonald's gravesite in Busan. He told Mary that.

"I've never seen the grave," Mary said.

"I'm sure Bill Allan would be glad to make you a copy."

Mary Robertson's inquiry, or as her sister described it, "Mary's whisper," began a process that would bring together thousands of veterans literally and spiritually for the first time since they had come home from Korea. It would also give the war that history forgot a permanent resting place. Between them, Mary Robertson and Bill Allan hatched the idea of fashioning a Korean War memorial for Canadians in Canada. At first, it was envisaged as a portable collection of photographs of the grave markers in Busan and Yokohama. The concept evolved to include a permanent monument built of stone and displaying 516 bronze replicas of the Busan grave markers. The Wall of Remembrance was unveiled at the Meadowvale Cemetery, near Brampton, on the forty-fourth anniversary of the Korean War's armistice.

The Wall provided survivors of the war and their families in Canada a place to gather in remembrance, As it turned out, the Wall and the ceremony also resolved at least one homecoming mystery.

On the morning of Sunday, 27 July 1997, a convoy of buses shuttled people from a staging area in Brampton to the Meadowvale Cemetery. Nearly six hundred Korea veterans from across Canada made the pilgrimage to the event. Nearly a thousand others – families, friends, media, politicians, and interested spectators – gathered in silence near the semicircular walkway in front of the wall or on the grassy hillside that rose above the wall from one end to the other.

Then came a most extraordinary moment. Following the dignitaries' speeches, the reading of a special poem in honour of the occasion, and much wreath laying, the veterans, who'd stood quietly, waiting in parade formation in front of the monument, were invited to approach the wall. The veterans, alone with their thoughts before the many bronze plaques, removed poppies from their lapels and pinned them on the wall. Some bowed their heads and closed their eyes. Others saluted smartly. Many wept openly. Then, in spontaneous response to the veterans' individual and collective grieving, many family members left their places adjacent to the memorial to join the vets at the wall.

Two middle-aged women emerged from the throng on the hillside and made their way through the sea of veterans to stand before the wall. One of the women caressed an eight-by-ten framed photograph of a young man in uniform. The picture faced out. The two women then held each other for emotional support as they knelt before the bronze plate commemorating one of the fallen, in all likelihood the man in the photograph.

A Korean War veteran separated himself from the clusters of men at the wall and introduced himself to the women. The three were suddenly frozen in recognition. The three quietly embraced, and tears flowed freely.

An interview revealed that the two women, Barbara Differ and Hazel Regan, were sisters. The framed photograph was a portrait of their brother Bill Regan. Early in July 1953, Regan's unit, 3rd Battalion, the Royal Canadian Regiment, had moved onto Hill 187 along the Commonwealth Division front. Sometime during the night of 17 July, the sisters learned by telegram that their brother had been wounded and taken to a MASH unit, where he died on 24 July, just three days before the armistice at Panmunjom. That's all the information official records ever gave them. In all the years after the war, none of Bill Regan's six sisters could discover anything more about their brother's wartime death.

"In 1991 we went to Korea," Hazel Regan explained later. "All of us except one [sister] went to Korea. We sort of expected while we were in Korea that we would meet someone who knew my brother and how he died. We found nothing ... In my heart, though, I always knew someday we would meet someone."[14]

That someone, it turned out, was the veteran who had approached them at the wall. His name was Clyde Pryor, an infantryman who'd served in Bill Regan's section of the regiment. Pryor remembered that the Chinese artillery fire had been particularly intense that night in July 1953. The shelling had broken a number of ground-laid communication lines. A volunteer pioneer patrol was assembled to work its way out into no man's land and repair the severed lines. Though both men were resigned to doing the repairs, they sensed the job didn't require two specialists, just one. Pryor said he and Regan flipped a coin to see who would go. Regan lost the toss. Then, Pryor told the sisters, during the repair operation, the Chinese shelling resumed, and Private Regan was mortally wounded.

"But for the toss of the coin, that would be me," Pryor told Hazel Regan as he pointed to the picture. In fact, Pryor admitted that one of the reasons he'd come to the unveiling was the hope of finding a member of Regan's family. "If not for the coin toss," he repeated, "I wouldn't be here. Your brother would be."[15]

An incredible coincidence. On a night so close to the end of the war, a young man from Toronto, Bill Regan, is felled by enemy shell fire. His family receives only the minimum notification, that he died while on active service with fellow Royal Canadian Regiment troops. The soldier's comrade is equally devastated, knowing he, not Regan, might well have been killed that night. Despite every attempt to learn more about his death, the Regan family finds nothing, not even after going to Korea. When Bill Regan's parents died some years after the war, the surviving sisters had a stone laid at their parents' gravesite. The inscription included their brother's epitaph: "Bill Regan, 1933–1953. Killed in Korea. July 24, 1953. Pax."

Then, at a ceremony and tribute created by Bill Regan's surviving comrades, a ceremony to give Canadian-bound mourners a place to grieve half a century later, Bill Regan's sisters meet the man who last saw their brother alive on the battlefield. He helps them carry the burden of grief. He fills in the empty spaces in their picture of their brother's last hours.

Hazel was asked: "Whatever possessed you to bring the framed photo of your brother Bill here to the wall unveiling today?"

"Because we felt it was important to put a human face on war," she said. "I brought Bill's picture so he wouldn't be forgotten."

Notes

1 Joe MacSween, "Lost Weight in Red Prison Camps, Freed Canadians Decline to Talk," *Canadian Press*, 30 August 1953.
2 Watson, quoted in MacSween, "Lost Weight."
3 Robert S. Peacock, *Kim-Chi, Asahi and Rum: A Platoon Commander Remembers Korea, 1952–1953* (Toronto: Lugus, 1994), 540.
4 Bill Jackson, interview, Calgary, Alberta, 2 August 1997.
5 Don Flieger, interview, Kitchener, Ontario, 15 April 1998.
6 Quoted in Merle Miller, *Plain Speaking: An Oral Biography of Harry S. Truman* (New York: Berkley Publishing, 1986), 290.
7 Barfoot, quoted in "Korea Conflict 'Forgotten War,'" *Canadian Press*, 14 November 1951.
8 Ted Zuber, interview, Petawawa and Seeley's Bay, 3 May 1997.
9 Jim McKinny, interview, Saskatoon, Saskatchewan, 4 August 1997.
10 Don Leier, interview, Saskatoon, Saskatchewan, 1 August 1997.
11 George Griffiths, interview, Petawawa, Ontario, 4 May 1997.
12 George Griffiths to Dick Ogden, 5 December 1952, with permission.
13 George Mannion, interview, Toronto, Ontario, 25 July 1997.
14 Hazel Regan, interview, Brampton, Ontario, 27 July 1997.
15 Clyde Pryor, interview, Brampton, Ontario, 27 July 1997.

14

The Korean War's Impact on the Republic of Korea Army and the Korean People's Army

Youngjun Kim

The Korean War was one of the most important events and tragedies in modern Korean history. It continues to shape the divided Koreas. The war's legacy is at the root of the contested security of the Korean peninsula today. The Korean People's Army invaded South Korea on 25 June 1950, but the origins of the conflict began much earlier. During the early twentieth century, facing occupation by imperial Japan, Korean nationalists in opposition formed Communist and Nationalist cadres that resisted the occupation and Japanese imperial policies in Korea and among Korean populations in Manchuria.[1] After the defeat of the Japanese empire in summer 1945, the Soviet Union's forces entered the northern part of Korea, and the United States occupied the southern part of Korea as part of the agreement that oversaw the Japanese surrender.

In the five years that followed, any hopes for Korean independence and reunification were waylaid. The Soviet Union supported the Korean People's Army (KPA) in North Korea while the United States aided the Republic of Korea Army (ROKA) in the South. Many KPA soldiers had experience and training through the Soviet Union's Red Army or the Chinese Communist forces during the Second World War. The officers and service personnel of the ROK were less experienced but had received training in the Japanese Army during the occupation and the US Army in the immediate postwar period. These formative influences shaped both armed forces. During the Korean War, the KPA and the ROKA were profoundly transformed by their bloody combat experiences. The war's deep legacies remain to this day.

Foundations of the ROKA and KPA

The ROKA originated from the Korea Independence Army, which was founded in 1940 during the Japanese colonial period but emerged with the birth of the Republic of Korea (ROK) government during the US occupation. When the ROK government was established on 15 August 1945, the ROKA had about fifty thousand soldiers and five brigades, commanded by the army chief of staff, General Lee Engjun. On 15 January 1946, the Korean Constabulary was established, based on Brigadier General L.E. Schick and Colonel A.S. Champeny's so-called Bamboo Plan, envisaged as a force of twenty-five thousand soldiers in nine regiments. The US Joint Chiefs of Staff approved an enlarged Korea Constabulary (up to fifty thousand soldiers) on 10 March 1948. The constabulary was to act as a militia and reserve force for the permanent army. From May 1949 to July 1950, the ROKA upgraded to eight divisions of roughly one hundred thousand soldiers. The ROK asked the United States to approve an expansion of the ROKA, which became more professional as combat experience mounted as the war drew on. Finally, the wartime emergency convinced US president Dwight Eisenhower to approve the ROKA's expansion to twenty divisions. In May 1953, it reached an establishment of 655,000 soldiers. The ROKA also adopted organization and tactics similar to American formations after years of training, instruction, and joint operations.[2]

ROK army officer students in the United States, 1952–56

	1952	1953	1954	1955	1956
Infantry School	300	336	360	368	320
Field Artillery School	201	248	289	274	164
Armor School	14	14	17	24	62
Engineer School	6	93	98	145	131
Signal Corps School	12	15	20	50	95
Aviation School	–	–	10	15	–
Medical School	4	64	28	48	48
Adjunct School	6	4	6	6	6
Paymaster School	–	2	4	5	5
Quartermaster School	4	12	12	17	29
Military Police School	2	8	8	12	10
Ordnance School	5	8	12	54	95
Intelligence School	–	1	–	5	10
Psychological School	58	–	–	–	–
Transportation School	2	2	4	3	18
Chemical School	5	5	7	10	10
Command and General Staff College	2	6	15	15	20
Total	621	827	886	1,050	1,041

Source: The Adjutant General's Office, Department of the Army, Tab M Summary of MDAP Training, 1954.5.17 (Washington DC: Department of the Army, 1954); and 김민식 [Min-sik Kim], "1950년대 한국군의 미국 군사유학 시행과 그 영향" [The Republic of Korea's army officers' military study abroad and its effects during the 1950s], 軍事 [Military] 98, 3 (2016): 285–321.

This table shows that thousands of ROKA officers had opportunities to benefit from US military education during and after the Korean War. These graduates became key players in shaping the ROKA's American approach to warfighting, introducing new equipment and institutions early in ROKA's postwar formation. These officer students not only learned English, technology, and tactics, but they also helped to forge closer bonds between the Republic of Korea and the United States. The training also had a lifelong impact on the young officers, whose service often lasted long after the war. In Korean society, not surprisingly in the aftermath of the war, Americanization was associated with modernization, and the American way of life became an aspirational model for the South Korean people. Koreans hoped to advance their society by embracing capitalism and establishing a safe and powerful homeland.

North of the thirty-eighth parallel, the Democratic People's Republic of Korea (DPRK) followed the role model of the Soviet Union. Kim Il Sung had been a junior officer in the Red Army, serving as company commander of the Soviets' 88th Special Reconnaissance Brigade during the Second World War in China. During Operation August Storm in 1945, the Soviet Army destroyed the Japanese Army in Manchuria. With the Japanese occupiers defeated, young Kim Il Sung and his colleagues had an ambitious plan to create a new army based on the Soviet model.

As a young soldier, Kim Il Sung had worked with the Chinese against the invading Japanese Army in Manchuria, from whom he fled, finding refuge in the eastern Soviet Union. He was meant to fight in Operation August Storm, but his unit did not enter combat because of the swift Soviet victory over the Japanese. When Kim Il Sung and his close colleagues returned to Korea from Manchuria, they brought with them a model for their new Korean army based on Red Army structures and concepts. Kim and his colleagues were initially a small faction among other political rivals who had fought the Japanese, including pro-Chinese Korean Communist groups who served in Korean territory during the Japanese period. However, with Soviet support before and during the Korean War, Kim Il Sung's faction gradually marginalized and ultimately removed his political rivals.[3]

On the eve of the Korean War, the KPA was a mixed force consisting of a small number of former Soviet-trained Koreans and a larger number of Korean Chinese veterans of Mao Zedong's forces who had joined the KPA after 1949. More than 70 percent of the KPA's battalion, regimental, and divisional commanders had former service in Mao's forces. With the strong influence of Chinese and Soviet officers, the KPA came to rely heavily on these countries' weapon systems. It might be said that the KPA's body – its organization, weapons, and doctrines – was derived from the Red Army, but its soul – its philosophy of life and military experiences – was grounded in Mao's Chinese Army and informed by the people's war or Maoist way of war.[4]

In the late 1940s, the DPRK drew its strength from poor Korean peasants, and prospective leaders with suitable family backgrounds often had an opportunity to study in the Soviet Union.[5] These young, passionate North Korean students benefited from this study abroad and usually rose to mid-career positions in industry, the party, universities, and other prominent institutions in North Korea. Kim Il Sung intentionally created a new middle class to become a new politically reliable backbone for North Korean society.

The KPA drew on this new class. Young KPA officers studied in the Soviet Union, where they learned military doctrines, field manuals, and drill exercises and techniques. As in the Americanization of the South Korean military, the Sovietization of North Korea led to the modernization of society with a focus on heavy industry. In the process, the KPA became an iconic symbol of the emerging Communist nation, a nation with advanced technology and strong self-defence capabilities.[6] Before the Korean War, Soviet military advisers also trained officers in North Korea, complementing the Sovietization process.[7]

The Korean War, the ROKA, and the KPA

When the Korean War broke out, the ROKA was in a crucial transition period. Most division commanders were new to their positions, and most had left units where they had established a working dynamic. On the other side, the KPA's commanders and staff were much more experienced because of their role in the Chinese Civil War. Around fifty thousand KPA soldiers had served in the Chinese forces, including 96 percent of the political commissars, who were directly guided by a party and more powerful positions than the commanding officers of units. Half of the general staff had also served in the Chinese forces, giving the entire force tremendous combat experience and providing Kim Il Sung with confidence in his invasion plan of the South.[8]

In the early stages of the war, the KPA advanced quickly, led by Pang Ho-san's 6th Division, which had a high proportion of Chinese Civil War veterans. The UN sided with South Korea; it condemned the invasion and encouraged its members to contribute to the South's defence as ROKA forces gave way in the face of the assault and retreated to the Nakdong River line. The Americans were also pushed back. Their formations consisted of many young and inexperienced soldiers who, as Brian McAllister Linn establishes in his chapter in this volume, had never heard of Korea and who had little understanding of Korean territory or the KPA's military capability.

But the ROKA and US Army survived and reversed the series of defeats in the Nakdong River Dense Line Battle, the defence of the Busan perimeter, and the Inchon Landing in September 1950. The Allied's advance northward led to the intervention of the Chinese People's Volunteer Force (CPVF), composed of more than 260,000 men and which Mao contributed to secure North Korea against the advancing UN Command.

The fighting that emerged in winter 1950 and spring 1951 was, as other contributors to this volume have noted, markedly different from the war's initial phases. When the trench lines finally solidified throughout 1951, around 40,000 insurgents, fifth columnists, and members of the South Korea Labour Party sympathetic to the North fought behind the lines. The ROKA, with reinforcements from contributing countries, was forced to divide some of its efforts to fight against the KPA along the line of confrontation and against the guerrilla forces in rear areas.[9] Battle-tested, the ROKA's combat performance steadily improved, aided by American and UN advisers and bolstered by overwhelming UN firepower.

The KPA soldiers were successful at first, but they were not the main players after the Chinese intervened and took over the direction of the war. Commander Peng Dehuai emerged as supreme commander of the CPVF-KPA's combined headquarters. Because the CPVF engaged in most of the fighting, the KPA did not develop more robust warfighting skills. As they lost the initiative, the North Korean soldiers were often relegated to the position of passive observers.

The partnership between the CPVF and the KPA was fundamentally different than the one between the US Army and the ROKA. Tension and fighting erupted between Pang and Kim, leaving the North Korean dictator furious. Part of the North Korean response was to develop the Juche ideology, a theory of self-reliance that supports self-determination and self-defence rather than reliance on independent foreign forces or alliances for security.[10] In contrast, the ROKA came to see the value of alliances as a foundational aspect of its self-defence. In pursuing the Juche ideology, North Korea became more isolated.

The Korean War's Long-Term Impacts and Legacy for the ROKA and the KPA

Two historical events shaped modern Korean history: the Japanese occupation of Korea and the Korean War. Contemporary Korean issues can be traced to these powerful incidents, including domestic political struggles, ideological battles, the Korean peninsula security crisis, and the ongoing tension between Korea and Japan. The Korean War is seen as particularly tragic since the Korean people were forced to fight each other, and its psychological shock and deep scars remain to this day. Approximately 3 million people in North and South Korea died or were injured and as many as 10 million families were separated by the war, including the more than 250,000 people who fled from the North to the South during the war.[11] The Korean War made South and North Korea what they are today and indelibly shaped the ROKA and the KPA.

For the ROKA, the Korean War had far-reaching lessons. First, the Korean War forged a relationship in blood between the ROKA and the United States. Young American soldiers who had never heard of Korea sacrificed their lives to liberate the South. In the war's aftermath, American soldiers garrisoned in South Korea had a special status, notwithstanding occasional periods of tension linked to the political environment.[12] To Korean soldiers, the US Army offered a role model for shaping the armed forces. These educated ROKA officers often rose to senior command in the army and Korean society. The ROKA has been deeply influenced by the US Army, drawing on its technology, doctrines, field manuals, human resource management, and logistics.

Second, although the Korean War turned the ROKA into an experienced fighting formation, it has developed its own unique culture. Before the war, many Korean officers were inexperienced or former officers from the Japanese occupation. They lacked the battle experience of KPA officers, who had served in the Chinese Civil War. The ROKA suffered more than 217,000 war dead during the war, but the survivors were hardened in battle. The officers guided the ROKA forward, drawing on American influence and their own experiences. While influenced by the US forces, the ROKA developed its own weapons, field manuals, and training curriculums. The ROKA has its own weapons, such as K-2 rifles, tanks, drones, missiles, ships, submarines, and aircraft; its own training systems, such as the Battle Command Training Program and the Korea Combat Training Center; and its own defence diplomacy, such as peacekeeping operations and military cooperation with many countries.

Third, lessons from the Korean War shaped the ROKA, which has been preparing to fight North Korean forces for the past seven decades. There has been significant planning and preparation for another invasion, with early warning technology such as signals equipment and space satellite surveillance. Because of the Korean War's influence, the infantry has always been privileged in defence planning, from education and training to weapons procurement and budget allocation. The study of geography and terrain is also crucial, especially along the Demilitarized Zone. Since 2019, the ROKA has prepared for war with advanced technology – such as AI, drones, unmanned autonomous vehicles, and cyber, space, information, and other operational concepts – that has been called Defense Innovation 4.0.[13] With this doctrine, the ROKA has a vision and blueprint: always prepare for a future war. The doctrine's origins were in the fear struck during the surprise attack that launched the Korean War.

Finally, the Korean War made South Korean citizens generally support the ROKA and endorse the importance of self-defence. In the postwar period, a strong military presence defended South Korea: 720,000 soldiers, including 660,000 in the army, 15,000 in the navy, 27,500 in the Marine Corps and 16,500 in the air force.[14] The war's history is taught to students at all levels and, since 1957, all able-bodied male South Koreans between the ages of eighteen and thirty-five must submit to mandatory military service for up to two years.

Consequently, the ROK's military has a central place in South Korean society. This phenomenon was only enhanced during the period of military dictatorship and national emergency that lasted between 1960 and 1989. Occupying a key place in government, the ROKA initiated advanced science and technology investment. The Park Chung Hee government's (1961–79) success in expanding economic development and infrastructure helped to mute public opposition to his rule. Park and his successor, President Chun Doo-hwan (1981–88), invested heavily in military capability. In particular, President Park supported the ROK military's gaining access to nuclear weapons. His government developed the so-called Yulgok force development plan from 1974 to 1981. For instance, the GDP to defence budget ratio ranged from 3.3 to 5.5 percent. The military industry played a role in fuelling the country's economic boom and technological innovations.

In the North, the KPA also learned complex and difficult lessons from the war. The KPA enjoyed early victories, but its defeat in fall 1950 cast a long shadow as Chinese forces had to come to its rescue and eventually assumed strategic control of the war. North Korea's leadership endured this humiliation, but afterwards, greater emphasis was placed on an army structure that could operate independent of the Chinese or Soviet forces. Unlike the alliance between the ROKA and the United States, the North Koreans were often shamed by their senior partners, pushed to the periphery, and given little role in the fighting from 1951 to 1953.

Desperate, Kim Il Sung had asked Stalin to deploy Soviet forces to save North Korea, but the Soviet dictator only advised Kim Il Sung to flee from the Korean peninsula to Manchuria and start a guerilla war like Mao had done in the Chinese Civil War. Later in the war, Stalin and Mao refused to join the armistice negotiations, seeking to prolong the war for their own gains. Recent Korean War historical writing has shown that Stalin's global-security strategy throughout the Korean War was not about securing victory in Korea but about distracting the United States to give the Soviet Union and Eastern European countries breathing space to rebuild and recover their own economies to forestall the buildup of the US military in Europe. Stalin ordered Peng, the Chinese commander of the Sino-North Korea Combined Forces, and Kim not to sign an armistice and to instead use everything, including POW issues, to prolong the negotiations for as long as possible.[15]

The Soviet direction ran counter to Kim's ambition to end the war quickly, given that the relentless US air-bombing campaign had destroyed North Korea's infrastructure and cities and killed more than 280,000 civilians. A postwar North Korean estimate suggested that between 1948 and 1953, the country lost 20 percent of its population to war and refugee movements.[16] Kim Il Sung remembered that he'd been used as a pawn when planning the future of North Korea and its armed forces. In 1956, an attempted coup by plotters seeking to overthrow Kim Il Sung's regime and put in its place a pro-Chinese faction of North Korean elites provoked Kim Il Sung to expel the Chinese volunteer forces from North Korea's territory, and it strained relations with Mao. North Korea's Juche ideology primarily targeted enemies such as the United States and South Korea, but an unnamed target was Kim's previous allies – the Soviet Union and China. North Korea's enormous expenditure on its armed forces and its refusal to host foreign troops reflected the war's legacy in the North's efforts to secure independence and to build a bulwark against foreign intervention.[17]

The KPA also suffered heavily from US strategic-bombing campaigns during the last two years of the war. The bombers dropped 430,000 bombs, destroying approximately 8,700 industrial facilities and inflicting psychological trauma on the North Korean people. More than half of North Korea's approximately 2 million wartime casualties were civilians.[18] This massive trauma influenced the North Korean way of war. The KPA built underground bunkers and hundreds of kilometres of tunnels throughout the demilitarized zone. It invested in air defence weapons in addition to its formidable field artillery and other offensive capabilities. The Korean War experience also led the KPA to develop an unexpected emphasis on asymmetric warfare. The combined military capability of the ROKA and the US military, based on massive firepower and airpower, led to crippling KPA casualties. The KPA turned to insurgency warfare, tactical surprise, and special operations during the war, including support for an insurgency in the Jiri Mountain region of South Korea during the last stages of the war.[19]

After the Korean War, the KPA strengthened its asymmetric warfare capabilities, including special forces, cyber warfare, information and psychological warfare, abduction, terrorism, and assassination. It also relied on the deterrent qualities of nuclear, chemical, and biological weapons. During the Cold War, North Korea initiated a program to send spies and special forces into South

Korea to kill and kidnap ordinary citizens as well as members of the intelligentsia. The program was meant to destabilize the South as well as to "restock" the North's human capital.[20] The North Koreans pursued this course with some urgency, as the Park government's establishment of diplomatic relations with Japan in 1965 led to greater diplomatic links between South Korea and external markets.[21] In January 1968, North Korean special forces tried to assassinate South Korean president Park and his spouse, Yuk Young Soo. The First Lady was later assassinated by a North Korean sympathizer in August 1974. North Korean attacks against ROK targets occurred outside of the peninsula, such as a bombing attempt on Chun Doo-hwan during an official visit to Myanmar in 1983 that killed twenty-one, or the bombing of Korea Air Flight 858, which killed 115 passengers and the crew.

North Korean asymmetric attacks continued into the post-Cold War period, including an attempted infiltration by submarine that led to a manhunt and firefights between the ROKA and North Korean commandos in September 1996.[22] Recent North Korean provocations have included the 2010 North Korean bombardment of Yeonpyeong Island and the same year's sinking of ROKS *Cheonan* by North Korean torpedo attack, which killed forty-six ROK sailors. Cyberattacks and nuclear and missile tests have also been directed at the United States, South Korea, and Japan. However spectacular, North Korea's asymmetric operations are attempts to compensate for the KPA's historical weaknesses in conventional warfare capability, especially its limited logistical and sustainment ability versus an American enemy allied with South Korean forces. The legacy of the Korean War is that it continues to influence the KPA's strategic priorities.

Conclusion

The Korean War never ended in the Korean peninsula. Divided Korea remains one of the most dangerous security issues in the world. History repeats itself. The two Koreas were icons of the divided Cold War, and they remain icons of the new twenty-first-century Cold War. North Korea is still allied with China and Russia, and South Korea is still defended by the United States and Japan. The ROKA and the KPA still target each other, and the Demilitarized Zone is still one of the most dangerous places in the world. North Korea has conducted numerous nuclear and missile tests, and the KPA has become a symbol of this unique garrison state with its closed borders. Even as both armies have modernized since 1953, the Korean War exerts a strong influence. The ROKA and the KPA are representative of the two Koreas' different approaches to war and peace in a divided peninsula that has been deeply shaped by war and the greater regional and global forces at play in the Cold War.

Notes

1 Robert A. Scalapino and Chong-Sik Lee, *Communism in Korea,* vol. 1, *The Movement,* and vol. 2, *The Society* (Berkeley: University of California Press, 1972); Suh Dae-Sook, *The Korean Communist Movement, 1918–1948* (Princeton, NJ: Princeton University Press 1967); Allan R. Millett, *The War for Korea, 1945–1950: A House Burning* (Lawrence: University Press of Kansas, 2005); and Allan R. Millett, *The War for Korea, 1950–1951: They Came from the North* (Lawrence: University Press of Kansas, 2010).

2 국방부 군사편찬연구소 [Institute for Military History, Ministry of National Defense], 한국군 전력증강사 1, 1945–1960 [Development of the ROK Armed Forces 1, 1945–1960] (서울 [Seoul]: 국방부 군사편찬연구소 [Institute for Military History, Ministry of National Defense, 2020]), 241–44.

3 Scalapino and Lee, *Communism in Korea*; Suh, *The Korean Communist Movement*; Dae-Sook Suh, *Kimi Il Sung: North Korean Leader* (New York: Columbia University Press, 1988); Erik van Ree, *Socialism in One Zone: Stalin's Policy in Korea, 1945–1960* (New York: St. Martin's Press, 1989); and Andrei Lankov, *From Stalin to Kim Il Sung: The Formation of North Korea, 1945–1960* (New Brunswick, NJ: Rutgers University Press, 2002).

4 Youngjun Kim, *Origins of the North Korean Garrison State: The People's Army and the Korean War* (London: Routledge, 2017), 35–63.

5 KPA officers could not have had any association with occupying Japanese forces. Nor could their families have been members of the landholding classes.

6 Youngjun, *Origins of the North Korean Garrison State,* 86–114.

7 Youngjun, *Origins of the North Korean Garrison State,* 86–114; and National Archives and Records Administration, RG 242, box 10, file 200775.

8 Youngjun, *Origins of the North Korean Garrison State.*

9 Youngjun, *Origins of the North Korean Garrison State,* 195–229.

10 Suh, *Kim Il Sung*; and Youngjun, *Origins of the North Korean Garrison State.*

11 Kook Sungha and National Museum of Contemporary History, *National Museum of Contemporary History,* trans. Andrew McCullough and Ron Youngju (Seoul: National Museum of Contemporary History, 2012), 187.

12 Anti-American demonstrations became more common, understandably, after the 1987 democratization and the end of the Cold War, and more overt displays of displeasure were linked with incidents involving US Forces Korea. Overall, public impressions of the United States through the Cold War were positive, notwithstanding disappointment over the United States' failure to condemn military rule. Chang Hun Oh and Celeste Harrington, "Democratization and Changing Anti-American Sentiments in South Korea," *Asian Survey* 47, 2 (2007): 335. See also Hyug Baeg Im, "The US Role in Korean Democracy and Security since the Cold War Era," *International Relations of the Asia-Pacific* 6, 2 (2006): 157–87.

13 "Defense Chief Stresses Need for 'Realistic, Practical' Defense Innovation," *Korea Times,* 17 November 2022, https://koreatimes.co.kr/www/news/nation/2022/11/205_339998.html.

14 Ministry of National Defense, Defense Budget, https://www.mnd.go.kr/mbshome/mbs/mnd/subview.jsp?id=mnd_010401020000.

15 Youngjun Kim, "Why Did Stalin Not Support a Quick Victory of the Korean People's Army? Stalin's Unspoken Global Security Strategy for the Korean War," *Korean Journal of International Studies* 17, 1 (2019): 79–102; Shen Zhihua and Neil Siver, *Mao, Stalin and the Korean War: Trilateral Communist Relations in the 1950s* (London: Routledge, 2012); Shen Zihua, "Sino-Soviet Relations and the Origins of the Korean War: Stalin's Strategic Goals in the Far East," *Journal of Cold War Studies* 2, 2 (2000): 44–68; Shen Zhihua and Danhu Li, *After Leaning to One Side: China and Its Allies in the Cold War* (Washington, DC: Woodrow Wilson Center Press, 2011); and Kim Donggil, "Stalin's Korea U-Turn: The

USSR's Evolving Security Strategy and the Origins of the Korean War," *Seoul Journal of Korean Studies* 24, 1 (2011): 89–114.

16 This estimate comes from Lieutenant-General V.N. Razuvaev, who counted 282,000 bombing dead in addition to 800,000 other deaths associated with wartime conditions or ground combat. See Cold War International History Project, "New Evidence on North Korean War Losses," Wilson Center, Insights and Analysis, 1 August 2001, https://www.wilsoncenter.org/article/new-evidence-north-korean-war-losses.

17 Youngjun, *Origins of the North Korean Garrison State,* 195–238; Youngjun, "Why Did Stalin?," 79–102.

18 Youngjun, *Origins of the North Korean Garrison State,* 219–22; Songbo Kim and Yi Chongsok, *Puk'anui Yoksa 1: Kon'guk kwa Inmin Minjujuui Kyonghom, 1945–1960* [North Korean history, vol. 1, State building and the people's democracy experience, 1945–1960] (Seoul: Yoksa Pip'yongsa, 2011), 158.

19 Youngjun, *Origins of the North Korean Garrison State,* 195–229.

20 Go Myong-Hyun and Ben Forney, "Kidnapping as Foreign Policy: North Korea's History of State Sponsored Abductions," Asan Institute for Policy Studies, 2018.

21 Major Daniel P. Bolger, *Scenes from an Unfinished War: Low-Intensity Conflict in Korea, 1966–1969* (Fort Leavenworth, KS: Combat Studies Institute, 1991), 4–5. Bolger documents no less than forty firefights between the US 2nd Division and KPA infiltrators during these three years, in addition to the other provocations listed in this chapter.

22 Sebastien Roblin, "In 1996, a Dead North Korean Spy Submarine (Armed with Commandos) Nearly Started a War," *National Interest,* 13 March 2017, https://nationalinterest.org/blog/the-buzz/1996-dead-north-korean-spy-submarine-armed-commandos-nearly-19750. The manhunt took months to conclude, during which the North Koreans killed eight ROKA soldiers and two civilians. All but two of the twenty-six crewmen died by suicide or in combat with the ROKA.

15

Canadian-Korean Relations since the Korean War

Tina J. Park

The history of Canada's relationship with the Republic of Korea (ROK) since 1953 is one of exceptional growth and transformation. Today, after more than sixty years since the establishment of their diplomatic relationship, Canada and Korea share a largely positive partnership in trade, defence, and cultural exchange. But the bilateral relationship has not always been so familiar. Before dispatching Canadian troops to the Korean War in 1950, Canada's minister of national defence, Brooke Claxton, quipped, "Korea was an obscure place on the Western side of the Pacific, a place of indeterminate status, best known perhaps because the people were known to wear strange hats."[1] Claxton's comment is significant because it underlines the fact that Korea was seen as a battleground of the Cold War rather than as a country of significance in its own right. Lester B. Pearson, Canada's secretary of state for external affairs, and at the time the president of the UN General Assembly, said of the Korean War armistice of 26 July 1953: "This is the end of one chapter of bloodshed and fighting. But it is only the beginning of a new and difficult one – the making of peace."[2]

For three years, Korea had come to exist in the Canadian mind as a mountainous battlefield with bitter winters but also as a potential trouble spot. In the immediate aftermath of the war, Canada seemed content to leave behind the peninsula and its problems, effectively dusting its hands of the Korea question when reunification talks in Geneva in 1954 were fruitless. However, some Canadian soldiers remained engaged in Korea until 1957, and development aid was dispersed during this time, which proved to be important to Korea's recovery. Since then, South Korea's rapid industrialization and commercial interests gradually elevated the Korean peninsula's importance in the minds of Canadian policy-makers. This chapter provides an overview of Canadian-Korean relations since the Korean War, with reflections on key areas of collaboration. Essentially, this chapter argues that it was Canadian economic interests and South Korea's potential as a commercial partner, rather than Cold War politics or shared sacrifices from the war, that deepened Canadian-Korean relations from the 1960s onwards.

Humanitarian and Development Assistance

Canadian veterans from the Korean War returned home with vivid memories of the violent and destructive nature of warfare, the threat of communism, Korea's dismal state of poverty, and the special plight of orphans.[3] The stalemate in 1953 left many issues unresolved, and an unprecedented level of political, financial, human, and social damage across the peninsula. In South Korea alone, more than six hundred thousand housing units had been destroyed, leaving many Koreans on the street, along with damaged manufacturing capacity and shattered infrastructure.[4] Perhaps the greatest losses for Korean society were human: out of a population of 20 million in 1950, more than 1.3 million people were killed, wounded, or went missing. Orphans, refugees, widows, and the injured scrambled for water, food, and housing on city streets and in the countryside.

On 4 February 1954, two days after his seventy-second birthday, Prime Minister Louis St. Laurent embarked on an ambitious tour around the world, which included a short trip to Seoul on his way to Japan.[5] Asia certainly remained at the top of St. Laurent's priorities considering Canada's rapid economic developments and the "astonishing rate" of interdependence between nations of the world. In his own words: "Our external policy has acquired a growing importance in the thinking of our people, and the importance of external relations has been reflected in the debates in the House and practically all aspects of the activities of those who are charged with the responsibilities of government." St. Laurent vowed to the House of Commons before his departure that he would "bring back with me and also leave behind not only useful information but perhaps a clearer picture of the problems which all of us have to face together."[6]

St. Laurent saw Korea as a distant country, but his visit also confirmed that it was a suitable venue for Canadian aid. Having fought for South Korea's survival with its own soldiers, Canada now had a vested interest in safeguarding stability on the Korean peninsula. Protecting the survival of the ROK state became another means of fighting the Cold War. Throughout the 1950s, Canada's engagement on the Korean peninsula was primarily focused on the domain of humanitarian activities. These aid efforts were facilitated at official levels through the UN Korea Relief Agency and the Colombo Plan, which South Korea would later join in 1963, as well as through nongovernmental organizations in Canada.[7]

Chief among such organizations was the Unitarian Service Committee (USC) of Canada, founded by Lotta Hitschmanova in 1945.[8] From its inception in the early 1950s until its eventual termination in 1978, the ROK program remained the single-largest program ever undertaken by the USC. By 1978, the USC had invested some CAD$13 million in South Korea, which was more than half of the USC's total income in funds and gifts in kind. At the time of the withdrawal from Korea, Hitschmanova called it "the USC's greatest success story during the past thirty-three years."[9]

Ordinary Canadians were also actively involved in these humanitarian efforts, through campaigns such as "Milk for Korea" and "Operation Codfish," aimed at helping orphans and school children. In 1953, the Canadian government donated salted codfish from Newfoundland and Quebec valued at CAD$300,000 as an in-kind contribution to the UN Emergency Relief Programme in Korea.[10] This was in addition to its fully paid financial contribution of CAD$7.25 million.[11] By March 1954, Ottawa had contributed an additional 1,500 tons of Canadian salted cod valued at CAD$450,000 to the UN Emergency Relief Programme in Korea. The emergency relief program, in which thirty-six countries participated, had been inaugurated by the UN Command shortly after the outbreak of hostilities in Korea. It aimed to provide immediate aid to the Korean people.[12]

Nevertheless, Ottawa still had no "Korea policy" to speak of, mainly because Korea was still seen as an underdeveloped country, secondary in importance to Japan or China. There was no urgency in establishing diplomatic ties or developing any policy on Korea while the public servants in Ottawa viewed Korea as little more than an aid recipient. Hence, humanitarian impulses, largely stemming from grassroots efforts by the Canadian public and through organizations such as the USC, effectively substituted for official policy-level engagement during this period.

Building Diplomatic and Commercial Relations

Following developmental aid efforts in the 1950s, Canada and the ROK finally established diplomatic relations in 1963. The ROK government, under the leadership of Park Chung Hee, a highly authoritarian leader, was intent on expanding diplomatic relations in the West to gain international legitimacy vis-à-vis North Korea. Civil servants in Ottawa followed Korea's economic, diplomatic, and political developments carefully, especially given ongoing South Korean pressure for a resident Canadian ambassador in Seoul and the country's pursuit of a bilateral trade agreement on a most-favoured-nation basis.[13] According to Department of External Affairs internal memos, Canada rejected South Korea's suggestion for a bilateral trade agreement on a most-favoured-nation basis because of concerns about "being flooded with South Korean low-cost textiles."[14] In the early 1960s, Korean affairs was a secondary concern handled by staff at the embassy in Tokyo. South Korea in the early 1960s was still heavily reliant on external aid and, with some 70 percent of the national budget going towards defence and the containment of communism, Korea still needed help to support its population. These views are acutely illustrated in a 1964 report from the Canadian ambassador to Japan, R.P. Bower (who was also cross-accredited to Korea), who noted that "uneasy over recent international developments, the Koreans grasp at any symbol of moral and physical support from the West."[15] Bower's report serves as a reminder that while South Korea is the dominant economic and cultural power of the two Koreas in the 2020s, this outcome was far from certain in the decades following the war. External support was key to South Korea's survival.

Under such circumstances, the signature of the first trade agreement between Canada and the Republic of Korea, on 20 December 1966, marked an important occasion, particularly considering how quickly South Korea turned from being an aid recipient to a viable trading partner. The agreement was largely beneficial to Canada, as it emphasized exports of wheat, barley, flour, softwood lumber, pulp and newsprint, asbestos, and base minerals.[16] South Korea also agreed to place voluntary restraints on its exports to Canada if they threatened domestic industries in the Canadian market.[17] As a result of the agreement, between 1970 and 1972, Canadian exports to Korea doubled each year in sales of goods, mainly asbestos, wheat, sulphur, and pulp. Canadian imports from Korea also increased exponentially during this period, including sweaters, wigs, footwear, cotton, and synthetic textiles.[18]

Transformation of Canada-ROK bilateral trade, 1970s

	ROK exports to Canada		Canadian exports to ROK		
Year	Amount*	% change	Amount*	% change	Net*
1970	19,553	29.4	23,165	3.8	−3,612
1971	28,935	48.0	38,960	68.2	−10,025
1972	58,915	103.6	35,993	−7.6	22,922
1973	124,881	112.0	82,545	129.3	42,336
1974	166,764	33.5	115,702	40.2	51,062
1975	197,347	18.3	150,175	29.8	47,172
1976	314,129	59.2	115,852	−22.9	198,277
1977	298,756	−4.9	149,634	29.2	149,122
1978	327,173	9.5	204,033	36.4	123,140
1979	387,643	18.5	326,348	59.9	61,295

Note: * CAD$1,000s
Source: Government of ROK, K-Stats.

Commercial Relations and the CANDU Reactor

In many ways, the 1970s were a special decade in the history of Canadian-Korean relations in terms of institutional mechanisms, the takeoff in bilateral trade, and the expansion of the relationship between the two peoples. While the official diplomatic relationship was established in 1963, it took a full decade until a resident Canadian embassy was set up in Seoul in 1973, largely in response to Korea's economic growth. Under Prime Minister Pierre Trudeau, Canada heralded a new "Pacific" direction in its foreign policy, in recognition of the growing importance of the Asia-Pacific region. While these efforts were delayed and did not entirely succeed at first, the 1970s marked a clear point of departure in terms of volumes of trade and Korean migration to Canada.

In particular, the export of CANDU (Canada deuterium uranium) reactors, designed by Atomic Energy of Canada Limited, became a central issue in Canadian-Korean commercial relations.[19] The commercial value of the CANDU reactor, at about $576.5 million, made for the biggest but also the most controversial deal ever signed between Canada and the ROK. Exporting the CANDU reactors became a matter of public importance, as Canada struggled with domestic economic pressures and the broader foreign-policy objective of nuclear nonproliferation.[20] To purchase CANDU reactors, South Korea eventually ratified the Nuclear Non-Proliferation Treaty in 1976, halted its efforts to acquire a French nuclear-reprocessing plant, and placed enhanced safeguards on nuclear reactors.[21]

Despite its high commercial value, there was nothing inevitable about the success of CANDU export to Korea, because of the Canadian public's fears about nuclear proliferation as well as complicated politics in the Western alliance. Just a few years earlier, in 1969, Canada had failed to sell a CANDU reactor to South Korea, when the Korean government sought out the cheaper and more accessible American reactors on offer. At the same time, Washington suspected that South Korea was planning to develop a nuclear weapons program under the disguise of nuclear energy development. Throughout the 1970s, Canadian-Korean relations were primarily driven by economic interests for Canada and geopolitical interests for South Korea under the context of the Cold War. The changing dynamic of Canadian-American-British collaboration on nuclear reactors influenced the CANDU deal and brought Ottawa and Seoul closer together in the process. Domestic interests also influenced Ottawa's position, including Atomic Energy of Canada Limited's interest in exporting the CANDU technology to developing countries.[22] Growing public discontent about the United States in South Korea, coupled with fears about North Korea's technological advancement, all played into the South Korean decision-making process.

In 1973, the South Korean government approached Canada for the CANDU reactors. It did not hold an international tendering process in the hopes of reaching a quick deal without alarming Washington. President Park understood that Washington was wary of South Korea's investment in nuclear technology, and he found that Canada had the type of reactor that could be useful. Canada, through the Export Development Corporation and a consortium of banks, provided a loan of over CAD$300 million to the South Korean government to facilitate this deal.[23] After the Indian Peaceful nuclear explosion debacle – during which India purchased a similar reactor and used it to enrich plutonium to create a nuclear weapon – Canada, too, had cause for wariness about how CANDU technology might be used.[24] When the agreement for CANDU reactor sales to South Korea was signed on 26 January 1976, Canada insisted on the most stringent of all safeguards agreements to date, including several important conditions to highlight that nuclear cooperation was for peaceful purposes only.[25] Canada also insisted on prior consent for the retransfer of all nuclear equipment, material, facilities, fuel, or technology as well as a prior-consent requirement for the reprocessing of all generations of fuel.

Without a doubt, the sale of the CANDU reactors became the single most important game changer in terms of the Canadian approach towards Korea, shifting Ottawa's traditional preoccupations with Japan and China in its Pacific policy. A 27 January 1975 memo from the Pacific Division of the Department of External Affairs outlined the significance of the CANDU deal in Canadian-Korean relations:

> Until the event of the CANDU sale to Korea, our general relations interest in Korea was [sic] largely derived from our interest in Japan for which the Korean peninsula has great economic and security significance. This sale alters the substance and significance of our bilateral relationship with Korea and because of its political and economic implications we will need to follow developments on the Korean peninsula closely.[26]

Beyond the commercial value, the CANDU deal marked the beginning of a real partnership between the ROK and Canada.

Evolving Canadian-Korean Relations

Canada's relations with the ROK continued to blossom from the 1980s onwards, most notably in the realms of trade, immigration, cultural exchanges, and security cooperation. As like-minded allies, Canada and the ROK came to share similar values and interests on many global issues, including promoting peace and security, the rule of law, and human rights. Both countries are firmly committed to multilateral institutions such as the UN, the Association of Southeast Asian Nations, Asia-Pacific Economic Cooperation, and the North Atlantic Treaty Organization and have a history of close partnership with the United States.

One of the key areas where relations continued to improve was in trade. The Canada-Korea Free Trade Agreement, Canada's first free trade agreement in the Asia-Pacific region, entered into force on 1 January 2015. It represents a milestone for both countries. Most significantly, the agreement gives Canada access to the fourth-largest economy in Asia, which is crucial considering South Korea's $1.8 trillion annual GDP and its market of 51 million people.[27] With full implementation, the agreement is expected to increase Canadian exports to the ROK by 32 percent and boost the Canadian economy by CAD$1.7 billion. As of 2023, South Korea is Canada's seventh-largest merchandise trading partner and export market. Merchandise trade between the countries was valued at over $16.7 billion in 2021. Canada's exports to Korea, including mineral ores, mineral fuels and oils, precious stones and metals, pulp, wood, and meat reached $6.3 billion in 2021. Key items for Korean exports to Canada include passenger cars, wireless phones, automobile parts, tires, and steel; in turn, primary Canadian exports to Korea include bituminous coal, copper ore, iron ore, uranium, and pulp. Both parties to the trade agreement believe that it will continue to foster collaboration and coprosperity between the two countries in fields such as medicine, rails, steel, aerospace, artificial intelligence, and defence procurement.[28]

Market forces were not the only element influencing the Canada-Korea relationship. Immigration and people-to-people relations formed an increasingly important element of the link between the countries over the past sixty years. South Korean immigration to Canada has grown steadily since the 1966 reform of Canadian federal immigration regulations that implemented a merit-based points system to screen would-be citizens. In 1969, there were only about two thousand Koreans in Canada. That figure grew to nearly twenty thousand by 1980. By the late 1990s, Statistics Canada reported that the ROK had become the fifth-largest source of immigrants to Canada. In 2023, there are more than two hundred thousand individuals of Korean origin living in Canada, which is the fourth-largest Korean diaspora overseas.[29] Korean Canadian communities are concentrated in Ontario, British Columbia, Quebec, and Alberta. In addition, there are some twenty thousand Korean students studying in Canada as well as some three thousand Korean-born adoptees. There are also growing numbers of Canadians who live and work in the ROK. The latest figures include some 27,000 Canadians living in Korea, 3,200 of them English-language teachers. These figures are roughly equal to the thirty thousand Canadians who served in Korea during and after the war.[30]

Active efforts have been made to institutionalize cultural and people-to-people ties between the two countries. In 1984, the Canada-Korea Society was founded in Ottawa by Canada's first resident ambassador to Korea, John A. Stiles. The society had the principal aim of promoting bilateral friendships, cooperation, and better understanding between Canada and Korea, as well as among Canadians and Koreans. The society, under the leadership of Young-Hae Lee, has been working in close partnership with the Canada-Korea Inter-Parliamentary Friendship Group and the ROK embassy. The society continues to host an annual Canada-Korea dialogue series at Parliament Hill every summer, featuring high-level speakers who discuss key political and economic issues between the two countries.

The uncertain security environment since the end of the Cold War has also brought the two countries together. The 2022 Russian invasion of Ukraine has elevated the importance of close security cooperation between like-minded partners. In November 2022, the Canadian government launched its Indo-Pacific Strategy, highlighting the Republic of Korea as a key partner for Canada in the Indo-Pacific.[31] Although official diplomatic relations between South Korea and Canada commenced in 1963, Korea did not send a defence attaché to its Ottawa embassy until 1977. Canada posted its first defence attaché to Seoul in 1979. Defence relations between Canada and the ROK have since become more solidified. In line with the 1953 Korean Armistice Agreement, which created the UN Command Military Armistice Commission to supervise the Demilitarized Zone, the commission has long included a Canadian officer. Canada's commitment consists of one colonel (the Canadian defence attaché) and one sergeant as part of a team that liaises with the United Nations Command, an international body that investigates guard posts and ceasefire violations, participates in ceremonies, and facilitates the repatriation of the remains of mostly American and South Korean soldiers discovered in North Korea.[32] Whenever there are incidents along the Demilitarized Zone, the military liaison is responsible for reporting to the UN Command. The defence attaché in the ROK is also there to inform Canadian senior leadership through the Department of National Defence about the current situation on the Korean peninsula to facilitate collaboration on enhancing stability, another priority of the Indo-Pacific Strategy.

Since 2009, the ROK has been invited to observe or participate in Canada's Exercise Maple Flag. Maple Flag, an annual six-week training operation hosted by Canada's air force tactical training centre at CFB Cold Lake, has become one of the world's most significant international air combat exercises since its introduction in 1978. The Cold Lake base is home to the largest unrestricted airspace in the world and the only tactical bombing range in Canada, covering 11,600 square kilometres and more than 640 tactical targets. While it initially started as an aircraft-centric exercise, Maple Flag now seeks to encompass all tactical airframes in the modern air combat environment to better reflect changing trends in warfare. Exercise Maple Flag is designed to train multinational forces and enhance interoperability using a simulated UN air campaign against a capable enemy. By bringing together air force personnel from Canada's partner nations, the exercise tests a full spectrum of capabilities aimed at improving interoperability such as command and control, air-to-air and air-to-ground operations, and intelligence, surveillance, and reconnaissance.

On the other side of the Pacific, Canada since 2009 has participated in the Key Resolve Exercise, an annual combined and joint military command post operation held by the more than twenty-four US forces stationed in South Korea and the ROK armed forces. Using computer-assisted simulations, the exercise's objective is to strengthen the ROK-US combined forces' operational capabilities in defence of the ROK. In the most recent iteration, held in 2013, more than three thousand US and ten thousand ROK forces participated, under the command of the ROK Military Joint Chiefs of Staff and supervised by the Swedish and Swiss Neutral Nations Supervisory Commission to ensure that it complied with the terms of the 1953 Korean Armistice Agreement. Under the agreement between the Canadian government and the ROK, classified information is shared between the respective governments. The Key Resolve Exercise is also designed to strengthen Allied readiness for protecting the Asia-Pacific region and promoting peace and stability on the Korean peninsula.[33]

Canada and the ROK have also engaged in an annual bilateral exchange of warships since 2000.[34] Both countries are members of the Combined Maritime Forces, a thirty-four-member maritime multinational partnership operating in the Gulf of Aden, Arabian Gulf, Indian Ocean, and Gulf of Oman. The Canadian and Korean navies have, as a result, enjoyed a close partnership on naval engagements in the region. In 2010, the ROK Navy assumed command of Combined Task Force 151, a counterpiracy operation in the Gulf of Aden. This was the first time that the ROK assumed the role of command within the Combined Maritime Forces and reflects the enhanced reputation of the Korean Navy, as seen in its leadership, in 2006 and 2008, of the Rim of the Pacific Exercise, the world's largest international maritime warfare exercise, hosted biennially, largely by the US Navy's Pacific fleet. Canada and the ROK, both Pacific Rim nations, have been enthusiastic participants in the exercise, hosted largely by the US Navy's Pacific fleet. The allied military forces from the Pacific Rim participate in this exercise to enhance interoperability, and Canada has taken part since 1971. In addition to the Combined Maritime Forces and the Rim of the Pacific Exercise, the Royal Canadian Navy regularly participates in trilateral exercises with the

ROK and US navies as well as a bilateral exercise with the ROK Navy on an annual basis.

Canada's relatively chilly relationship with North Korea, the ROK's volatile neighbour, is in noteworthy contrast to its generally friendly relationship with the South. In the recent past, Canada's interaction with the Democratic People's Republic of Korea (DPRK) has been generally limited, aside from the formation of diplomatic relations in 2001. In spring 2010, when a multinational investigation team, including three Canadian naval experts, found that a North Korean torpedo had sunk the ROKS *Cheonan*, then prime minister Stephen Harper announced measures to restrict trade with the DPRK and suspended bilateral senior-level contacts.[35] Furthermore, in autumn 2010, the Canadian government introduced a Controlled Engagement Policy towards North Korea, which was designed to restrict further government-level engagement with the DPRK, except for humanitarian assistance, human rights issues, or regional security concerns. In summer 2011, the Canadian government applied economic sanctions to the DPRK under the Special Economic Measures Act to reinforce its disapproval of aggressive actions such as the sinking of the *Cheonan*. At the time of writing, there is no official diplomatic channel for Canada to communicate directly with the DPRK regime.

Canada and Korea Today

China's rising economic and military influence, as well as the turbulent geopolitical security situation caused by North Korea's sabre rattling and tensions between China and Taiwan in the Indo-Pacific theatre, points to the need for Canada and Korea to work closely together in the coming decades. Canada's new Indo-Pacific Strategy makes a compelling argument for Canada to work with like-minded allies such as South Korea, especially considering ongoing security threats from North Korea, the growing importance of the cyber domain, and China's ambitious efforts in the Indo-Pacific theatre.

In terms of trade, there is already a focused and sustained interest in critical minerals and clean technologies. Canada certainly has a desire to establish its presence as an engaged party in the Indo-Pacific region while also looking for opportunities to use its ample natural resources to profit from the world's increasing reliance on semiconductors and transition to sustainable sources of energy.[36] South Korea, meanwhile, has established itself as one of the largest producers of both semiconductors and lithium-ion batteries, yet it lacks a substantial domestic source of critical minerals and therefore has to import about 97 percent of its mineral supply.[37] Promoting growth in trade of critical minerals has therefore been a goal of both Prime Minister Justin Trudeau and President

Yoon Suk Yeol. President Yoon explicitly stated that both nations "play crucial roles in global supply chains [and] will work together for the mineral resources sector to build a cooperative architecture."[38] The shared interest of the two leaders has already translated into various memoranda of understanding at various institutional levels.

Conclusion

Canadian engagement on the Korean peninsula began informally with reports by missionaries in the 1880s. These pioneers linked the two countries until Canada became involved in the Korean War and when official diplomatic relations were established in the 1960s. Europe, rather than Asia, was Ottawa's preoccupation in the early to mid-twentieth century. Canada's lack of engagement with Korea can also be seen as a reflection of a broader trend in the history of Canadian-Asian relations. Aside from a few diplomatic engagements, the country's reluctant importation of railway workers from China, and the forced relocation of Japanese Canadians during the Second World War, Canada's engagement with the Indo-Pacific countries in the first half of the twentieth century tended to be very limited and ad hoc. Ottawa established a legation in Japan in 1929 and opened an embassy in Nationalist China in 1943, but it waited until 1963 to establish diplomatic relations with South Korea. It then took another decade for the Canadian embassy to open in Seoul in 1973, which only materialized because of South Korea's insistence. Canadian participation in the Korean War in 1950, therefore, stemmed from Canada's desire to support the United Nations and Canada's ally the United States rather than any independent or real interest in the fortunes of the Korean peninsula.

Having fought in the Korean War, Canada's strategic interest and humanitarian impulse guided Canadian-Korean relations in the 1950s. Ultimately, South Korea's rapid industrialization and the sale of the CANDU reactors in the 1970s elevated the ROK's importance for Canadian policy-makers. Through trade, immigration, and strategic defence cooperation, Canadian-Korean relations continued to expand from the 1980s onwards, from limited contacts to the more complex and interwoven relationship seen today. On the whole, Canadian-Korean relations in the post-Korean War period transformed rapidly from humanitarian efforts to trade only because South Korea – through its exceptional economic growth – became a country of consequence for Canada's commercial interests. As the case of the CANDU reactors sale makes clear, South Korea's economic growth changed the general importance of the Korean market for Canadian industries. The Korean diaspora in Canada and the large number of Korean students who come to Canada annually point to the Korean public's largely favourable perception of Canada.

On the political and diplomatic front, Canada could certainly play a more active role in terms of promoting peace on the Korean peninsula, specifically in multilateral diplomatic efforts to tame North Korea's nuclear ambitions. Canadian recognition of the DPRK in 2001, a short-lived experiment in foreign policy, has essentially resulted in a policy of nonengagement between Canada and the DPRK. There may yet be unseized opportunities. In light of Canada's positive reputation on the Korean peninsula, Canada could play a unique role as an "honest broker" between the two Koreas as well as in broader regional dynamics. To have the necessary credibility and access to affect diplomatic developments on the Korean peninsula to do so, Canada would need to re-establish full diplomatic relations with the DPRK. In the aftermath of the Russian invasion of Ukraine in 2022, and in light of Canada's new Indo-Pacific Strategy, Canada and its NATO allies must learn to work closely together with partners in the region, particularly in the cyber and technological domains.

Moving forward, closer cooperation is expected between Canada and the ROK, so both countries can fully reap the benefits of the free trade agreement in fields such as artificial intelligence, science and innovation, and labour. On issues such as climate change, cyber security, and technological advancements, Canada should make a greater effort to engage with South Korea's expertise, both in the public and private spheres. In doing so, Canada would be able to take advantage of South Korea's geostrategic location as a gateway to the greater Asian market while also making meaningful contributions to promoting peace and stability in the Asia-Pacific region and the global community at large.

Notes

1 Library and Archives Canada (LAC), MG 32 B5, Brooke Claxton Fonds, vol. 97, file 1120.

2 United Nations Archives, "Statement by Lester B. Pearson," Canada File, 26 July 1953.

3 For interviews with Korean War veterans, see the Memory Project Archives, "Korean War," *Canadian Encyclopedia*, https://thecanadianencyclopedia.ca/en/collection/the-memory-project-archive-collection.

4 Young-Iob Chung, *South Korea in the Fast Lane: Economic Development and Capital Formation* (Oxford: Oxford University Press, 2007), 9.

5 "Louis St. Laurent Goes around the World in 42 Days," CBC News, broadcast, 14 March 1954.

6 "Louis St. Laurent Goes around the World in 42 Days,"

7 "ROK Joins the Colombo Plan," National Archives of the Republic of Korea, Department of Public Information, 1968, http://theme.archives.go.kr/next/daily/viewMain.do?selectDay=20140129.

8 Joy Thierry Llewellyn, "Lotta Hitschmanova," *Canadian Encyclopedia*, 12 July 2016, http://thecanadianencyclopedia.ca/en/article/lotta-hitschmanova/.

9 Report to the Unitarian Service Committee board, 14 May 1978, in Clyde Sanger, *Lotta and the Unitarian Service Committee Story* (Toronto: Stoddart, 1986), Appendix.

10 "Donation of Canadian Salted Cod for Korean Relief," Cabinet Conclusions, LAC, RG 2, Privy Council Office, series A-5-a, vol. 2653.

11 Department of External Affairs, press release, 7 December 1953, http://gac.canadiana.ca/view/ooe.sas_19531207EP/1?r=0&s=1.

12 This program was in addition to the long-range reconstruction program carried out by the UN Korean Reconstruction Agency, in which Canada, together with thirty-three other countries, participated, and towards which the Canadian government had contributed CAD$7.25 million.

13 The treaty would be signed by December 1966, but Canada's reaction to the Korean proposal was lukewarm at best in the early 1960s.

14 "DEA Memo: Suggested Visit by South Korean Foreign Minister, Feb 26, 1965," LAC, RG 25, Department of External Affairs, vol. 8776, file 20-1-2-ROK.

15 "Letter No. 561 from the Canadian Ambassador, Tokyo, Japan dated Nov 17, 1964," LAC, RG 25, vol. 8776, file 20-1-2-ROK.

16 "Visit of Dr. Tong Won Lee, Foreign Minister of the ROK to Canada, Dec 19–21, 1966," LAC, RG 25, vol. 8776, file 20-1-2-ROK.

17 "South Korea and Canada Sign Trade Accords," *Globe and Mail,* 21 December 1966.

18 "Canada, Korea Enjoy Rapid Trade Growth, Closer Relations," *Globe and Mail,* 15 March 1971.

19 From its creation in 1952, Atomic Energy of Canada Limited focused on developing peaceful applications of nuclear energy through the use of heavy water and natural uranium, although it did produce plutonium for the American weapons program earlier in its history. See Robert Bothwell, *Nucleus: The History of Atomic Energy of Canada Limited* (Toronto: University of Toronto, 1988).

20 Bothwell, *Nucleus.*

21 Robert Bothwell and Jean Daudelin, eds., *Canada among Nations 2008: 100 Years of Canadian Foreign Policy* (Montreal/Kingston: Norman Paterson School of International Affairs/Centre for International Governance Innovation/McGill-Queen's University Press, 2009), 222.

22 The 1970s Energy Crisis also affected South Korea's interest in atomic research and technology and the CANDU reactors, as did India's nuclear explosion, Canadian concerns about the nature of the political situation in South Korea, President Park's nuclear agenda, and a scandal involving the Atomic Energy of Canada Limited's agent, Shaul Eisenberg. See Jiwon Tina Park, "From Strangers to Partners: Canadian-Korean Relations 1888–1978" (PhD diss., University of Toronto, 2018), 239–43, https://tspace.library.utoronto.ca/bitstream/1807/101639/3/Park_Jiwon_T_201806_PhD_thesis.pdf.

23 Duane Bratt, *The Politics of CANDU Exports* (Toronto: University of Toronto Press, 2006), 114.

24 For more on this debate, see Ryan Touhey, *Conflicting Visions: Canada and India in the Cold War World, 1974–76* (Vancouver: UBC Press, 2015).

25 Ministry of Foreign Affairs Republic of Korea, "Daehanmin'guk chŏngbuwa k'anada chŏngbuganŭi p'yŏnghwajŏk mokchŏkŭl wihan wŏnjaryŏgŭi kaebal mit ŭngyonge issŏsŏŭi hyŏmnyŏkŭl wihan hyŏpchŏngŭi kaejŏngŭl wihan kyohwan'gaksŏ" [Agreement between the Government of the Republic of Korea and the Government of Canada for cooperation in the development and application of atomic energy for peaceful purposes], Seoul, 26 January 1976, file GOSI 446, http://treatyweb.mofa.go.kr/JobGuide.do#.

26 "Memo for the Minister: A Review of Canada's Relations with Korea since 1967," 27 January 1975, in "Political Affairs: Policy and Background for Canadian External Policy and Relations with the Republic of Korea," LAC, RG 25, vol 8776, file 20-1-2-ROK (1973–75).

27 ROK's GDP figure is based on US dollars.
28 "Canada–the Republic of Korea Relations," Government of Canada, 2023, https://www.international.gc.ca/country-pays/republic_korea-republique_coree/relations.aspx?lang=eng.
29 The largest diasporas are located in the United States, China, and Japan.
30 "Canada–the Republic of Korea Relations."
31 Global Affairs Canada, "Canada's Indo-Pacific Strategy," 2022, https://www.international.gc.ca/transparency-transparence/indo-pacific-indo-pacifique/index.aspx?lang=eng.
32 From 2018 to 2019, Canada provided UN Command's first ever non-US deputy commander, Lieutenant-General Wayne Erye, presently serving as the chief of defence staff for the Canadian Armed Forces.
33 7th Air Force, "Exercise Key Resolve," https://www.7af.pacaf.af.mil/About-Us/Fact-Sheets/Display/Article/408384/exercise-key-resolve/.
34 Korea's last ship visit to Canada was in 2015, and the visits have been annual since 2017. In 2021, sailors from HMCS *Winnipeg*, as part of their official visit, stopped at the UN Military Cemetery to mark the sixty-ninth anniversary of the attack on HMCS *Iroquois* in October 1952. The Canadian defence attaché and the Canadian War Museum collaborated to put together a package of information to help sailors during their visit. Correspondence with Andrew Burtch, 5 September 2021.
35 Prime Minister's Office, "Statement of the Prime Minister of Canada," 24 May 2010, https://www.canada.ca/en/news/archive/2010/05/statement-prime-minister-canada-534599.html.
36 Steve Scherer, "Canada, South Korea Seek Deeper Cooperation on Critical Minerals," Reuters, 23 September 2022, https://www.reuters.com/business/autos-transportation/canada-south-korea-seek-deeper-cooperation-critical-minerals-2022-09-23/.
37 Government of Canada, Trade Commissioner Service, "The Canada-Korea Free Trade Agreement: Benefits and Opportunities for the Canadian Mining Sector," 10 May 2021, https://www.tradecommissioner.gc.ca/korea-republic-coree-republique/157114.aspx?lang=eng.
38 Scherer, "Canada, South Korea Seek Deeper Cooperation."

16

Canada's Korean War in Commemoration, Memorials, and Memory

Tim Cook and Andrew Burtch

"He should have been there," Al McKelvey spat. McKelvey had been a twenty-one-year-old Canadian private when he fought in the Korean War.[1] The veteran was angry that Prime Minister Jean Chrétien had chosen not to attend a ceremony in Brampton, Ontario, to mark the fiftieth anniversary of the end of the Korean War on 27 July 2003.

Although many of Canada's thirty thousand veterans had passed away from illness and old age, more than 300 veterans had assembled at the site of the Korea Veterans Association memorial, built in 1997, to remember the 516 Canadians who died during the Korean War. They gathered near the memorial, a large arcing pavilion covered in the bronze nameplates of the Canadian dead, fashioned to resemble the memorial plaques dotting the UN Memorial Cemetery in Busan. McKelvey and other veterans' anger was compounded by decades of feeling neglected by the Canadian government, which had not given the war's history, and the sacrifice of veterans, the attention they believed was due. That the fallen Canadians were marked in Brampton, north of Toronto, and not in the nation's capital seemed further evidence of the challenges they'd face in commemorating the war. Indeed, as many veterans had remarked for decades, Canada's participation in the Korean War was so little studied, understood, or commemorated that it was known as the "forgotten war."

This chapter examines how the Korean War was presented, remembered, and commemorated in Canada over the seventy years following the armistice in July 1953. It investigates the role of the state in organizing events and memorials to mark the war as well as veteran-led initiatives to organize acts of remembrance. But assessing the place of the Korean War in Canadian social memory goes beyond memorials, and so we explore history and visual culture, veterans' kinship networks and associations, and the place of medals and national symbols of remembrance such as the Silver Cross Mother. While the Korean War has never had much resonance with the Canadian public, there has been a surge in commemorative activities focused on the war since the beginning of the twenty-first century. However, these efforts pale beside the outreach and public diplomacy of commemoration carried out by the Republic of Korea.

The Princess Patricia's Canadian Light Infantry's (PPCLI's) battle at Kap'yong in April 1951 was a point of great pride for the Canadian brigade in Korea. In some ways, it was reminiscent of the resistance of the Canadian division at Ypres in April 1915 in the face of the German chlorine gas attack. In the First World War, the Canadians, raw and untried, fought hard against overwhelming forces. Thirty-five years later, the efforts of the Canadians, Australians, Americans, and New Zealanders to prevent the Kap'yong Valley from being overwhelmed by a much larger assaulting force led the American government to award the units involved with the US Presidential Unit Citation "for extraordinary heroism and outstanding performance." However, senior Canadian military and diplomatic officials in Ottawa were affronted by the American award, especially as the decision was reached without consulting the Canadian government. Michelle Fowler, in her study of the government's response to the issue, speculated "that some wanted ... the Presidential Unit Citation to die a quick and silent death."[2]

Even though the Australians quickly received permission to wear the insignia, the members of 2 PPCLI had to wait years before authorization was forthcoming. Senior Canadian generals such as Lieutenant-General Guy Simonds, the chief of the general staff and one of Canada's most successful fighting commanders from the Second World War, felt the collective honour should not be worn by individuals, because it would be resented by all the other Canadian units. Press inquiries and condemnation from columnists put pressure on the Department of National Defence in 1953, but Simonds would not relent.[3] Following his retirement, objections disappeared, and in April 1956 it was decided that not only could members who served in Korea at the time wear the prized insignia, but all members of 2 PPCLI, past and future, should share the privilege.[4] And yet the delay is a symbolic reminder of the contested memory of the Korean War, a case where official recognition of wartime efforts came late, if at all, and in half-measures that served to increase veterans' skepticism and resentment.

Canada's official historian of the Korean War, Lieutenant-Colonel Herbert Fairlie Wood, deals only marginally with the delays over the awarding of the American citation in his 1966 work, *Strange Battleground*. The writing of an official history, often told in a series of volumes, has a long tradition in military forces. Victors and vanquished offer clinical accounts that are usually meant for staff officers to better understand the conflict, process lessons, and make sense of victory and defeat. They are written in crisp, dry language, and present battles from the point of view of generals (or, in the case of Korea, colonels or majors) rather than those at the sharp end.

In Ottawa, the Canadian Army Historical Section was under the command of famed historian Colonel Charles Stacey, who served during the Second World War while documenting the army's actions and was responsible for a series of official histories. Stacey well understood the value of collecting records while the war was unfolding.[5] During the Second World War, he put trained historical officers in the field to observe the unfolding conflict, to interview participants, and to encourage the creation and archiving of records.[6] Stacey won the generals' trust during that war by writing reports about organization, training, and operations for senior commanders, and while his focus in 1950 was on completing a multivolume history of the Second World War, he ordered several officers to East Asia.

The historical officers in the field were to document the war, write narratives of the battles, and interview officers. A short history of the Korean War was published in 1956 by Captain Frank McGuire, a Second World War veteran and permanent force officer who served as a historical officer in theatre. But a more substantial offering was later written by Lieutenant-Colonel Herbert Fairlie Wood. As a serving professional officer and commander of 3 PPCLI, he was not without a stake in how the fighting was presented.[7] Wood seemed to be particularly wary of giving credit to the 2nd Battalion units, made up of volunteers recruited specially for Korea who served in the first year of the war. Praise was more forthcoming in his assessment of his own professional soldiers of the 3rd Battalion, who served in the last year of the war. As William Johnston would show years later in his 2003 reassessment, *A War of Patrols,* and in his contribution to this volume, Wood's praise disguised how those units tended to underperform compared to the units that fought through the war's first year.[8]

Strange Battleground was a staid offering of the army's various rotations and battles based on war diaries, historical officers' reports, and American and British official records. The historical officers in the field, Captain Frank McGuire and Lieutenant R.I. Martin, drafted four of the eighteen chapters.[9] As with previous official histories, senior officers were shown early drafts to offer commentary. For example, Major-General J.M. Rockingham, the brigadier during the early part of the war and subsequently commander of 1 Canadian Infantry Division, offered his insight in March 1955. His surviving notes give no indication that he sought to shape his own reputation. In fact, one note, on assessing units in battle, offers the astute observation, "I think there is a great danger in assuming that a formation has encountered less opposition than another formation because it attains an objective earlier and because it has less casualties. Skill in using covering fire and manoeuvre, as well as the energy of the troops involved has much to do with this."[10]

In his history, Wood was at pains to rebuff some of the critical reports of officers such as Major W.H. Pope, who during the war offered a frank and damning assessment of the Canadians' lack of aggression and static patrolling patterns from 1952, writing in one critical report that the enemy "has raided our outposts and forward positions and ambushed our patrols at will."[11] Pope had served in combat during the Second World War as well as two tours in Korea with the Royal 22e Régiment, although Wood questioned his assessments and even his experience on the battlefield.

Robert S. Peacock, a platoon commander in Wood's battalion, did not think much of the official history and enjoyed far more the colonel's *The Private War of Jacket Coates* (1966), a fictionalized account of the Korean War from a Canadian antiheroic private. Peacock described it as a "rather ribald collection of real and half-real incidents" as well as "very readable and humourous ... I consider the book to be the unofficial history of the 3rd Battalion PPCLI."[12] *The Private War of Jacket Coates* followed in the long line of soldiers' embracing the antiheroic and satirical, from Bruce Bairnsfather in the First World War to William "Bing" Coughlin's *Herbie* in the Second World War. It was a surprisingly candid account that offered insight into fear and exhaustion, trading anything for Canadian rye whisky, and the brutality of combat.[13] One reviewer described the heroes of the book as "good soldiers all; pains in the fat red necks of provost sergeants, but God's gift to an infantry company commander."[14] Wood, who also wrote children's books pseudonymously as John Redmayne, died from heart problems the year after *Strange Battleground* was published. Perhaps he might have come back to the war in future publications.[15]

The navy also published an official history, although it paled in comparison to the Second World War army histories or, later, the navy studies that were published from the 1980s onwards.[16] The official histories were important publications, especially since little had been written about the war in the fifteen years since the armistice, although they were not meant as the last word on the conflict.

Historically, few Canadian soldiers, sailors, or pilots had taken to autobiography or memoir writing. The exceptions were a few brilliant memoirs and novels that emerged from the First World War, such as accounts from frontline soldiers Will Bird, R.J. Manion, and James Pedley. After the Second World War, save for a brief burst of writing from a handful of journalists, there were few memorable personal accounts. In 1919 and 1945, young men resumed lives interrupted by war, pursuing jobs and families while struggling, mostly in private, to make meaning out of their wartime experience. Perhaps more surprisingly, the senior commanders from the two world wars, from Sir Arthur Currie to Harry Crerar to Guy Simonds, did not publish memoirs, unlike their colleagues in the United Kingdom or the United States. The paucity of military biography in the country leaves us with a severe gap in Canadian military history.[17]

The Korean War is no exception to the trend. It was not until the 1990s that a trickle of life writing emerged concerning veterans' service in Korea. Bob Ringma, a junior officer in Korea who went on to have a long career in the Canadian Forces, wrote in a 2003 memoir, *M*L*B*U: Full Monty in Korea,* of one reason for the lack of writing: "The Canadian public was well aware of the Korean War in its first two years, but after that appeared to gradually lose interest. Better times were afoot in Canada and most people were concerned with improving their lot in life; they were little interested in a conflict in a far-off land."[18]

One of the ways the Canadian government has officially honoured its war dead was through the commissioning of a series of books of remembrance, housed in altars installed in Ottawa's Memorial Chamber of the Peace Tower in the centre block of Parliament. By spring 1962, the chamber included books of remembrance for the First World War, the Second World War, and the South African War and the Nile Expedition. The fourth book was bound in a dried birdseye maple cover and inlaid with ivory. On its pages, artist Alan Beddoe inscribed the names, ranks, regiments, and dates of death for the 516 Canadians who died as a result of Korea service. On Remembrance Day, 1962, the governor general, Georges Vanier, unveiled the book in the Peace Tower at an event attended by veterans and next of kin. "The Korean Book of Remembrance records and consecrates their glorious memory," said Vanier. Prime Minister John Diefenbaker described the Canadians' sacrifice and evoked the international commitment of Canada, as reported in *The Legionary,* "that the force in Korea had been not nationalist but internationalist, a concept of which men had dreamed for generations."[19]

The main impetus for the dedication of *The Korean War Book of Remembrance* in 1962, rather than in 1963, the ten-year anniversary of the armistice, is that the government was acceding to the requests of a body of dwindling South African War veterans, who fought from 1899 to 1902. The 1962 dedication by the governor general was timed to coincide with the sixtieth anniversary of the signing of the Treaty of Vereeniging, which ended the South African War. As both *The South African War Book of Remembrance* and the Korean book had been commissioned at the same time, the aged veterans of the earlier imperial war and the Department of Veterans Affairs felt that adding the Korean War book to the unveiling ceremony would help extend public interest in the South African War.[20] In the end, the South African War book was unveiled in May 1962, the Korean War book in November 1962. The War Service Records Division of the Department of Veterans Affairs compiled the total number of Canadian dead in the Korean War as 516, which included all men who died in North America while slated for overseas service in addition to those who died in Korea.[21] As with the First and Second World War books, the official casualty figures included Canadians who died after the war of natural causes or as part of duties after the armistice. The cut-off date for inclusion in the book was 31 December 1956; those who died afterwards, even if of lingering war wounds, were not considered eligible.[22]

The government planned to display *The Korean War Book of Remembrance* in the Memorial Chamber temporarily before moving it to a new national memorial that was to be built at Nepean Point, east of the Parliamentary Precinct overlooking the cliffs abutting the Ottawa River. This new monument would mark the fallen of all wars other than the First World War, which had its national memorial in downtown Ottawa. This war memorial would have been a powerful focal point to act as a site of remembrance for veterans, next of kin, and other Canadians, but it would ultimately never be built.

Canada's National War Memorial was initially titled *The Response*, based on sculptor Vernon March's bronze castings of twenty-two members of the Canadian Expeditionary Force marching through the memorial's central arch. Unveiled in May 1939, the memorial had its origins in the monument-building period after the First World War. With the fallen buried overseas or without identifiable remains, thousands of cenotaphs had been erected in communities across Canada, along with other forms of memorials, such as historical texts, stained glass in churches, returned war trophies from overseas, and other symbols and acts of commemoration.[23]

In the immediate postwar period, veterans of the Second World War believed that March's memorial in downtown Ottawa was too deeply tied to the First World War. The Canadian Legion appealed for a new monument, but the federal government refused the request. The country was looking forward, not backward, as wartime prosperity stimulated a boom in jobs, families, and new communities.[24] Undaunted, the Legion raised the issue with officials in Ottawa in 1954. Two years later, a memorial building on Nepean Point was tentatively approved.[25]

The new memorial would stand for all wars except the First World War. The Legion promoted it as the "National Shrine of Remembrance."[26] In February 1963, the Department of Public Works, charged with its construction, released the plans for the public. The memorial, complete with a chapel, would be topped with an eighty-foot-tall cenotaph and a tree-lined pathway for Remembrance Day congregations. But with a change in government in April 1963, Lester Pearson's Liberals were little enthused about building another cenotaph in Ottawa. An editorial in the *Globe and Mail* proposed that "we are surely more beyond the stage in which we thought it appropriate to honor our dead by erecting elaborate structures which have no practical use. The modern and more sensible trend ... is to invest money in some useful function." *The Globe* and other newspapers suggested that a more fitting tribute would be to dedicate a public space or hospital to the war dead, given that the National Memorial had been a de facto monument to the dead of the Second World War and Korea, especially given the national Remembrance Day ceremony was held there.[27] Some minor public criticism in the form of a few letters written to newspapers gave the re-elected Liberal government cover to postpone and then cancel the memorial's construction to the outrage of the Canadian Legion. Many veterans felt snubbed, but perhaps the government's action was more closely aligned with the emerging dominant values of Canada, which was leaving behind its military history and embracing new symbols that were often in opposition to war.

The Royal Canadian Legion (as it was known from 1960), established in the aftermath of the First World War, had welcomed Second World War veterans into their ranks, but these men often had to elbow their way into the halls that were filled with their fathers and uncles who had served on the Western Front. The Korean War veterans, a much smaller cohort, faced even more challenges: Canadians' general ignorance about what they'd endured overseas, having their war described as a "police action," relatively low casualties, and the dark and irreverent comedy *M*A*S*H* (1972–83) perhaps diminishing some of their hardships. "In Legion gatherings and other functions," wrote a veteran of the Korean War, "World War Two veterans would be quick to remark, 'Kap'yong couldn't have been much of a battle if you only had ten killed; why we had over 900 killed at Dieppe.'"[28]

In 1973, Clyde Bougie, who served as a hygiene and laboratory assistant with the Royal Canadian Army Medical Corps, established the Korea Veterans Association. Over the years, hundreds and then thousands would join. Bernard Cote, one of the survivors of the Battle of Kap'yong, overcame his reluctance to revisit his soldiering days at the urging of fellow veterans. Cote had left the army in 1955 and worked in private industry, but the Korea Veterans Association became a key organization for him as he reached retirement age.[29] Many veterans held dual membership in the Legion, too, and the biannual conference of the Royal Canadian Legion often voted on motions related to Korean War veterans. Some of the resistance to recognizing and commemorating Korean War service manifested locally rather than nationally. Members of the nearly two thousand legion halls across the country occasionally misinterpreted their rules and regulations or imposed their own ideas about who could be welcomed into the branch. And so, like other veterans' subgroups, such as the Hong Kong Veterans Association or the Merchant Navy veterans, the smaller number of Korean War veterans demanded a separate organization to care and fight for issues relevant to them.[30] The association's units were, accordingly, at the forefront of commemorative efforts and often worked with communities to have the names of the fallen and the dates of the Korean War added to First and Second World War cenotaphs. "It wasn't the Canadian Government doing this," said David Graham of the 2nd Battalion, Royal Canadian Regiment, "just Korean veterans."[31]

Anniversaries matter in commemorating military history. They focus the media and sometimes Canadians. The fiftieth anniversary of the First World War, between 1964 and 1968, led to a renewal of interest in that conflict and an outpouring of documentaries, films, plays, novels, and histories. The fiftieth anniversary of the Second World War was significant in renewing interest in what the aged veterans of that war did to destroy the Nazis.[32] In 1975, to recognize the twenty-fifth anniversary of the start of the war, American Korean War veterans organized a series of tours to return to South Korea. While some veterans made the trip to Korea individually throughout the century, judging from the actions of veterans of the two world wars, visits typically start to occur twenty to twenty-five years after the end of the war. Some never wanted to think about Korea again and were happy to leave it behind; others stayed in touch with comrades through the Korea Veterans Association or informal kinship networks. But by the mid-1970s, international travel became easier and cheaper, and that allowed some veterans to return to the sites of old wars.

The American Korea Veterans Association organized a series of tours from June to November for veterans, and it invited members of the Canadian association to participate. Vic Thompson of Manotick, Ontario, went with a small Canadian contingent and provided a first-hand account. Flying from Los Angeles on 25 September 1975 aboard Korean Air Lines 747, the party crossed the International Date Line and landed in Seoul. Thompson was surprised to discover a prosperous country, like almost every veteran of the war who remembered cities being ruined in the fighting. Seoul was a bustling city of almost 7 million. After a visit to the Demilitarized Zone – which was guarded and mined, and a fearful reminder that the war had left North and South divided – the small Canadian contingent received the Korean War Ambassador for Peace Medal, a commemorative medal presented by the South Korean government to veterans.

Tours to the old battlefields, museums, and monuments followed, including a visit to Panmunjom, the village straddling North and South Korea, where the armistice was signed. The Canadians were even allowed to cross into North Korea to take photographs of the North Korean guards. The veterans' group tried to find some of their old battle entrenchments, such as Hill 355, Little Gibraltar, but were unsuccessful. Time and development made it unidentifiable. At events and military parades, the Canadians and Americans were feted and cheered. Thompson wrote of being "touched by the spontaneous greetings." The final leg of the tour was to Busan to visit the UN Memorial Cemetery. The Canadians laid wreaths they had carried halfway around the world to honour "the graves of our comrades." Throughout the trip, Thompson was deeply impressed by South Korea's transformation and, he noted, the Koreans' "genuine affection for us."[33] The theme of South Korean gratitude to veterans would emerge in the coming decades and become an important component of how veterans made meaning of the war, even as their service was neglected in Canada.

During the late 1960s and 1970s, the Royal Canadian Legion struggled to overcome apathy among Canadians about their country's military history. Against the backdrop of the Vietnam War and the threat of thermonuclear annihilation, Canadians soured on almost anything related to the Canadian Forces other than peacekeeping operations. These United Nations missions had the advantage of being politically popular and relatively cheap, even as most of Canada's armed forces were dedicated to NATO deterrence in western Europe. Canadians had little interest in learning about the wars, teaching them to children, or creating cultural products that allowed for re-engagement. The Legion, Canada's largest veterans' association, believed part of the problem was the lack of a memorial in the capital separate from that of the national memorial unveiled in 1939 and deeply linked to the First World War. The Legion had periodically raised the issue of another national memorial in Ottawa to mark conflicts and wars after the Pearson government cancelled the National Shrine of Remembrance, but these appeals were unsuccessful.

Realizing that no memorial would be forthcoming, the Legion conceded that it must, instead, pressure the government to add the name and dates of the Second World War and the Korean War to the National War Memorial. It was a bittersweet victory. Governor General Edward Schreyer unveiled the new dates on 29 May 1982 at the rededication. He remarked: "It is appropriate at this sacred ceremony that we should pray that there will never be a need for further additions to the memorial – that Canadians along with peoples everywhere will never again be asked to experience the devastation of war." It was, alas, an aspirational hope; indeed, the dates of more wars would be added to the memorial over the years. The *Montreal Gazette* observed of the event that "Canadian veterans of the Second World War and Korea received long-overdue recognition." It didn't report that the governor general had referred to the Canadians in Korea as an "international peacekeeping" force.[34]

The following year, the Legion moved to mark the thirtieth anniversary of the Korean War armistice. *Legion* magazine (*The Legionary* renamed) admitted, "Our Korea veterans have not always been given their just due." Politicians tended to label Korea a "police action" instead of a war, a tendency those who served there singled out as infuriating.[35] The Legion also nominated Constance Wylie, the mother of Lloyd Wylie, who was killed on 7 March 1951 by machine-gun fire on Hill 532, to carry out the official duties of the National Silver Cross Mother on 11 November 1983. She was the first mother of a Korean War fatality and the first National Silver Cross Mother who served in remembrance of a soldier who had died after the Second World War. On a grey, windy day of drizzling rain, the eighty-year-old from Vancouver laid the wreath before some 2,500 participants and spectators. "My boy knew what he was in for," Wylie later said. "If it hadn't been him, it would have been someone else's son. That is the only way you can think about it. If you didn't, you would go crazy."[36] The Legion's decision to appoint Wylie was another sign that the organization was taking seriously Korea veterans' demands to be treated as equal to those who fought in the world wars.

"At last," noted an editorial in *Legion* in July 1991. The editor argued that that short phrase summed up the feelings of Canada's Korean War veterans following a surprise mid-June announcement of the creation of the Canadian Volunteer Service Medal for Korea. The veterans affairs minister, Gerry Merrithew, observed, "The medal recognizes the major contribution of those volunteers who served with the United Nations' forces in Korea."[37] The veterans had been asking for a separate medal for decades, and its creation took a combined submission from the Korea Veterans Association, the Royal Canadian Legion, the National Council of Veteran Associations in Canada, and the Army, Navy, and Air Force Veterans in Canada.

In summer 1988, to mark the thirty-fifth anniversary of the Korean War armistice, the Canadian government had offered a Korean Service Badge to veterans and the immediate families of Korean War dead. This lapel pin, similar to those issued during the Second World War, did not satisfy the veterans' desire for unique recognition.[38] Movement on a distinctly Canadian service medal for Korea gained traction as a result of the country's participation in the Persian Gulf War, which began in August 1990 when Iraq invaded Kuwait. Canada contributed approximately five thousand personnel at sea, in the air, and on land to a UN-sanctioned, US-led coalition that shielded other Gulf states from Iraqi aggression before unleashing a punishing air and land offensive that decisively expelled Iraqi forces from Kuwait before a ceasefire was signed in February 1991. By June 1991, service personnel who had participated in that mission were slated to receive the government-issued volunteer service medal. Less than two weeks later, before the Gulf War medals were awarded, the government announced it would mint and present a Canadian Volunteer Service Medal for Korea.[39]

The first fifty-nine Canadian veterans to receive the medal did so in a ceremony with Governor General Ray Hnatyshyn in early November 1991. The medal, suspended by a blue, yellow, red, and white ribbon, was marked with Queen Elizabeth II on the obverse and the simple inscription "Korea Volunteer 1950–1954 Voluntaire Coré" on the reverse. Merrithew told ceremony participants, "We have corrected the injustice."[40] For those veterans in attendance, such as the vice-president of the Korea Veterans Association, Roy Reid, it was "a most memorable occasion that will remain with us and our families forever."[41] Most Korean War veterans, however, received their medals through the mail, unceremoniously in a plain envelope, leading one member of Parliament to lament: "The hypocrisy of it all. How can this government mail out medals of honor?"[42]

The fiftieth anniversary of the Second World War led to a sea change in how Canadians thought about war. For decades, the public had embraced the comfortable image of Canada as peacekeeper. But the end of the Cold War led to a fragmentation of the world order and the rise of regional civil wars and ethnic conflicts. In the early 1990s, peacekeepers were ordered into hopeless, no-win situations in the former Yugoslavia, Somalia, and Rwanda. Seeking to bring aid, support, and peace, they found only lawlessness, war, and genocide.[43] This was the culmination of years of neglect of the Canadian Forces and veterans. The federal government finally acknowledged the gross inattention and devoted funds to mark anniversary years. The Battle of the Atlantic and the Italian Campaign were the focus of 1993, both of which resulted in official contingents of politicians and veterans being sent overseas. They were followed by even larger commemorative events – for D-Day, in 1994, and the liberation of the Netherlands, in 1995.

As part of these veterans' pilgrimages, in 1993 the "forgotten war" was marked with an official group of politicians and Korean War veterans returning to South Korea. To acknowledge the armistice's fortieth anniversary, twenty-four veterans were sent on a pilgrimage from October 17 to October 28. The delegation included Pat Bogert, who commanded the 25th Canadian Infantry Brigade, and

Gordon Ramsay, the national president of the Korea Veterans Association. Feted in Japan and then in South Korea, the veterans remarked upon these countries' remarkable reconstruction in the decades since they had served.

Marcel Richard, who fought in Korea and ended his career as a brigadier-general, recounted feeding many displaced refugees during the war and how he "felt very good about" aiding the war-torn nation.[44] Chi Kap-Chong, the chairman of the United Nations Korean War Allies Association, met the group at the Canadian Korean War Memorial Garden, built in the 1970s in the Kap'yong Valley to mark the 1951 battle. He told the veterans, "Korea has not forgotten."[45] It had not, although Canada had, even as the country was grappling with its military history and beginning to turn more attention to marking its past wars after decades of neglect and apathy. Korea remained a war, wrote veteran John Bishop in his 2000 memoir, which was "little known and too soon forgotten."[46]

And yet Canada's presence in the war was not forgotten in South Korea, especially where its soldiers lay buried. The UN Memorial Cemetery in Korea was a product of the chaotic first months of the Korean War. As UN contingents, including Canada's, arrived in Korea, the bulk of the fighting forces during the war's first months were American. Soldiers killed in the advance to the Chinese border in fall 1950 were buried in a variety of makeshift temporary gravesites with the intent of later consolidation. These graves had to be hurriedly exhumed and relocated or abandoned, as approximately 1,500 were overrun during the first phases of the November 1950 Chinese offensive, which succeeded in recapturing Seoul.[47] American remains that could be properly identified, embalmed, and returned to bereaved families in the United States began their transit home in January 1951, just as the Chinese offensive was blunted and the UN counterattacked. Graves that were recaptured as part of the advance were also exhumed, and the remains of the American dead were shipped home.[48] Tens of thousands of American forces would make this solemn journey by the war's end, creating an extensive and vital graves registration infrastructure that served the UN forces.

The remainder of the UN forces, including Canada's, did not follow a similar casualty repatriation policy. Traditions in the British Commonwealth governed the decision to bury soldiers near the battlefield. To avoid a repeat of the embarrassing and unfortunate loss of fallen soldiers to enemy offensives, Korean labourers prepared seven acres of territory at Tanggok, firmly within the secure Busan perimeter at the southern tip of the Korean peninsula. When the site was dedicated in April 1951, it was administered through the UN Command, and American grave registration companies oversaw the movement of non-American dead to their final resting places.[49] Before this, authorities in Ottawa considered whether to repatriate the remains from South Korea, with a concern for the fate of Canada's dead if South Korea fell to enemy forces. However, at a meeting to finalize Canada's "no repatriation" policy in July 1951, the Department of National Defence concluded, "If we were to remove our war dead from Korea, it would be tantamount to an admission that we expect South Korea to be overrun by the Communists, and what we fought for there undone."[50] Killed Canadians would remain in theatre, buried with their comrades and more than two thousand UN forces.

In 1955, following the Republic of Korea's parliamentary proposal to transfer the cemetery lands permanently to the UN, the UN General Assembly passed a resolution to maintain the cemetery permanently.[51] In the end, 378 Canadian soldiers would be buried in Korea far from their families. Under the Commonwealth's policy of nonrepatriation, then, the first and most obvious site of memory for international forces' involvement in the Korean War was the UN Memorial Cemetery. It would become a site of pilgrimage for family members and veterans in later years. It also emerged as a point of connection between South Korea and Canada.[52]

Canadian veterans of the war and Korean civilians mounted initiatives in the years following the war to forge a commemorative landscape. The first of these took place in 1975, to mark the Battle of Kap'yong, with the unveiling of a memorial stone near the battlefield with a plaque dedicated to the 2nd Battalion, Princess Patricia's Canadian Light Infantry. On 7 November 1975, before an audience of Canadians and South Koreans, a memorial stone was unveiled. A decade later, it was expanded with a much larger monument dedicated to the Canadian effort in Korea, in English, French, and Korean.[53]

"It has been a long time coming," Bill Allan said.[54] The president of the Korea Veterans Association, Unit 57, Mississauga, was remarking on the unveiling of the Wall of Remembrance at the Meadowvale Cemetery outside of Brampton, Ontario, on 27 July 1997.[55] Hundreds of veterans stood at attention in front of the wall, a semicircular structure of grey granite two feet in height and two hundred feet long with 516 bronze plaques. Allan and others had spent four years raising $300,000. The Royal Canadian Legion provided a third of the funding, but the federal government contributed nothing to the memorial project. Meadowvale Cemetery donated the land after the federal government denied the Korea Veterans Association's request for a place of prominence in Ottawa, further embittering the veterans behind the project and reinforcing in their minds that they would have to do it themselves if a memorial were ever to be erected.[56] The Korea Veterans Association's founder, Clyde Bougie, said at the event, "By building this lasting tribute, the children of the future will visit this historical wall and know that Canadians played their part in the Korean War."[57]

Other memorials followed. In 2001, to mark the fiftieth anniversary of the Korean War, Canadian veteran Vince Courtenay mounted an effort to build a memorial linking Canada and Korea. After being denied funding by the federal government, Courtenay privately raised money to hire Korean sculptor Young Mun Yoo. The artist sculpted a bronze figure of a soldier atop a dais marked with the names of all 516 Korean War dead for the memorial to be located in Windsor, Ontario.[58] Donations from the City of Windsor, local labour unions, the US Veterans of Foreign Wars, the Royal Canadian Legion, and Windsor-area veterans supported the memorial.[59] In the sculpture, the soldier lifts a Korean girl in his arms, and the girl cradles sixteen maple leaves, symbolizing the sixteen soldiers and sailors whose remains were never recovered. To the soldier's right, a Korean boy holds a bouquet of flowers. Two monuments were built. The first was integrated into the Canadian section of the UN Memorial Cemetery in Busan. Its twin was unveiled in Windsor, Ontario, in 2001 before it was moved and installed along the Mackenzie King Bridge in Ottawa in 2003. The monument, almost invisible to the thousands of pedestrians and commuters crossing the bridge daily, faces its twin thousands of kilometres away.[60]

Other regional tributes were mounted in the years following the unveiling of the national memorial at Brampton, often without federal support. These included a monument in Quebec City dedicated to the soldiers of the Royal 22e Régiment, a project mobilized by Roland and Carmen Boutot and the local chapter of the Korea Veterans Association.[61] In 2004, discussions began between the City of Burnaby, British Columbia, and the Korea Veterans Association to build a significant memorial to the Korean War. Unveiled in 2007, the Burnaby memorial is one of the most visually impressive memorials in Canada, though its connection to the Korean War is not immediately obvious. Commissioned through a million dollars raised by Burnaby's sixty-thousand-strong Korean Canadian community, *The Ambassador of Peace* monument is a three-metre-tall sculpture by Korean sculptor Hyun Kuk Cho of a woman with arms outstretched, standing atop a concrete plinth overlooking the entrance to Burnaby's Central Park.[62] It evokes the powerful link between Canada and South Korea and the role of Canadians in supporting the liberation of that country.

Memorials erected in Canada since 2022 include actual pieces of the Korean landscape. Gapyeong County officials in Korea sent large stone slabs from where Canadians soldiers fought in Kap'yong to form the centrepiece of memorials in Langley, British Columbia; Niagara Falls, Ontario; and Airdrie, Alberta.[63] Each stone, weighing six and a half tons, is engraved in English and Korean in remembrance of soldiers who fought in Korea.[64]

Even as the commemorative landscape in Canada and Korea became better populated by the turn of the century, veterans' efforts to mark their own service were not matched by pronounced public or political interest in commemorating the war. The Korean War remained vastly overshadowed by the world wars. In 1995, the fiftieth anniversary of the end of the Second World War was observed across the country, the same year that thousands of Canadian veterans returning to the Netherlands were greeted as heroes, causing a media sensation about the place of history, remembrance, and military history in public life. Nothing comparable greeted the Korean War veterans when the fiftieth anniversary of the Korean War armistice arrived on 27 July 2003. Although this is not surprising given that the Second World War involved far more Canadians and was part of a wider international series of commemorations.

However, as Korean War veterans had done in the past, they came together, and three hundred Korea Veterans Association members bore witness at their memorial in Brampton. The veterans were furious when Prime Minister Jean Chrétien declined to attend the event.[65] Even the wreath laid on behalf of the federal government was insufficient, wrote Gay Abbate for the *Globe and Mail,* and was "seen by many as another side of Ottawa's lack of appreciation for the sacrifice of those who fought and died in the Land of the Morning Calm."[66] The government's limited presence – ironically, during a "year of remembrance" dedicated to Korean War veterans – stood in stark contrast to the warm words of Ki-ho Chang, the Republic of Korea's ambassador to Canada, who spoke of his country's eternal gratitude: "To the veterans, we'll never forget the struggle you waged on our behalf."[67]

Veterans revisiting the Korean peninsula decades after their initial deployment would find ample evidence that the country they were sent to defend in the early 1950s had not forgotten them. Beginning in 1975, the Republic of Korea's Ministry of Patriots and Veterans Affairs launched an annual revisitation program by which up to six hundred UN veterans and their family members were offered heavily discounted travel to Korea and hospitality during their week-long stay.[68] Veterans revisiting Korea continued to be struck by how dramatically the country had transformed into an economic power and cultural hub in East Asia, especially in contrast to Communist North Korea.

There remained a small but growing number of Canadians who sought to ensure that the memory of Canada's service to South Korea was not forgotten. Senator Yonah Martin, the first Korean Canadian parliamentarian, took up this cause as the sixtieth anniversary of the Korean War armistice approached. Martin was born in Seoul and immigrated to Canada in 1972, living and teaching in Vancouver. Martin worked closely with both Korean Canadian community members and the veterans' association to build connections and create commemorative events.

Early efforts included a re-enactment of the historic Imjin Gardens hockey game between the Royal 22e Régiment and the Royal Canadian Regiment, originally contested on the frozen Imjin River in 1952. The anniversary was marked by the passage of a vote through Parliament to enact a National Korean War Veterans' Day each 27 July, beginning during the Year of the Korea Veteran in 2013. In July 2013, the Canada-Korea Society partnered with the Canadian War Museum to host a gala for hundreds of Korean War veterans and their families. It coincided with the opening of the museum's temporary exhibition about the anniversary and updates to its long-term displays, which had been visited by millions since the museum's opening in its present location in 2005. Other commemorative events have followed, especially around anniversaries of battles, campaigns, and the war.

"The children of the future must know about the war in Korea," recounted Bill Allan of the Korea Veterans Association. "When we die, so does the KVA."[69] In 2017, there were thirty-seven branches, known as units, across Canada, with a national council governing the body that was concerned about the welfare of veterans and their families. The importance of periodically coming together rekindled old memories and stoked morale among aging comrades. From 1992 to 2008, a biannual reunion was held among Korean War veterans. "It may be Canada's forgotten war," wrote veteran Rob Ringma, "but it isn't for the soldiers."[70] Indeed, that was the case, but what happens when the final veterans pass on?

Bill Nasby, a private during the war, recounted years later how he did not want "to forget the guys we left behind."[71] The ghosts of comrades ever haunted, but all veterans had to get on with their lives. Some war veterans remained in the Canadian Armed Forces, while others joined civilian society. For decades, there was little interest among Canadians in memorializing the war. And so it fell to the veterans to remember and commemorate the war that had deeply shaped their lives.

One of the ways that veterans made meaning of the war was to reflect on the success of South Korea and its people since the armistice, especially in relation to the horror show of North Korea, whose citizens suffered under despotic rule in a police state plagued by periodic bouts of starvation. "The loss of life was not in vain," recounted veteran Scotty Martin at the fiftieth-anniversary ceremony of the end of the war. "South Korea is still free today."[72] Andrew C. Moffat, upon returning to South Korea and marvelling at its transformation, recounted the "lumps in our throats and tears in our eyes" as the veterans were greeted by large crowds. People waved, cheered, and said, "Thank you for saving my Country."[73]

And so even as Canadians have paid little attention to the Korean War and the veterans of it, much of the memory making has come from grateful South Koreans who continue to honour those who served with the UN forces. "Our government never cared about us," reflected Bernard Cote, a veteran of the Battle of Kap'yong. "The Koreans did everything for us."[74] This recognition, albeit late in the lives of veterans, along with the Canadian state's episodic but growing attention to these neglected veterans, has also led to greater awareness in Canada, with more memorials, history books, veterans' memoirs, museum exhibitions, and a need to archive increasingly silenced voices. As Canada is a country that does not traditionally define itself through war and conflict, the Korean War will likely never resonate strongly among the broader public, especially in comparison to the total societal struggle of the world wars. But as this book has shown, there is room to better understand the war in its many nuances, including its impact on the Canadian Armed Forces and Canada's role on the world stage and in the Cold War. Most powerfully, however, the Korean War was a war that transformed those who served and came home, and those who never had a chance to return home and who remain buried there. The war imprinted itself deeply on the survivors even as they moved on with their lives and contributed to modern Canada.

Notes

1 "Vets Livid at Ottawa Snub of Korean War Ceremony," *Globe and Mail,* 28 July 2003. On American veterans' anger at Washington, see Judith Keene, "Lost to Public Commemoration: American Veterans of the 'Forgotten' Korean War," *Journal of Social History* 44, 4 (2011): 1099–117.
2 Michelle Fowler, "'For Extraordinary Heroism and Outstanding Performance': Kap'yong, 2 PPCLI and the Controversy surrounding the US Presidential Unit Citation," *Canadian Military History* 13, 4 (2004): 23.
3 See correspondence in Department of National Defence, Directorate of History and Heritage (DHH), file 113.003 (D23).
4 Herbert Fairlie Wood, *Strange Battleground: The Operations in Korea and Their Effects on the Defence Policy of Canada* (Ottawa: Queen's Printer, 1966), 165–66.
5 On official histories, see Tim Cook, *Clio's Warriors: Canadian Historians and the Writing of the World Wars* (Vancouver: UBC Press, 2006).
6 See C.P. Stacey, *A Date with History: Memoirs of a Canadian Historian* (Ottawa: Deneau, 1983).
7 Canadian Army Historical Section, *Canada's Army in Korea: The United Nations Operations, 1950–1953 and the Aftermath* (Ottawa: Queen's Printer, 1956).
8 William Johnston, *A War of Patrols: Canadian Army Operations in Korea* (Vancouver: UBC Press, 2003).
9 Wood, *Strange Battleground,* Preface.
10 Rockingham to Stacey, 14 March 1955, DHH, 681.013 (D68).
11 Major W.H. Pope, "Infantry Patrolling in Korea," 23 June 1953, 1, DHH, 41025.003(D5).

12 Robert S. Peacock, *Kim-chi, Asahi, and Rum: A Platoon Commander Remembers Korea, 1952–1953* (Toronto: Lugus, 1994), xi.

13 H.F. Wood, *The Private War of Jacket Coates* (Don Mills, ON: Longmans, 1966); on the antihero, see Tim Cook, "Anti-heroes of the Canadian Expeditionary Force," *Journal of the Canadian Historical Association* 19, 1 (2008): 171–93.

14 Hugh Laming, "Comrades of Kipling Characters," *Globe and Mail,* 24 September 1966.

15 "Army Historian Led Battalion in Korean War," *Globe and Mail,* 18 May 1967.

16 Thor Thorgrimsson and E.C. Russell, *Canadian Naval Operations in Korean Waters, 1950–1955* (Ottawa: Naval Historical Section, Canadian Forces Headquarters, 1965).

17 J.L. Granatstein and Dean Oliver, *The Oxford Companion to Canadian Military History* (Don Mills, ON: Oxford University Press, 2011), 38.

18 Bob Ringma, *M*L*B*U: Full Monty in Korea* (Burnstown, ON: General Store Publishing, 2003), 160.

19 "Remembrance Book Dedicated for Korean War Fallen," *The Legionary* (December 1962): 17.

20 Advisory Committee on the Books of Remembrance, 6 April 1961, Library and Archives Canada (LAC), MG 30 D252, Alan B. Beddoe Fonds, vol. 30.

21 "Notes on the Korea Book of Remembrance," DHH, 81/661.

22 Beddoe to Deputy Minister, Veterans Affairs, Progress Report No. 1, 25 November 1957, LAC, MG 30 D252, vol. 31.

23 Jonathan Vance, "The Great Response: Canada's Long Struggle to Honour the Dead of the Great War," *The Beaver* (October-November 1996): 29.

24 Tim Cook, *The Fight for History: 75 Years of Forgetting, Remembering, and Remaking Canada's Second World War* (Toronto: Allen Lane, 2020), 161–80.

25 "Statement on National Cenotaph and World War II Book of Remembrance," *House of Commons Debates,* 22nd Parl., 3rd Sess. (30 April 1956) (Hugues Lapointe), https://www.lipad.ca/full/permalink/1842957/.

26 "Advisory Committee on the Books of Remembrance," 6 April 1961, LAC, MG 30 D252, vol. 30.

27 "In Memoriam," *Globe and Mail,* 23 February 1963.

28 Robert Hepenstall, *Find the Dragon: The Canadian Army in Korea, 1950–1953* (Edmonton, AB: Four Winds, 1995), 344.

29 Interview with Bernard Cote, 2 June 2022, Canadian War Museum, Oral History Program, 31D 22 Cote.

30 Tim Cook and Matt Moore, "The Merchant Navy Redress Campaign and the Fight for Veteranhood," *Canadian Historical Review* 102, 3 (2021): 390–413.

31 Ted Barris, *Deadlock in Korea: Canadians at War, 1950–1953* (Toronto: Macmillan, 1999), 299.

32 See Dan Todman, *The Great War: Myth and Memory* (New York: Hambledon, 2005); and Cook, *The Fight for History.*

33 All citations from "Return to Korea," *Legion* (February 1976): 42–43.

34 "Schreyer Rededicates Ottawa War Memorial," *Montreal Gazette,* 31 May 1982; and "Memorial Honors All Veterans," *Ottawa Citizen,* 31 May 1982.

35 "A Ceremony to Remember," *Legion* (November 1983): 2.

36 Pat Sullivan, "A Time for Anniversaries," *Legion* (December 1983): 4.

37 "Korea Medal," *Legion* (July-August 1991): 2.

38 "Government Orders, Veterans Affairs," *House of Commons Debates,* 33rd Parl., 2nd Sess. (12 July 1988) (Allan Ernest Pietz), https://www.lipad.ca/full/permalink/3747514/.

39 Kathy Lynas, "Korea: Remembering Canada's Forgotten War," *Senior Times,* news clipping, LAC, RG7, G-30, vol. 45, file HNAT-801-15, pt. 1.

40 "Korea Vets to the Fore," *Legion* (December-January 1991–92): 8.
41 Roy Reid to H.E. Ray Hnatyshyn, Governor General of Canada, 14 November 1991, LAC RG7-G-30, vol. 45, file HNAT-801-15, pt. 1.
42 "Government Orders, Veterans Affairs," *House of Commons Debates,* 34th Parl., 3rd Sess. (10 December 1991) (George Albert Proud), https://www.lipad.ca/full/permalink/3891182/.
43 J.L. Granatstein, *Who Killed the Canadian Military? What Canada Must Do to Defend Itself in the 21st Century* (Toronto: HarperFlamingoCanada, 2004).
44 Tom MacGregor, "From Panmunjom to Taejon," *Legion* (December-January 1993–94): 19.
45 MacGregor, "From Panmunjom to Taejon," 21.
46 John Bishop, *The King's Bishop: A Canadian Corporal in Korea, 1950–51* (Duncan, BC: Fir Grove, 2000), 169.
47 Judith Keene, "Bodily Matters Above and Below Ground: The Treatment of American Remains from the Korean War," *Public Historian* 32, 1 (2010): 66.
48 Helen Cheek, "8204th Army Unit (Army Graves Registration Service Group)," *On Point* 11, 2 (2005): 26–28.
49 Colonel J. Wallis to AAG Plans, "Ag ADM Instruction, Canadian Army Special Force," 30 September 1950, LAC, R112, vol. 35557, file 1090-33/29, pt. 1.
50 Colonel John Wallis, "Burials in Korea," 25 July 1951, LAC, RG 24, 1983-84/215, vol. 8, file 1090-33/29, pt. 2.
51 United Nations General Assembly Resolution 997(X), 15 December 1955, http://www.worldlii.org/int/other/UNGA/1955/72.pdf.
52 Jiwon Tina Park, "From Strangers to Partners: Canadian-Korean Relations (1888–1978)" (Phd diss., University of Toronto, 2018), 23.
53 Jack Whittleton, Northeast Asia Division, Department of External Affairs, to W.A.B. Douglas, Director of History, 23 April 1979, DHH 79/391.
54 Ray Dick, "Korea War Veterans Get Long-Sought Symbol of Recognition," *Legion Magazine* (November-December 1997): 70.
55 For the challenge of Korean War memorials, see Suhi Choi, *Embattled Memories: Contested Meanings in Korean War Memorials* (Reno: University of Nevada Press, 2014); and Judith Keene, "Aesthetics versus Ownership: Artists and Soldiers in the Design of the National Korean War Veterans Memorial, Washington, DC," in *War Memories: Commemoration, Recollections, and Writings of War,* ed. Stéphanie A.H. Bélanger and Renée Dickason (Montreal/Kingston: McGill-Queen's University Press, 2017), 33–54.
56 "Vets Livid at Ottawa Snub of Korean War Ceremony," *Globe and Mail,* 28 July 2003.
57 Ray Dick, "Korea War Veterans Get Long-Sought Symbol of Recognition," *Legion Magazine* (November-December 1997): 70.
58 "Statement by Members, Korean War Veterans," *House of Commons Debates,* 37th Parl., 1st Sess. (8 May 2001) (Roy H. Bailey), https://www.lipad.ca/full/permalink/4185246/.
59 "Statement by Members, Korean War Veterans," *House of Commons Debates,* 37th Parl., 2nd Sess. (29 September 2003) (Brian Masse), https://www.lipad.ca/full/permalink/4258100/.
60 Andrew Burtch, "A Time to Remember the Canadian Dead of the Korean War," *Ottawa Citizen,* 15 November 2018.
61 "Statement by Members, Korean War Veterans," *House of Commons Debates,* 36th Parl., 2nd Sess. (19 September 2000) (Paul Mercier), https://www.lipad.ca/full/permalink/4166913/.
62 "Korean War Memorial: Ambassador of Peace," *City of Burnaby Art Gallery,* https://collections.burnabyartgallery.ca/detail/publicart11.

63 Gapyeong is the official romanized version of Kap'yong. As the county is discussed here, rather than the battle, we are respecting this spelling.

64 Liam Britten, "Critical but Little-Known Piece of Canadian Military History Is the Focus of Garden Planned for Langley," *CBC News*, 1 February 2022, https://www.cbc.ca/news/canada/british-columbia/critical-but-little-known-piece-of-canada-s-military-history-is-the-focus-of-garden-planned-for-langley-1.6334623.

65 "Vets Livid at Ottawa Snub of Korean War Ceremony," *Globe and Mail*, 28 July 2003.

66 "Vets Livid at Ottawa Snub of Korean War Ceremony."

67 "We'll Never Forget: South Korea Tells Vets," *Globe and Mail*, 28 July 2003.

68 Ministry of Patriots and Veterans Affairs, "Revisit Korea Program," https://www.mpva.go.kr/english/contents.do?key=956.

69 "Branches Back Korean War Monument," *Legion* (March 1996): 20.

70 Ringma, *M*L*B*U*, 161.

71 Brent Watson, *Far Eastern Tour: The Canadian Infantry in Korea* (Montreal/Kingston: McGill-Queen's University Press, 2003), 176.

72 "We'll Never Forget: South Korea Tells Vets," *Globe and Mail*, 28 July 2003.

73 Andrew Moffat, *Korean Memories: A Canadian Gunner's Experience in the "Forgotten War"* (Ottawa: Keshet Productions, 2006), 219.

74 Interview with Bernie Cote.

Selected Bibliography

Allard, Jean V., with Serge Bernier. *The Memoirs of General Jean V. Allard.* Vancouver: UBC Press, 1988.

Appleman, Roy E. *South to the Natkong, North to the Yalu (June-November 1950).* Washington, DC: Office of Chief of Military History, 1961.

Barclay, C.N. *The First Commonwealth Division: The Story of British Commonwealth Land Forces in Korea, 1950–1953.* Aldershot, UK: Gage and Polden, 1954.

Barris, Ted. *Deadlock in Korea: Canadians at War, 1950–1953.* Toronto: Thomas Allen, 2010.

Bercuson, David. *Blood on the Hills: The Canadian Army in the Korean War.* Toronto: University of Toronto Press, 1999.

–. *True Patriot: The Life of Brooke Claxton, 1898–1960.* Toronto: University of Toronto Press, 1993.

Bernier, Serge. *Le Royal 22e Régiment.* Montreal: Art Global, 2000.

Bevin, Alexander. *Korea: The First War We Lost.* New York: Hippocrene Books, 1986.

Bishop, John. *The King's Bishop: A Canadian Corporal in Korea, 1950–51.* Duncan, BC: Fir Grove, 2000.

Blair, Clay. *The Forgotten War: America in Korea.* New York: Anchor Books, 1987.

Bothwell, Robert. *Alliance and Illusion: Canada and the World, 1945–1984.* Vancouver: UBC Press, 2007.

Bothwell, Robert, and Jean Daudelin, eds. *Canada among Nations, 2008: 100 Years of Canadian Foreign Policy.* Montreal/Kingston: McGill-Queen's University Press, 2009.

Bothwell, Robert, and William Kilbourn. *C.D. Howe: A Biography.* Toronto: McClelland and Stewart, 1979.

Boutilier, James, ed. *RCN in Retrospect.* Vancouver: UBC Press, 1982.

Bowers, William T., William M. Hammond, and George L. MacGarrigle. *Black Soldier, White Army: The 24th Infantry Regiment in Korea.* Washington, DC: CMH, 1996.

Brock, Jeffry. *The Dark Broad Seas.* Vol. 1. Toronto: McClelland and Stewart, 1981.

Carew, Tim. *Korea: The Commonwealth at War.* London: Cassell, 1967.

Carruthers, Susan L. *The Good Occupation: American Soldiers and the Hazards of Peace.* Cambridge, MA: Harvard University Press, 2016.

Catchpole, Brian. *The Korean War, 1950–1953.* New York: Carroll and Graf, 2000.

Christensen, Thomas J. *Useful Adversaries; Grand Strategy, Domestic Mobilization, and Sino-American Conflict, 1947–1958.* Princeton, NJ: Princeton University Press, 1996.

Composition Committee, ed. *38 Xian shang de jiaofeng: Kangmei yuanchao zhanzheng jishi* [The fight over the thirty-eighth parallel: The recorded truth of the War to Resist the US and Aid Korea]. Beijing: PLA Literature Press, 2010.

Cook, Tim. *Clio's Warriors: Canadian Historians and the Writing of the World Wars.* Vancouver: UBC Press, 2006.

–. *The Fight for History: 75 Years of Forgetting, Remembering, and Remaking Canada's Second World War.* Toronto: Allen Lane, 2020.

Cooper, George. *Fight, Dig and Live: The Story of the Royal Engineers in the Korean War.* Barnsley, UK: Pen and Sword, 2016.

Cotton, James, and Ian Neary, eds. *The Korean War in History.* Manchester, UK: Manchester University Press, 1989.

Cowdrey, Albert E. *Medics' War.* Washington, DC: Centre of Military History, 1987.

Davis, Robert T. *The US Army and the Media in the 20th Century.* Fort Leavenworth, KS: Combat Studies Institute Press, 2009.

DeRosa, Christopher S. *Political Indoctrination in the U.S. Army from World War II to the Vietnam War.* Lincoln: University of Nebraska Press, 2006.

Donaghy, Greg J. *Grit: The Life and Politics of Paul Martin Sr.* Vancouver: UBC Press, 2015.

Donnelly, William M. *Under Orders: The Army National Guard during the Korean War.* College Station: Texas A&M University Press, 2001.

–. "The US Army during the Korean War." In *Raise, Train, and Sustain: Delivering Combat Power,* edited by Peter Dennis and Jeffrey Gray, 127–59. Canberra: Australian Military History Publications, 2010.

Dower, John. *Embracing Defeat: Japan in the Wake of World War II.* New York: W.W. Norton, 1999.

Dutil, Patrice, ed. *The Unexpected Louis St. Laurent: Politics and Policies for a Modern Canada.* Vancouver: UBC Press, 2020.

Eayrs, James. *In Defence of Canada.* Vol. 3, *Peacemaking and Deterrence.* Toronto: University of Toronto Press, 1972.

Epley, William W. *America's First Cold War Army, 1945–1950.* Arlington, VA: Association of the United States Army, 1999.

Farrar-Hockley, Anthony. *The British Part in the Korean War.* Vol. 2, *An Honourable Discharge.* London: Her Majesty's Stationery Office, 1995.

Field, James A., Jr. *History of United States Naval Operations: Korea.* Washington: Department of the Navy, 1962.

Fitzpatrick, Meghan. *Invisible Scars: Mental Trauma and the Korean War.* Vancouver: UBC Press, 2017.

Flint, Roy K. "Task Force Smith and the 24th Division: Delay and Withdrawal, 5–19 July, 1950." In *America's First Battles, 1776–1965,* edited by Charles E. Heller and William A. Stofft, 266–75. Lawrence: University Press of Kansas, 1986.

Foot, Rosemary. *A Substitute for Victory: The Politics of Peacemaking at the Korean Armistice Talks.* Ithaca, NY: Cornell University Press, 1990.

Fowler, Michelle. "'For Extraordinary Heroism and Outstanding Performance': Kap'yong, 2 PPCLI and the Controversy surrounding the US Presidential Unit Citation." *Canadian Military History* 13, 4 (2004): 19–28.

Gardham, John. *Korea Volunteer: An Oral History from Those Who Were There.* Burnstown, ON: General Store Publishing, 1994.

Gibby, Brian R. *Korean Showdown: National Policy and Military Strategy in a Limited War, 1951–1952.* Tuscaloosa: University of Alabama Press, 2021.

Goodman, Allan E., ed. *Negotiating while Fighting: The Diary of Admiral C. Turner Joy at the Korean Armistice Conference.* Stanford, CA: Hoover Institution Press, 1978.

Gow, J.I. "Les Québécois, la guerre et la paix, 1945–60." *Canadian Journal of Political Science* 3, 1 (1970): 88–122.

Granatstein, J.L. *Canada's Army: Waging War and Keeping the Peace*. Toronto: University of Toronto Press, 2002.

–. *A Man of Influence: Norman A. Robertson and Canadian Statecraft, 1929–68*. Toronto: Deneau, 1981.

–. *The Ottawa Men: The Civil Service Mandarins, 1935–1957*. Toronto: Oxford University Press, 1992.

Granatstein, J.L., and Dean Oliver. *The Oxford Companion to Canadian Military History*. Don Mills, ON: Oxford University Press, 2011.

Gray, Hub. *Beyond the Danger Close: The Korean Experience Revealed*. Toronto: Northwest Printing, 2003.

Grey, Jeffery. *Australian Brass: The Career of Lieutenant General Sir Horace Robertson*. Cambridge: Cambridge University Press, 1992.

–. *The Commonwealth Armies and the Korean War: An Alliance Study*. Manchester, UK: Manchester University Press, 1988.

Gugeler, Russell A. *Combat Actions in Korea*. Washington, DC: Government Printing Office, 1954.

Halberstam, David. *The Coldest Winter: America and the Korean War*. New York: Hyperion Books, 2007.

Hanson, Thomas E. *Combat Ready? The Eighth U.S. Army on the Eve of the Korean War*. College Station: Texas A&M University Press, 2010.

Hastings, Max. *The Korean War*. New York: Simon and Schuster, 1988.

Haydon, Peter, and Ann Griffiths, eds. *Canada's Pacific Presence: Purposeful or Peripheral*. Halifax, NS: Centre for Foreign Policy Studies, 1998.

Heppenstall, Robert. *Find the Dragon: The Canadian Army in Korea, 1950–1953*. Edmonton, AB: Four Winds, 1995.

Hermes, Walter G. *Truce Tent and Fighting Front*. Washington, DC: Office of the Chief of Military History, US Army, 1966.

Hickman, Tom. *The Call-Up: A History of National Service*. London: Headline, 2005.

Hillmer, Norman. *O.D. Skelton: A Portrait of Canadian Ambition*. Toronto: University of Toronto Press, 2015.

Holmes, John W. *The Shaping of Peace: Canada and the Search for World Order, 1943–1957*. Vol. 2. Toronto: University of Toronto Press, 1982.

Institute of Military History of Ministry of National Defense. *Development of the ROK Armed Forces 1, 1945–1960*. Seoul: Institute for Military History of the Ministry of National Defense, 2020.

–. *History of the Republic of Korea Armed Forces in Modern History*. Seoul: Institute for Military History of the Ministry of National Defense, 2019.

Isenberg, Michael. *Shield of the Republic: The US Navy in an Era of Cold War and Violent Peace, 1945–62*. New York: St. Martin's Press, 1993.

Jacobs, Jim. *From the Imjin to the Hook*. Barnsley, UK: Pen and Sword, 2013.

Joffe, Ellis. *The Chinese Army after Mao*. Cambridge, MA: Harvard University Press, 1987.

Johnston, William. *A War of Patrols: Canadian Army Operations in Korea*. Vancouver: UBC Press, 2003.

Kaplan, Edward. *To Kill Nations: American Strategy in the Air-Atomic Age and the Rise of Mutually Assured Destruction*. Ithaca, NY: Cornell University Press, 2015.

Kennedy, Paul. *The Parliament of Man: The Past, Present, and Future of the United Nations*. Toronto: HarperCollins, 2006.

Kim, Donggil. "Stalin's Korea U-Turn: The USSR's Evolving Security Strategy and the Origins of the Korean War." *Seoul Journal of Korean Studies* 24, 1 (2011): 89–114.

Kim, Youngjun. *Origins of the North Korean Garrison State: The People's Army and the Korean War.* London: Routledge, 2017.

Knight, Amy. *How the Cold War Began: The Gouzenko Affair and the Hunt for Soviet Spies.* Toronto: McClelland and Stewart, 2005.

Lankov, Andrei. *From Stalin to Kim Il Sung: The Foundation of North Korea, 1945–1960.* New Brunswick, NJ: Rutgers University Press. 2002.

Latham, William Clark, Jr. *Cold Days in Hell: American POWs in Korea.* College Station: Texas A&M University Press, 2012.

Lech, Raymond B. *Broken Soldiers.* Urbana: University of Illinois Press, 2000.

Leffler, Melvyn P. *A Preponderance of Power: National Security, the Truman Administration, and the Cold War.* Stanford, CA: Stanford University Press, 1992.

Li, Xiaobing. *China's Battle for Korea: The 1951 Spring Offensive.* Bloomington: Indiana University Press, 2014.

Li, Xiaobing, Allan R. Millett, and Bin Yu, trans. and eds. *Mao's Generals Remember Korea.* Lawrence: University Press of Kansas, 2000.

Li, Xiaobing, and Glenn Tracy, trans. and eds. "Mao's Telegrams during the Korean War, October-December 1950." *Chinese Historians* 5, 2 (Fall 1992): 65–85.

Li Ying et al. *40 jun zai chaoxian* [The 40th Army in Korea]. Shenyang: Liaoning People's Press, 2010.

Linn, Brian McAllister. *Elvis's Army: Cold War GI's and the Atomic Battlefield.* Cambridge, MA: Harvard University Press, 2016.

Mackenzie, Hector. "Canada's International Relations in the Early Cold War: The Impact and Implications of the Gouzenko Affair." In *The Gouzenko Affair: Canada and the Beginnings of Cold War Counter-Espionage,* edited by J.L. Black and Martin Rudner, 15–27. Ottawa: Penumbra Press, 2006.

–. "Knight Errant, Cold Warrior or Cautious Ally? Canada on the United Nations Security Council, 1948–1949." *Journal of Transatlantic Studies* 7, 4 (2009): 453–75.

Marshall, S.L.A. *Bringing up the Rear: A Memoir.* San Rafael, CA: Presidio Press, 1979.

McGibbon, Ian. *New Zealand and the Korean War.* Vol. 2, *Combat Operations.* Auckland, NZ: Oxford University Press, 1996.

Melady, John. *Korea: Canada's Forgotten War.* Toronto: Macmillan, 1983.

Meyers, Edward C. *Thunder in the Morning Calm: The RCN in Korea, 1950–1953.* St. Catharines, ON: Vanwell, 1992.

Middlemiss, Dan. "Economic Considerations in the Development of the Canadian Navy since 1945." In *RCN in Transition, 1910–1985,* edited by W.A.B. Douglas, 254–79. Vancouver: UBC Press, 1988.

Millett, Allan R. *The War for Korea, 1945–1950: A House Burning.* Lawrence: University Press of Kansas. 2005.

–. *The War for Korea, 1950–1951: They Came from the North.* Lawrence: University Press of Kansas, 2011.

Milloy, John C. *The North Atlantic Treaty Organization, 1948–1957: Community or Alliance?* Montreal/Kingston: McGill-Queen's University Press, 2006.

Mossman, C. Billy. *Ebb and Flow: November 1950–July 1951.* Washington, DC: Center of Military History, 1990.

Munro, John A., and Alex. I. Inglis, eds. *Mike: The Memoirs of the Right Honourable Lester B. Pearson.* Vol. 2, *1948–1957.* Toronto: University of Toronto Press, 1973.

Naval Historical Branch. *British Commonwealth Naval Operations, Korea, 1950–1953.* London: Ministry of Defence, 1967.

O'Neill, Robert. *Australia in the Korean War, 1950–1953.* Vol. 2, *Combat Operations.* Canberra: Australian War Memorial, 1985.

Park, Jiwon Tina. "From Strangers to Partners: Canadian-Korean Relations (1888–1978)." PhD diss., University of Toronto, 2018.

Pears, Maurice, and Fred Kirkland. *Korea Remembered: The RAN, the ARA, and the RAAF in the Korean War, 1950–1953*. Georges Heights, NSW: Combined Arms Training and Development Centre, 1998.

Peng Dehuai. *Peng Dehuai junshi wenxuan* [Selected military papers of Peng Dehuai]. Beijing: CCP Central Archival and Manuscript Press, 1988.

Peters, Richard, and Xiaobing Li. *Voices of the Korean War: Personal Stories of American, Korean, and Chinese Soldiers*. Lexington: University Press of Kentucky, 2003.

Pope, William Henry. *Leading from the Front: The War Memoirs of Harry Pope*. Waterloo, ON: Laurier Centre for Military and Disarmament Studies, 2002.

Price, John. *Orienting Canada: Race, Empire, and the Transpacific*. Vancouver: UBC Press, 2011.

Rawling, Bill. *Death Their Enemy: Canadian Medical Practitioners and War*. Quebec: AGMV, 2001.

–. *Myriad Challenges of Peace: Canadian Forces Medical Practitioners since the Second World War*. Ottawa: Canadian Government Publishing, 2004.

Reid, Escott. *Radical Mandarin: The Memoirs of Escott Reid*. Toronto: University of Toronto Press, 1989.

Ridgway, Matthew B. *The Korean War*. Garden City, NY: Doubleday, 1967.

Ringma, Bob. *M*L*B*U: Full Monty in Korea*. Burnstown, ON: General Store Publishing, 2004.

Scalapino, Robert, and Chong-Sik Lee. *Communism in Korea: The Movement*. Berkeley, CA: University of California Press, 1972.

–. *Communism in Korea: The Society*. Berkeley, CA: University of California Press, 1972.

Schwartz, Mildred A. *Public Opinion and Canadian Identity*. Berkeley, CA: University of California Press, 1967.

Shen, Zhihua. *Mao, Stalin and the Korean War: Trilateral Communist Relations in the 1950s*. Translated by Neil Silver. London: Routledge, 2012.

–. "Sino-Soviet Relations and the Origins of the Korean War: Stalin's Strategic Goals in the Far East." *Journal of Cold War Studies* 2, 2 (2000): 44–68.

Shen, Zhihua, and Li Danhu. *After Leaning to One Side: China and Its Allies in the Cold War*. Washington, DC: Woodrow Wilson Center Press, 2011.

Shin, H.K. *Remembering Korea, 1950: A Boy Soldier's Story*. Reno: University of Nevada Press, 2001.

Shrader, Charles R. *History of Operations Research in the United States Army*. Vol. 1, *1942–1962*. Washington, DC: Office of the Deputy Undersecretary of the Army of Operations Research, 2006.

Shuang Shi. *Kaiguo diyi zhan: Kangmei yuanchao zhanzheng quanjing jishi* [The first war since the founding of the state: The complete story of the War to Resist the US and Aid Korea]. Beijing: CCP Party History Press, 2004.

Shuguang Zhang, and Chen Jian, trans. and eds. *Chinese Communist Foreign Policy and the Cold War in Asia: New Documentary Evidence, 1944–1950*. Chicago: Imprint Publications, 1996.

Srinivasan, Krishnan. *The Rise, Decline and Future of the British Commonwealth*. Basingstoke, UK: Palgrave, 2005.

Stairs, Denis. *The Diplomacy of Constraint: Canada, the Korean War, and the United States*. Toronto: University of Toronto Press, 1974.

Suh Dae-Sook. *Kim Il Sung: North Korean Leader*. New York: Columbia University Press, 1988.

–. *The Korean Communism Movement, 1918–1948.* Princeton, NJ: Princeton University Press, 1967.

Tan Jingjiao et al. *Kangmei yuanchao zhanzheng* [The War to Resist the US and Aid Korea]. Beijing: China Social Science Press, 1990.

Thomson, Dale C. *Louis St. Laurent: Canadian.* Toronto: Macmillan, 1967.

Thorgrimsson, Thor, and E.C. Russell. *Canadian Naval Operations in Korean Waters, 1950–1955.* Ottawa: Naval Historical Section, Canadian Forces Headquarters, 1965.

Touhey, Ryan. *Conflicting Visions: Canada and India in the Cold War World, 1946–1976.* Vancouver: UBC Press, 2015.

Van Ree, Erik. *Socialism in One Zone: Stalin's Policy in Korea, 1956–1960.* New York: St. Martin's Press, 1989.

Vatcher, William H. *Panmunjom: The Story of the Korean Military Armistice Negotiations.* New York: Praeger, 1958.

Wang Yan et al. *Peng Dehuai zhuan* [Biography of Peng Dehuai]. Beijing: Contemporary China Press, 1993.

War Compilation Committee. *History of the United Nations Forces in the Korean War.* Vol. 2. Seoul: Ministry of National Defense, 1973.

Watson, Brent Byron. *Far Eastern Tour: The Canadian Infantry in Korea, 1950–1953.* Montreal/Kingston: McGill-Queen's University Press, 2002.

Whitby, Michael. "A Letter from Korea by Lieutenant L.A. 'Andy' Collier." *Canadian Naval Review* 6, 2 (2010): 22–25.

Williamson, Corbin. "Fighting with Friends: Coalition Warfare in Korean Waters, 1950–1953." *Joint Forces Quarterly* 83, 4 (2016): 99–104.

Wood, Herbert Fairlie. *The Private War of Jacket Coates.* Don Mills, ON: Longmans Canada, 1966.

–. *Strange Battleground: The Operations in Korea and Their Effects on the Defence Policy of Canada.* Ottawa: Queen's Printer, 1966.

Xu Yan, trans. Xiaobing Li. "Chinese Forces and Their Casualties in the Korean War." *Chinese Historians* 6, 2 (1993): 45–64.

–. *Mao Zedong yu kangmei yuanchao zhanzheng* [Mao Zedong and the War to Resist the US and Aid Korea]. 2nd ed. Beijing: PLA Press, 2006.

Yang Dezhi. *Yang Dezhi huiyilu* [Memoir of Yang Dezhi]. Beijing: PLA Press, 1992.

Yang Di. *Zai zhiyuanjun silingbu de suiyueli: Xianwei renzhi de zhenshi qingkuang* [My years at the CPVF General HQ: Untold true stories]. Beijing: PLA Press, 1998.

Zhao Jianli, and Liang Yuhong. *Fenghuo 38 xian: Diwuci zhanyi zhanshi baogao* [The flames of battle raging across the thirty-eighth parallel: Combat report on the Fifth Campaign]. Beijing: Military Science Press, 2007.

Zhu, Pingchao. "Disgraced Soldiers: The Ordeal of the Repatriated POWs of the Chinese People's Volunteer Army from the Korean War." *Journal of Chinese Military History* 4, 2 (2015): 162–200.

Contributors

Ted Barris is a journalist, author, and broadcaster. He taught journalism at Toronto's Centennial College for eighteen years. His bestselling and award-winning books include *Deadlock in Korea: Canadians at War, 1950–1953; The Great Escape: The Untold Story; Dam Busters: Canadian Airmen and the Secret Raid against Nazi Germany;* and *Rush to Danger: Medics in the Line of Fire,* which was long-listed for the 2020 RBC Taylor Prize for nonfiction. He is a recipient of a Minister of Veterans Affairs Commendation and the Queen Elizabeth II Diamond Jubilee Medal and Platinum Award. He is a Member of the Order of Canada.

Andrew Burtch is the Canadian War Museum's historian for the post-1945 period and an adjunct research professor in the Department of History at Carleton University. He is the author of *Give Me Shelter: The Failure of Canada's Cold War Civil Defence*, which received the C.P. Stacey Award for Military History. For his contributions to Canada's Korean War history, he was awarded a Civil Merit Medal from the Republic of Korea in 2021.

Tim Cook is the chief historian and director of research at the Canadian War Museum. He is a frequent media commentator and the author of over a dozen best-selling books. Cook is a four-time winner of the Ottawa Book Award for Literary Non-Fiction, a two-time winner of the J.W. Dafoe Award, two-time winner of the C.P. Stacey Award for Military History, and recipient of the Charles Taylor Award for Literary Non-Fiction. He is a member of the Royal Society of Canada and the Order of Canada.

Meghan Fitzpatrick is a strategic analyst and an adjunct professor of war studies at the Royal Military College of Canada. She specializes in military mental health and resilience, and her work has appeared in such distinguished publications as *Social History of Medicine* and *War and Society.* She is also the author of *Invisible Scars: Mental Trauma in the Korean War.*

Norman Hillmer is Chancellor's Professor of History and International Affairs at Carleton University. Among his publications are *O.D. Skelton: A Portrait of Canadian Ambition*; the 1947 volume of *Documents on Canadian External Relations*; and *Nearly Neighbours: Canada and the Soviet Union from Cold War to Détente and Beyond* (with J.L. Black).

William Johnston retired in 2023 after forty-one years as a historian at the Department of National Defence. He is the author of *A War of Patrols: Canadian Army Operations in Korea* and a coauthor of the RCAF and RCN official histories *The Crucible of War, 1939–1945; The Seabound Coast*; *No Higher Purpose;* and *A Blue Water Navy.*

Youngjun Kim is a professor at National Security College, Korea National Defense University. He is the author of *Origins of the North Korean Garrison State: People's Army and the Korean War.* He is a member of the National Security Advisory Board of the Republic of Korean President's Office, as well as the Advisory Board for the Department of Unification. He is a managing editor of the Korean *Journal on Nuclear Nonproliferation and Energy,* sponsored by the Ministry of Foreign Affairs of the Republic of Korea. He is an executive director of the Korea Nuclear Policy Society and has led a Nuclear Leadership Policy Initiative between the Republic of Korea and the United States.

Xiaobing Li is professor of history and Don Betz Endowed Chair in International Studies at the University of Central Oklahoma. He is the editor of the *Chinese Historical Review* and editorial board member of the *Journal of Military History* and *Journal of Chinese Military History.* He served in the People's Liberation Army (PLA) in China. Among his recent books are *China's New Navy*; *Sino-American Relations: A New Cold War* (with Qiang Fang); *The Dragon in the Jungle: The Chinese Army in the Vietnam War*; *Attack at Chosin*; *East Asia and the West* (with Yi Sun and Wynn Gadkar-Wilcox); and *China's War in Korea.*

Brian McAllister Linn is the Ralph R. Thomas Professor in Liberal Arts at Texas A&M University. He is the author of six books, including *Real Soldiering: The US Army in the Aftermath of War, 1815–1980* and *The Philippine War, 1899–1902*, and over fifty articles and book chapters. He has given numerous international lectures, been awarded a John Simon Guggenheim Memorial Foundation Fellowship, and held visiting professorships at the US Army War College, the University of Birmingham, the American Academy in Berlin, and National University, Singapore. In 2023, he received the Society for Military History's S.E. Morrison Prize for lifetime achievement.

Hector Mackenzie was for three decades the senior departmental historian at Canada's Department of Foreign Affairs. His extensive scholarship centres on the Second World War and the Cold War, including the impact of the gay purges on the Canadian foreign service. He is the editor of the 1948 and 1949 volumes of *Documents on Canadian External Relations.*

S.P. MacKenzie is the Caroline MacKissick Dial Chair in the Department of History at the Univerity of South Carolina. He teaches, among other things, courses on the evolution of warfare, and is the author of various books and academic articles on military matters, including several works on aspects of British and Commonwealth participation in the Korean War.

Richard Mayne works for the Department of National Defence as the chief historian and director of RCAF History and Heritage, having served eighteen years as a reserve officer in the Canadian Armed Forces. He has authored, co-authored, and coedited publications on aspects of Canadian military history and defence issues. He sits on board of directors for various organizations related to defence and aviation issues, including as deputy chairman of the RCAF Heritage Fund.

Tina J. Park is the chief executive officer of The Park Group, a boutique consulting firm specializing in global governance and international security. She is also a vice president of the NATO Association of Canada and teaches Canadian history at the University of Toronto.

Ryan M. Touhey is associate professor at St. Jerome's University, University of Waterloo. He is the author of *Conflicting Visions: Canada and India in the Cold War World, 1947–76,* and coeditor of *Reassessing the Rogue Tory: Canadian Foreign Relations in the Diefenbaker Era.*

Jonathan Vance is Distinguished University Professor and J.B. Smallman Chair in the Department of History at the University of Western Ontario. He is the author of more than a dozen monographs, the codirector of the online educational resource Wartime Canada, and a frequent consultant for government and corporate public history projects.

Michael Whitby is a senior naval historian at the Directorate of History and Heritage, Department of National Defence, and coauthor of *The Official History of the Royal Canadian Navy in the Second World War.*

Index

Note: Page numbers with (f) refer to figures.

Abbott, Douglas, 33, 37, 39, 43
accidents, battle, 194, 196–98
Acheson, Dean, 36, 217, 229
air power: and Berlin Blockade, 143–44; bombing of North Korea, 150–51; Canadian government attitude toward, 143; and rail transportation, 85; and war at sea, 74. *See also* Royal Canadian Air Force (RCAF); US Air Force (USAF)
air transport, 33, 34, 35, 64, 142, 145–49
aircraft: Avro CF-100 Canucks, 152; B-29 Superfortress bombers, 149–50, 151, 152, 155; Canadair Sabres, 152; carriers, 75, 82; F-51 Mustang fighters, 145; F-86s, 149, 150, 155; ground-controlled approach (GCA) system, 147; helicopters, 64; maintenance, 148; MiGs, 149–53, 155; North Star, 34, 35, 145, image 16; RF-80 reconnaissance, 153; transport, 33, 34, 35
Akinam, John, 209*n*25
Albany Line, 92
alcohol, 184–85, 202, 204–5; deaths from, 198–200; rum ration, 80, 184, 198
Allan, Bill, 243–44, 284, 287
Allard, Jean V., 111, 117, 123, 125, 126, 133, image 22
anniversaries: federal government and, 282, 286; fiftieth, 272, 285, 286; of First World War, 279; fortieth, 282–83; Legion and, 281; military history/historiography and, 279; of Second World War, 279, 282, 285; seventieth, 7; thirtieth, 281; thirty-fifth, 281; veterans and, 272, 286
antibiotics, 179, 182–83, 202
Appleman, Roy E., *South to the Natkong, North to the Yalu*, 58
armed forces (Canada): attitudes toward, 280; in Second World War, 17, 18. *See also* Canadian Army; Royal Canadian Air Force (RCAF); Royal Canadian Navy (RCN)
armistice: Canadian 1953 election and, 44–45; and Cold War, 8; discussions, 215; Kim and, 254; North vs South Korean difference re commemorative dates, 14*n*12; Pearson on, 258; and POWs, 224–25; seventieth anniversary, 7; signing, 171; Stalin and, 254. *See also* peace talks
Army, Navy, and Air Force Veterans in Canada, 281
Army Public Information Office (US), 62
artillery: 2 PPLCI at Kap'yong, 96; of Canadian group, 101–2; along coastal routes, 74; CPVF, 106; creation of Commonwealth Division and, 103; deaths by, 194; importance of, 60; importance of firepower, 3. *See also* New Zealand Army: artillery; Canadian Army: Royal Canadian Artillery; US Army: Field Artillery Branch
asymmetric warfare, 254–55
Atomic Energy Commission (UN), 22
Atomic Energy of Canada Limited, 262, 270*n*19, 270*n*22

attrition, war of, 57, 60, 66, 167, 236
Auden, W.H., 18
Austin, Maurice "Bunny," 133
Austin, William James Lewis, 203, 209*n*41
Australian Army
in Commonwealth Division, 131, 132, 133–34, 137*n*22
ground forces for Korea, 36
relations with Canadians, 133–34
Royal Australian Regiment (RAR): casualties, 94; criticisms of 25th Brigade, 122; headquarters driven back, 94; at Hill 355, 122; at Kap'yong, 96, 100; patrolling by, 122
Royal Australian Regiment, 1st Battalion (1 RAR), 141*n*60
Royal Australian Regiment, 3rd Battalion (3 RAR), 94; casualties, 92; at Hill 504, 94, 166; and Hill 532, 92; at Kap'yong, 166; Presidential Unit Citation award, 100; PVA 118th Division contact with, 94
Australian Navy: *Bataan*, 76, 77, 78; *Sydney*, 82; *Warramunga*, 76, 77

Badowich, Len, 223, 228
Baikie, Elburne, 85
Bairnsfather, Bruce, 275
Baker, Arthur, 225, 226
Bamboo Plan, 248
Barfoot, Walter Foster, 11, 237
Barris, Ted, 11
Bates, Art, 240–41
The Battle at Lake Changjin (film), 10
battle exhaustion, 183–84, 203
battlefield medicine. *See* military medicine
Beaman, W.J. "Bill," 227
Beddoe, Alan, 276
Beech, Keyes, 62
Belzile, Charles, 182
Bercuson, David, 34, 46*n*1; *Blood on the Hills*, 5
Berlin Blockade, 25, 56, 143–44, 145
Berton, Pierre, 147
Bigart, Homer, 62
Bingham, Peter, 121
Bird, Will, 275
Bishop, John, 283
Black Watch, 199
blockade operations, naval, 73–74, 82
Bloody Ridge, Battle of, 169
Bogert, M.P., 117, 282–83; assuming command from Rockingham, 117; leadership, 110–11, 118, 123, 126; on 23 October raid, 122; and patrolling, 118
Boss, Bill, 227–28
Bothwell, Robert, 19
Bougie, Clyde, 239, 278, 284
Boutin, Benoit, 200
Boutin, Hughette, 200
Boutot, Carmen, 285
Boutot, Roland, 285
Bovey, John, 85–86
Bower, R.P., 261
Bowling Alley, 111, 115
Bradley, Omar N., 5, 54, 217
brainwashing, 10
Brennan, M.L., 197
Brennan, Patrick, 42
Bretland, P.M., 181
Bridge of No Return, 242
Britannia Camp, 226
British Army: 29th Brigade, 93; attitudes of personnel within Commonwealth Division, 128, 133, 134, 135; contributions to Commonwealth Division, 128, 137*n*22; at Kap'yong, 96; relations with Australians, 132, 133, 139*n*43; relations with Canadians, 133, 139*n*43; relations with New Zealanders, 139*n*44; Royal Military Police, 134–35
British Commonwealth General Hospital, 178, 180
British Commonwealth Zone Medical Unit, 178, 188*n*36
British Field Ambulance, 26th, 177
British General Hospital 29, 177, 178
Brock, Jeffry, 73, 74–75, 76, 77–80, 88*n*21
Burden, Wallis, 85, image 21
Burke, B.A., 94, 96
Burtch, Andrew, 10, 185
Busan: Eighth Army breakout from, 91; retreat to, 56–57; ROKA/US forces driven back to, 90; UN Memorial Cemetery, 194, 205, 243–44, 272, 280, 283, 284, 285
Butler, David, 130

Calkins, James Alvin, 193
Campbell, Herbert Peter, 195
Canada: 1949 election, 31; 1953 election, 43–45, 46; balancing UN vs US demands, 8; budget, 39–40, 43; and Cold War, 8, 20–21, 36; in Commonwealth, 19, 20–21; contribution to Second World War, 17; as creditor nation, 17; diplomatic relations with People's Republic of China, 32; economy, 42, 43, 45–46; international involvement during 1930s, 18–19; international outlook/policies, 27; international standing, 17; as internationalist, 144; and Kashmir dispute, 23; as middle power, 19, 22; North Atlantic alignment, 18; in North Atlantic Triangle, 17; and nuclear energy, 21–22; numbers of Canadians serving in Korean War, 9; and Palestine mandate, 22–23; peacekeeping/peacemaking, 22, 144, 282; post–Second World War foreign policy, 19–20; as trading nation, 17; and United Nations Commission on Korea, 26; and UNSC, 22–24; and UNTCOK, 26. *See also* federal government; North Atlantic alignment/Triangle
Canada-Korea Free Trade Agreement, 264
Canada-Korea Inter-Parliamentary Friendship Group, 265
Canada-Korea Society, 287
Canada–North Korean relations: Canada's recognition of DPRK, 269; Controlled Engagement Policy, 267; diplomatic, 267, 269; limited nature of, 267; non-engagement in, 269
Canada–South Korea relations, 10, 258–59; CANDU reactor exports in, 262–63, 268; Cold War and, 258, 259, 262; cultural, 263, 265; diplomatic, 260–61, 262, 265, 268; energy in, 267–68; Exercise Maple Flag, 265–66; history of, 268; humanitarian aid in, 259–60, 261, 268; immigration in, 263, 264, 268; Key Resolve Exercise, 266; Korea policy, 260; maritime exercises, 266–67, 271*n*34; and multilateral institutions, 264; and partnership with US, 264; people-to-people, 263, 264–65, 268; security cooperation, 263, 265–67; shared values/interests in, 263–64; St. Laurent's visit to Seoul, 259; strategic interests in, 268; trade, 260, 261, 262–63, 264, 267–68, 269
Canada-UK relationship, 18–19. *See also* North Atlantic alignment/Triangle
Canada-UN relationship: Canadian volunteer brigade for Korea, 35; and response to North Korean invasion of South, 33, 34
Canada-US relationship, 19; and response to North Korean invasion of South, 33, 34–35. *See also* North Atlantic alignment/Triangle
Canadian Army
25th Infantry Brigade: 2 PPCLI rejoining, 103; Allard as commander, 123; Australian criticisms of, 122; Bogert's leadership, 110–11; C Company, 102; casualties, 106; at Ch'orwon, 103, 168; creation of Commonwealth Division and, 103; D Company, 102; in divisional reserve, 122; enlistment into, 90; formation of, 90; in Han'tan River Valley, 102; at Hill 210, 115; and Hill 355, 106, 115; at Hook, 122; at Imjin River, 103, 106; at Jamestown Line, 110; leadership, and performance of, 111; and Operation Commando, 106; and Operation Pepperpot, 112–13; patrols/patrolling, 118–19, 122; prisoner capture, 119–20; professional soldiers and change in character of, 117–18; professionalism of, 107, 110; Rockingham's leadership/qualities and, 110; rotations of units/commanders, 110–11, 112; at Sami-ch'on River, 122; during stalemate, 110; in US Infantry Division, 25th, 102
1st battalions, 111, 118, 126
2nd battalions, 90, 101, 111
3rd battalions, 111
Princess Patricia's Canadian Light Infantry, 1st Battalion (1 PPCLI): A Company, 112–13; casualties, 117, 119; at Hill 132, 117; and Hill 156, 113; and

Hill 210, 115; and Hill 227, 116; and Hill 355, 115; 120; at Hook, 117; in Operation Pepperpot, 112–13; regular force soldiers vs volunteers in, 112; replaced by 3 PPCLI, 122; replacing 2 PPCLI, 112; strength, 112
Princess Patricia's Canadian Light Infantry, 2nd Battalion (2 PPCLI): 5 Platoon, 97; 6 Platoon, 97; 10 Platoon, 98–100; 11 Platoon, 98; 12 Platoon, 98; A Company, 94, 95(f), 98; actions against hilltop positions, 92; and alcohol, 198–99; B Company, 94, 95(f), 96, 97–98; C Company, 94, 95(f), 98; C Company at Hill 444, 193; casualties, 92, 93, 100; and Chinese casualties, 100; at Chip'yong-ni, 163; condition, 91, 92, 100–1; D Company, 93, 95(f), 96, 98; end of tour of duty, 111–12; in First World War, 273; and Hill 532, 92; at Hill 677, 94, 101, 116, 166; and Hill 795, 93; joining 27th Commonwealth Brigade, 91–92; at Kap'yong, 90, 94, 95(f), 96, 97, 107, 273, 284; memorial at Kap'yong, 284; in Operation Claymore, 103, 106; and Operation Commando, 106; Presidential Unit Citation awarded to, 100, 107, 273; professionalism of, 107; rejoining 25th Brigade, 103; replacement by 1st Battalion, 112; Second World War veterans in, 92, 100, 110; sexual assault/murder of Koreans by soldiers, 135; to "show flag" with UN forces in Korea, 91; training, 91; US Shermans firing on, 94
Princess Patricia's Canadian Light Infantry, 3rd Battalion (3 PPCLI): on Jamestown Line, 112; posting to Far East, 112; replacing 1 PPCLI, 122
Royal 22e Régiment (R22eR), image 8; in Commonwealth Division, 133–34; Imjin Gardens hockey game, 287; Quebec City monument to, 285
Royal 22e Régiment, 1st Battalion (1 R22eR): on Hill 159-210 ridge, 120; at Jamestown Line, 118
Royal 22e Régiment, 2nd Battalion (2 R22eR): acclimatization exercises, 101, 102; casualties, 102; at Chail-li, 102; criticisms of, 133–34; and Hill 166, 113; at Hill 172, 106; and Hills 210 and 355, 115–16; in Operation Claymore, 103, 106; in Operation Dirk, 103, 106
Royal 22e Régiment, 3rd Battalion (3 R22eR), 123
Royal Canadian Regiment (RCR): casualties, 119; and Hill 156, 113; and Hill 166, 113, 116; at Hill 187, 169; at Hill 355, 120, 169; Imjin Gardens hockey game, 287; at Koje-do, 220; at Maryang-san, 169; 23 October raid, 121–22
Royal Canadian Regiment, 1st Battalion (1 RCR): arrival home in Canada, 235; casualties, 121; and Hill 113, 119; and Hill 355, 121; at Jamestown Line, 118; prisoner capture, 120; raid on Hill 227, 121
Royal Canadian Regiment, 2nd Battalion (2 RCR): A Company at Hill 355, 241; acclimatization exercises, 101, 102; B Company at Hill 355, 194, 240–41; at Hook, 117; at Kakhul-bong, 168; repatriation, 235
Royal Canadian Regiment, 3rd Battalion (3 RCR): arrival in Korea, 123; casualties, 123; at Hill 187, 123, 171; at Hill 387, 245; Royal Canadian Artillery, 81st Field Regiment and, 3
Australian relations in Commonwealth Division, 133–34
Canadian Administrative Unit, No. 2, 196, 197
Canadian Field Ambulance: 25th, 177; 38th, 226
conscription, 35
contributions to Commonwealth Division, 130, 134–35, 137*n*22
ground forces deployment, 34, 36, 37, 90
Historical Section, 274
Lord Strathcona's Horse (LdSH) (Royal Canadians), 101, 102, 115
New Zealand relations in Commonwealth Division, 133
official history, 274–75
Operational Research Team, No. 1, 182
performance of volunteers vs regular force successors, 9
Provost Corps, 134–35

Royal Canadian Army Medical Corps, 177, 239, 240
Royal Canadian Artillery, 81st Field Regiment, and 3 RCR, 3
Royal Canadian Horse Artillery, 238–39; 2nd Field Regiment, 101–2, image 9
rush to volunteer, 39
training, 90
volunteer brigade group for Korea, 35, 36
and western European defence, 40
Canadian Institute of Public Opinion, 43, 44
Canadian Legion. *See* Royal Canadian Legion
Canadian Military Mission Far East, 151–52
Canadian Volunteer Service Medal for Korea, 281–82
Canadian War Museum, 3, 12, 238, 271*n*34, 287, image 1
CANDU reactors, 262–63, 268, 270*n*22
Canning, Laurie Albert, 209*n*25
Carr, Maurice, 99
Cassels, A.J.H. "Jim," 103, 116, 120, 129, 130–31
casualties: battle vs nonbattle, 197; Canadian Infantry Brigade Group, 25th, 106; Casualty Identification Program, 206; Casualty List No. 88, 222; Casualty List No. 174, 222; at Ch'orwon, 103; civilian, 252, 254; classification of, 193, 197; Commonwealth death-to-wounding rate, 178–79; Commonwealth Division, 106, 178; from friendly fire, 154; at Hill 132, 117; at Hill 210, 115; at Hill 355, 115, 194, 241; at Hill 467, 102; at Hill 532, 92; at Hill 795, 93; at Kap'yong, 92, 93, 94, 100, 121; NKPA, 163; numbers of Canadian, 45; Operation Commando, 106; Operation Pepperpot, 113; POWs on lists, 221–22; 1 PPCLI, 117, 119; 2 PPCLI, 92, 93, 100; during prisoner capture raids, 119–20; protection of nonrepatriates and numbers of, 230; psychological, 183–84; 2 R22eR, 102; RAR, 94; 3 RAR, 92; RCAF and, 148; RCN, 85; 1 RCR, 119, 121; 3 RCR, 123; recording of, 193; ROKA, 125, 252, 259; Second World War compared, 207; Spring Offensive, 168; suicide as percentage of, 200; total numbers, 192, 230, 252; transport, 179–80; treatment of Korean vs Canadian, 237–38; US Cavalry Division, 107; US X Corps, 162; USAF combat losses, 152; during war of attrition, 167. *See* also deaths; illness/injuries; military medicine
casualties (CPVF): at Chip'yong-ni, 163; at Ch'orwon, 103, 161; at Hill 132, 117; at Kakhul-bong, 168; at Kap'yong, 92, 93, 94, 96, 100, 166, 167; in Operation Commando, 106–7; during Third Campaign, 162; totals in Korean War, 160; at Triangle Hill, 170; at Unson, 161; during war of attrition, 167
ceasefire, 113, 116–17, 123. *See also* armistice; peace talks
cenotaphs. *See* memorials
CFB Cold Lake, 265–66
Chail-li, 102, 168
Chambers, W.T., 197
Champeny, A.S., 248
Chang Ki-ho, 286
Chenpongchon (Chenpeongchon), 166
Cheonan (ROKS), 255, 267
Chi Kap-Chong, 283
Chiasson, Michel Paul, 209*n*25
China: Canadian embassy in, 268; Civil War, 27, 31, 250, 252, 254; and Cold War, 10; Cold War, and international relations, 172; Communism in, 56; and Communist Bloc, 6; effect of Korean War on, 171–72; establishment of People's Republic, 27; government materials/supplies for war, 160; in Indo-Pacific area, 267; intervention in Korean War, 39–40; land war with, 53, 65; military spending, 160; recognition of People's Republic, 31; and UN, 10; as vanguard of Communist countries, 172
Chinese People's Volunteer Force (CPVF), 10; around 40th parallel, 161; anti-landing defence system, 170; artillery, 106; and Bloody Ridge battle, 169; at Chail-li, 102; in Chinese Civil War,

161; at Chip'yong-ni, 163; at Ch'orwon, 167–68; concentration of attacks on ROK, 125; CPVF-NKPA Joint Command, 167; deaths, 207; exhaustion of resources, 167; in Fifth Campaign, 164–65(f), 166–68; fighting patrols, 119; fighting style, 97; in Fourth Campaign, 163; in Han'tan River Valley, 102; at Hill 132, 117; at Hill 187, 169, 171; at Hill 227, 115, 116; at Hill 275 (Old Baldy), 170; and Hill 317, 113; at Hill 355, 115, 169; imitation of western forces, 171; intervention in war, 53, 57, 251, 253; invasion of, 91; at Kakhul-bong, 168; at Kansong/Samcheon-ri/Konangpo-ri line, 168; at Kap'yong, 92, 93, 94, 96–97, 98–100, 166–67; and KPA, 249–50, 251, 253; at Kumsong, 171; lack of preparedness, 160; length of time in Korea, 160; MiGs, 149–53; numbers of missing in action, 160; numbers of POWs, 160; Operation Commando and, 106; and Operation Pepperpot, 112–13; in Operation Showdown, 170; patrols by, 119, 120; personnel strength, 160, 162, 163, 169; piecemeal offensives, 170–71; at Pork Chop Hill, 171; protection of North Korea, 161; raid on 1 RCR, 121–22; raid on 3 RCR, 123, 124(f); RCR capture of, 120; reinforcements, 93; and reunion of Korea, 162; and ROK forces, 161; in Second Campaign, 162–63; during stalemate, 118; strategic/tactical changes, 169, 171; in Third Campaign, 163; and trench warfare, 169; and UNF, 161; at Unson, 161–62; and US troops, 161; at White Horse Hill, 170; withdrawal to north, 167. *See also* casualties (CPVF)

Chinese People's Volunteer Force (CPVF), units: 9th Army, 166; 12th Army, 31st Division, 170; 15th Army, 170; 19th Army, 168, 169; 20th Army, 166, 169; 26th Army, 166; 27th Army, 166; 40th Army, 166, 167; 47th Army, 107; 63rd Army, 167–68; 64th Army, 169; 68th Army, 169; 116th Division, 161–62; 118th Division, 94, 96–97, 100, 166–67; 172nd Regiment, image 17; 189th Division, 168; 192nd Division, 106–7

Chinnamp'o, 76–78

Chip'yong-ni, battle of, 163

Ch'o-do, guerrilla landing near, 83–84

Chongchon River, 162

Ch'orwon (Cheorwon), 103, 106, 167–68, image 6

Chosin Reservoir, Battle of, 162

Chrétien, Jean, 272, 286

Christie, Robert Allan, 199–200

Chun Doo-hwan, 253, 255

Ch'unch'on hydro dams, 93

Churchill, Winston, 21

citations: American Distinguished Flying Cross, 151, 154; Canadian Korean medal, 155; Commonwealth Distinguished Flying Cross, 154; federal government and, 273; at Kap'yong, 100–1; Korean Service Badge, 281; Korean War Ambassador for Peace Medal, 279, image 28; Legion of Merit, 155; Military Cross, 120; Military Medal, 120; to 2 PPCLI, 273; for RCAF, 149; UN Korean medal, 155; US Air Force medal, 150; US Presidential Unit Citation, 273

Clark, Mark, 217

Claxton, Brooke, 39; and 1953 election, 43; and air force, 144, 148; Bercuson on, 46*n*1; and Berlin Blockade, 25; on contribution of destroyers and transport aircraft, 33; on contribution of ground forces, 34; and defence spending, 33, 34, 35; and Department of Defence, 40; on economy, 41; increased defence budget, 144; on Korea, 258; on navy vs air force, 143; on POWs, 222; on response to North Korean invasion of South, 33, 39; and volunteer rate for Special Force, 37

Clements, Bennie, 209*n*25

Coke, W.L., 184–85

cold injuries, 181

Cold War: armistice and, 8; and Asian vs western Europe defence, 53; Canada and, 20–21, 36; and Canada-ROK relations, 258, 259, 262; Canadian attitude toward, 8; China and, 10, 172; Commonwealth and, 21; and divided Korea, 255; end of, 282; heightening of tensions, 56; Korean War and, 5, 6, 12, 66;

literature regarding, 7–8; North Korean program to destabilize South, 254–55; North Koreans as Soviet agents, 54; peacekeeping during, 11; RCAF and, 143–44; RCN and, 81, 87; UNSC and, 22
Cold War Crucible (Masuda), 5
Collier, Andrew, 75, 77, 78
Collins, J. Lawton, 65
Colombo Plan, 31, 46, 259
Colson, Charles, 219
Combat Actions in Korea (Guegler), 58
Combined Maritime Forces, 266
Combined Policy Committee, 22
Combined Task Force, 266
commemoration, 11; absence of events, 12; Korean War Ambassador for Peace Medal, 279, image 28; North vs South Korean difference regarding dates of, 14*n*12; ROK and, 273; South Korean government support for, 11; South Korea's attitude toward, 286–88. *See also* anniversaries
Committee of the Chinese Congress of the Defenders of World Peace (Beijing), 222
Commonwealth formations
1st Commonwealth Division, 3, image 14; in I Corps reserve south of Imjin River, 122–23; 1 PPCLI in, 130; achievement of, 129; appreciation/admiration for comrades within, 131–32; atmosphere within, 129–30; Australian Army contributions to, 131, 137*n*22; Australian-British relations within, 132, 133, 139*n*43; Australian-Canadian relations within, 133–34; British Army contributions to, 137*n*22; British attitudes within, 128, 133; Canadian Army contributions to, 131, 137*n*22; Canadian reputation in, 134–35; Canadian-British relations in, 133, 139*n*43; Cassels as commander, 129, 130–31; casualties, 106; change in deployment, 134; command structure, 130–31; and Commonwealth spirit, 9–10, 128–30, 132, 134, 135–36; creation, 103, 128, 132; cultural divisions within, 135–36; deactivation of, 132–33; detention barracks, 134; and First Battle of Maryang-san, 129; friction/rivalry within, 129–30, 132, 133–34; general staff officers, 131; idea of maintaining in Asia, 139*n*39; Indian Army contributions to, 131, 137*n*22; infantrymen in, 134; at Jamestown Line, 123; mutual relations within, 131–32; naming of, 136*n*7; New Zealand Army contributions to, 131, 137*n*22; New Zealand–British relations in, 139*n*44; New Zealand–Canadian relations within, 133; in Operation Minden, 106; pay differentials within, 140*n*52; personnel strength, 93; praise for, 129–30; reputation, 128; Second World War veterans in, 128; sports within, 135, 141*n*61; during stalemate, 107, 110; and Third Battle of the Hook, 129; US influence and, 135; West as commander, 129, 131
27th Commonwealth Brigade, 163; 2 PPCLI joining, 91–92; in IX Corps reserve, 101; across 38th parallel, 92; and Albany Line, 92; attachment to 25th US Infantry Division, 102; composition, 91; at Han River, 102; at Kap'yong, 93–94, 96, 102, 166, 167; numbers of personnel, 93; Philippine battalion attached to, 102; PVA 118th Division contact with, 94; up Kap'yong River valley, 92–94
28th Commonwealth Brigade, 106, 113, 115, 129, 132
29th Commonwealth Brigade, 163
See also Australian Army; Canadian Army; Indian Army; New Zealand Army
Commonwealth of Nations: Canada in, 20–21; Canada-UK relationship, 18–19; and Cold War, 21; and Indonesian independence, 23; lack of definition, 136*n*7; navies, 73; spirit in Commonwealth Division, 128–30, 132, 134, 135–36
communicable disease, 181
communism/Communists: in China, 56; China as vanguard of Communist countries, 172; and Chinese Civil War, 27, 31; Colombo Plan and, 31; involvement in Korea to combat, 39;

neutrality of US and advance of, 54; numbers of personnel in Command, 93; and POW exchanges, 218, 220
Connolly, Donald, 146
Connors (combat engineer), 237
continental defence: Canadian spending on, 40; RCAF and, 152, 155; RCN and, 73; US Army and, 54
Controlled Engagement Policy, 267
Convalescent Depot, 177
Cormack, John, 130
Cornish, V.K., image 9
Cote, Bernard, 278, 288
Coughlin, William "Bing," *Herbie,* 275
Courtenay, Vince, 285
Cowan, Stuart Franklin, 203
Cowdrey, Albert, *The Medic's War,* 185
Crerar, Harry, 276
Crown News, 135–36
The Crowsnest, 78, 80, 86
Cumings, Bruce, 13*n*5; *The Origins of the Korean War,* 13*n*9
Currie, Sir Arthur, 276
Curtis, Wilf, 145, 152
Czechoslovakia coup, 6, 56, 143

Daegu (Taegu), 235
Daido-ko, 77, 78
Daily Worker, 222
Daly, Thomas, 129–30, 137*n*29
Danby, E.D., 131
D'Artois, Guy, 205
deaths: from accidental firearms discharges, 194–95, 204–5; from accidents, 192–93, 194–99; in action, 192, 193–94, 197, 206; from alcohol consumption, 198–200; by artillery, 194; battle accidents, 194, 196–98; from cancer, 203, 204; Chinese small arms fire, 193–94; classification, 196, 197, 201; Commonwealth death-to-wounding rate, 178–79; CPVF, 207; from disease, 202–3; during disembarkation leave, 200; EHF mortality rates, 180; families of victims, 193, 196–98, 205–7; from friendly fire, 196, 197; from heart disease, 203–4; from homicide/manslaughter, 193, 204–5; from illness, 193; from injuries, 194; at Kap'yong, 278; from landmines, 196, 197; missing/presumed dead, 192, 205–7, 214–15; mortality rates among veterans, 186–87; mortality rates among wounded, 178–79; numbers of, 192–93, 277; of POWs, 214–15, 222; records, 207; repatriation of remains, 283–84; by suicide, 193, 199, 200–2, 209*n*30; during training, 195–96; from wounds, 192
Defence Production, Department of, 40–41
defence spending (Canadian), 33, 34, 35, 37, 39–41, 43. *See also* military spending
DeMara, Walter, 79–80
Demilitarized Zone, 90, 215, 252, 255, 265, 279
Democratic People's Republic of Korea (DPRK). *See* North Korea
Deng Hua, 171
Deschenes, Joseph Arthur Adelaide, 195
DeWolf, Harry, 81
Dexter, Grant, 42
Dextraze, Jacques, 101, 115
Diefenbaker, John, 276
Differ, Barbara, 244–46
The Diplomacy of Constraint (Stairs), 13*n*5
diplomatic relations: with North Korea, 267, 269; with South Korea, 260–61, 262, 265, 268
Directorate of Personnel Records, 196–97, 206
diseases, 202–3
Dodd, Francis, 219
dressing stations. *See* field dressing stations
Drew, George, 32, 41
drug misuse, 184, 185–86
Dugal, Paul, 222, 225, 226, image 22
Dumas, Jean Berchmann, 198
Dyer, George, 84
dysentery, 202

Earhart, Albert Clifford, 199–200
Eden, Anthony, 217
Eisenberg, Shaul, 270*n*22
Eisenhower, Dwight D., 64, 231, 248
Elmendorf Field, 146
Empey, Jim, 204

epidemic hemorrhagic fever (EHF), 180–81, 203, 236
Essential Materials (Defence) Bill, 40
Europe, defence of, 40; Asian mainland vs, 53; force sent to, 46; Korean War vs, 152; NATO deterrence in, 280; South Korea vs, 27; US Army priorities and, 65; US commitment to, 27
EUSAK-ROKA KATUSA program, 62
Exercise Maple Flag, 265–66
Export Development Corporation, 263
External Affairs, Department of, 19

Far East Command, 60
Far Eastern Tour (Watson), 5, 185
federal government: achievement, 45–46; and air power, 143; and anniversaries, 282; and Berlin Blockade, 25; and citations, 273; and fiftieth anniversary of Korean War, 286; initial response to Korean War, 31–32; and Korean Veterans Association, 284; and memorials, 277–78, 284, 285; and military spending, 143, 144; public opinion regarding, 43; unpreparedness for Korean War, 155; veterans' response to attitude of, 272; and Wall of Remembrance, 284
Fehrenbach, T.R., *This Kind of War,* 58
Ferguson, George, 42
field dressing stations, 194, 239, 240, image 19; 25 Canadian (25 FDS), 177–78, 184, 188*n*36, image 4, image 18
Field Surgical Team, 22, 177
First World War: book of remembrance, 276; conscription during, 35; fiftieth anniversary, 279; Korean War compared to, 5, 12; memoirs/novels emerging from, 275; memorial in Ottawa, 277; and national unity, 38; PPCLI in, 273; in public memory, 11; trench warfare, 169
Fitzpatrick, Meghan, 10
Fleet Mail Offices, 79
Fleming, S.B., 152–53
Flieger, Don, 236
Foulkes, Charles, 34, 37
Fowler, K.E., 120
Fowler, Michelle, 273
Fraser, Blair, 38, 41, 42
Freedom Village, 226, 227, 228, 242
friendly fire, 94, 154, 196, 197
friendly islands, 82–85
Fu Chongbi, 167–68

Gabreski, F.S., 154
Gagnon, P.E., 38
Galarneau, R.J., image 9
Gapyeong (Kap'yong), 285
Gardiner, Jimmy, 36
Gardner, H.R., 120, 121, image 12
Gavin, James M., 61, 65
Geneva Convention Relative to the Treatment of Prisoners of War (1949), 213, 214, 216; Article 109, 225; Article 110, 225; Article 118, 215, 217, 225; refugee vs POW provisions, 221. *See also* prisoners of war (POWs)
germ/biological warfare, 223–24
Gill, John, 237, 238
Gillis, Donald Hugh, 229
Globe and Mail: on Canadian response to North Korean invasion of South Korea, 36–37; on Korean War fiftieth anniversary, 286; on memorials, 278
Glover, E.A., 154
Gouzenko, Igor, 21
Gow, J.I., 38–39
Graham, David, 279
Granatstein, J.L., 46*n*1
Grant, Harold, 72
Gray, Hub, 194
"Great Bugout," 57, 58
Griffiths, Barbara, 242, 243
Griffiths, George, 223, 240–43
Griffiths, Verdon, 243
Guegler, Russell A., *Combat Actions in Korea,* 58
guerrilla warfare, 251, 254
Gulf War, 281–82; MASH units, 179; medals, 282
Gunn, James, 224, 227

Haean Basin (Punchbowl), 169
Hale, E.B., 153–54
Halliday, Hugh, 152
Han River, 102
Haneda Airport, 146

Hangang River, 163
Hant'an River, 102, 103
Harper, Stephen, 267
Harrison, William K., 221
Hartman, Charles, 73
Hassett, Frank, 130, 133
heart disease, 203–4
Heartbreak Ridge, 169
Heath, R., 88*n*42
Hees, George, 220
helicopters, 64; Bell H13D, 180; in MEDEVAC roles, 180
hemorrhagic fever. *See* epidemic hemorrhagic fever (EHF)
Hendrick, M.M., 152
Herbie (Coughlin), 275
Hermes, Walter G., *Truce Tent and Fighting Front,* 230
Hibbard, J.C., 82, 84
Hill 97, 123
Hill 113, 119
Hill 123, 123
Hill 132, 117
Hill 156, 113
Hill 159, 111, 115, 120, 125
Hill 166, 113, 116
Hill 172, 106
Hill 187, 123, 169, 171
Hill 210, 111, 115, 120
Hill 227, 111, 115, 116, 121
Hill 275 (Old Baldy), 170
Hill 317, 106, 113
Hill 355, 111, 114(f), 125, 224, 225, 242, image 10; Canadian Infantry Brigade Group, 25th and, 106, 115; casualties, 115, 194, 231; CPVF at, 115; 1 PPCLI at, 120; RAR at, 122; 1 RCR at, 121; 2 RCR, B Company at, 194, 240–41; RCR at, 120, 169; 7th US Infantry Division at, 115; veterans revisiting, 280
Hill 387, 245
Hill 444, 193
Hill 467, 102
Hill 504, 94, 166
Hill 532, 92, 281
Hill 677, 94, 96, 97, 98, 100, 101, 116, 166
Hill 690, 169
Hill 795, 93
Hill 865, 97, 98, 197
Hill 1089, 169
Hillmer, Norman, 8, 144
Hiroshima nuclear attack, 65
Hitschmanova, Lotta, 259–60
Hnatyshyn, Ray, 282
Hoge, William, 93–94
Hollyer, Ed, 3, image 1
Home by Christmas offensive, 162
homicide/manslaughter, 193, 204–5
Hong Kong Veterans Association, 279
Hook, battles of, 117, 122, 129, 237–38
Hope, Bob, 147
Howe, C.D., 33, 36, 39–41
Human Resources Research Organization Project Fighter, 61
humanitarian aid: in Canada-ROK relations, 259–60, 261, 268; to North Korea, 267
Hutchinson, Bruce, 42
Hyan Kuk Cho, 285
hygiene, 180, 181, 202

illness/injuries: alcohol and, 184–85; burns, 181–82; causes, 180; deaths from injuries, 194; diseases, 202–3; drug misuse and, 184, 185–86; epidemic hemorrhagic fever (EHF), 180–81; patient evacuation/repatriation, 186; psychological, 183–84; venereal disease (VD), 182–83; wintertime, 181–82. *See also* casualties; mental health
Imjin River, 103, 106, 199–200, 207, 235, 287
Inchon amphibious landing, 39, 53, 57, 62, 76–77, 84, 91, 162, 251
India, 162; and Canadian involvement with Asia, 31; in Commonwealth, 21; and Indonesian independence, 23; and Kashmir, 23; neutrality, 229; Peaceful nuclear explosion, 263
Indian Army: contributions to Commonwealth Division, 131, 137*n*22; Field Ambulance and Surgical Unit, 60th, 177, 179; Indian 60th (Para) Field Ambulance, 131
Indonesian independence, 23–24
Indo-Pacific Strategy, 265, 267, 268, 269
Iron Triangle, 103, 106, 170

Jackson, Bill, 235–36
James, W.J., 177

Jamestown Line, 107, 110, 111, 118, 123. *See also* stalemate
Japan: defeat of, 247; defence of South Korea, 255; Korea as buffer zone for China against, 161; nation-building in, 55; North Korean asymmetric attacks against, 255; occupation of Korea, 247, 251; South Korean diplomatic relations with, 255; US occupation of, 54, 55
Japanese Army: Soviet Army destruction of, 249; training of ROKA, 247
Jenkins, Orval, 222, 228
Johnston, William, 9, 139*n*45; *A War of Patrols*, 5, 274
Jordan, Kelly C., 59
Joy, Turner, 215, 221
Juche ideology, 251

Kaesong, 162
Kakhul-bong, 168
Kansong (Kanseong), 168
Kap'yong, Battle of, 92–101, 116, 166–68, 193, 194, 273; Canadian Korean War Memorial Garden, 283; casualties at, 121; deaths, 278; memorial stone, 284, image 26; withdrawal from valley, 101, 102
Kashmir, 23
KATUSA (Korean Augmentation to the US Army), 62
Kelly, S.G., 76, 77–78, 88*n*21
Kendall, Paul W., 129
Key Resolve Exercise, 266
Kim Il Sung, 6–7, 73, 249, 250, 251; Stalin and, 6, 253, 254
Kim Youngjun, 11
Kimpo Airport, 236
King, William Lyon Mackenzie: and Berlin Blockade, 25, 143–44; and Canadian participation in Second World War, 19; death of, 36; and Gouzenko affair, 21; hesitation of, 31, 32; and Palestine mandate, 23; post–Second World War foreign policy, 19; retirement, 26; and Soviet espionage, 21; and UNTCOK, 26
Kipling, Rudyard, 58
Knowles, Stanley, 32
Koch, Kenneth, 167
Koje Incident, 219–20
Koje-do Island (Geojedo), 219–20
Konangpo-ri, 168
Korea Air Flight 858, 255
Korea Veterans Association, 239, 272, 278–79, 284, 285
Korean Armistice Agreement, 265
Korean Constabulary, 248
Korean Peninsula: Canada as honest broker within, 269; Canadian attention to, 27, 258, 259, 263, 265, 268, 269; Cold War and, 255; Demilitarized Zone, 90; Korean War impact on, 247; legacy of war on, 7, 247, 255; maritime environment, 73; occupation zones, 25–26; reunification two Koreas, 6, 57, 162, 168, 258; ROKA/KPA representative of approaches, 255
Korean People's Army (KPA): 6th Division, 250; antilanding defence system, 170; asymmetric warfare, 254–55; casualties, 163; Chinese Army influence over, 249–50; and Chinese Civil War, 250, 252; composition, 249; CPVF and, 251; CPVF-NKPA Joint Command, 167; driven north across 38th parallel, 91; formation of, 249–50; and future war with ROKA, 252–53; impact of defeat on, 253; impact of Korean War on, 11, 253–54; initial assault on South Korea, 90; invasion of Republic of Korea, 54; officers, 250, 252; preparedness, 250; rapid advance of, 250; Soviet support for, 247; structure, 253; and Task Force Smith, 56–57; underestimation of, 56
Korean Service Badge, 281
Korean Service Corps, 140*n*49
Korean Veterans Association (US), 279
Korean War: addition to National War Memorial, 280–81; and aerial transport, 64; as attritional war, 66, 167; and Cold War, 5, 6, 12, 66; command of sea and, 73; damage to South Korea, 259; effect on China, 171–72; European threat vs, 152; federal government initial response to, 31–32; fiftieth anniversary, 272, 285, 286; as "forgotten war," 11, 53, 169, 172, 230–31, 234–35, 237, 272; fortieth anniversary, 282–83; impact of, 251–52; impact on KPA,

253–54; impact on ROKA, 252–53; impact on US Army, 53, 66; and importance of battlefield command, 125–26; lack of knowledge regarding, 3–4; legacies, 7, 10–11; life writing, 276; as local, 6; in military history, 3, 5, 12, 66; military medicine turning point during, 10, 176, 178–79, 186; multifaceted nature of, 9; names/dates of fallen added to cenotaphs, 279; as not the kind of war to fight, 64; numbers of Canadians serving in, 9; origins, 247; as "police action," 186, 236, 239; protection of nonrepatriates and prolongation of, 230–31; public attitudes toward, 8–9, 272; and rapid-response capability, 155; seventieth anniversary, 7; sixtieth anniversary, 286–87; thirtieth anniversary, 281; thirty-fifth anniversary, 281; unsettled outcomes of Second World War and, 5–6; and US imperialism, 12; and Vietnam War, 5, 66; as war of attrition, 57, 236; as "war of patrols," 179; world wars overshadowing, 12; Zuber as artist for, 238
The Korean War: An International History (Stueck), 14*n*14
Korean War Book of Remembrance, 192, 193, 199, 200, 201, 203, 204, 207, 276–77
Kowang-san. *See* Hill 355
Kuam-san, 169
Kubrick, Stanley, *Paths of Glory*, 229
Kumsong, 171

Lachine, QC, 148
LaFrance, Claude, 153
landmines, 196, 197
Langley memorial, 285
Laporte, Pierre, 38
Larby, John, 130
LaRiviere, Andrew, image 19
League of Nations, 19, 23
Lee Engjun, 248
Lee Young-Hae, 265
Leffler, Melvyn, 21
Legion. *See* Royal Canadian Legion
Leier, Don, 239–40
Leier, Lisa, 239–40
Levesque, Omer, 149, 150, 151, 153
Levy, M.G. "Mike," 93, 98–99
Li Dezhang, 166
Li Xiaobing, 10, 93
Lie, Trygve, 34, 36, 45, 237
Lilley, C. Vance, 97, 205
Lindsay, J.D., 154
Linn, Brian McAllister, 9, 250
Little Gibraltar. *See* Hill 355
Liu Yuzhu, 166
Low, Solon, 32

MacArthur, Douglas: on Eighth Army, 55; and EUSAK, 56; and "Great Bugout," 57; Home by Christmas offensive, 162; and Inchon amphibious assault, 91; in military historiography, 53; and Operation Chromite, 76; presidential ambitions, 55; and press, 58; Ridgway relieving, 53; Truman and, 53; on US defence of South Korea vs Europe, 27; and war with China, 65
MacBrien, J.J., 88*n*42
MacDonald, Bernard "Tunny," 243–44
MacDonald, Bruce, 99
MacDonald, G.F.M., 137*n*29
MacDonald, John, 129
MacEachron, Harry Blake, 204–5
Mackay, Elliott Gordon, 193, image 20, image 28
Mackenzie, A.P.P., 96
MacKenzie, A.R. "Andy," 154, 226–27
Mackenzie, Hector, 8, 144
MacKenzie, S.P., 9–10
Mackenzie King Bridge, Ottawa, memorial, 285
Macklin, W.H.S., 192, 206
MacSween, Joe, 234
malaria, 202–3
Manion, R.J., 275
Mannion, George, 243–44
Mao Anying, 162
Mao Zedong, 163; and Chinese Civil War, 254; on Chinese intervention as victory, 171; contribution of CPVF, 251; and CPVF Spring Offensive failure, 168; on crossing 38th parallel, 162; death of son, 162; and Fifth Campaign (Spring Offensive), 166; and guerrilla warfare, 254; and Korea as buffer zone against Japan, 161; on total victory vs defence of North Korea, 162–63; and

unification of Korea, 162; on war of attrition, 163
March, Vernon, 277
Marine Corps (US), 64
maritime geography/environment: and Chinnamp'o evacuation, 76–77; East vs West Coasts, 82; RCN and, 73
Marshall, George, 216
Marshall, S.L.A., 61, 62
Martin, Paul, 36
Martin, R.I., 274
Martin, Scotty, 287
Martin, Yonah, 286–87
Maryang-san, battles of, 129, 169–70
*M*A*S*H,* 240, 278
Masuda Hajimu, *Cold War Crucible,* 5
Mayhew, Robert, 36
Mayne, Richard, 10
McChord Air Force Base, 145, 146, 147
McDermot, Terry, 39, 41
McGuire, Frank, 274
McKelvey, Al, 272
McKinny, Jim, 238–39
McNamara, Ted, 112
McNaughton, A.G.L., 22, 23, 24
media: on Canadian response to North Korean invasion of South Korea, 33, 36–37, 38–39; *Globe and Mail,* 36–37, 278, 286; Liberal Party relationship with, 42; MacArthur and, 58; *Maclean's,* 41, 42; on Pearson, 42; and POWs, 227–28
medicine. *See* military medicine
The Medic's War (Cowdrey), 185
Memorial Cemetery (UN), 272, 280, 283, 284, 285
Memorial Chamber, Peace Tower, 276, 277
memorials: Airdrie, 285; Battle of Kap'yong, 284; Burnaby *Ambassador of Peace,* 285, image 29; Canadian Korean War Memorial Garden, 283; cenotaphs, 239, 277, 278, 279; First World War, 277; Kap'yong memorial stone, 284, image 26; Langley, 285; linking Canada and South Korea, 285; on Mackenzie King Bridge, 285; at Nepean Point, 277–78; Niagara Falls, 285; Royal 22e Régiment in Quebec City, 285; stone slabs from Korea, 285; types of, 277; Wall of Remembrance, 244–46, 284–85, 286, images 24, 27; in Windsor, 285
Menon, Krishna, 229
mental health, 184, 186; antidepressants, 184; antipsychotic medication, 184; battle exhaustion, 183–84, 203; neuropsychology, 202; post-traumatic stress disorder (PTSD), 183, 186; psychological casualties, 183–84, 186
Merchant Navy veterans, 279
Meredith, Brian, image 3
Merrithew, Gerry, 281, 282
Meyers, Edward, 80
Middlesex Regiment, 1st Battalion, 94
Military Air Transport Service (MATS), 145, 147, 148
military history/historiography: anniversaries in commemoration of, 279; historical officers in field, 274; Korean War in, 3, 5, 12, 66; life writing, 275–76; Office of the Chief of Military History, 59; recording of wartime experience and, 59; US, 5, 53; writing of, 274. *See also* official histories
military medicine: Commonwealth integration vs national differences in services, 178; evacuation (MEDEVAC), 180; evacuation/repatriation of patients, 186; Korean War as turning point in, 10, 176, 186; personnel, 176, 188*n*36, image 18; personnel and survival of soldiers, 186; preventative medicine, 180, 181, 182, 202; resource shortages, 188*n*36; Royal Canadian Army Medical Corps, 177; services/support, 177–78; surgical treatment, 179, 180, 184; US Army Medical Corps, 177; war and, 176. *See also* casualties
military spending: Canadian, 143, 144; by China, 160. *See also* defence spending (Canadian)
Millett, Allan, 106–7
Mills, J.G.W, 98, 99
mines: land, 196, 197; sea, 73, 74
missing in action: Chinese, 160; as POWs, 214–15, 225
Mitchell, Humphrey, 36
*M*L*B*U: Full Monty in Korea* (Ringma), 276

mobile army surgical hospitals (MASH) units, 179, 181, 194, 238, 245
Mobile Dental Teams, 177
Moffat, Andrew C., 287
Monague, Kenneth Roger, 199
monuments. *See* memorials
morale: alcohol and, 184–85; enemy raids and, 122; mail delivery and, 79; MEDEVAC helicopters and, 180; operational success and, 80; of professional soldiers, 117–18; in RCAF, 148; in RCN, 72, 80, 87
Morris, Frederick, 196, 198
Morrison, William Earl, 209*n*25
Morton, R.E.A., 225
Mulroney, Brian, 206
Munsan, 228
murder. *See* homicide/manslaughter
Mydans, Carl, 62

Nabu-ri, 111
Nabu-ri Valley, 112, 118–19
Naech'on, 94, 96
Nakdong River line, 250–51
narcotics, 185–86
Nasby, Bill, 287
National Council of Veterans Associations in Canada, 281
National Defence, Department of: Casualty Identification Program, 206; Casualty List No. 88, 222; Casualty List No. 174, 222; and citations, 273; no repatriation policy, 284
National Guard (US), 61
National Korean War Veterans Day (South Korea), 287
National Shrine of Remembrance/Nepean Point memorial, 277–78, 280
National War Memorial, 278, 280–81
Natkong River, 56–57
NATO. *See* North Atlantic Treaty Organization (NATO)
Navaneelan, Tanya, 202
navies. *See* Australian Navy; Royal Canadian Navy (RCN); US Navy
Navy (South Korean), and Rim of the Pacific Exercise, 266
negotiations. *See* peace talks
Nehru, Jawaharlal, 31
Nepean Point memorial site, 277–78
Netherlands, Indonesian independence and, 23–24
Neutral Nations Repatriation Committee, 229
Neutral Nations Supervisory Commission, 266
New Zealand Army: artillery, 93, 94, 96, 99, 131–32; contributions to Commonwealth Division, 131, 137*n*22; ground forces for Korea, 36; relations with Canadians in Commonwealth Division, 133; Royal New Zealand Transport Corps, 132
Niagara Falls memorial, 285
Nile Expedition, 276
Nixon, G.W., 152–53
North, G.W., image 9
North Atlantic alignment/Triangle, 17, 18, 20, 22–23, 24–25. *See also* Canada-UK relationship; Canada-US relationship
North Atlantic Alliance, 5
North Atlantic Treaty Organization (NATO), 24–25, 65, 144, 149, 152; deterrence in western Europe, 280; Netherlands and, 23; RCAF and, 144, 155; RCN and, 72, 73, 81, 82, 87; US and, 9; US Army priorities and, 65
North Korea: air force, 149; attack on South Korea, 56; bombing of, 150–51; civilian casualties, 254; Cold War program to destabilize South, 254–55; and Communist Bloc, 6; emigrants to South Korea, 252; humanitarian aid to, 267; invasion of South Korea, 7; and Juche ideology, 251; middle class creation in, 250; military and civilian casualties, 252; Russian alliance with, 255; sea strategy, 73–74; Soviet Union and, 6, 54, 249, 250; US bombing campaigns against, 14*n*9, 254; veterans visiting, 280. *See also* Canada–North Korean relations; Korean People's Army (KPA)
North Korean People's Army (NKPA). *See* Korean People's Army (KPA)
nuclear energy/weapons, 54, 270*n*22, 280; aerial transport and, 64; CANDU reactors, 262–63, 268; combat troops

vs, 64; Soviet Union and, 21–22, 64; US and, 22; US Army and, 65–66; USAF and, 65
Nuclear Non-Proliferation Treaty, 262

Office of the Chief of Army Field Forces, 65; "lessons learned" publications, 59
official histories, 273–75; of Korean War, 192; US Army, 230; US POWs in, 230. *See also* military history/historiography
Ogden, Dick, 242
Operations: August Storm, 249; Big Switch, 226, 228; Chromite (*see* Inchon amphibious landing); Claymore, 103, 106; Commando, 104–5(f), 106, 110; Dirk, 103, 106; Hawk, 145–49, 152, 155; Little Switch, 225; Minden, 104–5(f), 106; Pepperpot, 112–13, 235; Scatter, 218; Showdown, 170
Operations Research Office, 61
Organized Army Reserve, 61
Orienting Canada (Price), 13*n*5
The Origins of the Korean War (Cumings), 13*n*9
Orson, Don, 234, 235
Osan, 56
Owen, C.G., 228

Palestine mandate, 22–23
Pang Ho-san, 250, 251
Panmunjom: armistice signed at, 171; Operation Little Switch at, 225; peace talks at, 110, 113, 116–17, 122, 242; prisoner releases at, 226; veterans visiting, 280
Park, Tina J., 10
Park Chung Hee, 253, 255, 260, 263
Paths of Glory (Kubrick), 229
Patrick, A.R., 155
patrols/patrolling, 103, 116–17, 118–19, 122, 125, image 13; fighting, 118–19, 122, 123; "jitter," 119; reconnaissance, 111, 113–14, 118–19, 120, 122, 123, 125–26; school, 123, 126
Patterson, George, 26
Payne, Donald M., 148, 149
Payton, Gerald, 198
peace talks, 83–84, 110, 113, 116–17, 122, 123, 144, 168, 215, 224–25. *See also* armistice
peacekeeping/peacemaking, 11, 12, 22, 144, 280, 281, 282
Peacock, Robert S., 134, 275, image 2
Pearson, Lester B.: on Anglo-American collaboration, 21; on armistice, 258; and Canada as middle power, 19; and Colombo Plan, 31; on deployment of destroyers, 34–35; and Koje Incident, 220; media on, 42; Menon and, 229; and National Shrine of Remembrance/Nepean Point memorial, 278, 280; Nehru's visit and, 31; on North Korean invasion of South Korea, 32–33; on policy goals for Cold War, 36; on response to North Korean invasion of South, 33, 35–36; as secretary of state, 31–32; St. Laurent and, 20; and UNTCOK, 26; and US defence of South Korea vs Europe, 27; on volunteer brigade force for Korea, 36
Pedley, James, 275
Peng Dehuai: and armistice, 254; calling off first phase of Spring Offensive, 167; and Chongchon River, 162; and Ch'orwon, 168; and counterattacks, 169; on CPVF as protecting North Korea, 161; and Fifth Campaign (Spring Offensive), 166; and first battle as success, 162; and Fourth Campaign, 163; on modernization of Chinese force, 171; perception of differences between western and Chinese forces, 160; request to Mao for pause until spring, 162; and second phase of Spring Offensive, 167; Stalin and, 254; as supreme commander, 251; and Third Campaign, 163; on trench warfare, 169
People's Volunteer Army (PVA). *See* Chinese People's Volunteer Force (CPVF)
personnel records, 193, 207
personnel strength: of Commonwealth Division, 93; of Communist command, 93; CPVF, 160, 162, 169; RCAF, 142, 143, 145; RCAF pilots flying with USAF, 154; RCN, 72, 81; of UN forces, 93; US Army, 53, 54, 55, 57, 61, 63, 65; US Eighth Army, 56; US I Corps, 162; US IX Corps, 162; US X Corps, 162

Philippine battalion, 102
Pickersgill, Jack, 38, 45, 46, 46*n*1
Plomer, James, 83–84
Pope, Henry William "Harry," 119, 122, 123, 275
Pork Chop Hill, 171
post-traumatic stress disorder (PTSD), 183, 186
Presidential Unit Citation, 100, 107
preventative medicine, 180, 181, 182, 202
Price, John, *Orienting Canada*, 13*n*5
Prince, Robert, 36
prisoners of war (POWs): I Corps on capture of prisoners during stalemate, 119–20; accounting for, 221–22; armistice negotiations and, 215, 224–25; and brainwashing, 10, 221, 223, 227–28; camp conditions, 216–17, 221, 222, 225–26; Canadian, 213–14, 222–23, 224, 227–28, image 22; Chinese, 160, 215–16, 228, image 12; collaboration, 215, 217, 229; collective importance of, 213–14; concerns regarding conduct after capture, 10; conditions, 241–42, 243; deaths, 214–15, 222; dilemma of, 10; escape attempts, 218–19, 227, 230; exchanges, 171, 217–18, 221, 224–26; expectations of, 230; forced labour, 215; and germ warfare, 223–24; Griffiths as, 241–43; ideological extremes between, 216–17; indoctrination of, 213, 223; intelligence officer interrogations, 227–28; international law and, 213, 224; Koje Incident, 219–20; media and, 227–28; missing in action as, 214–15, 225; North Korean, 125, 215–16, 218–19; numbers of, 214, 218–19, 221–22, 224–25; numbers of Chinese, 160; pilots as, 154; politicization of, 213, 216; protection of nonrepatriates, 230–31; psychological warfare and, 213; records, 214; release after armistice, 222; repatriation, 122, 160, 215–19, 221, 224–29; ROK release of anti-Communist, 125; screening of, 218–19, 220; during Second World War, 213, 215, 222; treatment of, 222–23, 224; UN Command and, 215, 216; US, 214, 215, 221, 222–23, 224, 228–29; US Code of Conduct for, 230; in US official history, 230; US remaining in China, 215; violence between, 216–17, 219–20. *See also* Geneva Convention Relative to the Treatment of Prisoners of War (1949)
The Private War of Jacket Coates (Wood), 275
Project Visa, 61
Prugh, George S. Jr., 230
Pryor, Clyde, 245–46
psychological casualties, 183–84, 186
Public Works, Department of, and Nepean Point memorial, 277–78
Pukhan (Bukhan) River, 94, 169
Pusan Perimeter, Battle of, 57
Pyle, Ernie, 63
Pyongyang, 162; POW transit facility at, 218–19

Quinn, John, 85

radar, 83, 85, 155
railway strike, 37–38
Rainer, Doug, 237
Ramsay, Gordon, 283
Ramsay, Lady Patricia, 198–99
Rangeraja, A.G., 177
Rangers (US), 60
RCN. *See* Royal Canadian Navy (RCN)
rearmament, 37, 39–40
reconnaissance patrols. *See* patrols/patrolling
Red Cross Society (Canadian), 222
Redknap, Donavan "Reg," 3, 12, image 1
Redmayne, John, 275
Regan, Bill, 244–46
Regan, Hazel, 244–46
Reid, Roy, 282
remembrance. *See* commemoration
Remembrance Day, 277, 278
repatriation: of casualties, 186; of POWs, 122, 160, 215–19, 221, 224–29; protection of nonrepatriates, 230–31; Soviet Union and, 215
Republic of Korea (ROK). *See* South Korea
Republic of Korea Army (ROKA): 2nd Division, 170; 6th Division, 93, 94, 166; and alliances, 251; Battle Command Training Program, 252; casualties, 125, 252; central place in society, 253;

Chinese concentration of attacks on, 125; citizen support for, 253; culture, 252; Defense Innovation 4.0, 252–53; fighting against guerrilla forces vs KPA, 251; and future war with North Korea, 252–53; government and, 253; impact of Korean War on, 11, 252–53; Japanese Army training of, 247; at Kap'yong, 93, 166; Korea Combat Training Centre, 252; at Kumsong, 171; military strength, 247–48; at Nakdong River line, 250–51; nuclear weapons, 253; numerical strength, 253; officers, 252; in Operation Showdown, 170; origins, 247–49; at outbreak of Korean War, 250; recruits, image 24; retreat to Busan, 56–57; retreat to Seoul, 90; training, 252; US Army relationship with, 252; US influence on, 248–49; US support for, 247; weapons, 252

The Response, 277

Rethinking the Korean War (Stueck), 9

Rhee, Syngman, 6, 220

Richard, Marcel, 283

Richards, Cyril Williams, 196, 198

Richardson, John, 130

Ridgway, Matthew B.: and blame-the-troops narrative, 58; and EUSAK, 57; on future wars, 64; along Hangang River, 163; on Koje-do, 219; in military historiography, 53; and public relations, 62; on release of POWs, 222; on US national security strategy, 64

Rim of the Pacific Exercise, 266

Ringma, Bob, 287; *M*L*B*U: Full Monty in Korea,* 276

Ritchie, Charles, 19

Ritchie, Elspeth Cameron, 185–86

Robertson, Mary, 243–44

Robertson, Norman, 36, 46*n*1

Robertson, Sir Horace, 139*n*43

Rockingham, John, 90; and acclimatization training, 101; Bogert assuming command from, 117; on British attitude to Canadians, 133; during ceasefire, 116; at Chail-li, 102; creation of Commonwealth Division and, 103; and Hill 166, 113; and Hills 210 and 355, 115; leadership, 110, 114, 118, 122, 125; at Nabu-ri, 111; and patrols/patrolling, 103, 106, 113–14, 116, 123, 125–26; qualities, 110, 114; on relations within Commonwealth Division, 130; in *Strange Battleground,* 274–75; West and, 131

Ronning, Chester, 32, 227

Ross, Harold, 97

Rothwell, Thomas, 224, 226, 228

Route 17, 93–94, 97, 100

Royal 22e Régiment (R22eR). *See under* Canadian Army

Royal Australian Regiment (RAR). *See under* Australian Army

Royal Canadian Air Force (RCAF): 1 Canadian Air Division, 152, 154, 155–56; air transport squadron, 33, 34, 35, 142, 145; aircraft maintenance, 148; airmen at Shemya, image 15; and Berlin Blockade, 143–44; casualties, 148; citations, 149; close calls, 148–49; and Cold War, 143–44; competing priorities, 10; and continental defence, 152, 155; contribution, 10, 34, 142–43, 145, 155, 156; electronics expertise, 155; European presence, 154; flights to Korea, and mail to RCN, 79; flying hours/month, 147; freight amount, 148; lack of losses, 147; living conditions, 148; loan of fighter pilots to USAF, 149–55; MiGs and resources of, 155; morale, 148; and NATO, 144, 155; Operation Hawk, 145–46; personnel strength, 142, 143, 145; post–Second World War cuts to, 142, 155; post–Second World War demobilization, 143; rebuilding of, 144–45, 152; during Second World War, 142; Second World War veterans in, 153; sortie numbers, 148; spending on, 144; and UN electronic warfare, 142; and USAF, 142

Royal Canadian Legion: and Canadian Volunteer Service Medal for Korea, 281; exclusion of Korean War veterans, 207; First vs Second World War veterans in, 236; and Korean veterans, 235–36, 239, 278–79, 281; *Legion,* 281; *The Legionary,* 276; and Nepean Point memorial, 277, 278; and public attitudes toward military, 280; and thirtieth anniversary of Korean War, 281;

and Wall of Remembrance, 284; and Windsor memorial, 285
Royal Canadian Navy (RCN)
Accelerated Defence Program and, 87
assets devoted to Korea, 80–81
Athabaskan, 34, 71; arrival in Japan, 72; condition, 72; at evacuation of Chinnamp'o, 76, 77, 78; number of tours, 80; operational effects on, 78
blockade duty, 71
bombardment by, 74–75
budget, 87
casualties, 85
Cayuga, 34, 71; arrival in Japan, 72; to Busan, 73; condition, 72; DeMara treating on, 80; at evacuation of Chinnamp'o, 76, 77, 78; flying UN flag, 75; and guerrilla landing near Ch'o-do, 83–84; number of tours, 80; weather, and clothing on, 80; at Yosu, 74
at Chinnamp'o, 76–78
and Ch'o-do guerrilla landing, 83
clothing, 79
and coastal artillery, 74
and Cold War, 81, 87
and Commonwealth navies, 73
competing priorities, 10
composition, 72, 81–82
conditions in Korea, 78–80
and continental defence, 73
contribution/deployment, 10, 33, 34–35, 71
Crusader, 80, 85–86
and East vs West Coasts of Korea, 73
expenditure on, 72
fighter-bomber squadrons, 82
friendly islands defence, 82–85
Haida, 80
Huron, 80, 81, 86, 89*n*60
and Inchon amphibious assault, 76–77
interwar periods, 71–72
Iroquois, 74, 80, 85, 86, 271*n*34, image 21
Magnificent, 81, 82
mail delivery to, 79
matériel, 78–79
morale, 72, 79, 80, 87
and NATO, 72, 73, 81, 82, 87
Naval Services Headquarters (NSHQ), 72, 82
new warship construction, 87
Nootka, 80, image 7
official history, 275
Ontario (HMCS), 71, 82
and Operation Chromite, 76
personnel strength, 72, 81
political profile, 81
post–Second World War cuts to, 71–72, 86–87
Québec, 82
radar, 83
recreation, 79
reputation, 73
response to North Korean invasion of South, 33–34
rotation of destroyers, 81
sailing to Korea, 72–73
sailor health, 79–80
screening of aircraft carriers, 75
and sea mines, 74
during Second World War, 71
sickly season, 71–72, 81, 86–87
Sioux, 34, 71; accommodations on, 79; arrival in Japan, 72; condition, 72; at evacuation of Chinnamp'o, 76, 77; number of tours, 80–81; operational effects on, 78
supply depot at Sasebo, 79
"trainbusting," 85–86
training in, 81, 82
trilateral exercises with ROK and US, 266–67
and UN, 81, 86
and US Navy, 73
weather and, 80
Welfare Committees and, 80
Winnipeg, 271*n*34
Royal Canadian Regiment (RCR). *See under* Canadian Army
Ryan, William Joseph, 194

Sabbatis, Frederick James, 204
Samcheon-ri, 168
Sami'ch-on River, 117, 122
Sangnyong-ni, 107
Sangok-dong, 169
Sanscartier, Emile Joseph, 205
Sasebo, Japan, 72–73, 79
Schick, L.E., 248
Schreyer, Edward, 280–81

Scott, Cuthbert, 222
Scott-Moncrieff, Alan, 84
Sea of Japan, 73
sea power, 71, 76, 85
Second World War: addition to National War Memorial, 280–81; army histories, 275; book of remembrance, 276; Canada's middle power status during, 19; Canadian forces in, 17, 18; casualties during, 207; conscription during, 35; deaths by suicide during, 201–2; Dieppe raid casualties, 207; documentation of experience during, 59; fiftieth anniversary, 279, 282, 285; historical officers in field, 274; Korean War compared to, 5, 12; legacy of, 5–6; life writing, 275–76; mortality rates among wounded, 178, 179; and national unity, 38; POWs in, 213, 215, 222; psychological casualties, 183; in public memory, 11; radar during, 83; RCAF in, 142; RCN in, 71; St. Laurent's principles of foreign policy during, 20; unsettled outcomes of, 5–6; venereal disease rates, 182. *See also* veterans (Second World War)
Selective Service Administration (US), 61
Seoul, 162, image 3; abandonment of defence of, 57; Canadian embassy in, 268; capture-recapture of, 7, 39, 93, 163, image 5; Fifth Phase Offensive and, 93; North Korean initial capture of, 32; St. Laurent's visit to, 259; veterans revisiting, 279
Shemya, 146, image 15
Silver Cross Mother, 272, 281
Simonds, Guy, 273, 276
South African War, 12, 267–77; *The South African War Book of Remembrance,* 276–77
South Korea: Americanization in, 249; asymmetric attacks against, 255; attitude toward veterans, 280, 286–88; birth of Republic of Korea (ROK), 247; Canadian attitudes toward, 258; commemoration by, 273; commercial interests, 258; emigrants from North Korea, 252; external support, and survival of, 261; industrialization, 258; Japanese defence of, 255; and Korean War Ambassador for Peace Medal, 279, image 28; military and civilian casualties, 252, 259; Ministry of Defence Agency for Killed in Action Recovery and Identification, 206; Ministry of Patriots and Veterans Affairs, 286; North Korean invasion of, 7, 56; Northern Cold War program to destabilize, 254–55; and nuclear energy/weapons, 262, 263, 270*n*22; strategic interest to US, 56; support for Canadian remembrance, 11; UNSC resolution to assist, 32; US defence of, 255; US defence of, vs western Europe, 27; US occupation of, 6, 25–26, 247; veterans' tours to, 279–80, 282–83, 286; war damage to, 259; warship exchanges with Canada, 266, 271*n*34; Year of the Korea Veteran, 287. *See also* Canada–South Korea relations; Republic of Korea Army (ROKA)
South Korea Labour Party, 251
South to the Natkong, North to the Yalu (Appleman), 58
Soviet Union: Air Force divisions, 169; and Berlin Blockade, 25, 143–44; and Communist Bloc, 6; destruction of Japanese Army, 249; espionage, 21; fear of invasion in West Germany, 61–62; and iron curtain, 21; and KPA, 247, 249–50; NATO and, 24; non-repatriation of POWs, 215; North Atlantic partners' split from, 20; North Atlantic Treaty and, 24; and North Korea, 6, 7, 54, 249; and nuclear energy/weapons, 21–22; nuclear war with, 64; occupation of northern Korea, 247; sea-mining, 74; threat in Europe, 60; war with, 53, 54, 61–62, 65–66
Sperry High Definition Warning Surface (HDWS), 83, 86
Spring Offensive (Fifth Campaign), 93–101, 166–68
St. Laurent, Louis: at 25 Field Dressing Station, image 4; in 1949 election, 31; and 1953 election, 43–45, 46; becoming prime minister, 26, 144; on Canada's contribution to war effort, 145; Fraser

on, 41; on ground forces for Korea, 37, 90; leadership, 46; and national unity, 38; and North Atlantic Treaty, 24; and Palestine mandate, 22–23; and Pearson, 20; on principles of foreign policy, 20; public opinion regarding, 41–42; and railway strike, 37–38; replacing King, 144; and response to North Korean invasion of South, 33, 36, 38; and support for South Korea, 32; and UNTCOK, 26; welcome to 1 RCR, 235; world tour, 259
Stacey, Charles, 274
Stairs, Denis, *The Diplomacy of Constraint*, 13*n*5
stalemate, 168; Commonwealth Division during, 107; first year of war contrasted with, 90, 110; mortality rates during, 179
Stalin, Joseph, 215; death, 224; and Kim Il Sung, 6; and Korean War, 253–54; and Mao on war of attrition, 163; and POWs, 215; supplying arms, 169
Stiles, John A., 265
Stone, J.R. "Jim," 91, 92, 94, 96, 97–98, 99, 100–1, 112–13, 193, 199, 202
Strange Battleground (Wood), 273, 274–75
Stratemeyer, G.E., 151–52
strength. *See* personnel strength
Stueck, William: *The Korean War: An International History*, 14*n*14; *Rethinking the Korean War*, 9
suicide, 193, 199, 200–2, 209*n*30
Sui-ho reservoir area, 153

Taejeon, Battle of, 214
Tanggok, 283
Task Force 77, 86
Task Force Smith, 53, 56, 60, 66
Taylor, Paul, 77
Taylor, Ronald Harvey, 204
Theseus (HMS), 74–75
thirty-eighth parallel, 57, 91, 92–93, 162, 163
This Kind of War (Fehrenbach), 58
Thomas, R.C.W., 131
Thompson, Vic, 279, 280
Thomson, Dale, 37
Tong, Darryl, 179
Toole, John Richard "Dickie," 205–7
Toole, Nellie, 206, 207
Touhey, Ryan, 8–9
"trainbusting," 85–86
training: 2 PPCLI, 91; 2 R22eR, 101, 102; 2 RCR, 101, 102; Canadian Army and, 90; RCN, 81, 82; ROKA, 252; Second World War veterans and, 90; US Army, 55, 56, 61, 63; US Infantry, 60
Transfusion Team 9, 177
Tremblay, George, 209*n*25
Tremblay, Yves, 201–2
trench warfare, 169
Triangle Hill (Shangganling (Tall Hill)), 170
truce. *See* armistice
truce talks. *See* peace talks
Truce Tent and Fighting Front (Hermes), 230
Trudeau, Pierre, 262
Truman, Harry S.: and air power, 150; authorization of ground forces from Japan, 54; and Churchill's US visit, 21; committal of US troops vs atomic strikes, 64; and defence of South Korea, 27; and desegregation of forces, 62; indecision regarding army's role, 55; and MacArthur, 53; military criticism of, 58; and POW repatriation, 216; and Soviet Union, 21
Turner, Robert, 183

UK-US-Canada relationship. *See* North Atlantic alignment/Triangle
UN Command: China's struggle against, 10; driven out of North Korea, 91; electronic warfare, 142; mandate, 265; Military Armistice Commission, 265; numbers of personnel, 93; and POWs, 215, 216, 217–18, 219–22, 226; RCN and, 73, 86; and sea power, 71, 76
Unitarian Service Committee (USC), 259–60
United Kingdom: ground forces for Korea, 36; in North Atlantic Triangle, 17; response to North Korean invasion of South Korea, 32–33. *See also* British Army
United Nations (UN): Atomic Energy Commission, 22; Canada and, 22; China

and, 10; Commission on Korea, 26; contradictory interests, 18; Emergency Relief Programme in Korea, 260; establishment of, 18; Korea Relief Agency, 259; Korean Reconstruction Agency, 270*n*12; Korean War Allies Association, 283; and Korean War as "police action," 236; and North Atlantic Treaty, 24–25; Observer Corps, 33; RCN and, 81; Security Council (UNSC), 22–24, 32; Special Commission on Palestine, 22; Temporary Commission on Korea (UNTCOK), 26
United States: asymmetric attacks against, 255; and atomic energy, 22; Canada-ROK relations and, 264; defence of South Korea, 255; effect of intervention on allies, 27; Korean War, and imperialism of, 12; and NATO, 9; neutrality, and Communist aggression, 54; in North Atlantic Triangle, 17; occupation of southern Korea, 6, 25–26, 247; response to North Korean invasion of South Korea, 32–33; in South Korea, 6; support for ROKA, 247; unilateral action by, 22; and western European defence, 24
Unson, Battle of, 161–62
US Air Force (USAF), 99; 4th Fighter Interceptor Wing, 153; 187th Airborne Regiment and Koje Incident, 219–20; air-bombing campaign, 254; atomic weapons, 65; bombing campaigns against North Korea, 14*n*9; combat losses, 152; at Kap'yong, 100; and Korean War vs Air Division, 152; Military Air Transport Service (MATS), 145, 147, 148; RCAF and, 142; and RCAF air transport squadron, 145; and RCAF aircraft, 152; RCAF loan of fighter pilots to, 149–55; as support for Army, 64; as unreliable source of support, 64
US Army
- I Corps: aggressive patrolling/raiding policy, 119; at Hant'an/Imjin Rivers, 103; numerical strength, 162; and Operation Commando, 106; and Operation Minden, 106; and Philippine battalion, 102; on prisoner capture, 119–20
- IX Corps, 101; at Kap'yong, 93; personnel strength, 162
- X Corps: at Bloody Ridge, 169; at Chosin Reservoir, 162; at Heartbreak Ridge, 169; personnel strength, 162
- 1st Cavalry Division, 56, 107; 8th Regiment in Unson battle, 161–62; at Chip'yong-ni, 163
- Eighth US Army Korea (EUSAK), 57; 1952 study, 58; aggressive patrolling/raiding policy, 118; blame for early defeats, 58–59; breakout from Busan, 91; counteroffensive driving Communists back to 38th parallel, 92; designation as, 56; equipment, 56, 57; facilities, 56, 57; and Fifth Phase Offensive, 93; in final act of war, 125; Headquarters analytical branch, 59; in Japan as occupation force, 55; lessons of 1950, 59–64; MacArthur's view of, 55; media reporting on, 57–58; personnel strength, 56, 57; retreat to South Korea, 162; training, 56; withdrawal from Kap'yong valley, 101
- 72nd Tank Battalion, 94, 100, 166
- Field Artillery Branch, 60
- Infantry Branch, 59–60; Rangers, 60
- Infantry Division: 7th, 62, 115, 170; 24th, 56, 59, 94, 166, image 6; 25th, 56, 102, 166, 168; 45th, 170
- air force as support, 64
- Armor School, 64
- atomic weapons, 65–66
- Command Conference program, 63–64
- and Commonwealth Division, 129, 135
- composition, 61–62
- conscripted vs volunteer, 53, 61–62
- and continental defence, 54
- criticism of, 66
- cuts to, 55, 60
- in Europe, 54
- and firepower vs personnel, 65
- in future war, 54–55
- impact on, 53
- in Japan, 54
- lessons learned from Korean War, 53–54, 59–66
- and limited wars, 64
- media relations, 62–63

Medical Corps, 177
mental conditioning, 63–64
mobilization, 54
and NATO/Europe as decisive theatres, 65
Officer Candidate Schools, 62
officer corps transformation, 62
official history, 230
personnel strength, 53, 54, 55, 61, 63, 65
post–Second World War, 54–55
and POWs, 216–17
racial integration, 53, 62
relationship with ROKA, 248–49, 252
Reserve Officer Training Corps, 62
reserve pool, 61
social composition, 53
in South Korea, 7
in Task Force Smith, 66
as temporary occupational force to permanent garrison, 53
training, 55, 61, 63
transformation during war, 9
Troop Information and Education, 63
war with Soviet Union, 54–55
US Marine Division, 1st, 94, 162, image 17
US Navy, 64; *DeHaven*, 86; *Forrest Royal*, 76, 77, 78; *Marsh*, 85; *Orleck*, 85; Pacific fleet, 266; RCN and, 73
US-UK-Canada relationship. *See* North Atlantic alignment/Triangle
USSR. *See* Soviet Union
Utah Line, 93

Valley Forge Army Hospital, 229
Van Fleet, James, 101, 107, 129, 166, 170
Vance, Jonathan, 10
Vanier, Georges, 276
venereal disease (VD), 79, 182–83
veterans (First World War): and Legion, 278; Second World War veterans vs, 236
veterans (Korean War): attitudes toward, 234–35; biannual reunions, 287; Canadian Volunteer Service Medal for Korea, 281–82; deaths by suicide, 201; and fiftieth anniversary of end of war, 272, 286; gala at Canadian War Museum, 287; homecoming, 11, 12, 234, 235–36, 237, 238–40, 242–43; isolation, sense of, 187; Korean Service Badge, 281; lack of understanding of experiences of, 186–87; Legion attitudes toward, 235–36, 278–79; mortality rates, 186–87; negative health outcomes, 187; pilgrimages to South Korea, 282–83; and remembrance/commemoration, 11, 12; South Korean gratitude to, 280; tours to South Korea, 279–80, 286; and veterans' loans, 239, 243; visiting North Korea, 280; and Wall of Remembrance, 244–46, 284–85; wearing of collective citations, 273; wish to forget war, 234, 239; Year of the Korea Veteran in South Korea, 287. *See also* Korea Veterans Association
veterans (Second World War): in 1 Commonwealth Division, 128; in 1st battalions, 111; in 2 PPCLI, 92, 100, 110; in 3rd battalions, 111; attitudes toward Korean veterans, 235–36; enlistment in 25th Canadian Infantry Brigade Group, 90; First World War veterans vs, 236; Legion and, 278; and National War Memorial, 277; Netherlands tour, 286; pilgrimages, 282; in RCAF, 153; in Special Force, 92
veterans (South African War), 276
Veterans Affairs, Department of, 243; and *Korean War Book of Remembrance*, 276–77; and number of dead, 192; War Service Records Division, 277
Veterans of Foreign Wars (US), 285
Vietnam War, 280; Korean War and, 5, 66; MASH units, 179
Vipond, Milton, 182

Walker, Walton, 56, 57, 180
Walton, W.J., 88*n*42
A War of Patrols (Johnston), 5, 274
War to Resist the United States and Aid Korea, 10
Warkworth Institution, 243
wars fading over time, 11–12
Watson, Brent Byron, 182, 203; *Far Eastern Tour*, 5, 185
Watson, Ron, 234, 235
Watt, A.W., 205
Weapons System and Evaluation Group, 61

Welland, Robert, 77, 78
Wen Yucheng, 166
West, Mike, 129, 130, 131, 134
West Point Military Academy, 62
Whitby, Michael, 10
White Horse Hill, 170
wintertime accidents, 181–82
Wonsan (port), 74
Wood, Herbert Fairlie, 122, 274; *The Private War of Jacket Coates,* 275; *Strange Battleground,* 273, 274–75
Woodside, Willson, 220
Woodward, Stanley, 36
Wrong, Hume, 19, 25, 35–36
Wylie, Constance, 281
Wylie, Lloyd, 281
Wyoming Line, 103, 106

Xi Jinping, 172

Yalu River, 57, 150, 161, 227
Yang Dezhi, 167–68
Yeltsin, Boris, 206
Yeonpyeong Island, 255
Yoon Suk Yeol, 268
Yosu, 74
Young, Charles, 230
Young Mun Yoo, 285
Yuk Young Soo, 255

Zhou Enlai, 224, 227
Zuber, Ted, 237–38, image 10, image 13, image 23

Studies in Canadian Military History

John Griffith Armstrong, *The Halifax Explosion and the Royal Canadian Navy: Inquiry and Intrigue*

Andrew Richter, *Avoiding Armageddon: Canadian Military Strategy and Nuclear Weapons, 1950–63*

William Johnston, *A War of Patrols: Canadian Army Operations in Korea*

Julian Gwyn, *Frigates and Foremasts: The North American Squadron in Nova Scotia Waters, 1745–1815*

Jeffrey A. Keshen, *Saints, Sinners, and Soldiers: Canada's Second World War*

Desmond Morton, *Fight or Pay: Soldiers' Families in the Great War*

Douglas E. Delaney, *The Soldiers' General: Bert Hoffmeister at War*

Michael Whitby, ed., *Commanding Canadians: The Second World War Diaries of A.F.C. Layard*

Martin F. Auger, *Prisoners of the Home Front: German POWs and "Enemy Aliens" in Southern Quebec, 1940–46*

Tim Cook, *Clio's Warriors: Canadian Historians and the Writing of the World Wars*

Serge Marc Durflinger, *Fighting from Home: The Second World War in Verdun, Quebec*

Richard O. Mayne, *Betrayed: Scandal, Politics, and Canadian Naval Leadership*

P. Whitney Lackenbauer, *Battle Grounds: The Canadian Military and Aboriginal Lands*

Cynthia Toman, *An Officer and a Lady: Canadian Military Nursing and the Second World War*

Michael Petrou, *Renegades: Canadians in the Spanish Civil War*

Amy J. Shaw, *Crisis of Conscience: Conscientious Objection in Canada during the First World War*

Serge Marc Durflinger, *Veterans with a Vision: Canada's War Blinded in Peace and War*

James G. Fergusson, *Canada and Ballistic Missile Defence, 1954–2009: Déjà Vu All Over Again*

Benjamin Isitt, *From Victoria to Vladivostok: Canada's Siberian Expedition, 1917–19*

James Wood, *Militia Myths: Ideas of the Canadian Citizen Soldier, 1896–1921*

Timothy Balzer, *The Information Front: The Canadian Army and News Management during the Second World War*

Andrew B. Godefroy, *Defence and Discovery: Canada's Military Space Program, 1945–74*

Douglas E. Delaney, *Corps Commanders: Five British and Canadian Generals at War, 1939–45*

Timothy Wilford, *Canada's Road to the Pacific War: Intelligence, Strategy, and the Far East Crisis*

Randall Wakelam, *Cold War Fighters: Canadian Aircraft Procurement, 1945–54*

Andrew Burtch, *Give Me Shelter: The Failure of Canada's Cold War Civil Defence*

Wendy Cuthbertson, *Labour Goes to War: The CIO and the Construction of a New Social Order, 1939–45*
P. Whitney Lackenbauer, *The Canadian Rangers: A Living History*
Teresa Iacobelli, *Death or Deliverance: Canadian Courts Martial in the Great War*
Graham Broad, *A Small Price to Pay: Consumer Culture on the Canadian Home Front, 1939–45*
Peter Kasurak, *A National Force: The Evolution of Canada's Army, 1950–2000*
Isabel Campbell, *Unlikely Diplomats: The Canadian Brigade in Germany, 1951–64*
Richard M. Reid, *African Canadians in Union Blue: Volunteering for the Cause in the Civil War*
Andrew B. Godefroy, *In Peace Prepared: Innovation and Adaptation in Canada's Cold War Army*
Nic Clarke, *Unwanted Warriors: The Rejected Volunteers of the Canadian Expeditionary Force*
David Zimmerman, *Maritime Command Pacific: The Royal Canadian Navy's West Coast Fleet in the Early Cold War*
Cynthia Toman, *Sister Soldiers of the Great War: The Nurses of the Canadian Army Medical Corps*
Daniel Byers, *Zombie Army: The Canadian Army and Conscription in the Second World War*
J.L. Granatstein, *The Weight of Command: Voices of Canada's Second World War Generals and Those Who Knew Them*
Colin McCullough, *Creating Canada's Peacekeeping Past*
Brandon R. Dimmel, *Engaging the Line: How the Great War Shaped the Canada–US Border*
Meghan Fitzpatrick, *Invisible Scars: Mental Trauma and the Korean War*
Patrick M. Dennis, *Reluctant Warriors: Canadian Conscripts and the Great War*
Frank Maas, *The Price of Alliance: The Politics and Procurement of Leopard Tanks for Canada's NATO Brigade*
Geoffrey Hayes, *Crerar's Lieutenants: Inventing the Canadian Junior Army Officer, 1939–45*
Richard Goette, *Sovereignty and Command in Canada–US Continental Air Defence, 1940–57*
Geoff Jackson, *The Empire on the Western Front: The British 62nd and Canadian 4th Divisions in Battle*
Steve Marti and William John Pratt, eds., *Fighting with the Empire: Canada, Britain, and Global Conflict, 1867–1947*
Steve Marti, *For Home and Empire: Voluntary Mobilization in Australia, Canada, and New Zealand during the First World War*
Douglas E. Delaney and Serge Marc Durflinger, *Capturing Hill 70: Canada's Forgotten Battle of the First World War*
Peter Kasurak, *Canada's Mechanized Infantry: The Evolution of a Combat Arm, 1920–2012*
Sarah Glassford and Amy Shaw, eds., *Making the Best of It: Women and Girls of Canada and Newfoundland during the Second World War*

Alex Souchen, *War Junk: Munitions Disposal and Postwar Reconstruction in Canada*

George Belliveau and Graham W. Lea, eds., *Contact! Unload: Military Veterans, Trauma, and Research-Based Theatre*

Tim Cook and J.L. Granatstein, eds., *Canada 1919: A Nation Shaped by War*

Arthur W. Gullachsen, *An Army of Never-Ending Strength: Reinforcing the Canadians in Northwest Europe, 1944–45*

Peter Farrugia and Evan J. Habkirk, eds., *Portraits of Battle: Courage, Grief, and Strength in Canada's Great War*

Andrew L. Brown, *Building the Army's Backbone: Canadian Non-Commissioned Officers in the Second World War*

Matthew Barrett, *Scandalous Conduct: Canadian Officer Courts Martial, 1914–45*

Alex Souchen and Matthew S. Wiseman, eds., *Silent Partners: The Origins and Influence of Canada's Military-Industrial Complex*

David Roberts, *Boosters and Barkers: Financing Canada's Involvement in the First World War*

Studies in Canadian Military History

Published by UBC Press in association with the Canadian War Museum

Printed and bound in Canada

Set in Swiss Condensed and Minion by Artegraphica Design Co. Ltd.

Copyeditor: Lesley Erickson

Proofreader: Kristy Lynn Hankewitz

Indexer: Noeline Bridge

Cartographer: Eric Leinberger

Cover designer: George Kirkpatrick

Cover image: Private Morris J. Piche is helped to an aid station behind the front lines in the Kap'yong Valley by Lance Corporal W.J. Chrysler, both of the 2nd Battalion, Princess Patricia's Canadian Light Infantry. | Imperial War Museum, MH 33026.